Gleaning from decades of meticulo
toward cultural trends as a trained s
along a journey through the books of
and providing soul-nourishing insights along the way. With the release
of *Sixty-Six*, readers will come to garner wisdom from one known as a
gifted professor, inspirational wordsmith, and passionate devotee of
Scripture.

Charles L. Perabeau, Ph.D.
Dean of the School of Theology and Christian Ministry
Olivet Nazarene University

Dr. Kent Olney takes us on an in-depth trip through the sixty-six books
of the Bible. The totality gives the reader a unique and perceptive "lay of
the land." As a long-time Christian, I have a new appreciation for how
the sixty-six books of the Bible fit together. Olney even shows how the
"begats" books make sense by illustrating their relevance to twenty-
first-century problems associated with redefining gender and marriage
as well as family breakdown. He also shows how the books of the Old
Testament can be grouped together to show various purposes.

Each chapter consists of fresh and contemporary analysis and commentary. In addition to the depth of research and the solid theological
foundation, the book gives penetrating social and cultural understanding. Olney's scholarly background in theology and sociology makes for
a wonderfully enticing way of looking at Scripture. The depth of scholarship and breadth of cultural implications are enriching. This book is
solidly grounded theologically with stories and sociological insights that
provide a deep and unique message from each book. Olney's advice to
take one chapter at a time is very apropos because there is such richness
in each chapter that it's worth taking the time to let it all sink into the
mind and heart of the reader.

Janice Shaw Crouse, Ph.D.
Author, speaker, columnist, and social commentator

The Bible's size and complexity intimidate readers, who default to sermons alone for their spiritual food. But Dr. Olney . . . does great labor
for us by capturing four or five essentials per book. Aloof Old Testament books become accessible. Doctrinally dense New Testament books
find focus. This sociologist—who observes, analyzes, and counts—is
a reliable expositor who keeps pointing out the window to the most
important landmarks along Route 66.

Gregg Chenoweth, Ph.D.
President, Olivet Nazarene University

Sixty-Six is a work that reflects the communication skills, spiritual insights and leadership of Dr. Kent Olney. This book offers a practical, fresh look at the Bible that should be a must read for every church leader in America. What has always impressed me about Dr. Olney's teaching is the way everything he writes as a sociologist is also so saturated with God's Word. Not only is his teaching practical and principle-driven, it is always delivered in a spirit which is winsome, helpful and encourages personal reflection. Read this book and be encouraged—this book is a winner!

Larry McKain, D.Min.
Superintendent, Chicago Central District
Church of the Nazarene

Kent Olney's sociological perspectives provide theological insight and offer a practical source of guidance that helps his readers grow. It is a privilege to recommend his thoughts.

Ronald E. Smith, Ph.D.
President, Ohio Christian University

SIXTY-SIX

A SOCIOLOGIST REFLECTS ON SCRIPTURE, ITS THEMES, AND THEIR RELEVANCE

Francis Asbury Press
Wilmore, Kentucky

THE FRANCIS ASBURY SOCIETY
PO Box 7
Wilmore, KY 40390
859-858-4222
800-530-5673
fas@francisasburysociety.com
www.francisasburysociety.com

ISBN: 978-0-915143-54-2
Cover design by D. Curtis Hale and Jennie Lovell
Printed in the United States of America

This book is dedicated to:

My Grandchildren

Autumn, Kamden, Kolton, Benedict, Claire

Since my youth, O God, you have taught me,
and to this day I declare your marvelous deeds.
Even when I am old and gray,
do not forsake me, O God,
till I declare your power to the next generation,
your might to all who are to come. (Psalm 71:17–18)

And I will make every effort to see that after my departure you
will always be able to remember these things. (2 Peter 1:15)

Contents

OLD TESTAMENT THEMES

NEW TESTAMENT THEMES

Acknowledgments

We are all the product of many social relationships and influences. None of us arrives or achieves on his or her own. Birth itself illustrates the fact in that every human—the exceptions being the original Adam and Eve—came into this world the result of a mother's and father's joint contribution. We are inextricably linked to one another, making it impossible to take sole credit for any accomplishment. That certainly holds true when writing a book.

This volume did not develop out of a vacuum. I am the product of many social, intellectual, and spiritual influences. First and foremost, I was born to parents, Harold and Sharon Olney, who instilled in me morals, discipline, responsibility, and a love for God's Word and the church. As a teenager, my home and church were significantly transformed by the 1970 Asbury College Revival, planting a thirst in my heart to know God more deeply.

Choosing to attend Asbury College and then Asbury Theological Seminary in the 1970s, on the heels of God's extraordinary movement in that community, was formative. Words fail to express my debt of gratitude to the clear preaching and teaching of local pastors and Asbury College president Dr. Dennis F. Kinlaw. They regularly whetted my appetite for a deeper relationship with God and his Word and made me hunger for more. My college and seminary professors—and respected biblical scholars—William Coker, Victor Hamilton, Gerald Miller, John Oswalt, and David Thompson, to name a few, fed both my mind and soul while daily modeling godly living. As a young man, I aspired to become like them. I will be forever grateful for their example in making God's Word so appealing to students like me.

This project would never have occurred without the support and encouragement of well over one hundred individuals and other guests who attended the Scripture & Society Sunday school class between 2002 and 2022. The class, part of College Church of the Nazarene in Bourbonnais, Illinois, was more than a group of eager participants. These individuals seriously desired to live out the biblical principles we studied and discussed on a weekly basis. Consequently, class members became family and cared for one another, much like the early church described in Acts 2:42–47. This book would not have been written without such dear friends and fellow pilgrims on the journey to our eternal home. Many from our number have already gone ahead of us to heaven and will be there to welcome us when we make that same trip one day.

The team at the Francis Asbury Society, of course, has been indispensable to this work. Without the assistance, vision, creativity, editorial skills, guidance, and encouragement of Vic Reasoner and Jennie Lovell, this project would still be languishing in a file somewhere. Words of appreciation do not fully express the sentiments of my heart. Nonetheless, to both Vic and Jennie, thank you! Your acts of kindness, adaptability, and professionalism came just when I needed them most.

My inspiration for so much of life over the past half-century, whether contemplating writing a book or moving across the country, has been my college sweetheart and wife of nearly fifty years, Beth. She has stood by me and made me a "we." Together we have known the joy of marriage, ministry, teaching, praying, parenting, and grandparenting—and the heartache sometimes associated with each area. She knows my love for her surpasses adequate expression; and I know the same about her love for me. Our two sons, Kyle and Luke, their wives (both named Amber), and our five grandchildren have indulged me on more than one occasion when I have shared some of the thoughts now contained in this book around our Sunday dinner table. Thank you, one and all, for being such a good audience when I have wanted to share an idea. The family laughter that often followed was good medicine for my soul and helped keep my feet planted squarely on the ground of reality. May we Olneys continue to love and follow Jesus all our days. Nothing matters more.

Finally, I owe all that I am and any good I might have accomplished—in this project or in any other—to the Lord Jesus Christ. His sacrifice for the whole world and His work in my individual life, though the latter is still in progress, are worthy of eternal praise. To God be the glory!

Introduction

A century ago, in 1926, the construction of Route 66 began. The project was designed to provide a continuous roadway from Chicago, Illinois, to Los Angeles, California. When completed in 1938, the eight-state project produced the first fully paved highway in the United States to connect the upper Midwest to the West Coast. Route 66 was an architectural wonder designed at a time when the automobile was quickly beginning to symbolize America's independence and wanderlust spirit. For over half a century people traveled the 2,400-mile two-lane road, seeking new opportunities and satisfying their thirst for adventure. Many dreamed of the good life that awaited them in California, at the end of Route 66.

Numerous stories have been written about people's experiences along this legendary highway. For example, John Steinbeck's classic novel, *The Grapes of Wrath* (1939), describes early travelers on what he called "the main migrant road . . . the long concrete path across the country . . . the mother road" (p 118). Because Route 66 cut through so many of our country's major towns—Chicago, St. Louis, Tulsa, Oklahoma City, Amarillo, Santa Fe, Albuquerque, Flagstaff, Los Angeles, and others—the highway also earned the designation as "the main street of America." It was a thread that tied one community to the next. Various descriptive historical accounts have been produced to document life and travel along the road that defined so many Americans' experiences during the early automobile age (e.g., Atonson, 2012; Dedek, 2007; Krim, 2005; and Wallis, 1990).

Our country's fascination with the mother road was further evident when songwriter Bobby Troup, in 1946, wrote a song entitled "Route 66." Singer Nat King Cole popularized these lyrics:

If you ever plan to motor west
Travel my way, take the highway that is the best
Get your kicks on Route 66

It winds from Chicago to LA
More than two thousand miles all the way
Get your kicks on Route 66

Now you go through Saint Looey
Joplin, Missouri
And Oklahoma City looks mighty pretty
You see Amarillo
Gallup, New Mexico
Flagstaff, Arizona
Don't forget Winona
Kingman, Barstow, San Bernardino

Won't you get hip to this timely tip
When you make that California trip
Get your kicks on Route 66

Won't you get hip to this timely tip
When you make that California trip
Get your kicks on Route 66
Get your kicks on Route 66
Get your kicks on Route 66

In addition to books and songs that featured America's favorite road, an early 1960s television program—again simply named, "Route 66"—ran for over three years on CBS. The adventure drama had a straightforward plot that included two young men crossing the country in a Corvette convertible inherited from the father of one of the characters. The series was filmed entirely on location along Route 66, where the travelers met a variety of challenges, worked odd jobs, and interacted with numerous people along the way. The black-and-white series, consisting of 116 episodes, depicted the vibrancy of American life experienced by those bound together by the nation's "main street."

Why has there been such fascination with Route 66? Why did books, songs, and TV programs focus so much attention on this road during the middle of the twentieth century? Why have historians been drawn to research and write on this piece of the American experience? Why do numerous museums in multiple states continue to tell the story of and display memorabilia from Route 66 today? The answer is two-fold in that the road symbolized and connected both the possibility of future promise and the security of past roots, values long held dear by Americans. First, the highway beckoned people to new opportunities. Americans believed a better life—away from the hard work of eking out an existence in wind-swept, dusty fields across the Midwest and South—awaited them in sunny and fertile California. A new world filled with hope and promise lay just ahead for those who journeyed this road. Opportunity has always enticed people to travel uncharted pathways in hopes of realizing a dream. Route 66 invited ambitious adventure-seekers westward in pursuit of delights and pleasures they believed to be at the end of the road.

Second, however, Route 66 also allowed people to stay connected to their roots even while exploring new horizons. A new destination, by its very nature, implies something is being left behind. Those traveling this unknown and extended highway were not only going somewhere to seize an opportunity but also were leaving a place that held cherished memories and deep meaning in their lives. Traveling Route 66 brought people to new land and communities, yet it also afforded the possibility of returning to their roots with relative ease. Earlier travel, whether it was by boat across a harrowing ocean or by covered wagon across the sun-scorched prairie, made returning nearly impossible. This newly paved two-way highway was different, signifying that one's roots need not be so completely severed. Opportunities ahead held promise and potential, but the prospect of returning to one's roots—which many people did on this same two-lane highway—was also an option. These dual factors, then, future opportunities and past roots and memories, contributed to the widespread appeal of Route 66.

The book you hold in your hands, *Sixty-Six*, describes another road-way that links opportunity and roots. Like Route 66, the construction of this road was intentional, required the cooperation of untold numbers of contributors, has a rich history, and promises a delightful destination. I am speaking, of course, of the sixty-six books that comprise the Holy Bible. These sacred books, when they are read thoroughly and system-

atically and seriously reflected upon, provide a road leading to meaningful life both now and in the hereafter. That road points to remarkable
opportunities while rooted in a magnificent past. Both the future and
the past come together and make sense when one travels this hallowed
highway. It is a road I recommend taking, as have many saints and sages
down through the centuries before me. Journeying through these sixty-
six sacred books is a trip that will not disappoint.

There are several parallels between America's Route 66 and the
collection of sixty-six books that comprise the Bible. First, as noted
above, both these pathways have long represented opportunity and
roots. The roads were designed so that the traveler might simultaneously look forward to bright possibilities and point backward to one's
origins and ancestry.

Second, both emphasize social connections. Route 66 not only connected Chicago to Los Angeles but linked dozens of smaller towns and
their inhabitants along the way. Similarly, the books of the Bible contain
numerous themes and events that are connected. These connections are
designed to help us maximize the potential for which we were created.
We are poorer individuals and a more deprived and contentious community when we fail to consider and build on the truths discovered in
Scripture—truths intended to enhance life and social wellbeing.

Third, the purpose of both roads was to provide a smoother trip.
Anyone who has driven across the United States knows it is a long
journey. One can only imagine the bumps and mishaps of that journey prior to a paved road. Route 66 changed all that, allowing one to
leave Chicago and drive more than two thousand miles to California on
solid pavement. The journey became easier on both the vehicle and the
human body. Scripture, too, was designed for the purpose of offering a
smoother and easier trip. The Word of God offers us a paved road and
an accurate map through life. While not guaranteeing perfect conditions
along the way, this road sure beats the alternative of trying to navigate
the journey on one's own. God paved the way through the gift of his
written Word.

Fourth, both roads were built to carry people through all kinds of
weather. Extremes in weather once made cross-country travel a nightmare. Rain and mud, snow and ice, sun and wind—all these elements
could slow or ruin a trip. Route 66 promised consistent road conditions upon trustworthy pavement, regardless of the weather. The elements became less of an issue. The Bible, too, was built for all sorts

of weather. Despite circumstances, God's road—leading through the pages of the Holy Bible—can be trusted to carry weary travelers onward. When the storms of discouragement, anxiety, uncertainty, and despair come, the Word of God provides the rock upon which we can stand and move forward.

Fifth, and finally, both roads have gradually grown obsolete. In 1985, with a fully functioning network of interstate highways operating, Route 66 was officially decommissioned. The mother road became antiquated and too narrow to handle the increasing traffic demands of the late twentieth century. Thus, a more advanced and efficient highway system was devised. Furthermore, more options were provided. No longer was there a singular route to take one from the Midwest to California. Several highways, each spanning diverse landscapes and terrain, could lead one to the same destination.

What happened to Route 66 over the years also has happened to the sixty-six books that constitute the Bible. Both have followed similar trajectories toward obsolescence. With the onset of the information age and the proliferation of multiple sources from which to draw guidance, the Bible—like Route 66—came to be viewed as antiquated and narrow to the modern mind. Rather than looking to the Bible as our primary source for wisdom and life's direction, we are now told there are several options one might take to find guidance and fulfillment. Each option offers something unique and each, it is widely argued, leads to the same end point. We are told that what matters is having the freedom to choose where we want to go and how we get there. Consequently, fewer and fewer people give serious thought to the sixty-six books of the Bible and the messages those books contain. Like Route 66, whose story is remembered in books and museums today, the sixty-six books of the Bible have produced no shortage of descriptive commentary around a story increasingly marginalized and relegated to museums and cathedrals. In short, irrelevance has become the dominant collective response to 66—whether referring to the Route or the Bible.

ॐ ॐ

Sixty-Six is intended to offer a counter-perspective. Its premise is that the Bible is as relevant and applicable to life as ever. The book's subtitle—*A Sociologist Reflects on Scripture, Its Themes, and Their Relevance*—captures this central thought and provides insight regarding the book's overall purpose. Perhaps a few comments on the five key words contained in the subtitle will help one understand the author's intent more fully. I will take these words in reverse order, beginning with *relevance*. As implied above, I am operating with the belief that God's Word has as much to say to us today as it did to its original readers centuries ago. Its message is timeless, pertinent, and life-giving in every generation. In a fast-moving information age like ours, of course, it is tempting to dismiss the ancient text of the Bible in favor of new words, ideas, and interpretations that bombard us 24/7 through our smartphones and cable news. The challenge of the believer, as well as the task of Bible teachers and preachers, is to understand that God's inspired written Word remains our compass for life. We still need, and benefit from, the collective message of these sacred sixty-six books.

Themes form another emphasis here. The Bible's authors, like all authors, wrote to communicate an intentional message related to certain essential truths. Each book, therefore, has themes that get repeated. I have chosen in the pages that follow to focus on a theme from each book. The reader should not misunderstand me to be suggesting there is only one theme found in every book, for the reality is most books contain several important themes. I acknowledge that another person might highlight alternate themes if he or she undertook the same project. In fact, at another juncture in my own life, I might emphasize other themes as well. The pages that follow focus on those themes that caught my attention at the time I was studying and writing.

The themes typically emerged in one of three ways. First, most themes came from the fact that a particular word or phrase is repeated in a given book. For example, the repetition of "vanity" in the book of Ecclesiastes, "sovereignty" in the book of Ezekiel, "kingdom" in the book of Matthew, and "joy" in the book of Philippians made those easy and natural themes to identify. Repetition of words often reveals what a person values. Biblical authors communicated what mattered to them by referencing particular words multiple times. Second, other themes arose not so much from repetition of a word as from an overarching emphasis in the narrative. Examples include themes like the raw "courage" found in Daniel, the bold "witness" of early believers in the book of Acts, the importance of "actions" in James, and the "persistence" encouraged in Jude. An author's emphasis through stories and illustrations often demonstrates the primary theme and purpose of writing. Third, a few themes were derived from some unique aspect of the book. In a sense, this represents the opposite of the first two categories, repetition and emphasis. Some books are known for a singular or unusual characteristic. We see that when Esther highlights life in a "citadel," when the Song of Songs accentuates "romance," when Jonah keeps heading "down," and when Luke offers a careful "account" of the gospel. In these latter cases, a rare feature of a book seems to point to its central message and, therefore, suggests its theme.

The late Bible scholar and former president of Asbury College, Dr. Dennis F. Kinlaw, in his daily devotional *This Day with the Master* (2002), talked about the importance of biblical themes and how they contribute to understanding the overall truth of God's Word. Kinlaw had this to say in his July 24 reading, entitled "The Symphony of Scripture:"

> One of my professors in graduate school shocked a number of us when he said, "I get a bit afraid for many of you who underline what you like in the Bible." Furtively, I closed my Bible. He continued, "I suspect that I can tell you which verses you have underlined." And then he gave a remarkably accurate depiction of the portions that I had marked.
>
> He explained his point, informing us that what we did not underline was as much the Word of God as that which we did. He warned us that we should not study just the portions of the Scripture that we liked. The Scripture must be faced as a whole.
>
> Then he said, "You read a verse and it has meaning for you, so you highlight it. But what you want to do is move from a verse to a paragraph so that you can see the larger unit of which your favorite verse is only a part. You need to begin putting these units together so you can see whole segments of biblical truth. From that you will start to see biblical themes and how they are developed through the various parts of Scripture." If we did that, he insisted, we could begin to see the unity and beauty of the Word of God.
>
> It was then that I began to see that Scripture is a whole, though it is divided into sixty-six books written across many centuries. It is like a Beethoven symphony with its various themes, each of which is different, but each of which contributes to the beauty and power of the whole.

Sixty-Six attempts to portray what Kinlaw and his graduate school professor discovered. Scripture is indeed a symphony, with each movement building on what has come before and contributing to what comes next. Its themes do communicate an unparalleled "unity and beauty." Those who carefully pay attention to the message found in these sixty-six books will come to understand why the apostle Peter spoke with great confidence about "the living and enduring word of God" (1 Peter 1:23).

The third key word, and the basis of this entire project, is *Scripture*, by which I mean the standard sixty-six books central to the Christian faith. Back in 2002, I began teaching an intergenerational Sunday school class that went by the name "Scripture and Society." For nearly twenty years I had the wonderful privilege of leading fifty to eighty participants in a weekly study of God's Word. Six convictions, or principles, guided me then; they still do.

First, *Scripture is God's Word to us.* It is the primary way by which God speaks to his people today. Therefore, we ought to be familiar with the Bible and its message. How else will we know what God wants to tell us?

Second, *all Scripture is from God.* The whole Bible—Old Testament and New Testament books alike—demands our attention. Every book of the Bible has a message we need to hear. Difficulty in ascertaining that message or discomfort in hearing it does not excuse us from attending to what God says. We need to know the entirety of Scripture—the Old Testament and the New, the law and the prophets, the proverbs and the parables, the heart-warming stories and the heart-wrenching stories, the familiar favorites and the obscure passages. All of it comes from God, and is intended "for teaching, rebuking, correcting and training in righteousness" (2 Tim 3:16).

Third, *Scripture is relevant and applicable.* As noted earlier, its message is timeless and universal. The Enemy works to convince us otherwise. Nonetheless, the witness of countless people across history and nations tells a different story, a story corroborating the value and inspiration of God's Word regardless of time or place.

Fourth, *Scripture is best studied as it was written.* In other words, we are best served when we read and study one book at a time, from its beginning to its end. Though this is the standard way to read any book, I fear we have turned the Bible into a dictionary or recipe book, going to it to extract a limited text from a much larger context. Many well-meaning preachers do this, contributing unintentionally to the confusion and lack of interest people in the pew have toward opening their Bibles. Who wants to read a disjointed dictionary? Consequently, meaningful overarching themes and threads that a biblical author is trying to weave through a book are routinely missed. We have our much-loved passages that we post on the office wall or on social media but fail to realize that Scripture is a library of sixty-six books, each with beginnings, endings, characters, and themes. Lost are the deeper truths that a more comprehensive and systematic approach to reading the books of the Bible would help us gain.

Fifth, *Scripture is needed by all.* No age group or people group is exempt. When I was asked to consider teaching the adult Sunday school class referenced earlier, two options were suggested. The church was looking for someone to lead a group of young adults and someone else to begin a class for senior citizens. "Let's combine them," I said, probably somewhat naively. My response, however, was based on the belief that we all share the same basic need: to be immersed in the Word of God and discover its relevance. An intergenerational class—ranging in age from eighteen to ninety years old—was born; it was also international and interracial. University professors, students, business leaders, young moms and dads, medical professionals, housewives, and retired folks studied the Word together. God—through his Word—has something to say to all of us.

Sixth, *the study of Scripture happens best when it includes a good dose of joy, laughter, hope, and optimism.* Even when topics are tough and challenging, the student of Scripture can throw his or her head back and laugh because of knowledge that the overall story ends in victory. It is my belief, therefore, that laughter and delight—not to be mistaken for frivolity or disrespect—are indispensable. What a shame to understand or promote God's Word as dry theology or rigid orthodoxy, void of winsomeness and appeal. Those of us who teach the Word of God are obliged to do all we can to make it attractive and meaningful, without compromising its message. Joy and laughter are appropriate ingredients that enrich the study of Scripture.

These six guiding principles have influenced the writing of *Sixty-Six*. The degree to which I have been successful and kept true to my convictions will be determined by you, the reader. Human shortcomings and limitations notwithstanding, the design here is to encourage honest reflection on significant overarching biblical themes across all sixty-six books that comprise this ancient, sacred, and still relevant text.

The subtitle further suggests that what is contained in this volume are *reflections.* This is my way of saying that the material here should not be viewed as "the last word" on any of the subjects or themes. Rather, these are contributions from one individual seeking to understand God's Word and its relevance to life today. As mentioned above, another student of the Word might suggest alternate themes suitable for some, or all, of the sixty-six books in the Bible. That is the nature of God's Word; its richness and depth prohibit any single person from ever exhausting it. While Scripture's message is universal, it also speaks uniquely and pointedly to each individual soul. My prayer is that the reader will allow the reflections contained within these pages to inspire him or her to engage in further reflection on God's Word. I have confidence that the Holy Spirit will guide individuals who dare to do so.

Because these are reflections, the reader will find I have often shared experiences from my own personal life that illustrate or describe a given topic. For example, I grew up with deaf siblings and worked for years in a world where sign language was used and Deaf community values were prized. Therefore, occasional stories pertaining to those experiences have made their way into this volume. Numerous other entries include brief personal or family stories intended to illuminate a particular point. In summary, the sixty-six reflections on Scripture that fill these pages frequently draw from those areas of life with which I am most familiar. I hope in the process that I have enhanced the clarity of the book's message.

Finally, reference is made in the subtitle to the author being a *sociologist*. I have been shaped by graduate education that has included both seminary and sociology. The former lit the fires for the study of God's Word; the latter gave me tools and strategies that influence how I study God's world. For nearly three decades I have served as a professor of sociology. Not surprisingly, then, the reader will note numerous entries in this volume that specifically reference sociology. Beyond explicit references, however, one will find other evidence that the author is operating as a sociologist. Four markers of a sociologist at work are all on display in this book.

Observation. Sociologists are trained to observe details in human behavior. Not surprisingly, then, observations form the heart of this book, some pertaining to Scripture and some pertaining to society at large. For example, we will observe the prophet Jonah going down to Joppa, falling down into the sea, sitting down in the shade, and sinking down in despair; the trajectory of his life was unmistakably downward. We will observe that the apostle John references love more than any other biblical writer, with nearly ninety percent of his references occurring as verbs; love is what we do. We will also observe behaviors of contemporary life such as the use of iPhones, unrest in city streets, family breakdown, and more. All these observations and others like them—whether of God's written Word or of human activity—provide insight into social behavior and often signal repeated patterns. One can learn a great deal about the Bible and his or her neighbor by simple observation. We will do that in the pages ahead.

Counting. Sociologists like to count. Quantifying populations, behaviors, problems, or any other social phenomena is what sociologists do. Counting provides measurement of and insight into the magnitude of trends, strengths, or emphases. We will notice that the prophet Jeremiah called the people of God to "listen" or "hear" nearly 150 times, whereas the prophet Ezekiel referenced "the Sovereign Lord" over 200 times. The title "Christ" is mentioned over 560 times across the New Testament. Observing and then counting these and many other words provide perspective that can be gained no other way, often underscoring a biblical author's focus on a particular theme. Counting allows us to make important comparisons. The practice is a useful tool regularly employed by sociologists in their work.

Analysis. Sociologists contend that meaning and relationships are best understood when observations and measurements (counting) are followed by careful thought and examination. Such a process allows us to explore possibilities and make informed interpretations of a variety of social behavior, including the behavior of authors. Thus, we will strive to analyze the messages and purposes of biblical writers. For example, why does the romantic and sensuous Song of Songs appear in the middle of the Bible? Why are "evil," "judgment," "anger," and "warning" all major themes if God is loving? Why do Matthew and Revelation—the bookends of the New Testament—both reference heaven so often? Analysis encourages intentional exploration and evaluation of that which our eyes see and our minds process; it pushes us to look for elusive answers to tough questions.

The Sociological Imagination. Sociologist C. Wright Mills, in his 1959 book *The Sociological Imagination*, popularized the idea of finding connections between an individual experience and larger social forces. The concept has to do with stretching one's mind beyond the obvious and recognizing there are bigger things going on than what the human eye can perceive. *Sixty-Six* will suggest, for example, that Ruth's character, Daniel's courage, Hosea's predicament, and Timothy's hardship had meaning and purpose far beyond how they were experienced by the respective individuals. God was doing something in the larger community of his people—indeed, in the wider world itself—of which these individuals were only a small part. The sociological imagination, while acknowledging and respecting individual experience, understands that external social influences, relationships, and forces are also operating. We will find that to be true over and over again as we make our way through this book.

In summary, the book's subtitle—*A Sociologist Reflects on Scripture, its Themes, and their Relevance*—is descriptive of what the reader will discover in the following pages. My hope is that those who read through the chapters ahead will find the content insightful, instructive, and encouraging, while stimulating even further exploration of the sixty-six books that comprise the Bible.

ℰ   ℭ

The inspiration for *Sixty-Six* can be traced back to late 2019, when my wife and I determined to read through the entire Bible over the course of the subsequent year, 2020. For most of the previous four decades, my approach to studying Scripture had been to do so book by book, chapter by chapter, in a methodical and detailed manner. In so doing, I had read through the entire Bible—some books, in fact, multiple times—but due to the slow pace, it took me years to get through all sixty-six books in their entirety. Nonetheless, the practice shaped my own study and understanding of Scripture and provided regular nourishment to my needy soul. I highly recommend the routine, especially to those who like to journal and savor details.

This alternate approach to reading the Bible was different for one accustomed to plodding through its 1,189 chapters and pondering words and phrases along the way. By reading several chapters a day, in order to keep on schedule and complete the whole reading assignment in a year, I saw things in a new light. The experience might be likened to a fly-over of a particular geographical area, after having spent years traversing the same area on the ground. I discovered I had spent so much time on details that I had forgotten the overall lay of the land, perhaps like a botanist who spends years studying the floor of the Amazon rainforest, but never flies over the area to see its expanse, design, and magnitude.

After a few weeks into the year—with only a handful of books from the Bible under my belt—I began to see themes emerge that, at times, I did not remember seeing earlier. Then the COVID-19 pandemic hit and slowed life down for everyone around the world. The slowdown, while troublesome and tragic on so many levels, provided me more time to keep up my scheduled Bible reading. The result was that I reached my goal; by the end of 2020, I had completed all sixty-six sacred books I had set out to read (as did my wife). Somewhere along the year's journey I began to assign a title, or theme, to each book I had read. The theme summarized my reflections on what I perceived to be a central message from that particular book.

Due to the pandemic and its corresponding shutdown, the Scripture & Society Sunday school class that I was leading was not gathering in person for weekly class sessions but began operating on a remote basis. I sent out weekly email lessons to a class list of nearly 120 individuals. As I prayed and thought about the direction of the class for the new year ahead, 2021, I sensed God's Spirit direct me to the sixty-six books and themes I had studied throughout 2020. Consequently, starting the first Sunday of January 2021, I sent out the initial installment of what became sixty-six consecutive weeks of themes from every book in the Bible. *Sixty-Six* is a collection of those emailed themes and reflections, revised and edited for publication here.

ॐ ॰

This book, by its very design, is not intended to be read hurriedly from beginning to end. Optimally, I would recommend no more than one chapter, or theme, be read a day. Some may prefer to read only one entry per week, as the sixty-six themes were originally developed and delivered. I suspect readers will benefit most when they take adequate time to pause and reflect on what God is communicating through a given book of the Bible and its corresponding theme.

Each entry, or chapter, will begin with key verses from a book in the Bible, followed by reflections on a significant theme from that same book. The reflections typically will combine insights from Scripture, a connection to contemporary society, and often some personal reference to illustrate an aspect of the theme. A short prayer follows each reflective thought. Then some questions are asked that might be used for either personal consideration or discussion with other trusted individuals.

Finally, longer recommended readings from the Bible are offered at the end of each respective entry. These are provided for those who want to dig deeper into a book and its suggested theme. In most cases, reading one recommended Bible chapter per day will allow a person to complete all the supplemental readings within a week.

§Ͻ   ϹΆ

Finally, in keeping with the title of this book, most of what the reader will find in the following pages was written when I, the author, was age sixty-six. Perhaps that is mere coincidence. Or perhaps it provides further evidence to the enduring relevance of God's Word in that it still speaks even when one is well into his seventh decade of life. What I know for certain is this: the Bible and its themes continue to captivate me, assist me to understand my world, and animate me to respond in meaningful ways. I still get my kicks by traveling 66—the route that God's people have taken before me. I invite you to join me on the journey.

OLD TESTAMENT THEMES

෨ ෬

1

GENESIS: Family

So God created man in his own image, in the image of God
he created him; male and female he created them. God
blessed them and said to them, "Be fruitful and increase in
number; fill the earth and subdue it." (Genesis 1:27–28)

The LORD then said to Noah, "Go into the ark, you
and your whole family, because I have found you
righteous in this generation. (Genesis 7:1)

Joseph stayed in Egypt, along with all his father's family.
He lived a hundred and ten years .... (Genesis 50:22)

The Bible begins with the creation story, culminating with the human family. Several times throughout the creation narrative God looked at his handiwork and called it "good." However, after creating complementary male and female humans, instituting marriage between them, giving them the capacity and the command to procreate (i.e., to join God in the act of creation), and establishing the family unit as the prototype for all future social relationships, God elevated his appraisal by announcing his work was "very good" (Gen 1:31). Indeed, it was.

What follows in the book of Genesis is the story of family life. The families of Adam, Noah, Abraham, Isaac, and Jacob—and their interactions with God, family members, and neighbors—make up the content of the first book of Holy Scripture. The Bible begins with neither a theological explanation of God nor a philosophical description of man, nor even a list of expectations for those who mine the pages of this sacred text. Plain and simple, the dominant theme as the Bible opens is the genesis of the family. Once God is established as the timeless, eternal Creator ("In the beginning God created . . ."), and once creation is set in motion in the first chapter of Genesis, the book proceeds with forty-nine additional chapters of family life. Every page contains a mixture of ordinary and dramatic circumstances experienced by individuals who come to us in families. These events would become the repeated ebb and flow of family life that would mark human existence for millennia thereafter, and still does today.

Like every family that has ever existed, biblical families are remembered for both their contributions and their disappointments. I have never met a perfect family in my lifetime. As I search the pages of Scripture, I find the same to be true there. The sin that occurred in Genesis 3 tainted every individual and family that followed. Adam and his family were known for the kind of work they did, caring for God's creation. However, pride, jealousy, and sin soon destroyed their idyllic home and small community. Noah and his family were known for being righteous, godly, and obedient. Nonetheless, near the end of his life, Noah's sons were involved in an act of disrespect that resulted in a tragic curse. Abraham, Isaac, and Jacob formed a three-generation family that would be remembered for its faith for centuries to come. Unfortunately, they would also be remembered for multiple acts of deception that marked their family line. Families are like that. They teach and nurture us and, because of fallen human nature, sometimes embarrass and shame us. Despite the imperfections, we dare not miss the family's priority in the eyes of God. The family was God's design, his first social institution, his intention for how humans would live and thrive in the world.

Families make several important contributions to their members and to wider society. Sociologists often refer to these as social functions. Examples abound in the book of Genesis. Adam and Eve illustrated the primary family function of reproduction. Cain, Abel (4:1–2), and Seth (5:3) were all mentioned by name; but "other sons and daughters" (5:4) also became part of this initial family. Noah protected his family from the flood that engulfed the world (7:1, 5–7). Families were designed not only to reproduce but to protect and care for one another. Abraham "believed the LORD" (15:6), taught his son Isaac to do the same (22:7–8), and has long been remembered as the father of our faith (Rom 4:12–18).

Thus, we see the important role that the family plays in the formation of one's relationship with God. When famine and starvation threatened his family, the patriarch Jacob rallied his sons to go and "buy grain from Egypt" (42:1–3) so that they might provide food for their entire extended family. Time and again in the very first book of the Bible we see the family functioning in ways that contribute to society and that help foster social order. Reproduction, protection and care, matters of faith, and economic provision are all significant social functions carried out by the family. God had a practical purpose in mind when he designed us to live in families. Family life was neither arbitrary nor the result of a cosmic accident. Personal and social good were part of God's family plan.

Is it any wonder, then, that the Enemy—known throughout Scripture as Satan and referred to in Genesis as "the serpent" (3:1)—would marshal all his forces to attack what God valued, prioritized, and intended to use for human flourishing? What God created for noble purposes, the Enemy sought to degrade and destroy. That has not changed today. Gender, marriage, childbearing, and family life—all parts of God's "very good" creation—remain favorite targets of the Adversary. God's creative design for family life continues to experience the Enemy's relentless and vicious assaults. Consider the following social issues that mark family life in the twenty-first century:

- Gender confusion, wherein people now reject what they perceive to be limitations resulting from God's dual categories of male and female.
- Instability of marriage, wherein relationships are built on feelings rather than the commitment God intended, thus making divorce far too common.
- Redefinition of marriage, wherein the complementarity of both sexes—so beautifully united by God—is now seen as optional and largely irrelevant in a marriage.
- Devaluation of childbearing, wherein children, once seen as gifts of God (Ps 127:3), are routinely aborted, abandoned, marginalized, or even avoided altogether.
- Family breakdown, wherein fathers are too often absent, mothers are too often disadvantaged economically, and children too often suffer serious anxiety and behavior problems, leaving God's priority institution in shambles.

While certainly not a comprehensive list, the consequences of the Enemy's ruthless and ongoing attacks on family life have been catastrophic for both individuals and communities. God's design has been shattered and the carnage is evident everywhere one looks.

Though the specifics have changed over time, the assault on the family itself is not a new phenomenon. The roots of the assault can be traced back to the earliest families in Genesis. Whereas God designed the family for reproduction, care, protection, faith in God, and provision of its members, the Enemy was quick to introduce to the family the destructive practices of murder (4:8), polygamy (4:19), deception (12:13; 20:2; 27:19), disrespect (25:29–34), betrayal (37:23–28), promiscuity (38:15–18), and more. God's divine design was tarnished early, and the effects continue to wreak havoc in homes in this current century.

Despite the tragic consequences and distortion of sin, however, the family has remained one of the most distinguishing features of social life everywhere. There is not a people group known to anthropology or sociology that does not exist in families. Human beings continue to form and live in family units. What began in Genesis became the pattern for all generations to follow. People became known for whose son or daughter they were, to what tribe they belonged, and who their ancestors were. Families carried with them identity, social status, and distinction. For example, to be from the tribe (family) of Judah made one distinct from those who were from the tribe (family) of Levi. While Judah's family became known for its royalty, Levi's family became known for its priestly role and duties. Family names still carry with them meaning among community members long after the accounts in Genesis.

Nonetheless, by the late 1800s, as the Bible increasingly became the object of criticism and skepticism, its teachings became suspect. Among the many casualties were the once widely accepted views pertaining to all elements of creation, including the human family. Early family scholars from the fields of anthropology and sociology began proposing an evolutionary model for understanding the family's origin. Rejecting the creation account and the subsequent narrative found in Genesis, these social critics looked for another way to describe the family's roots. What that meant was that God's design was no longer seen as the starting point for our understanding, a starting point that sin then distorted. Rather, an evolutionary explanation was adopted, suggesting there had been a series of family types throughout human history that eventually led to the model with which we have become most familiar:

the male-female, monogamous, permanent, childbearing model. Like all previous models—according to the evolutionary argument—this one too, over time, should be expected to give way to new forms of the family.

Karl Marx's friend and collaborator, Friedrich Engels, provides a case in point. Marx and Engels tied the current form of family life to capitalism. Not long after Marx died, Engels wrote a lengthy essay entitled, "The Origin of the Family, Private Property, and the State" (1884). Engels noted that the modern family was a product of capitalism, not the product of a creative and sovereign God, who the atheistic Marx had long before dismissed. According to Marx and Engels, once capitalism was abolished the current family form would disappear with it. New ways of forming intimate relationships—new designs for the family—would then emerge. With this understanding, of course, no one need be surprised or concerned with subsequent changes to family life. This view, or some form of it, became the dominant position held by family scholars in secular universities. The implication, of course, was that family changes are simply evolutionary adaptations and adjustments to new and better ways of relating that fit the current generation. With this logic, no one need be alarmed at what has happened to the family over the past half-century. In fact, we should expect to see still other evolutionary changes in years to come.

Could Satan have devised a more cunning plan than his multifaceted attack on the family? Questioning the family's design, origins, definition, and purpose has had the cumulative effect of challenging the Creator. Could there be a more effective strategy to defy God and reject his intentions and lordship? The serpent's original question to our ancestors—*"Did God really say . . . ?"* (3:1)—continues to echo through the corridors of time. In few arenas has the answer to the question been more consequential than in how we understand, define, and live as families. God's authority has been usurped and his design distorted.

May God forgive and restore us. Families matter. They always have. Social order and civility are products of healthy family life. All one must do is read through the book of Genesis to catch a glimpse of the practical plan and immeasurable possibilities inherent in this first social institution.

PRAYER

Our Father in heaven (even in praying we acknowledge the family, for we call you "our Father"), thank you for your design and order. Forgive us for neglecting your creative intent when it comes to our families. Restore sanity to our land once again in our understanding of gender, marriage, childbearing, and families. You have created these for our good. Help us to value what you have made. May we give our families the attention they deserve. May we live in harmony with those you have placed within our care. May our relationships exhibit godliness and obedience to your Word. May our families reflect and honor you in all our ways. AMEN.

QUESTIONS

1. What are two or three positive values you have inherited from your family? What contributions has your family made in your development? How have those shaped you?

2. What are some practical strategies society might employ to strengthen marriages and families today? How might people respond if we encouraged such strategies?

3. Why do you think family problems are often the cause of such intense emotional human pain? How is such pain best addressed or resolved?

4. Why does it matter what people think about the origins of the family? What practical difference does it make? What outcomes might we expect from having different views?

SUGGESTED READING

Genesis 1–3, 12, 21–22, 24, 37

2

Exodus: Obedience

*Pharaoh said, "Who is the LORD, that I should
obey him and let Israel go?" (Exodus 5:2)*

*Now if you obey me fully and keep my covenant, then out of all
nations you will be my treasured possession. (Exodus 19:5)*

Obey what I command you today. (Exodus 34:11)

The theme of obedience dominates the book of Exodus. Once God
created the world and established the family, the matter of obeying the Creator needed to be addressed. In fact, this need existed long
before Exodus. The first sin of the first family was an act of disobedience (Gen 3). Not surprisingly, then, the second book of Holy Scripture
emphasizes obedience. It is as if God said to his people (his new family):
"Let me make this clear. If you want to thrive, reach your potential, and
experience all that I have planned for you, you must obey me. Ignoring
me and insisting on your own way will result in tragic consequences."

Then the entire Exodus account proceeds to illustrate the need for obedience and the consequences of disobedience. Consider the following:

1. Near the beginning of the book Moses had several exchanges with God (chs 3–6) wherein the central issue was whether Moses would obey God and return to Egypt.

2. Pharaoh scoffed at the idea of obeying the Lord, Yahweh (5:2). Not only was Pharaoh the ruling authority in Egypt but the Egyptians had their own gods if one was needed.

3. Pharaoh's hard heart (7:13, 22; 8:15, 19, 32; etc.) and disobedience resulted in multiple plagues inflicting his people and land in Egypt (chs 7–11).

4. God gave his people special instructions for Passover (ch 12). Those instructions were to be carefully obeyed that night. The events also were to be remembered and repeated annually as a reminder of God's intervention and deliverance (see 12:24).

5. Obedience was the key to the Israelites safely crossing the Red Sea (ch 14) and later in obtaining water, manna, and quail to sustain them on their journey (chs 15–17).

6. At Mount Sinai, God gave Moses the Ten Commandments and expected complete obedience to those commands (chs 19–20).

7. Instructions for building the tabernacle and its furnishings were to be strictly followed and obeyed (chs 25–31).

8. While Moses was delayed on the mountain listening to God, Israel disobeyed and built a golden calf (ch 32). Then we read these words: "the Lord struck the people with a plague because of what they did with the calf Aaron had made" (32:35).

It would be difficult to read Exodus and miss this emphasis: God's people—his family—would not have much of a future unless they obeyed him. The rest of the Old Testament includes a collection of stories describing those who obeyed and disobeyed, and the consequences associated with each.

Obedience is so fundamental to human and social flourishing that everything else flows from this principle. For example, physical health depends on following basic dietary and exercise laws. Social order grows out of adherence to principles of communication and respect. Spiritual vitality rests on consistent obedience to God and his Word. Is it any wonder the prophet Samuel would one day rebuke King Saul with these words: "To obey is better than sacrifice" (1 Sam 15:22)? Valued rituals, social activism, personal initiative, and good intentions all must take a back seat to uncompromising obedience. Conformity to the will of God is the timeless foundation upon which all subsequent human activity and devotion derive their purpose and meaning. Obedience is the cornerstone upon which every aspect of life—physical, social, or spiritual—works best.

There are several fundamental truths discovered in Exodus that provide helpful insight regarding the nature of obedience:

- Obedience is best learned in a family.
- Obedience assumes a higher authority.
- Obedience requires an awareness of expectations.
- Obedience demands individual submission.

Failure to appreciate and understand any one of these assertions lies at the root of why people of every generation have struggled to obey. Therefore, each is worthy of further exploration.

The family and obedience. The order and presentation of dominant themes at the beginning of Scripture are not accidental. The family, emphasized in Genesis, is the most fertile ground for learning obedience, emphasized in Exodus. God revealed himself in a family—Father, Son, and Holy Spirit. And one of the characteristics we know about the Son is that he obeyed his Father (see Matt 26:38, 42; Phil 2:6–8). So even the obedience of God's Son took place in a family context. What an example for the human family, wherein it is expected that obedience will be taught, modeled, and required of each new generation. Is anyone surprised, then, that as family life has continued to unravel over the past half-century, we have witnessed increasing civil disobedience, disorder, and incarceration rates in our society? A quick check of the daily news reminds us of the crises that result from family breakdown and the disturbing acts of disobedience that inevitably follow in its wake. Those who fail to teach, model, and demand obedience at home do a tragic disservice not only to their family members but ultimately to wider society. When families—fathers and mothers—fail to instill obedience, society is charged with the task and the results are never pleasant. The tantrum of a child is much easier to address and correct than the tantrum of an adult. Obedience is best learned in a family, the principle being passed from one generation to the next.

Higher authority and obedience. By its very nature, obedience acknowledges a higher authority. Obedience requires an object or individual to which it responds. It implies there is someone who knows more than I do, someone to whom I ought to listen for direction. The Bible declares that "someone" is *Yahweh*—the great I AM, the God of Abraham, Isaac, and Jacob. He is both Creator and Authority. Obedience recognizes him as the supreme and ultimate expert. Early in Exodus (5:2), Pharaoh rejected that fact, asking, "Who is the LORD [*Yahweh*], that I should obey him . . . ?" The implication was that Pharaoh himself was in charge; he answered to no one else. Other world leaders before and after Pharaoh have done the same, denying any external authority above themselves. This has been a tendency among not only political leaders but also the brightest academic minds. Higher education encourages specialization that delves deep into a subject. When someone does so, exploring the intricacies of a singular topic, we are prone to call that person an expert in his or her field, an authority to whom others turn for guidance. The danger, of course, is that such people—whether world rulers or world-renowned academic experts—begin to believe their authority extends beyond the boundaries of their limited area of knowledge and influence. Interestingly, as civilization has progressed in recent years, there is evidence that we have witnessed a simultaneous decline in our trust of authority. Advancements in technology, science, and information have given us greater trust and confidence in our own ability to function without outside input. We have convinced ourselves that we now stand as our own authority. Who needs God when we have confidence in ourselves and access to infinite resources at our fingertips? Higher authority has given way to inner authority. We consider ourselves to be in charge, masters of our own destiny. When such thinking dominates, obedience falls by the wayside and civility gives way to anarchy as everyone demands his or her own individual rights.

Awareness of expectations and obedience. One cannot obey unless one is clear regarding what is expected. Fortunately, God did not leave his people wondering. Exodus makes clear that God—our Authority—went to great lengths to explain his expectations. Details and restrictions regarding the Passover (Ex 12), the ten specific commandments (Ex 20), and instructions for building the ark and the tabernacle (Ex 25–30; 37–40) all point to a God who was concerned that his people know what was expected of them. Moses walked and talked with God, as did many other notable biblical characters, thus hearing what the Divine Authority had to say. Once those early followers of God heard from him, they obeyed him. In fact, the Hebrew word for "obey" and "hear" are one and the same. To hear was to obey; no reasonable person would have the audacity to do otherwise. Today one of the primary ways a believer hears from God and gains awareness of what he expects is from the Bible, the written Word of God. We read it, study it, hear it declared, and put its teaching into practice. Failure to take God's Word seriously jeopardizes life. Limited awareness and shallow knowledge delude us into assuming we know more than we do and can function as our own authority. Sadly, society and its media are littered with examples of those who are self-proclaimed experts, obeying only their selfish desires and passions. Awareness of what God expects is shallow and marginal to life—if such awareness exists at all.

Submission and obedience. Obedience is ultimately an act of submission, and therein lies a major problem. The people of Israel struggled with this during Moses' day, and that struggle has persisted in every generation since. The stories of Scripture are the stories of individuals and groups who repeatedly had to make a choice: would they submit to the Lord God (*Yahweh*), or would they reject him and choose another god? Would they attempt to usurp God's authority and elevate themselves as the supreme power? That same question has confronted every group of people over the centuries. We should not be surprised, then, that in a cultural climate like ours that has long advocated independence, assertiveness, and self-expression, submission to anyone or anything continues to be rare. Force and even violence, if necessary, are viewed as much more effective and utilitarian than compliant surrender. We have convinced ourselves that submissive obedience may have had a place in a bygone era but has little relevance to the kind of world we inhabit today. Sadly, however, without a willingness and recognition of one's need to submit, there will never be the obedience required by God; and without obedience, a relationship with the Creator will be distorted and soon nonexistent.

Social analysts widely agree that family chaos and civil disobedience are two characteristics that mark twenty-first-century American culture. Are these just realities we must get used to and live with today? No! The first two books of Holy Scripture point to a better way, the way of obedience lived and modeled in families. When that becomes the pattern—when God's way is embraced rather than scorned—entire communities benefit.

Let us determine to refocus on God's Word that speaks of family design and encourages obedience to Divine Authority. Therein lies our hope during tumultuous and distressing times. Therein lies our foundation for social order. Therein lies the way to please the Lord our God.

PRAYER

O Lord, our God, you have called us to obey and yet too often we have failed to do so. Forgive us and our many excuses. Forgive our pride and independence. Forgive our failure to recognize our need for your direction. From this day forward help us to be an obedient people concerned about doing your will rather than our own. May we submit to your Lordship. May our desires be in alignment with your desires, and may we do what you command. Give us strength to do so even when others do not. We offer this prayer in the name of your Son, Jesus Christ, who submitted himself "and became obedient . . . even [to] death on a cross" (Phil 2:8). AMEN.

QUESTIONS

1. After reviewing the list of major stories found in Exodus (see page 34), which one do you think makes the strongest case for obedience? Why is that story so meaningful?

2. Looking back over your own life, does an example come to mind of a time you willingly disobeyed an authority? What were the consequences of that act of disobedience?

3. Why are some people more inclined to obey authority than others? What factors do you think make the difference? How is obedience best taught?

4. In general, what makes it hard to obey the Lord today? Do you think it is harder or easier to obey the Lord today than it was during Moses' day? Why?

SUGGESTED READING

Exodus 3–4; 12–14; 16; 20

3

LEVITICUS: Holiness

*You must distinguish between the holy and the common,
between the unclean and the clean. (Leviticus 10:10)*

*I am the LORD your God; consecrate yourselves and be
holy, because I am holy . . . I am the LORD who brought
you up out of Egypt to be your God; therefore be holy,
because I am holy . . . You must distinguish between the
unclean and the clean . . . (Leviticus 11:44–47)*

*You are to be holy to me because I, the LORD, am holy, and I have
set you apart from the nations to be my own. (Leviticus 20:26)*

God called his family—represented by Abraham, Isaac, Jacob, and
their descendants (Genesis)—to be obedient (Exodus) and holy
(Leviticus). Throughout Scripture these fundamental marks, or characteristics, of God's people remained unchanged. Obedience *to* God
and being holy *like* God always have distinguished the faithful. Other
characteristics such as love, joy, peace, and hope would flow from these
two descriptions and further identify God's family. Obedience and holiness, however, were the foundational and indispensable attributes that
continued to define God's people across the pages of Scripture. Those
who fail to obey and fail to live a holy life undermine their relationship
with the Creator God and harm their witness to the world.

The word *holy* is found more times in Leviticus than in any other book of the Bible, occurring over eighty times there. What makes it so important that it would be given such emphasis early in sacred Scripture? In part, the answer has to do with ownership. God is making a people who are his "own" (20:26). To be called "holy," then, establishes one's identity as belonging to God and no one else. Paul amplified and applied that idea centuries later when he wrote these words to the Corinthians, "You are not your own; you were bought at a price. Therefore honor God with your body" (1 Cor 6:19–20). The context of Paul's admonition was keeping oneself from sexual immorality. When writing to the Thessalonians, Paul made a similar connection when he said, "It is God's will that you should be sanctified; that you should avoid sexual immorality; that each of you should learn to control his own body in a way that is holy and honorable" (1 Thess 4:3–4). To be holy is to belong to God. To belong to God is to keep one's body from sexual immorality and distortion. To keep oneself from sexual immorality is to stand against the teachings and practices of the culture. In other words, holiness is a big deal with big consequences.

Not surprisingly, over the years there has been significant confusion and mischaracterization regarding what it means to be holy. Anything that God values so much is likely to get contested in every generation. Such is the case here. What, then, can we learn from this early scriptural emphasis on holiness that might help us today? A closer look at how holiness is described in Leviticus reveals at least three ways to understand the term: to be holy is to be Godlike, distinct, and set apart. None of these traits is popular in contemporary society. In fact, all three descriptions run counter to the social norms of the twenty-first century, adding to the discomfort most people feel when they open the book of Leviticus. Pausing to reflect on each of these portrayals of holiness, however, may prove helpful.

First, we are told repeatedly that we should be holy because God is holy (11:44, 45; 19:2; 20:26; 21:8). Holiness describes God's very nature, or essence. Now he invites us, his people, to share that nature. To be holy, then, means to be like God, plain and simple. Holy people look and act like God. How does one do that? How does one become like God? I suspect this happens the same way a person becomes like anyone else: by spending time in the other's presence and listening to what the other has to say. That is certainly how a husband and wife become like each other over time, or how a child becomes like a parent, or a student like a teacher, or a disciple like his or her mentor. For the follower of God this implies becoming familiar with his Word, so we really do know what he has to say or how he might respond. It implies talking with him regularly—in prayer—and living in his presence so that conversation can continue all day long. The words "be holy, because I am holy" (11:44) come as an invitation to be Godlike: Be like him. Act like him. Talk like him. Love like him. See like him. Care like him. How different the world would be if holy people inhabited it.

The reality is too few people today who claim to be Christians, and who attend respectable churches in their communities, give serious attention to becoming more like God. Unfortunately, I fear our distorted view of what it means to be Godlike looks to outsiders as if we are trying to be sovereign and in control rather than sacrificial, loving, and oriented toward serving others. Do we aim to be like God? If so, what does that look like? What do others see in our lives that indicates we are holy like him? The command has not changed over the centuries, as Peter made clear when he later wrote: "Be holy, because I am holy" (1 Pet 1:16; cf. Lev 11:44, 45).

Second, to be holy means one "must distinguish between the holy and the common, between the unclean and the clean" (10:10). Distinctions are associated with holy living. Sadly, our politically-correct, fragile culture has frightened us away from making distinctions about almost anything today. Distinctions imply acts of judgment or discrimination, which cultural experts have convinced us ought to be categorically despised and rejected. The result of this extreme position has led not only to human tragedy but to widespread neglect of a key divine principle. Distinctions occur on the first page of Scripture, at the time of creation (Gen 1), and on the last page of Scripture, describing those who will be included and excluded from that eternal and holy city known as heaven (Rev 22:14–15). Throughout God's Word, his people are called to distinguish, or discern, between the holy and the common, the clean and the unclean, good and evil, and truth and falsehood. There are certain God-ordained distinctions put in place for humanity's good; these dare not be ignored. The idea that we should avoid making any distinctions is anti-biblical, anti-historical, and anti-rational. This modern inclination grows out of a yearning to be affirmed for any decision or lifestyle choice one makes and out of fear that someone may be offended by God's standard. And what is that standard? Be holy. Be distinct. Be different than the surrounding world and its values.

Over one hundred years ago the French sociologist Émile Durkheim, in his study of religion that resulted in his writing the book *The Elementary Forms of the Religious Life* (1915), distinguished between the sacred and the profane, or that which is holy and that which is common. Drawing upon his Jewish upbringing (his father and grandfather were both rabbis), Durkheim recognized the distinction found in Leviticus that would become the foundation for Judeo-Christian orthodoxy. He understood that daily social life depicts a difference between that which is considered holy and that which is not. That difference, according to Durkheim, is perceptible, definitive, and worthy of social maintenance. Whatever is set apart to be holy—or "sacred," to use Durkheim's term—helps form and maintain a religious community. In other words, distinction lies at the heart of a community of believers and provides meaning to the group and to the surrounding society. Without such a distinction there would be no community of faith, no church, no reason for religious expression.

Third, to be holy carries the idea of being "set . . . apart from the nations" (20:26). The King James Version states it this way: "severed . . . from other people." Separation is emphasized. Many will not like the sound of this, especially after having endured months of separation and isolation due to the COVID-19 pandemic. Some may ask: "Do you mean I have to live like this permanently?" All I know is this: God is seeking a holy people—those "set apart" for him—to accomplish his purposes in the world. He knows the human tendency to act like one's peers and do what they do. That was clearly illustrated early in the garden when the first family listened more to each other than they listened to God (Gen 3). Ever since then, God has been seeking those who would listen to him. He found such a person in Noah, then Abraham, and then Moses. These were holy individuals "set apart" for God's work. There is no indication that this divine calling has changed; God still looks for holy men and women. He seeks those who are more interested in what he says and does than they are in what their peers say and do. Such people are rare. They are more attuned to God than they are to Hollywood, Wall Street, Washington politics, cable news, Facebook, or any other social media outlet. They have set themselves apart and live *for* and *like* God. They are holy.

To summarize, holiness means looking like God, making distinctions, and separating oneself from the surrounding world's influence. However, all of this creates a problem today because we are more comfortable living like our peers than like God. We have been told repeatedly that making distinctions is a sign of bigotry and moral weakness. Separation is anathema to a generation that thrives on staying connected and making comparisons with neighbors. Nonetheless, God calls his people to be holy. Could it be that he is looking for such a people in these unsettling and extraordinary days? Is it possible that holy people not only please our Lord but provide the most effective witness to our watching neighbors?

Two final thoughts are worth noting:

1. We cannot become holy on our own. Our efforts will not bring this about. The writer of Leviticus is clear that it is God who makes us holy (20:8; 21:8, 15, 23; 22:16, 32). All we can do is come to him humbly and obediently, surrendering and letting him do the work in us. When that is our posture, he will make us holy—like himself, distinct, and set apart.

2. The standard of holiness is timeless. As noted earlier, the call to be holy occurs well beyond Leviticus. For example, Peter repeated the admonition in his New Testament letter centuries later: "Be holy because I am holy" (1 Pet 1:16). However, he was not alone in drawing attention to this matter, for the apostle John reported that the creatures gathered around the throne in heaven "never stop saying: Holy, holy, holy is the Lord God Almighty" (Rev 4:8). One day we will join them. God's Word makes clear that holiness is designed for all people, for all time. Apparently, it will be one of the most striking characteristics of heaven itself.

What would happen if God's family—those who call themselves by his name—truly obeyed and lived holy lives here and now? I suspect the impact would surprise us and point others to our Holy God.

May we so live here, embracing that which is holy, as we plan to live in the hereafter when we are gathered around the throne of "the Lord God Almighty."

Prayer

O Lord, our God, we acknowledge you as the Holy One and recognize that you are drawing to yourself a family of obedient and holy people. Forgive us for failing to see and aspire to the plan you have had since the beginning of time. Have mercy on us and make us like you, distinct, and set apart for your purposes. Yes, make us holy. May your holiness be lived out in our lives in a winsome and attractive way, drawing others to you. We offer this prayer humbly, in the name of your Holy Son, Jesus Christ. AMEN.

QUESTIONS

1. In what ways have we mischaracterized what it means to be holy today? What might be done to correct some of the common misunderstandings regarding holiness?

2. Who do you know who is Godlike? In what way? What features make him or her so?

3. What distinctions did the people of God (the Church) once have that we no longer have? Why do you think things changed?

4. How does one separate from the world (be set apart) while still being in the world and being an influence and witness to that world?

SUGGESTED READING
Leviticus 4, 10–11, 18–20, 26

4

NUMBERS: Order

Take a census of the whole Israelite community by their clans and families, listing every man by name, one by one. (Numbers 1:2)

Then the Tent of Meeting and the camp of the Levites will set out in the middle of the camps. They will set out in the same order as they encamp, each in his own place under his standard. (Numbers 2:17)

Count the Levites by their families and clans. (Numbers 3:15)

This was the order of march for the Israelite divisions as they set out. (Numbers 10:28)

Are you an orderly person? Do lists, sequences, regulations, systems, and structures help you navigate life? Do consistency and patterns ease or add to stress in your daily activities? I confess I am a person who likes order. I do not think I am obsessive about it, though at times my wife may disagree with that assessment. My garage is not the neatest in the neighborhood, nor is my lawn meticulously manicured. Nonetheless, I do tend to put things back where I found them, traverse the same route during my morning walk, keep my desk neat and free from clutter, and practice several repetitive daily habits. I like order. The late television personality Mr. Rogers and I probably would have been good college roommates, given our shared propensity for consistency and orderliness.

In the spirit of full transparency, maybe I am a bit more obsessive than I wish to admit. For example, for as long as I can remember I have placed my wallet in a particular spot on the dresser in my bedroom. It faces a certain way, with other objects lying around it in an orderly manner. The pattern makes it easy to detect when someone has moved it or removed something from it. More than once over the years, I have called out to my wife and asked, "Were you or one of our boys getting money out of my wallet?" The predictable response was, "How did you know? I was very careful to put it back just the way you left it." Yet something was out of alignment; my eye noticed a detail that my wife did not see. The order had been compromised ever so slightly. Occasionally I have been teased as a college professor for having a desk that is far too neat and orderly. The truth of the matter is I have a hard time accomplishing a task until clutter is removed and my immediate space has a semblance of order. Do you know anyone like that?

One of the themes found in the Old Testament book of Numbers—implied in the very title of the book—is order. God thought his people ought to stop on occasion, take a careful count, and order their lives. Apparently, there was value in doing so, whether that value was fully appreciated by his people or not. This emphasis on numbers and order early in Scripture may indicate God's concern with the overall operation and conduct of life. I even see it among my grandchildren who, as young as two years of age, began making efforts to line up their cars, crayons, and books in a particular order. Apparently, the characteristic is built into human nature and reveals itself early in one's life, perhaps showing again that we were created in the image of God. Design and details matter, especially those that speak of our relationship and obedience to the Lord.

Before proceeding further with the topic of order, however, the title of the biblical book under consideration here deserves attention and an explanation. The English title of this fourth book of the Bible is not its earliest and oldest title. The book, like the vast majority of the Old Testament, was originally written in the Hebrew language. Its Hebrew title was "In the Desert," taken from the book's opening line (1:1). However, early Greek translators came along and referred to the volume as Numbers because of the prominence given to taking a census and listing how many people belonged to various family groups in Israel. A census, or count of the population, was taken and recorded multiple times (e.g., 1:2; 4:2, 22; 26:2). Those who later translated the Bible into

English generally adopted the Greek title. Both the Hebrew and Greek designations are apt descriptions of the content and offer important complementary perspectives. In other words, the book chronicles the repeated numbering and ordering of God's people while they wandered for forty years in the desert, after their exodus from Egypt.

Nowhere in Scripture does one read more about counting, numbering, taking a census, and ordering activities than here in the book of Numbers. Counting the people of God and ordering the work of God are dominant themes throughout the book. If we are honest, this very feature is one of the reasons we rarely read the book, publicly or privately. The exercise feels pointless because we only see ancient and irrelevant lists and useless details. However, in our haste to move beyond such scriptural passages to a more engaging text we risk missing a central life lesson: orderly patterns have a purpose, resulting in enhanced human productivity. Thus, the arrangement of people, their movements, and their social activities in a sequential manner is intentionally emphasized here. For example, early in Numbers God instructed the Israelites to camp (ch 2) and travel in a specific and orderly way (10:11–28). Near the end of the book, an orderly report of where they had journeyed since leaving Egypt was provided (ch 33), followed by a description of important geographical boundaries they would need to know once the Israelites entered Canaan (ch 34).

It should be noted that this focus on order is not limited to Numbers. The theme is found several places throughout Scripture. Creation (Gen 1) reveals order in multiple ways: night follows day, the seasons follow one another, the creatures have their designed habitats (e.g., land, water, air), and more. In Proverbs 28:2, the principle of order gets elevated when we read, "A man of understanding and knowledge maintains order." Over in the New Testament, Luke expressed his desire "to write an orderly account" of the life and ministry of Jesus (1:3). Paul, concerned that the church in Corinth was out of control, reminded the local believers that "God is not a God of disorder" and, therefore, "everything should be done in a fitting and orderly way" (1 Cor 14:33, 40). On another occasion he commended the Colossians for being "orderly" and firm in their faith (2:5). There is ample scriptural evidence that structure and order matter to God and are designed for social health. The lack of order is always presented as a cause for concern, something to be resolved or restored.

A fair question to ask is: Why does any of this matter? What is there about order that would draw this kind of attention? In addition to order being a crucial building block and pattern at the time of creation, there are other reasons to embrace this blueprint for living. Order promotes *predictability, security, efficiency,* and *learning.* Let's explore each of these briefly.

Chaos and uncertainty are minimized when order is established, giving way to that which is expected and *predictable.* Thus, a God of order is seen as predictable, reliable, and trustworthy—someone who can be approached with confidence. We do not have to wonder if God will be loving, gracious, forgiving, or holy. These describe his nature; there is an order and predictability to the very essence of God. In the same manner, he created the world with predictable patterns—such as the seasons—that allow us to operate with assurance that winter will give way to spring, spring will give way to summer, and so on.

One feels safe and *secure* in an orderly environment. The French sociologist Émile Durkheim noted that order was the basis for society itself; community cohesion unravels without it, leaving people unsettled and insecure. Perhaps this is most evident whenever there are riots in our cities. The lack of order in the streets produces chronic and harmful stress among the local citizens who feel threatened and vulnerable.

The existence of order increases *efficiency,* making one more effective and less wasteful of time and resources than if operating in a disorderly or unsystematic manner. More can be accomplished at a reduced cost when organization and order trump clutter and confusion. We have all encountered someone trying to run a business or lead a classroom of students who struggled due to a lack of organization. The disorganized individual must change his or her ways quickly or change careers. Success, whether in business, education, or any other endeavor, requires the efficiency that order brings.

Learning is also related to order. Consider several basic processes in development. For example, one learns to swallow soft foods before learning to chew fibrous foods, one learns to crawl before learning to walk, one learns basic mathematics before conquering calculus, and one learns to write a sentence before publishing a book. We learn and grow in an orderly way. God knew his people would only succeed if they paid attention to his orderly design. The book of Numbers, positioned early in Scripture, emphasizes this guiding and timeless principle.

The value of orderliness is worth noting in another kind of learning as well. The study of Holy Scripture, whether done as an individual or in a group of believers, benefits students most when it is done in an orderly fashion. Since the Bible's message and presentation are purposeful and orderly, we would do well to investigate it the same way. Too often well-meaning students, and even scholars, settle for an unsystematic approach when reading God's Word—it might be called the *dictionary* approach—wherein one jumps into the middle of a book and pulls out an isolated concept or message. While we would never read another book that way, we have convinced ourselves that such an approach to Scripture is suitable, or at least "better than nothing." The result is that we miss valuable context and treasures contained in sacred Scripture and remain woefully ignorant of God's Word that is intended to be life-giving. How much better to read entire books, as each author designed, methodically mining its meaning in its larger context. Sadly, I fear that the dictionary approach to the Bible, rather than a more comprehensive and orderly approach, has contributed to growing biblical illiteracy among God's family. We have more access to the written Word of God than people have ever had in history; we even have it available on our computers and phones. However, we may know God's Word and apply it less than any generation before us. Perhaps one reason for this deficit is our failure to engage Scripture in an orderly and methodical way. We learn best when order is recognized and followed. Design and organization have a purpose that we miss when we adopt a haphazard approach to something so valued as Holy Scripture.

Do you remember the two titles suggested for this book centuries ago, one by the Hebrews and one by the Greeks? The first one spoke of being "in the desert," while the second one spoke of numbering and ordering the people for God-ordained tasks. We would do well to heed this dual focus today: When life seems to be an aimless wandering in the desert—and we have all been there—we would do well to pause and number, or order, our days for a higher purpose. That was God's design from the start.

Only one entry in the large collection of the Psalms is attributed to Moses, Psalm 90. There he wrote these words: "Teach us to number our days aright, that we may gain a heart of wisdom" (Ps 90:12). Apparently, Moses thought ordering our days was not only wise advice but the pathway to gaining even more wisdom.

Let us commit to doing so. Numbering, or ordering, our days and lives is the way of wisdom.

Prayer

O Lord, we confess that we too often and too easily drift far from your design. Forgive us. We see order all around us in the created world—in seasons, cells, and sunsets. Help us to understand and embrace the order that comes from your creative hand, order that has valuable purpose. Then teach us and help us to live orderly lives under your sovereign Lordship. When we find ourselves wandering in the desert, help us to so order our days that you alone are exalted and honored. Show us once again that following your intentions, your patterns, pleases you and results in our ultimate good. We pray this in the name of Jesus, whose death has brought order and purpose to our lives. AMEN.

Questions

1. Review the elements said to be associated with order: predictability, security, efficiency, and learning. Which of these do you see as most related to order in your life? How so?

2. How do you read Scripture? How would you describe the pattern (the order) that guides your study of God's Word? Is it time to try a new pattern?

3. In what way do you need to give more attention to order? Is there an area of life that needs to be more orderly? What strategy would help you get there?

4. How does one guard against becoming obsessive to the point that order becomes rigid and demanding? How might one balance order with freedom and spontaneity?

Suggested Reading

Numbers 1–3, 10, 18, 33–34

5

DEUTERONOMY: Law

Hear now, O Israel, the decrees and laws I am about to teach you. Follow them so that you may live. (Deuteronomy 4:1)

These are the commands, decrees and laws the LORD your God directed me to teach you to observe . . . so that you may enjoy long life. . . . Impress them on your children. (Deuteronomy 6:1–7)

Cursed is the man who does not uphold the words of this law by carrying them out. (Deuteronomy 27:26)

For I command you today to love the LORD your God, to walk in his ways, and to keep his commands, decrees and laws; then you will live. (Deuteronomy 30:16)

The fifth book of the Bible emphasizes the law. Deuteronomy literally means "second law" or "repetition of the law." Students of the Bible will remember that the law was initially given to Moses at Mount Sinai back in Exodus. Now Deuteronomy records the event once again (Deut 5; cf. Ex 20), underscoring its importance and calling for the Israelites to give their full allegiance to God and his laws as they anticipate entering the promised land.

The primary Hebrew word for law, "torah," occurs twenty-two times in Deuteronomy. Across the Old Testament, only in the Psalms is the word found more often—and most of those references are found in Psalm 119, a unique psalm written as an acrostic to celebrate the law, or word, of God. Over in the New Testament, in Romans and Galatians, Paul has much to say about the law. Clearly, then, the law is a favorite theme in Judeo-Christian teaching. Several observations might be made pertaining to the law after reading Deuteronomy. Four will be considered here.

First, the law is probably best understood by dividing it into categories, or types. Creation laws, social laws, and personal laws are categories that work well. *Creation laws* point back to God's original design found in the first two chapters of the Bible. These laws govern such things as our relationship with and obedience to the Creator; the laws of nature that include such forces as gravity, the seasons, and plant life; regulations that guide human life, gender, and marriage; the need for work and rest, and maintaining a balance between the two; and more. All of these were set in place by God at the time of creation. *Social laws* are intended to guide our relationships with others, especially in a fallen world. How we treat one another matters. Justice, civility, and respect are to be practiced. Thus, numerous laws define relationships with parents, other family members, neighbors, aliens (outsiders), and enemies. Such laws were designed for the flourishing of social relationships. *Personal laws* are primarily concerned with maximizing health. Laws related to diet, disease, and devotion to God—including the keeping of the Sabbath and other religious festivals—are included in this category. Following personal laws benefit individuals in a variety of practical ways. All these laws, regardless of type, are scattered over the first five books of the Bible which is why this collection of books is commonly referred to as the "Torah." Such laws are intended for the welfare of God's family.

Second, the law demands our attention. I find it interesting that the phrase "Hear, O Israel" is a common refrain repeated in Deuteronomy and elsewhere in the Old Testament. It is often used to draw attention to the importance of following God's law (e.g., 4:1; 5:1; 6:3, 4; 9:1). God does not want this behavior left to chance. Thus, he says: *Hear me now. I want to make sure you get this. Are you listening? Everyone, please pay attention.* The law of God is so foundational that we dare not miss it. In practical terms today, that means we need to read God's Word— his law—and hear it preached and taught. We need to find ourselves in places where we are exposed to the law of God so that we can then practice its principles. Unfortunately, that has become an increasingly rare experience these days and we are reaping the consequences. When laws are disregarded civilization breaks down. Consider the recent lawlessness witnessed in places such as the streets of Minneapolis, Seattle, Portland, and Washington, D.C. Simply stated, a community cannot function, nor will a nation long exist, without laws. They form the building blocks of society; their absence will lead to collapse. History provides ample evidence.

No wonder so many pages early in the Bible were devoted to the law. Of course, this has disturbed many people over the years, sometimes even standing as an impediment to reading these texts or accepting the claims of the Judeo-Christian faith altogether. On the surface, beginning with this emphasis on law seems uninviting, rigid, and legalistic. Sadly, such thinking misses the fact that God is building a foundation upon which grace, love, and liberty will later have meaning. Adherence to divine laws is indispensable for all that will follow, ultimately leading to human fulfillment and purpose. *"Hear, O Israel."* God wants our attention. He wants to teach us his ways—not to burden or oppress us, but to help us soar and reach our full potential. Are we listening?

Third, the law is to be passed on to subsequent generations (Deut 6:7; 11:19). That means parents and grandparents have a major role to play, ensuring their children are taught God's law. In part, this explains why fatherlessness is such a tragedy—it removes the primary teacher from the home. Author David Blankenhorn, in his 1995 book *Fatherless America*, declared fatherlessness our nation's "most urgent social problem." He may have been more prophetic than he realized at the time. This dereliction of duty that continues to plague our nation has created what writer Mary Eberstadt later called "the fury of the fatherless" (*First Things*, Dec 2020). Eberstadt's thesis is that too many children are growing up without dads, without an authority figure to teach them the boundaries of law and order. We are witnessing the results in angry and destructive behavior in our communities. Children need models in their daily lives who elevate and honor laws, while teaching them to appropriately channel their anger and frustration. This begins at home with dad. Indeed, parents are implored to "impress [these laws] on your children" (Deut 6:7). Parents in general—and dads in particular—are counted on to model and explain the purpose and value of laws. We dare not neglect this admonition. Future generations are at stake. Failure here will result in consequences that are both severe and long-lasting.

Fourth, the law holds the secret of life. Look around. Are the lawless, those who defy law and order, living optimally and flourishing? Are they getting the most out of life? Of course not. Following the law leads to life (4:1; 30:9–20). Individuals, and even nations, can only reach their potential when they acknowledge God, the Lawmaker and Lawgiver. Life is maximized not by breaking free from laws but by surrendering to them. We would do well to remember the words from our nation's first president, George Washington. In his 1789 inaugural address he declared that "the propitious smile of Heaven can never be expected on a nation that disregards the eternal rules of order and right, which Heaven itself has ordained." His warning was clear: America cannot ignore God-given laws and expect to be free from consequences. Disregarding law and order not only jeopardizes the stability of a nation but also destroys life among those who live there (30:11–20). Both our biblical and national ancestors seemed to understand this principle. Do we?

Deuteronomy completes what is often referred to as the "Pentateuch"—the Greek word for "five books." Together these first five books of the Bible provide a foundational blueprint for how God's people are to live. In a sense, everything that follows in the remaining sixty-one books of the Bible derives its meaning from this foundation. We cannot fully understand and appreciate God's activity throughout history without a solid grasp of the early pages of Scripture. Therefore, a summative review of key themes may be helpful at this point:

- Genesis points to the *family*. Gender, marriage, and family relationships were God's idea and design. They matter. Attempts to redefine them are audacious and haughty acts that usurp God's authority.
- Exodus points to *obedience*. God's family must decide early on who will be Lord, or Master, of life. The choice is significant; the consequences are severe. Life and death are in the balance.
- Leviticus points to *holiness*. God desires a distinct people who will look and act like him rather than follow the sinful and rebellious ways of their neighbors. He wants full commitment and allegiance.
- Numbers points to *order*. Efficiency, learning, and growth are maximized when life is marked by order. One's full, God-given potential will never be realized without it. Disorder and chaos will be the result.
- Deuteronomy points to *law*. There are certain fundamental truths and patterns that come from God and lead to life. They

are neither options to consider nor drafts to be edited and re-written but commands to follow.

God has a plan for his creation. That plan includes human wellbeing and eternal fellowship with the Creator. The plan, however, will only work if his people follow the blueprint and build their lives on his foundational principles. The Enemy will whisper (or perhaps even shout) that these designs are nothing but partisan political or cultural values and concepts. Do not believe it. We should not be surprised by such a charge from God's Enemy. After all, his first words to a human (Gen 3:1) came in the form of this question: "Did God really say [that]?" And ever since then, God's authoritative word has been questioned. Today his law is largely disregarded and seen as irrelevant, perhaps intended for another time and place, but with little use or application for people living in the twenty-first century.

The reality is this: God is still seeking our attention. He is calling us back to his Word, his law. We are harmed, as individuals and as a society, when we neglect it. On the other hand, life in its fullness becomes possible to those who follow God's law. The choice is ours.

Prayer

O Lord, we acknowledge you as the Creator who has a plan for your creatures. Forgive us for too often failing to live according to that plan. We confess to making a mess of things on earth because of our self-centered arrogance and separation from you. We humbly ask you to restore us to your design and intention. Help us to return to your Word, embrace its teaching, and live by its message. We recognize that your Word alone offers life that is abundant. Therefore, may we, our churches, our nation, and the world follow your blueprint and obey your law all the days of our lives. AMEN.

Questions

1. Why are some people, by nature, compliant while others are resistant when it comes to following laws or rules? What factors contribute to these attitudinal differences?

2. Why does God have such a hard time getting the attention of his people? Why do they not naturally listen to him? What about you? How do you ensure you listen to God?

3. How does one determine whether a law has roots in God's design and justice—and, therefore, needs to be honored—or whether it is an unjust law of human design that stands in opposition to God—and, therefore, to be rejected? How ought one to respond when God's law and man's law collide? (For example, see Acts 4:18–19; 5:29.)

4. Which of the key themes (see page 54) from the first five books of the Bible is most troubling or challenging to you personally? Why? What might you need to do to address it?

SUGGESTED READING

Deuteronomy 4–6, 8, 11, 28, 30, 34

6

JOSHUA: Promise

*I will give you every place where you set your
foot, as I promised Moses. (Joshua 1:3)*

*Do not let this Book of the Law depart from your mouth; meditate
on it day and night, so that you may be careful to do everything
written in it. Then you will be prosperous and successful.
Have I not commanded you? Be strong and courageous. Do
not be terrified; do not be discouraged, for the LORD your
God will be with you wherever you go. (Joshua 1:8–9)*

*The LORD your God fights for you, just as
he promised. (Joshua 23:10)*

God's people have always been a promise-focused, forward-looking people. Regardless of their circumstances, their best days are
ahead of them in a future promised by God. One cannot advance too
far in reading the Bible before realizing that God makes promises to his
family—promises that he keeps. The Bible's sixth book, Joshua, highlights that fact. The book records the people of Israel leaving their desert
wanderings and entering the land God promised their ancestors.

The theme of promise is so central to one's overall understanding of
Scripture that Dennis Kinlaw opens his 2002 devotional, *This Day with
the Master*, by focusing on this thought. His January 1 reading refers to

the "radical promise" that God makes to his followers. Kinlaw's words are helpful:

> God is the God who wants to make all things new, and His presence can be recognized by the element of radical promise that confronts us when we come to know Him. With God comes the word that the future can be better than the present. When Abraham met God, the experience contained a promise staggeringly large. It was that the barrenness of an old woman and the emptiness of a home would change. When God met Moses, in that meeting was the assurance that Moses was made for more than defeat and shepherding. The promise was given to him that God would use him to set his people free. In fact, Moses was to be God's man to build a nation. In Joshua's relationship to God was the promise that God had a land for his wandering people.

God's promises continue with each succeeding generation of followers. While many of these promises are specific to individuals (as noted above), there are other promises intended for the entire community of God. Joshua highlights three such promises that continue to be emphasized throughout Scripture. Those three are the enduring promises of property, prosperity, and presence. It is important to note here that God's promises are always conditioned on our obedience. Though that message is stated and illustrated repeatedly (e.g., Deut 28:1, 15; Josh 1:8; 24:14–15), perhaps nowhere is it more clearly seen than in the dismal failure at Ai immediately after the exhilarating victory at Jericho (see Josh 6–7). Israel's experiences confirmed that unfaithfulness and disobedience would lead to ultimate disaster, whereas faithfulness and obedience would lead to the fulfillment of God's promise. That pattern is a recurring one found throughout the pages of Scripture and across the centuries of history. God's promises stand when his people obey and faithfully devote themselves to him.

The promises of property, prosperity, and presence are all found in the opening chapter of Joshua and then expanded upon elsewhere. Each of these promises is worthy of further consideration.

The promise of property. "I will give you every place where you set your foot" (1:3). "You will lead these people to inherit the land I swore to their forefathers to give them" (1:6). Joshua restated and fulfilled what Moses had written earlier (Deut 6:3, 18; 11:24): God had promised them a wonderful land. It was the same land God originally promised Abraham (Gen 12:1, 7; Heb 11:9). The two primary features or descriptions of this promised land were that it was a place of plenty ("a land flowing with milk and honey," Josh 5:6) and a place of peace and rest. The promised land later became a metaphor used by followers of Jesus to describe heaven. Believers still look forward to the place, or property, that Jesus is preparing for them (John 14:2). Indeed, new property awaits all who walk with God.

The promise of prosperity. "Be careful to do everything written in [this Book of the Law]. Then you will be prosperous and successful" (1:8). Prosperity is promised to those who obey God's law. Unfortunately, *prosperity* has come to be narrowly defined as achieving wealth and fame. This limited understanding of the term is unwarranted. Both the original Hebrew word and its English counterpart can mean more than just financial or material abundance. To be prosperous means to thrive, flourish, or succeed. Implied is the idea of enjoying a good and satisfying life because one is pleasing God and reaching his or her potential. For example, Abraham's servant prospered by finding a wife for Abraham's son Isaac (Gen 24:56), and Daniel prospered when he survived the lion's den (Dan 6:28). In both cases prosperity meant a life rich with meaning and purpose. We, too, are promised prosperity. Paul put it this way: "We know that in all things God works for the good of those who love him, who have been called according to his purpose" (Rom 8:28). Stated another way, those who love and follow God will ultimately prosper with a life that is meaningful.

The promise of presence. "I will never leave you nor forsake you" (1:5). "The LORD your God will be with you wherever you go" (1:9). Arguably, the greatest promise of all is that of God's presence. This theme has a long history. God promised never to leave Jacob (Gen 28:15). He repeated the promise to Joshua (Deut 31:6; Josh 1:5, 9). Isaiah foretold the coming of Immanuel—"God with us" (7:14)—the fulfillment of which occurred in Matthew (1:23). Jesus's last words to his disciples prior to his ascension were a reminder that he would always be with them (Matt 28:20). He promised these same disciples that "the Father . . . will give you another Counselor to be with you forever" (John 14:16–17). The promise of God's eternal, accessible presence is a thread that weaves its way through Scripture. Missionary friend Jeannine Brabon, who for three decades has taken the gospel to inmates at the notorious Bellavista Prison in Medellín, Colombia, has claimed this promise. When a well-meaning individual questioned her regarding the wisdom of a woman engaging in such dangerous prison ministry, Jeannine responded: "Security is not found in the absence of danger but in the presence of Jesus." God's presence is our protection. We believers know that God is with us.

With these great promises one would expect God's people to be the most joyful, confident, victorious people known to mankind. While some are, far too many are not. We—God's children, the Church—seem to have lost our focus when it comes to God's promises. We too often live as discouraged and defeated people. While evidence of the trend is abundant, perhaps nowhere is it more obvious than in our music, our politics, and our pursuits.

Our music lyrics and tunes have grown increasingly depressing and melancholy. Woeful expressions and tones have replaced hopeful victory when we sing. Focus on the problems of this life has replaced focus on the glories of heaven. We are promised a bright future, but our music today seldom reflects that message.

Our politics have left us schizophrenic. On the one hand we claim that "the government will be on [the Lord's] shoulders" (Isa 9:6), while on the other hand we despair when the wrong person or party is in power. Feverishly working to get our side elected—and disappointed when that does not happen—we fail to remember the sovereignty of God. We are promised a bright future, but our political anxiety still ties us in knots.

Our pursuits betray and disappoint us. An insatiable desire exists for accumulating temporary, disposable treasures. We chase after the next adventure, hoping it will satisfy and make us the envy of others as we post yet more images of our happiness on social media. We have become obsessed with our perceived need of new experiences and possessions. We are promised a bright future, but our pursuits and passions tell a different story. Our gaze is seldom heavenward when there is so much that delights and captivates us here.

What has happened? Why have God's promises been forgotten, or at least marginalized, in our lives and communities? What interferes with us being a triumphant people who cling to and proclaim those eternal promises that speak of future property, hopes for prosperity, and the security of his daily presence? How have we lost the sense of promise and optimism that is so dominant in God's Word? Several factors have likely contributed, but at least two are mentioned in Joshua—one at the beginning of the book and one at the end. First, too many have lost their yearning for "this Book of the Law" and so fail to talk about it and "meditate on it day and night" (1:8). Every generation will struggle to act as the people of promise if they fail to read the Book (the Bible) that reminds them of the promise. There is no substitute for reading, knowing, and reveling in the Book. Second, Joshua concludes with a choice: "choose for yourselves this day whom you will serve" (24:15). Sadly, some opt for the wrong master, adopting their neighbors' gods rather than the God of promise. This was a problem that continued to afflict God's people. Centuries after Joshua was written, the prophets called for God's chosen ones to repent from their idolatry and disobedience. A choice must be made in every generation as to whom one will serve. We will never live like people of promise without intimate familiarity with God's Word and an intentional choice to make him the uncontested Lord of life.

Kinlaw concludes his first devotional entry with these words: "The very mark of the people of God in the Old Testament was that their faces were turned toward the future and were marked by confidence and expectation." The promise of God drew, sustained, and animated his people. May it do the same for us today.

Let us be a promise-focused, forward-looking people despite the condition of our fallen world. Others are likely to take notice and be encouraged when we do so.

PRAYER

O Lord, thank you for your timeless, magnificent promises—promises that reflect your goodness, compassion, and kindness. Forgive us for too often failing to embrace what you desire to give. Set our faces forward, beyond the trials and travails of this fallen world, so that we clearly see you and what you have prepared for us. Thank you for the promise of land we will enjoy throughout all eternity. Thank you for the promise of hope and prosperity that results in meaning rather than mere existence. Thank you for the promise of your constant presence and companionship. We acknowledge we are a blessed people with a bright future. Help us to live as the people of promise that you have designed us to be. AMEN.

QUESTIONS

*1. Would you describe yourself as a promise-focused, forward-looking person? If not, why not? What do you need to change to make that more of a reality?

2. What other contributing factors come to mind that might help explain why too few believers live and look like people of promise?

3. Why does every generation need to be reminded again of God's promises, even though those promises are recorded in the written Word of God?

4. What promise of God is most meaningful to you? Why? Is it property, prosperity, or his presence? Or is it perhaps another promise?

SUGGESTED READING

Joshua 1, 3–4, 6–8, 23–24

7

JUDGES: Disaster

*The fighting was so heavy that the Benjamites did not
realize how near disaster was. (Judges 20:34)*

*The men of Benjamin were terrified, because they realized
that disaster had come upon them (Judges 20:41)*

*In those days Israel had no king; everyone
did as he saw fit. (Judges 21:25)*

A tragic, unnecessary, and repeated sequence unfolded in Israel's history. The final statement found in the book of Judges summarizes the problem: "everyone did as he saw fit" (21:25; cf. 17:6). The result of that singular decision produced one disaster after another. Little has changed across the centuries. Whenever people do as they see fit—rather than as God wills and commands—lost potential, tragedy, and disaster follow. History is replete with heartbreaking examples.

Two types of disaster are described in the book of Judges. One is more public in nature, whereas one is more private. The first type of disaster typically results from external forces or events. The second type often comes from internal forces or personal decisions. Before looking further at how both types are described in the historical account of Judges, perhaps two relatively contemporary stories will allow us to understand better the nature and cause of each type of disaster, respectively.

A few years after my family moved to the village of Bourbonnais, Illinois, situated fifty miles south of Chicago, a disaster shook our community. Late in the evening on March 15, 1999, an Amtrak train carrying over two hundred passengers and heading southbound from Chicago collided with a semi-trailer truck loaded with heavy steel. The truck driver with his enormous load had misjudged his ability to clear the railroad crossing. When the train's engineer was unable to brake in time, the speeding train smashed into the bed of the truck. The train's two locomotives and eleven of its fourteen cars derailed. The disaster caused by the crash changed the lives of the Amtrak passengers, the surrounding community, and even the ways trains would operate at railroad crossings thereafter. Eleven people were killed and 122 were injured that night. The accident was assessed to cost over $14 million. The train's passengers and mourning family members could never have anticipated the disaster. External forces—a large, steel-laden, semi-trailer truck—blocked the train's movement forward just about the time many had settled in and were ready to doze off to sleep. Our village eventually erected a memorial to the victims of the train wreck, a perpetual reminder of the disaster and pain that can come so unexpectedly to fragile and innocent lives. Surviving passengers and surrounding community members will never forget the tragedy that occurred that night in 1999.

Whereas many people, like the Amtrak passengers, suffer disasters not of their own making, some experience disaster of another sort. Sometimes we find ourselves in a mess we have created on our own. I remember such an incident when I was a high school senior. It was late October and Halloween was just around the corner. A friend and I thought we would treat some of our church youth group to a haunted house adventure. We knew of an old farmhouse a few miles southwest of Flint, Michigan, that sat deserted on a quiet gravel road. Had we determined to take our friends directly to the designated location, we would have avoided the catastrophe that ensued. However, wanting to increase the suspense and anticipation of the evening excursion, my friend and I had scouted out a way to the house by entering a farmer's field on the opposite side of the country square mile. We would have to quietly bypass the farmer's house and navigate his lengthy field in the dark. The added challenge was part of the thrill for us imprudent teenagers. Three cars filled with spooked, yet enthusiastic, youth made up the convoy. With our headlights off, we successfully avoided detection as we snaked our way past the neighbor's occupied home and back through

64

his field, nearing our destination. Then the problems began. Because it had rained earlier in the day, the field we were traversing was soft and muddy. My friend's car got off the path and ended up stuck in the muddy field. To make matters worse, he repeatedly revved his engine and spun his tires in a desperate attempt to get free from his predicament. A few youth jumped out to push, but nothing helped. The noise and commotion, of course, caught the attention of the farmer in whose field we were trespassing. He came out to us on his tractor and, when he arrived, he found three cars, more than a dozen young people, and two sheepish and mortified ringleaders stranded in his field. What a mess we had created—both literally and figuratively. Our poor judgment had produced a disaster that was completely of our own making. The only thing that would have made it worse was if the farmer had opted to turn us in to the local authorities. Fortunately, he did not. I suspect he knew our humiliation and mud-covered cars, shoes, and clothes were punishment enough.

Both types of disasters—those arising from external forces and those arising from poor personal decisions—have the same effect. Despite the source, the result is a calamity that overwhelms those it touches. Disasters inevitably leave a group of people experiencing negative consequences. Pain, anguish, frustration, humiliation, regret, or a combination of all these are common when disaster hits. Both types of disasters and their corresponding consequences are found in the book of Judges.

Judges divides itself naturally into two major sections. The first sixteen chapters of the book describe the chaos God's people endured at the hands of outside forces. For example, their repeated inclination toward evil resulted in their subjugation to the Canaanites (4:1–3), Midianites (6:1), and Philistines (13:1), among others. Worth noting is that in each case these national disasters lasted for years, sometimes even decades, before God raised up a leader, or "judge," to deliver them. The final five chapters of the book, Judges 17–21, form what some Bible scholars describe as an epilogue or appendix. Regardless of the label, what is clear is that the content turns to the chaos created when inside forces or influences get distorted. The picture emerges of God's people participating in crass idolatry (chs 17–18), brutal rape (ch 19), civil war between its tribes (ch 20), and a form of kidnapping and human trafficking (ch 21). The whole book presents one embarrassment after another, finally concluding—almost in a sigh of exasperation—with these poignant words: "everyone did as he saw fit" (21:25). Disaster and chaos reigned.

What is written in these pages is appalling. Why would such events, or such a book, even be included in the Bible? Stories like these keep many people from wanting to read the Old Testament. Could this human ugliness not be sanitized or abridged and rendered in a more reader-friendly style? We prefer happy endings to our stories, not the brutality and carnage found in this book—particularly in its closing chapters.

Caution needs to be exercised lest our revulsion cause us to miss an important lesson. Disasters often serve as warnings. Is it possible, then, that this book of disasters was strategically prepared and placed in Scripture intentionally to warn future generations? Perhaps the book's repeated tragedies and tawdry ending are purposeful. The message is that life did not have to end this way for God's people then, nor does it have to end that way for God's people today. Both types of disasters discussed earlier—whether coming from external or internal sources—were needless tragedies tied to the fact that God's people ignored him and his design. When God's plan for life and family are rewritten (Genesis), when obedience is shrugged off (Exodus), when holiness is minimized (Leviticus), when order is compromised (Numbers), when law is abandoned (Deuteronomy), and when selfish desire trumps God's promises (Joshua), the fiascoes detailed in the book of Judges should not come as a surprise. This predictable pattern, or trajectory, is no less true today than it was in Bible times.

The root of the social chaos was a combination of evil and self-promotion. Two repeated phrases in Judges communicate this truth:

1. "The Israelites did evil in the eyes of the Lord" (2:11; 3:7, 12; 4:1; 6:1; 10:6; 13:1).

2. "Everyone did as he saw fit" (17:6; 21:25).

Thus, the overarching and unmistakable theme here is disaster. What is significant is this: the Hebrew word *ra* that gets translated "disaster" near the end of the book (20:34, 41) is the same word that is most often translated "evil" throughout Judges and the entire Old Testament. When we read that evil begets disaster, the message is literally that evil begets yet more evil—*ra* produces more *ra*. There is a snowball effect wherein evil and its resultant problems, left unchecked, increase in magnitude and scope. As noted earlier, history provides several examples of this. In addition to Israel's growing idolatry and self-sufficiency, consider Rome's growing paganism and hedonism, Nazi Germany's growing sense of superiority and barbarism, and modern America's growing appetite for materialism and sexual perversion. Evil begets evil; disaster follows and expands.

No, we ought not turn away from a book like Judges. Rather, we need to learn its timeless lessons as the people of God and as a nation. Disaster awaits anyone who ignores God and chooses to do "as he [sees] fit" (Judg 21:25). Evidence is as plentiful in America today as it was in Israel then.

The same God who promises property, prosperity, and presence in the book of Joshua punishes those who willfully disobey and choose their own way. God's promises are conditioned upon human surrender to him. Choosing what seems best to me and making my own pathway forward without listening to God invites disaster. Solomon later confirmed this when he wrote: "There is a way that seems right to a man, but in the end it leads to death" (Prov 14:12; 16:25). Doing what seems right to me, without reference to God, is always a recipe for tragedy. Unfortunately, humans in every generation keep making the same mistake, often failing to realize just "how near disaster" is (Judg 20:34).

The message is clear: we have a choice to make. We can choose God's way which leads to promise and prosperity, or our way which leads to ultimate disappointment and disaster. May God grant us wisdom and courage . . . and save us from ourselves.

PRAYER

Oh, Sovereign Lord, save us. Deliver us from the disasters that come when we ignore you. We confess that too often we act on our own, trusting our own intelligence, intuition, and judgment. Then disappointment and calamity come. We have experienced this as individuals, as communities, and as a nation. Forgive us for our haughtiness and audacity. May we—who call ourselves your followers—constantly seek you and your will, lest we make a mess of things. We pray this in the name of Jesus, who modeled for us complete submission to you, the Father. AMEN.

QUESTIONS

1. What examples come to your mind of everyone doing as he or she sees fit today? What have been the ramifications of that behavior personally? Nationally?

2. Why is it important that God's people in the twenty-first century still read and become familiar with the Old Testament? What lessons might we learn by doing so?

3. What example comes to mind of a disaster that could have been prevented and avoided? How? What needed to happen to bring about a better outcome?

4. After reviewing the opening paragraphs of this chapter, would you say most disasters you have witnessed or experienced have come from outside or inside forces? Explain.

SUGGESTED READING

Judges 1–2, 6–7, 13–16, 20

8

Ruth: Character

But Ruth replied, "Don't urge me to leave you or to turn back from you. Where you go I will go, and where you stay I will stay. Your people will be my people and your God my God." (Ruth 1:16)

All my fellow townsmen know that you are a woman of noble character. (Ruth 3:11)

The book of Ruth comes as a welcome relief after the disaster described in Judges. The opening words link the two books: "In the days when the judges ruled, there was a famine in the land" (Ruth 1:1). We know by reading the end of Judges that the famine was spiritual as well as physical; morals and meals were both lacking among God's people. This tender little book of four chapters and three main characters—Naomi, Ruth, and Boaz—serves as a bridge of hope, taking God's people from a ravaging famine to a redemptive future.

There is so much to enjoy about the story found in Ruth. Love, loyalty, hard work, kindness, and God's sovereignty and provision are all highlighted here. However, perhaps nothing is as noteworthy, especially given the distressing cultural climate of the day (Ruth 1:1), as Ruth's character. One can only assume that in an environment wherein "everyone did as he saw fit" (Judg 21:25), character was in short supply. How remarkable, then, to read that the people around Bethlehem were soon referring to Ruth, an outsider from Moab, as "a woman of noble character" (3:11). Could there be any higher compliment given to an individual?

In the midst of social decadence, national disintegration, and general moral decline, an individual of character was certainly needed. The irony, of course, is that the individual described here was a foreigner, a woman, a widow, childless, and one struggling to fend off poverty. She had no credentials, no impressive résumé, and no resources. Part of Ruth's appeal was that her story had so many unexpected elements.

The description found in Ruth 3:11 is interesting. Whereas "noble character" is the phrase used by translators of *The New International Version of the Bible*, the older *King James Version of the Bible* describes Ruth as being a "virtuous woman." Either translation is suitable because character and virtue can be synonyms; in other words, to have character is to be virtuous. *Merriam-Webster's Collegiate Dictionary* (2011) defines character as "moral excellence and firmness," while virtue is defined as "moral excellence and strength." The Hebrew word—*chayil*—that is rendered "noble character" supports the idea of strength or force. The word is often used of soldiers or armies. Putting all this together, the meaning of *character* that emerges is this: moral fortitude that does not waver under pressure or adversity. Character is marshaling the soldier within to stand and fight for what is honorable and good even in the face of unfavorable circumstances. That described Ruth from the beginning to the end of the story.

Just as character was obvious in the new resident of Bethlehem, it is obvious in those who have it today. Everyone knows good character when he or she sees it. But how is it developed in a person's life? Hints are offered in Scripture, especially over in the New Testament where the word *character* occurs three times. A review of these three uses is instructive.

First, **character is developed by what we read**. Acts 17:11 tells us that "the Bereans were of more noble character than the Thessalonians, for they received the message with great eagerness and examined the Scriptures every day to see if what Paul said was true." Though we know little else about the Bereans, we know they read and carefully studied God's Word and had a reputation for noble character. Luke, the writer of Acts, assumes a causal link—their character was a result of reading and absorbing Scripture. What one takes into his or her mind will indeed shape character. That's why time spent in God's Word is so important.

However, reading other material besides the Bible also forms us and begs the question: *what are we reading?* Our character will never exceed what we feed our minds. If we gorge ourselves on websites and social media messages, we should not be surprised when our character comes up lacking. From time to time, we need to evaluate what we are reading—or if we are reading at all. Biographies of those known for their faith, achievements, and character ought to be on one's reading list. We are influenced by what we read and allow to circulate in our minds. Though there is no record of Ruth reading literature, there is evidence that she "read" Naomi's life over the years to the extent that Ruth declared with determination: "Where you go I will go, and where you stay I will stay. Your people will be my people and your God my God" (1:16). I suspect Ruth's noble character was formed, at least in part, by a careful reading of Naomi's life. Our character, too, can be traced to what and whom we are reading.

Second, **character is developed by the people with whom we associate**. Borrowing a line from Greek literature, Paul warned the Corinthians that "bad company corrupts good character" (1 Cor 15:33). Implied, of course, is the opposite maxim that good company results in good character. Our associations affect our disposition and outlook. God created us as social beings; we influence one another. Within five minutes of meeting a new person, we can usually identify with amazing accuracy the kinds of friends that person has, for a person's character is shaped by his or her associates. After Ruth associated with Naomi for years, she developed additional relationships with Boaz and the people of God around Bethlehem. No wonder her memory is cherished; no wonder she is affectionately included in the genealogy of Jesus that opens the New Testament (Matt 1:5). As her circle expanded, those in it influenced her and no doubt she influenced them. Character is not formed in isolation but as we interact with others. Just as we benefit from evaluating what we are reading, we also benefit by pausing to consider with whom we spend our time. Our character will certainly show it.

Third, **character is developed by the hardship we experience**. Romans 5:3–4 reads: "We also rejoice in our sufferings, because we know that suffering produces perseverance; perseverance, character; and character, hope." If we are honest, we would rather ignore this biblical reference to character. Many of us look back and can identify plenty of suffering during recent times. We have experienced a lengthy pandemic resulting in isolation, social unrest that has left us all on edge,

nonstop political denunciations in the news, frigid winter tempera-
tures and scorching summer heat, and numerous individual struggles
of which few others are even aware (e.g., health, finances, loneliness,
uncertainty regarding the future). The suffering has been real and personal. What kind of person would rejoice in all of this? Are you kidding
me? And yet here Paul says that suffering teaches us to persevere, and
perseverance develops character. Ruth was not a stranger to hardship.
She married into a family suffering from a famine. She suffered the loss
of her husband while very young. Her life was turned upside down by
moving to a new area. She joined the poor servant girls of Bethlehem in
gathering just enough grain to survive. One hardship after another defined her life. Nonetheless, her perseverance, grit, and diligence earned
the community's respect and a reputation for having "noble character."

No one chooses to suffer. However, the plain truth is that character
grows out of such experience. We humans are prone to despise hardships like famines and pandemics. We detest losses whether they come
in the form of loved ones, jobs, or basic freedoms and privileges. We
disdain having to accept menial work that makes us feel like second-
class citizens. In the process we forget that God is at work; character is
being formed.

So why do you suppose character is emphasized in this little book
of Ruth, placed as it is strategically after the exploits of Moses and
Joshua and before the celebrated reign of David? I would argue that
the answer to that question lies in the fact that both character and hope
had been lost. When character disappears hope always goes with it,
leaving the future dark and dismal. Consider again the last part of Paul's
progression in Romans 5:4, "character [produces] hope." Sadly, hope
had been lost during Ruth's day and in its place were the narcissism,
chaos, and disaster described at the end of Judges. Naomi confessed her
own hopeless condition when she said to her widowed daughters-in-law
(1:12–13), "Even if I thought there was still hope for me . . . would you
wait? . . . No, my daughters. It is . . . bitter for me." Beyond assessing her
own hopeless condition, Naomi unknowingly provided an apt depiction
of Israel as a whole. The future looked bleak indeed. Hope was gone.

Ruth is the story of God intervening and changing the narrative
for his people. He used a poor, unsuspecting, foreign-born widow with
noble character to do so. He gave her a son, whose offspring (her great-
grandson, David) would one day rule the nation of Israel (4:13–17). Does
this sound familiar? It should. Centuries later many of the details of this

story would be repeated in a descendant of Ruth and Boaz, resulting in the birth of Jesus, the Ruler of the entire world.

God looks for one with noble character. He always has. And when he finds such an individual there is no telling what he will do with him or her. One person with character sparks hope, becoming the catalyst to change a community, a nation, or even the world. Will you be such a person in this generation?

Prayer

Our Father in heaven, make us more like you. Make us people of noble character. Perhaps never in our lifetime has the need been greater. If you can use an unlikely, unsuspecting Moabite widow, we dare to believe you can use us. Help us to give attention to the development of character in our lives—by considering what we read, by considering those with whom we associate, and by re-evaluating those hardships that come our way. Give us strength, vision, and perseverance, we pray, so that character develops and marks our daily lives. AMEN.

Questions

1. Who is there in your world that stands as a person of noble character? What makes him or her so? What are the identifying traits?

2. Which of the three ways for developing character identified above most needs attention in your life? What practical steps might you take to experience the change you need?

3. Why and how do you think character is related to hope? What is there about character that links it to future confidence and anticipation?

4. How would you advise someone who has a problem with his or her character? What words of wisdom might you offer? Why does character even matter?

Suggested Reading

Ruth 1–4

9

1 SAMUEL: Leaders

Samuel said to all Israel . . . "Now you have a king as your leader.
As for me, I am old and gray, and my sons are here with you. I have
been your leader from my youth until this day." (1 Samuel 12:1–2)

The LORD has sought out a man after his own heart and
appointed him leader of his people, because you have
not kept the LORD's command. (1 Samuel 13:14)

Finding a good leader is rare. Keeping a good leader is rarer still. History is littered with stories that illustrate both challenges. A reading of 1 Samuel reveals a great deal about leadership—both its possibilities and its hazards. Leaders would do well to mine the pages of this Old Testament book.

After the disasters described in Judges, the standard of noble character is raised in Ruth. First Samuel continues the emphasis on character, this time displaying it—both good and bad—in specific leaders. Four leaders dominate the book: two of them were tragic figures, two of them were exemplary. The two tragic figures were Eli the priest and King Saul; the two exemplary leaders were Samuel the prophet and young David. As the book opens the attention is on Eli (chs 1–4). His inability to lead his sons properly culminated in the deaths of both sons and of Eli himself. Then the spotlight shifts to Samuel (chs 7–16), described as the "leader of Israel" (7:6). Under his leadership, the Lord directed that the people be given the king they have requested (8:6–9). Samuel proceeded to anoint Saul as the first king of Israel. Saul's rocky years as king are emphasized throughout much of the remainder of the book (chs 8–16, 28, 31). Disobedience, jealousy, obsessions, family problems, remorse, witchcraft, loss, and an ignoble death tell the sad tale of Saul's leadership. David is introduced in the middle of the book (16:13) and soon his leadership traits develop and shine, albeit under awkward and difficult circumstances (chs 16–26).

What makes the difference in the trajectory of a leader? What makes one leader collapse in tragedy while another leader rises in triumph? Why do some leaders find disgrace and humiliation while others prompt praise and admiration? Why does history routinely distinguish between good leaders and bad leaders? The truth of the matter is that many leaders begin with much promise but fall from favor. That was certainly the case for Saul, whose life illustrates how hard it is to keep a good leader. Let me restate that thought this way: Saul illustrates how hard it is to keep a leader *good*. Because so many temptations, intrusions, and distractions assault a leader, the risk of failure is high.

The book of 1 Samuel—particularly chapter 15—provides helpful insight and instruction regarding leadership qualities. The paths of respectable leaders and corrupt leaders often begin similarly, but ultimately diverge and lead to distinct outcomes. Leaders are defined by choices and behavioral patterns that result in those outcomes. While time and space prohibit an exhaustive analysis of the leaders found in this and other Old Testament books, the following observations provide relevant comparisons when it comes to defining leaders.

First, **leaders are defined by how well they listen** (15:1). Saul failed to listen to God and the consequences were severe. Disobedience followed (15:1–11), and he soon lost his kingdom. Interestingly, earlier in the book, young Samuel was taught to listen to the voice of God. Samuel's response was, "Speak, for your servant is listening" (3:9–10). King Saul, unfortunately, had trouble listening to and obeying the voice of God (15:22). One gets the impression that David also listened carefully to God. How else would he have written so many personal, prayerful psalms? Listening is foundational to being a good leader. The practice starts by learning to listen to God and then extends to listening to the counsel of wise advisors (see Prov 12:15; 15:22). Failure to listen, as Saul discovered, results in painful calamities that could have been avoided.

Many leaders have a short tenure due to the fact that they refuse to listen to the wisdom available around them.

Second, **leaders are defined by the degree to which they compromise** (15:9). Saul spared the Amalekite king and the best of the animals when God had specifically ordered their total destruction (15:3). This compromise seemed reasonable at the time, as do all compromises. The problem is that God had ordered otherwise. Compromise of God's commands or design is always insidious, regardless of its justification. Leaders who compromise moral and ethical positions and then rush to explain their decisions and behaviors are a danger to their people. In this regard, Saul stood in contrast to both Samuel and David. The best leaders are those who refuse to compromise their morals when pressure mounts.

Third, **leaders are defined by how much they seek their own honor** (15:12). After a restless night during which Samuel agonized over Saul's disobedience, Samuel went to search for the king. However, Samuel was told, "Saul has gone to Carmel. There he has set up a monument in his own honor." Self-promotion has doomed many leaders. Building one's own monument is not only a sure sign of arrogance but also often a sign that a downfall is imminent. Centuries later the Babylonian king, Nebuchadnezzar, spoke from first-hand experience when he said, "those who walk in pride [the Most High] is able to humble" (Dan 4:37). Sadly, history reveals that too many leaders stumble over their own monuments and end in disgrace. Finding ways to honor oneself is a red flag of warning that communicates self-centeredness rather than service on behalf of other people.

Fourth, **leaders are defined by whom they fear** (15:24). Those seeking popularity fear people. Those seeking holiness fear God. Saul confessed to being "afraid of the people and so I gave in to them." David, on the other hand, stood in contrast to Saul in that he feared God rather than the people. Near the end of his life, David attributed these words to God: "When one rules over men in righteousness, when he rules in *the fear of God*, he is like the light of morning at sunrise" (2 Sam 23:3–4, emphasis added). Just as one welcomes the morning sunshine so does one welcome a leader who fears God and uses that as the standard for governing. Leaders who fear people are unpredictable and untrustworthy, changing with the latest popular trend of society. Consequently, they are leaders in name only; in practice they are followers. Those who fear God, however, lean on "the Rock" (2 Sam 22:2; 23:3) that is dependable, stable and, as David would one day write, "higher than I" (Ps 61:2).

Fifth, **leaders are defined by their ability to exercise restraint** (13:7–14; 24:1–7). One of the unmistakable contrasts presented in 1 Samuel relates to Saul's inability to wait, while David waited patiently. Saul struggled to wait a week for Samuel to arrive and offer the appropriate sacrifices prior to going into battle (10:8; 13:7–14). Finally, Saul took matters into his own hands. His actions displeased God and resulted in Saul losing his kingdom. Impatience got the best of him, and he could not restrain himself. David, however, practiced restraint repeatedly and waited years for God to establish him as king over Israel. This is brought into sharp focus when David had an opportunity to kill Saul as the king was relieving himself in a cave; and yet David refused to lift a hand against God's chosen king (24:1–7). David would not interfere with God's timing. One leader was impatient after waiting a week; the other surrendered matters to God though it meant waiting for years. Restraint—the ability to wait—is a mark of a good leader. It is also uncommon.

Sixth, **leaders are defined by their hearts, not their heads** (16:7). Is it mere coincidence that Saul is described by reference to his head, whereas David is remembered for his heart? Saul was said to be "impressive . . . a head taller than" his peers (9:2). David, on the other hand, has long been remembered for being "a man after [God's] own heart" (13:14). Later, in the New Testament, God's own testimony regarding David clarified what this phrase means: "I have found David son of Jesse a man after my own heart; he will do everything I want him to do" (Acts 13:22). David's heart (i.e., his passion, his striving, his focus) was to please God above all else. There is an important message here, perhaps especially for those of us engaged in the enterprise of education. Hearts, not heads, are the ultimate measure of leaders. Several years ago, I heard Dr. Leo Thornton, then president of Western Evangelical Seminary in Portland, Oregon, say, "Some people are educated beyond their intelligence." I suspect it was his way of cautioning an erudite and cultured audience that effectiveness is based on more than what one holds in his or her head. A good leader understands the importance of the heart.

Not much has changed over the centuries. Leaders are still distinguished and defined by these and related criteria. Listening, compromise, self-promotion, fear, restraint, and the heart continue to define and distinguish leaders. The differences between good and bad leaders, in fact, often comes down to these matters. Though leaders and their characteristics may be magnified more than ever in our information age, 1 Samuel provides a relevant contrast of styles that remains instructive to all future generations. The picture of leaders that gets painted in this book is clear and worthy of reflection: leaders vary. Not all of them are good. Not all are trustworthy.

May God grant us godly leaders. Furthermore, when we have a choice, may God help us *choose* godly leaders. Yet even more important, may God shape us to *be* godly leaders. The reality is that every one of us leads someone—at a job, at home, at church, or in the community. People watch and follow. Our influence touches untold numbers of impressionable individuals. Let us be leaders who please God in every way. A good and godly leader is a great gift to a community.

Prayer

O Lord, we recognize you as our supreme leader and king. Help us to live our lives in complete submission and surrender to you. We also recognize that you raise up earthly leaders to govern the affairs of society. So, grant us good, godly leaders—in our nation, our state, our community, our churches, and our other institutions. We pray that our leaders will rely on you for wisdom and strength, serving as reliable models for all who are under their influence. And do the same for us, by making us godly leaders. May our interactions, decisions, and behaviors consistently and humbly point to your lordship in our lives. AMEN.

Questions

1. What quality matters most to you in a leader? In what leader have you seen that quality most prominently displayed?

2. In your own words, why would you say leaders are so prone to abusing their position and power? What factors contribute to such abuse?

3. Do you think leaders today are more likely to fear people than ever? In other words, given the volume and speed of communication with our computers and social media options, is fearing what people will say more challenging than in years past? If so, how does one effectively lead in such a time as this?

4. Review the list of six criteria, or definitions, of leaders. Which of these most needs attention in your own life as a leader? How might you address this need?

SUGGESTED READING
1 Samuel 3, 9–10, 12, 15–18

10

2 SAMUEL: Consequences

Why did you despise the word of the LORD by doing what is evil in his eyes? . . . you despised me and took the wife of Uriah the Hittite to be your own. This is what the Lord says: "Out of your own household I am going to bring calamity upon you. . . ." Then David said to Nathan: "I have sinned against the LORD." (2 Samuel 12:9–13)

Decisions have consequences; and bad decisions have bad consequences. Arguably, no book in the Bible illustrates this more clearly than 2 Samuel. After Saul's death, David ascended to the throne of Israel. The first ten chapters of 2 Samuel record David's accomplishments and victories as king, but the next ten chapters reveal the dire consequences resulting from his poor decisions. The division of the book and the contrasts contained therein could not be more distinct, sending a resounding message to its readers.

Have you ever noticed how short-sighted humans are in their decisions and behaviors? Too many people operate as if their actions will have no adverse consequences. Why is that? What leads people to think they are exempt, or the exception, to natural consequences or penalties? Such human tendency seems to be increasing. Among other explanations, I suspect well-intentioned, protective parents may contribute to this trend. Some parents remove so many consequences from young children's lives that by the time they are grown they are unaccustomed to the law of cause-and-effect. One of the best gifts a parent can give a child is the gift of consequences. We do our children a disservice when we run to rescue them from every unpleasant outcome. There are long-term consequences for failing to experience immediate and natural consequences as children.

I see the problem among my college students. Growing numbers act surprised that poor attendance might somehow adversely affect their grade, or they are puzzled that a paper that has not been carefully proof-read and edited would result in a low grade. The same pattern exists in wider society. Many express disbelief when tragedy strikes a celebrity or cultural hero, who we somehow assume is immune from consequences. For example, sports fans around the world were shocked in February 2021 when they heard that golf legend Tiger Woods had a serious roll-over accident that crushed his right leg and put his golfing future in jeopardy. Bad things are not supposed to happen to people like him. Investigators spent months trying to figure out the cause of his near-fatal accident, ultimately concluding that excessive speed on a winding California road caused the single-vehicle crash. Tiger's actions—travel-ing 30 to 40 mph over the speed limit—had consequences that saddened his fans and the world. Or consider the tragic and unexpected death of 41-year-old former basketball star Kobe Bryant, just one year earlier. The morning air around Los Angeles was unusually foggy on January 26, 2020, when Bryant and his thirteen-year-old daughter, along with seven others, climbed into a helicopter to travel to the daughter's bas-ketball game. All nine people aboard the helicopter died when it crashed into an unseen mountain. Decisions and behaviors have consequences, regardless of one's status.

Consequences are a law of life, built into every human action. The choices we make—what we read, what we say, how we spend our money, what we eat, what time we go to bed, what career we pursue, where we vacation, who we marry, whether we exercise, our entertainment and hobby choices, how we treat our neighbors and more—all have conse-quences. The prevalence and nature of consequences likely explain the emphasis given them in this early book of the Bible.

The truth of the matter is that consequences are described in Scrip-ture long before David's time. Genesis 3 reveals the consequences of Adam and Eve disobeying God in the Garden of Eden. We humans con-tinue to suffer from those consequences; theologians call the condition original, or inherited, sin. Numbers 14 tells the story of the Israelites wandering and suffering for forty years due to their wickedness and grumbling against God (Num 14:29, 34–35). On the heels of the great victory in Jericho, Joshua 7 records a humiliating defeat at Ai when Achan secretly tried to keep plunder that God had ordered to be destroyed. Judges 16 vividly describes how Samson "did not know that the LORD had left him" (v 20) after he unwisely divulged the secret of his power to Delilah. The history of consequences is long, humiliating, and sordid. There is no shortage of examples by the time we reach David, nor is there an excuse. The horrible outcome of David's adulterous affair with Bathsheba, followed by his sinister plot to get rid of her husband Uriah (2 Sam 11), was predictable. What do we learn from this embarrassing incident in the life of David? Five lessons, or warnings, are worth our attention.

The first lesson is that **decisions have consequences**. Though the point was made earlier, it bears repeating. We dare not miss this fact as we examine the story that unfolds in 2 Samuel 11. David's decisions unleashed a host of disastrous outcomes that he never anticipated at the time. Decisions often lead to a cascading sequence of unforeseen events.

The second lesson is that **no one is exempt from consequences**. David, long remembered as a man after God's own heart (Acts 13:22) and Israel's greatest king, was not an exception to the rule. Whether one is a man after God's own heart, a golf legend, or a basketball all-star does not change the law of consequences. The rich and famous, my college students, your next-door neighbor, and you and I will all reap what we sow (Gal 6:7–8). There is no exemption clause for those who have achieved fame, fortune, or success. A poor decision, regardless of the status of the one who made it, will still lead to a poor outcome.

The third lesson is that **confession and repentance do not erase the consequences**. When Nathan the prophet confronted David with his sin, immediate confession followed (2 Sam 12:13). Psalm 51 records David's heart-felt confession, remorse, and repentance. Over the years many believers have gained encouragement and strength from this psalm, and rightfully so. However, even though David's relationship with God was restored by divine mercy and grace, the physical and relational consequences experienced on earth were not removed. Regrettable wreckage remained.

The fourth lesson is that **consequences are often painful and destructive for entire families**. Those cherished the most, one's family members, often end up experiencing the burden and devastation of poor choices and selfish actions. That was certainly the case for

David and his family. After Nathan confronted David and assured him that God knew of his sin and deception (2 Sam 12), the next six chapters detail the ugly undoing of David's family. Incest, rape, murder, a son's attempt at a coup, and the tragic deaths of several of David's children follow. The sexual encounter with Bathsheba that initially appeared to be nobody else's business (a phrase that has naively grown popular over the years) had become everyone's business. The pain was real, family relationships were irreparably torn, and victims were plentiful among David's family. Little has changed today. Families and the communities they inhabit always pay a stiff price when individual rights, unyielding independence, and instant gratification are promoted without regard for how others might be affected. Personal and private decisions often play out in very public ways.

The fifth, and final, lesson is that **consequences are often long-lasting**. David's family would be affected by his decisions for generations to come. Long after he was gone, his family line would continue to experience fallout from his actions. We should not be surprised by this. After all, as noted earlier, we are still living with the consequences of Adam and Eve's decision made thousands of years ago. Furthermore, the second of the Ten Commandments, forbidding idolatry, adds this warning: "I, the LORD your God, am a jealous God, punishing the children for the sin of the fathers to the third and fourth generation" (Ex 20:5; cf. Ex 34:7). Consequences often endure and get passed on to future generations. Therapists' offices are filled with individuals trying to shake the consequences of family sins and patterns that continue to dominate long after an initial decision or behavior occurred. We dare not be deceived: our decisions today will be felt by our children and grandchildren tomorrow and for years to come.

The message of 2 Samuel makes me pause and think twice about how my current decisions may unintentionally create consequences— for myself and others down the road. Anyone need to pause with me?

ℰℭ

This is a good place to stop and review what the opening ten books of Holy Scripture are trying to tell us. The Bible begins with God creating the world and the human *family* (Genesis). The family was intended to walk with God in *obedience* (Exodus) and *holiness* (Leviticus), demonstrating *order* (Numbers) and *law* (Deuteronomy) as its members operated in their daily lives. Though sin quickly distorted creation, the future was filled with *promise* (Joshua) for all who would follow God's design. Rejection of God's plan, however, resulted in *disaster* (Judges) that would need a deliverer. That deliverer—ultimately the Messiah from the line of David—would come through an unlikely, foreign-born woman known for her noble *character* (Ruth). *Leaders* (1 Samuel) would emerge in the years to come, some possessing good character and some not. Tragic *consequences* (2 Samuel) resulted whenever a leader ignored God and made poor decisions. The message of the Bible—from book to book—is intentional, sequential, and cohesive. We understand each successive book best when we understand what has preceded it. Therefore, reading the Bible orderly and chronologically has great practical value.

Paul declared that "all Scripture is God-breathed and is useful for teaching, rebuking, correcting and training in righteousness" (2 Tim 3:16). Yes, God's Word is useful for our development and maturation in the faith.

May God grant us eyes to see, ears to hear, minds to comprehend, and hearts to embrace his written Word.

PRAYER

O Sovereign Lord, we thank you for your faithfulness. Though we have known the pain, embarrassment, and consequences of our sins and failures, you have never abandoned us. You have continued to love us and have repeatedly brought us back to yourself. Thank you. Help us to live, from this day forward, as your representatives, making choices and decisions that honor you and avoiding those consequences that will hurt us and others for generations to come. We pray these things in the name of your son, Jesus. AMEN.

QUESTIONS

1. What factors have increasingly led people to think they can avoid consequences? How might we correct that faulty and harmful idea?

2. Think about the fact that confession and repentance do not automatically erase consequences. What are the implications of this? What examples can you provide?

3. What family pain or patterns can you identify that are likely the consequence of poor decisions made by earlier generations? How might you address those issues today?

4. In your opinion, what major theme found in the first ten books of the Bible needs more emphasis in the church today? In your own life today? Explain.

SUGGESTED READING

2 Samuel 7, 11–15, 18

11

1 KINGS: Evil

*Solomon did evil in the eyes of the LORD; he did not follow the
LORD completely, as David his father had done. (1 Kings 11:6)*

*Jeroboam did not change his evil ways, but once more appointed
priests for the high places from all sorts of people. (1 Kings 13:33)*

*You have done more evil than all who lived before you. You have
made for yourself other gods, idols made of metal; you have
provoked me to anger and thrust me behind your back. (1 Kings 14:9)*

*[Nadab son of Jeroboam] did evil in the eyes of the LORD,
walking in the ways of his father and in his sin, which
he had caused Israel to commit. (1 Kings 15:26)*

Evil is stubborn and universal. Ever since Adam and Eve ate from "the
tree of the knowledge of good and evil" (Gen 2:9) we have been dealing with evil and its consequences. The thread of evil runs throughout
Scripture; indeed, it is referenced in every book of the Bible except the
three small books of Ruth, the Song of Songs, and Philemon. We noted
its presence and destructiveness in Judges when we discussed *disaster*.
Now in 1 Kings we discover that evil takes center stage and dominates
the lives of Israel's leaders.

The book of 1 Kings opens with David passing on his reign to his
son Solomon. Despite a record of notable expansion and exploits (e.g.,
building the temple, dispensing wisdom, accumulating wealth), Solo-

mon is remembered for his evil (1 Kgs 11:6) rather than for the complete devotion to God that marked his father's life. After Solomon's death a national rebellion took place, dividing the kingdom into northern and southern territories. The southern kingdom, which operated under the rule of Solomon's son, Rehoboam, became known as Judah. The northern (and larger) kingdom was ruled by the competitor Jeroboam and retained the name Israel. The books of 1 and 2 Kings report that forty kings ruled over the combined kingdoms after Solomon's death, twenty over each kingdom. The majority of those rulers (25 of the 40 kings, 62%) are remembered for their evil. It was even worse in the northern kingdom, where 16 of the 20 kings (80%) were evil. The repeated emphasis is hard to miss. One almost gets the sense that the kings' tombstones read: "here lies yet another evil king."

Three primary characteristics of evil are identified in the book of 1 Kings, each worth a brief explanation. First, **evil is defiant**. At its core it is a rejection of God or a usurping of his authority. Evil (the Hebrew word is *ra*) is best understood as any act or disposition that rejects God's design and order. In the books of 1 and 2 Kings combined, the phrase "evil in the eyes of the LORD" occurs over thirty times (e.g., 1 Kgs 11:6; 15:26; 16:30; etc.), revealing that evil is first and foremost an affront to God. Furthermore, evil is closely tied to idolatry—rejecting the God of Israel and worshiping other gods. That was the case for Solomon, who followed the gods of his foreign wives (11:1–6) and, as a result, is remembered for doing "evil" (11:6). Jeroboam, the first of the twenty kings to rule the divided northern kingdom, set up his own religious places, practices, and priests (12:31). He refused to "change his evil ways," and it was this "sin of the household of Jeroboam that led to its downfall and to its destruction from the face of the earth" (13:33–34). Idolatry, or rebellion against God and his ways, consistently characterized evil throughout the Old Testament.

Little has changed today. Every act of evil, at its root, is defiance against God and his design. Consider the following examples:

- Murder is evil because it intentionally destroys a life created by God.
- Slavery is evil because it denies the dignity of humans created in the image of God.
- Abortion is evil because it snuffs out God's unique and intricate creation in the womb.

- Pornography is evil because it denigrates the inestimable value of humans and degrades the beauty of the sex act, both of which are purposeful gifts from God.
- Child abuse is evil because it robs a young person, created by God, of his or her self-worth and potential in the eyes of God.

We could add to the list, but the point should be clear. Defiance against God the Creator is the common thread of all these examples. Evil is the rejection of his design and order in favor of human ingenuity and self-centered desire. Idolatry, though it has many forms, is always evil because it seeks a substitute for God. We continue to witness the proliferation of idolatry in our own generation. Like the ancient kings of Israel, many leaders still operate out of defiance, idolatry, and evil.

Someone once noted that the word *evil* is "live" spelled backwards. This is an apt description of the condition we are trying to understand. The prophet Ahijah, speaking for God, hinted at this when he confronted Jeroboam with these words: "you have provoked me to anger and thrust me behind your back" (1 Kgs 14:9). Evil is a stubborn defiance wherein a person places God behind his back. Rather than facing and embracing God's design, he turns his back to God and ignores God's divine order. Such a person moves away from God rather than toward him. To live backward, contrary to God's call and plan, is always evil.

Second, **evil is progressive**. Jeroboam is described as having "done more evil than all who lived before" him (14:9). A few generations later, Ahab, too, "did more evil in the eyes of the LORD than any of those before him" (16:30). In fact, he "did more to provoke the LORD, the God of Israel, to anger than did all the kings of Israel before him" (16:33). The nature of evil is that it expands and finds new manifestations and new depths of depravity. Novel forms emerge that were unimaginable in previous generations. History gives testimony to this fact.

For example, consider the sexual revolution that began in the 1960s. Many social historians point to the pioneering work of Indiana University sex researcher Alfred Kinsey—in the 1940s and 1950s—as the catalyst for what followed. Pandora's box was opened and a whole array of aberrant sexual behaviors and consequences was unleashed upon society. Over the past half-century, we have watched in disbelief at the speed of the degeneracy around us. Society moved from concern over unwanted pregnancies to an explosion of STDs, to pornography addictions, to a hook-up culture, to endorsing a growing number of sexual orientations, to providing our children drugs and medical procedures to change their sex at will, to rewriting laws and regulations pertaining to those who may access public bathrooms and showers, to silencing those who dare maintain that there are sexual differences between males and females, to punishing people who dare point out the lunacy of it all. Where will this end? Evil grows over time; each new stage is more destructive than the preceding one. Ravenous and insatiable evil operates like a cancer in society as we proceed to do "more evil than all who lived before" us (14:9). Certainly, other contemporary examples could be noted. One thing is abundantly clear, however: these ancient Old Testament books are more relevant than we think. The progression of evil, while disturbing, is not new. Israel's behaviors are antecedents to our own actions, offering severe warnings intended to steer us away from all forms of evil.

Third, **evil is infectious**. It is rarely contained, but like a contagious disease it spreads to others. We see that clearly when we read that Jeroboam's evil was passed on to his son Nadab who succeeded Jeroboam as king (1 Kgs 15:25–26), then to the next king after him (15:34), and to subsequent kings as well (e.g., 16:19, 25–26, 30–31). Evil's influence spread not only to the rulers of Israel but also to the entire nation. Several times we read that the sin unleashed by her nation's kings "caused Israel" to sin as well (15:26; 16:19, 26). Such is the nature of evil. The book of 1 Kings closes as we might expect. Israel's ninth king since its separation from Judah—Ahaziah—was on the throne (22:51–53). Sadly, like those before him, Ahaziah is remembered for being infected by the same pernicious evil that dominated his father Ahab and their predecessor Jeroboam. These final words tell once again, in summary fashion, Israel's pattern: "He did evil in the eyes of the LORD . . . and provoked the LORD, the God of Israel, to anger, just as his father had done" (22:52–53). What a tragic national legacy. The entire nation of Israel succumbed to the virulent disease of evil that was passed from one leader to the next. A pandemic of wickedness and immorality was unleashed, and few stood to stem the tide.

Unfortunately, many nations have followed the same trajectory throughout human history. Our own nation is not exempt. Unless revival soon comes to America, all signs indicate that we may be headed in the same direction as ancient Israel. On our own, of course, we are incapable of fighting off the communicable and devastating effects of sin. God is needed in our land. Hope is found in turning to him.

Two final thoughts pertaining to evil—both underscoring our need for God—seem appropriate. First, Isaiah the prophet captured both the seriousness and distortion that accompanies evil when he said, "Woe to those who call evil good and good evil" (Isa 5:20). Apparently, there is a long history of confusion and mislabeling when it comes to evil. Humans, left on their own, have a propensity for inverting good and evil. It is incumbent that we stay alert if we are to avoid this deceptive tendency. Second, the last plea Jesus uttered in the Lord's Prayer was "deliver us from evil" (Matt 6:13). Jesus understood the destructive nature of evil and recognized that only those who gain victory over it will ultimately prosper. He also knew that only those who surrender completely to the Father's will have hope of such victory. Thus, he prayed: "Our Father in heaven . . . your will be done . . . deliver us from evil."

Indeed, may God deliver us from minimizing, mislabeling, or participating in evil. So much is at stake.

PRAYER

Our Father who art in heaven, forgive *us* and deliver *us* from evil. We confess that too often we have followed the ways of the world and participated in its sinful practices. At times we have been blinded and confused to the point wherein we have called evil good and good evil. Forgive us. Make us clean, pure, and holy—always surrendered to your will and design. Keep us from influencing others toward anything that displeases you. We pray this humbly, in the name and power of your Son, Jesus. AMEN.

QUESTIONS

1. What other examples of evil in the world today come to your mind? In what ways do these acts of evil exhibit a defiance toward God?

2. Why do you think leaders (kings) are so prone to committing evil? What makes them particularly susceptible?

3. What compromise toward evil do you see in our nation today? In the church? In your family? In your own life? Are there steps you might take to change things?

4. What contemporary example can you provide wherein we call evil good and good evil (Isa 5:20)? What can be done to avoid these kinds of moral inversions?

SUGGESTED READING

1 Kings 2–3, 11–15, 18

12

2 KINGS: Downfall

So the LORD was very angry with Israel and removed them from his presence. Only the tribe of Judah was left, and even Judah did not keep the commandments of the LORD their God. They followed the practices that Israel had introduced. (2 Kings 17:18–19)

The Israelites persisted in all the sins of Jeroboam and did not turn away from them until the LORD removed them from his presence, as he had warned through all his servants the prophets. So the people of Israel were taken from their homeland into exile in Assyria. (2 Kings 17:22–23)

The whole Babylonian army, under the commander of the imperial guard, broke down the walls around Jerusalem. . . . So Judah went into captivity, away from her land. (2 Kings 25:10, 21)

Unchecked evil leads to a nation's downfall. Second Kings documents that reality twice. First, because "the Israelites persisted in all the sins of Jeroboam and did not turn away from them" (17:22), they fell to the Assyrians (ch 17). Second, a century and a half later, history repeated itself when Judah fell to the Babylonians for the same reason (chs 24–25). God's chosen people lost their position of strength and prosperity and endured the hardship and humiliation of captivity due to their incessant rebellion against God. Their exile, or their downfall, is perhaps best summarized in the phrase "the LORD removed them from his presence" (2 Kgs 17:18, 23; 23:27). The truth and the tragedy are that the pattern is consistent: stubborn evil always leads to a downfall, defined here as being removed from the presence of God. Downfalls are still witnessed today.

Of course, as with so many other biblical truths, people often deny the fact that evil desires and practices could somehow be responsible for personal, organizational, or national demise. We look for other explanations when downfall and ruin take place. Poor financial management, lack of vision, or uncooperative citizens are more widely accepted reasons than an admission of evil. Yet a careful reading of 1 and 2 Kings will not allow one to escape the fact that evil and a nation's downfall are related. The warning of consequences described in 2 Samuel and the expansion of evil witnessed in 1 Kings resulted in Israel's downfall by the end of 2 Kings. Again, attentive Bible students are struck by how the sequence of themes in God's Word is purposeful and instructive when one reads these inspired accounts in an orderly and systematic fashion. Important clues regarding factors that contribute to a downfall emerge from the text. Four central ones will be mentioned here.

First, **a downfall occurs one person and one decision at a time over an extended period**. Though an observer might only see the final big mistake of a leader's fall, he should not be deceived. Typically, there are a series of smaller decisions and actions that lead to the final, and often public, cataclysmic event that ultimately marks the downfall. Second Kings illustrates the existence of antecedents to the final event historians now call Israel's exile. One king after another continued the evil practices of his predecessor, making yet other decisions that perpetuated defiance against God. As noted in the reflections on 1 Kings, after the reigns of Saul, David, and Solomon, the divided kingdoms of Israel and Judah each had a succession of twenty kings. Under those kings, Israel persisted over two hundred years before Assyria invaded and took control of the land in 722 BC (2 Kgs 17:3–6). Judah continued even longer—lasting well over three hundred years beyond Solomon's reign—before falling in 586 BC at the hands of the Babylonian army that destroyed Jerusalem and took its occupants captive (2 Kgs 24:10–12; 25:10, 20–21). Two to three hundred years is a significant amount of time. One might assume that would provide ample opportunity for God's people to make corrections, get things right, and change the trajectory of history. Unfortunately, that rarely seemed to happen and, when it did, was never sustained. Decision after decision was made to follow the evil practices of their neighbors and predecessors rather than follow the ways of God. When such a pattern endures over time, a downfall is predictable.

Unfortunately, history records numerous examples of such a trajectory. Too many powerful politicians, successful business leaders, charismatic religious personalities, and Hollywood celebrities have come crashing down in recent years. The handwriting is often on the wall long before the final collapse. Repeated patterns of abuse, manipulation, or ethical compromise are justified and go unchecked. Warning signs are ignored and excuses multiply. Eventually, however, the moral decline catches up with the individual and the downfall is complete. What was true in Israel's history is still true today: over time poor decisions have a cumulative effect that bring down leaders. The principle is universal and timeless.

Second, **a downfall occurs when God's message and messenger are largely ignored and marginalized**. Two of history's best-known prophets are found in the books of 1 and 2 Kings. The stories of Elijah (1 Kgs 17–19; 2 Kgs 1–2) and Elisha (2 Kgs 2–8) have inspired generations of Bible readers. Yet during their day these two prophets were often seen as some combination of eccentric, entertaining, or threatening. Evidence indicates that Israel's kings failed to take these prophets' message, let alone the messengers themselves, too seriously. When that happens repeatedly a downfall is to be expected. Tragically, that pattern also has been repeated down through history. Centuries later, when Jesus engaged in his earthly ministry, he told the parable of the rich man and Lazarus. Jesus concluded the story by noting the human tendency to ignore the prophets (Luke 16:31). The whole point of Jesus's parable is that the rich man's family had plenty of opportunities to hear God's warning through a variety of messengers and prophets, but they would not listen.

This should not surprise us, for we observe the same pattern today. For example, despite all the good accomplished by the late Rev. Billy Graham, very few national or world leaders seriously heeded the prophetic message that Graham proclaimed worldwide for more than half a century. Upon Graham's death in 2018, his son, Franklin, took his father's mantle and expanded his global outreach and ministry. National and church leaders around the world have certainly acknowledged the role played by both Billy and Franklin Graham and have appreciated their presence and assistance during a time of crisis or when a prayer has been needed at a high-level ceremony. Nonetheless, the Grahams—

much like Elijah and Elisha before them—have been largely ignored and marginalized by cultural leaders and celebrities around the world. They are valued when a solemn occasion requires a well-known religious representative to connect us to God, but otherwise few individuals want to disturb their life habits by too closely adhering to the Grahams' gospel message. The result is predictable: ignoring God and his message leads to both personal and national downfalls.

Third, **a downfall occurs when worship gets compromised and distorted**. Nowhere is this seen more clearly than in 2 Kings 17, where the contrast is made between worshiping God (*Yahweh*) and bowing down to other gods. In fact, the Hebrew word for worship (*shachah*) means "to bow down." Scripture reveals that when leaders and their people will not bow down before God on their own, God eventually removes them from his presence, and they go "down" another way. One way or another, people will go down. They will either do it on their own, in humility before God, or God will see that they ultimately go down as a result of their arrogance and compromise. Worship, wherein we humbly bow before God our Creator, is an acknowledgement and demonstration of our position before the sovereign Lord.

This whole topic, of course, raises an important question: Do we sincerely worship (bow down before) God? Or have we compromised and distorted worship so that it no longer means we bow down before him? Does our worship direct us to other gods? Those other gods may not be made of wood and stone as they so often were during Bible days; they may not be named Baal (17:16). However, gods of popularity, status, pleasure, and prestige can be just as offensive and deadly. History sadly notes that far too many people have met their downfall at the altar of such gods. From time to time we would do well to reconsider our worship practices lest they become compromised, distorted, and lead us to a tragic and needless downfall. Israel's history offers us a sober warning in this regard.

Fourth, **a downfall occurs when leaders and their people persist in sin and refuse to repent**. This takes us right back to our first observation above. Forty kings followed Solomon over a period exceeding three hundred years, and yet only rarely is there a record of repentance or reform. The story of Israel's behavior is described in these disturbing words: "The Israelites persisted in all the sins of Jeroboam and did not turn away from them until the LORD removed them from his presence, as he had warned through all his servants the prophets"

(2 Kgs 17:22–23). Persistent sin is mentioned three times in chapter 17 (vv 22, 34, 40). There was no turning away, no repentance. Instead, God's people continued to ignore the prophets and their warnings. Persistent patterns of sin, failure to turn and repent, and a stubborn refusal to heed the message of God's prophets led to Israel's downfall. The same formula always ends in ruin regardless of time, people, or place. Refusing to repent is a theme that runs throughout the pages of Scripture. Whenever such stubbornness prevails, we find that it breaks the heart of God, causes untold personal pain, and results in widespread calamity and a downfall that could have been avoided.

The tragedy of a downfall, while predictable when these factors are present, is that it is preventable. Prevention requires God-honoring decisions in the little matters of life, decisions that may differ from those made by individuals who have gone before us or from those who surround us in our present communities. Prevention comes when we take God's message and messengers seriously and heed God's Word even when few others seem to do so. Prevention is tied to our worship; before whom or what we bow and give our allegiance matters to God. Prevention happens when we are quick to identify, confess, and repent of any sin rather than continuing in it and hoping God does not notice.

Those who take these preventive steps will enjoy God's presence—forever—while those who chart their own way will one day find that his presence has been removed. Ultimate victory awaits the former; ultimate downfall awaits the latter. Scripture is clear.

PRAYER

Lord, our prayer is that you would deliver us from evil and keep us from downfall and ruin. Do not take your Spirit, your presence, from us. May we learn the lessons of history found in your holy Word. Help us to live in such obedience to you—heeding your message, worshiping you alone, repenting quickly when we have sinned—that we never experience the tragic downfall described here and experienced by so many. Save us. Save your people. Save our nation. Revive us, we pray, before it is too late. We humbly turn to you now and acknowledge you as the sovereign Lord of all history and all life. AMEN.

QUESTIONS

1. In addition to the factors noted above, what other factors do you think might contribute to a personal or national downfall? Explain why you think so.

2. What are some common false gods that compete with worship of the true God today? Which of these false gods most tempt you personally?

3. Though the pattern, or formula, for a downfall is quite predictable, why does every generation think they are the exception that will escape such an outcome?

4. If you could advise a leader today—whether national or local—regarding steps needed to avoid a downfall, what would you say? What succinct, practical advice would you offer?

SUGGESTED READING

2 Kings 1–2, 4–6, 17, 24–25

13

1 CHRONICLES: Teamwork

Then King David went in and sat before the LORD, and he said:
"Who am I, O LORD God, and what is my family, that you have
brought me this far? And as if this were not enough in your
sight, O God, you have spoken about the future of the house
of your servant. You have looked on me as though I were the
most exalted of men, O LORD God. (1 Chronicles 17:16–17)

David said, "Of these, twenty-four thousand are to supervise
the work of the temple of the LORD and six thousand are to be
officials and judges. Four thousand are to be gatekeepers and four
thousand are to praise the LORD with the musical instruments
I have provided for that purpose." (1 Chronicles 23:4–5)

Young and old alike, teacher as well as student,
cast lots for their duties. (1 Chronicles 25:8)

Repetition is often used in Scripture as a way to emphasize what is of utmost importance. The use of repetition also allows a familiar story to be told from a different perspective. For example, the four gospel accounts in the New Testament all emphasize the ministry, death, and resurrection of Jesus. Clearly, these events carry significance, forming the central message of the Christian gospel. However, the repetition by four distinct authors also allows the reader to see things from different, yet complementary, points of view. The same pattern exists in the Old Testament, particularly in the books of 1 and 2 Chronicles. Much of the content found there is a repeat of information found in 1 and 2 Kings. However, the unique perspectives of the respective authors result in unique themes. First Chronicles, after opening with long genealogical lists (chs 1–9), focuses on King David and his reign (chs 11–29). The word *chronicle* means an orderly record of historical events. When reading the record, or chronicle, of David's administration, one cannot help but be struck by the extensive teamwork that contributed to its success.

Teamwork is a concept found throughout Scripture, but one that gets far less attention than it probably deserves. The "suitable helper" (Gen 2:18, 20) that Adam needed in the Garden of Eden was an early endorsement of teamwork. Every successful marriage since then has formed a partnership of cooperation and mutual support. The ordering of the Israelites noted in the book of Numbers is further endorsement of teamwork. In the New Testament, Jesus sent out the disciples two by two (Mark 6:7). Later, the apostle Paul reminded members of the early church that they all had different gifts, all intended for strengthening the entire body of believers (1 Cor 12, Eph 4:11–12). Stated succinctly, "there are many parts" that work together as a team "but one body" (1 Cor 12:20). These references, and others like them, point to the value of teamwork. That theme is found here in 1 Chronicles when we read, first, the lists of genealogies that comprised the human family and, second, how David assigned various roles and duties for carrying out the work of God. Teamwork is a thread that runs through the entire book. Of course, none of this should surprise us since God has revealed himself to us in the form of a team—Father, Son, and Holy Spirit. Teamwork is a characteristic of our trinitarian God.

If God's people were to properly represent him in their world and become firmly established in the land, it would take a team. First Chronicles makes this abundantly clear when it begins by listing key members of the early human team that extended from Adam to Abraham (ch 1). The spotlight then shines on Abraham's grandson, Israel, noting how Israel's sons formed a team that would long represent God's people (chs 2–9). Along the way special attention is given to Israel's sons Judah (chs 2–4) and Levi (ch 7)—the former became the line that produced David, who would assume governmental responsibilities, the latter became the line of priests that would oversee matters pertaining to religious practice and the temple. Teamwork was at the heart of God's design for his people.

When the book shifts its focus to David and his leadership, teamwork remains a defining feature. Though it would be David's son Solomon who would eventually build the temple to worship God, it was David who prepared the elaborate operation. The detailed system included a variety of positions. Priests were identified, as well as the Levites who would assist them (23:2, 28–32). Musicians were gathered (ch 25), gatekeepers assigned (26:1–19), financial officers put in place (26:20–28), and civic officials given responsibilities in the community away from the temple (26:29–32). To further ensure a smooth operation, Israel had military leaders and personnel (27:1–15), local tribal officers (27:16–24), and business leaders who were assigned various tasks (27:25–34). The message was clear: teamwork would be needed to carry out the ministry and work required of God's people. Everyone had a job to do; everyone was expected to perform assigned duties for the good of all citizens. Failure to do so would jeopardize the entire community.

Across the centuries teamwork has continued to mark the people of God in some notable ways. Let me illustrate. Several years ago, I was surprised to learn that John Newton wrote what has arguably become the most widely sung hymn of the past 250 years, *Amazing Grace*, after being inspired by 1 Chronicles. At the time, I confess to thinking: how could anyone find inspiration for a song in an old book of genealogies like this? I had long assumed the well-known hymn's inspiration came from some of Paul's eloquent writings on grace in the New Testament. History, however, tells a different story. Newton was preparing to preach his 1773 New Year's Day message to those gathered at his church in Olney, England. He planned to use David's prayer found in 1 Chronicles 17:16–17 as his text, "Who am I, O LORD God, and what is my family, that you have brought me this far? . . . You have looked on me as though I were the most exalted of men." As was Newton's custom, he proceeded to pen the lyrics to a song as a way of amplifying his sermon. That song was *Amazing Grace*.

Most of us recognize the last stanza of this familiar hymn, beginning with the words: "When we've been there ten thousand years . . . ." The inspiring message clearly places the emphasis on how God's grace will provide for us an eternal home in heaven, wherein we will praise our Lord forever. As meaningful as these lyrics are, however, this was not how Newton ended his song. Rather, these familiar words were a later addition from an unknown author. Newton apparently ended the song with these less-familiar words:

> *The earth shall soon dissolve like snow*
> *The sun forbear to shine*
> *But God, who call'd me here below*
> *Will be forever mine*

Newton marveled that God had "called" him—great sinner though he was—and knew that nothing could sever that relationship, not even the end of this physical life and the surrounding world to which we have become so accustomed. Implied here is that the grace of God not only "saved a wretch like" Newton, a former slave trader, but "called" him to participate in the teamwork needed for the redemption of the world. Newton often expressed his amazement that God would employ him as a minister of the gospel. For fifteen years Newton served a church congregation in Olney, followed by twenty-eight years doing the same in London.

However, there is more to the story. Newton's biographer, Jonathan Aitken (*John Newton*, 2007), suggests there may have been another reason Newton wrote *Amazing Grace* when he did. While the song is largely a personal testimony—one only need observe the first-person singular pronouns (I, me, my, mine) that dominate the song to reach that conclusion—Aitken suspects teamwork also played a role in its inspiration. The English poet William Cowper moved to Olney to work with Newton and be under the latter's ministry. Together they wrote lyrics and produced the *Olney Hymns* (1779). Though most of the volume's 350 hymns were written by Newton, over sixty of them came from the hand of Cowper (including the well-known song, "There Is a Fountain Filled with Blood"). In fact, Newton considered Cowper far his superior when it came to writing poetry and hymns. Newton gained from Cowper's creativity and style. Their ambitious hymn project was a result of their close friendship and teamwork. By late 1772, however, Cowper was struggling with serious bouts of depression; his productivity had come to a standstill and his very life was at risk. Newton's *Amazing Grace* may well have had his friend in mind as much as he had his own past in mind. Just as Newton drew much of his creativity from Cowper, Newton may have been hoping that Cowper would now draw confidence in the grace of God during his dark hour of need and despair. Teamwork operates like that, serving and contributing to one another for the good of all.

After his conversion from the slave business to a minister of the gospel, Newton spent the rest of his life amazed that God would choose one like him for his team. In the last days of life—he died in 1807, at age 82—as Newton grew physically weak and worn, he is said to have spoken these words to a visitor: "My memory is nearly gone, but I remember two things: That I am a great sinner and that Christ is a great Savior" (Aitken, p 347). Newton was right. It is nothing short of amazing grace that God would choose any of us—sinners that we are—to be on his team. That choice, of course, has little to do with us and everything to do with the "great Savior" who, frankly, has no other options, for we are all great sinners and recipients of undeserved grace.

Teamwork is always needed in the family of God. Whether it is King David overseeing the needs of temple worship and community life, John Newton writing hymns by which to teach and inspire his people, or those who are trying to be salt and light in a twenty-first century world that has lost its moral bearings, God uses teamwork to get the job done.

He still calls us today to be part of his team. He recruits "young and old alike" (25:8). What will your contribution be?

Prayer

Our Father in heaven, we acknowledge you as Lord and Master of all. Your plan is not only to save us from sin, but you also call us to participate in your great work. You want us on your team. You have a role for us to play, a job for us to do. We confess that we marvel at the thought. Like David and John Newton before us, we ask, "Who am I . . . that you have brought me this far?" And then we remember your amazing grace. Thank you for that grace. Thank you for giving us a role to play in your work. Whatever our role—whether we are gatekeepers, financial officers, musicians, or business leaders—help us to engage in the work you have set before us with eagerness and purpose, always recognizing you as the Captain of the team. AMEN.

Questions

1. Why do you suppose God designed us for teamwork? Why is that the primary pattern we see over and over in Scripture?

What might teamwork imply about God and our relationship with him?

2. What are some of the challenges inherent in teamwork? What makes teamwork so hard at times?

3. What part of the song, "Amazing Grace," most speaks to you? Why? How has God's grace made a difference for you? Be specific.

4. Do you have a William Cowper in your life—someone who is unusually gifted in some manner but who struggles emotionally or spiritually? What might you do to encourage that person and engage him or her in meaningful teamwork?

SUGGESTED READING
1 Chronicles 16–17, 22–27

14

2 CHRONICLES: Humility

If my people, who are called by my name, will humble themselves and pray and seek my face and turn from their wicked ways, then will I hear from heaven and will forgive their sin and will heal their land. (2 Chronicles 7:14)

[Zedekiah] did evil in the eyes of the LORD his God and did not humble himself before Jeremiah the prophet, who spoke the word of the LORD. (2 Chronicles 36:12)

Pride is a recurring theme across the pages of the Old Testament. The word is found nearly one hundred times there, with strong warnings against it. The antidote, or remedy, to pride is repentance and a life of humility. Pride exalts oneself; humility lowers oneself. The biblical meaning of humility—in both the Old and New Testaments—has to do with bringing oneself down while acknowledging a higher authority. The characteristic is all too rare among those who have achieved position or success.

No book of the Bible references and points out the significance of humility more than 2 Chronicles. The first time the concept is mentioned is after Solomon has completed and dedicated the temple. What a majestic structure it must have been. The Lord appeared to Solomon shortly after this grand architectural accomplishment and spoke words that have become well-known and repeated often over the years: "If my people, who are called by my name, will humble themselves and pray and seek my face and turn from their wicked ways, then will I hear from heaven and will forgive their sin and will heal their land" (2 Chron 7:14). Several things are worth noting here. First, the preceding verse (v 13) makes clear that this was the response God deemed appropriate when drought, devastation, or plague ravaged the land. Second, the invitation was for God's people; they were the ones called to humility. Third, the act of humbling oneself was the initial response God required—coming before prayer, seeking God's face, and turning, or repenting. The implication is that the latter three steps would be ineffective without the former, humility. Fourth, God promised to respond to such humility by hearing, forgiving, and healing the land. The message was clear and hopeful: humility unlocks the door to restoration.

The first-time reader of the Bible might reasonably expect such clear instruction to have solved the problem of pride and arrogance once and for all. Scripture and history, however, tell a different story. Ironically, one cannot even leave the book of 2 Chronicles without realizing that the lack of humility was destructive for the very people to whom God gave the instruction. While there were occasional instances of humility among Judah's kings (e.g., 12:6–12; 34:27), the humility never lasted. Tragically, by the end of the book—and some 350 years after God spoke to Solomon—King Zedekiah was described as one who "did evil in the eyes of the LORD his God and did not humble himself before Jeremiah the prophet, who spoke the word of the LORD" (36:12). Zedekiah refused to "humble himself" and receive God's message from the prophet Jeremiah. The next thing we read about God's people is that "God handed all of them over to Nebuchadnezzar," the king of Babylon (36:17). The temple was ransacked, Jerusalem's walls were knocked down, and seventy years of agonizing exile followed (36:18–21). God meant what he said: humility, or the lack thereof, is a big deal with big consequences.

What was true for Israel and Judah, and their leaders, has proven true for other nations across the centuries. Examples abound in both ancient and recent history in the likes of Babylon, Greece, Rome, Germany, Japan, and the Soviet Union, to name a few. Moreover, there are numerous writers and speakers today who suggest the United States— unless there is widespread repentance and turning to God—may soon be added to the list. The absence of humility always spells disaster, both personally and nationally.

One would be justified in asking whether we have learned anything from history in this regard. Why do we, citizens of the twenty-first century, still find humility so rare? Why is it so seldom genuinely exhibited among leaders everywhere—whether in business, education, politics, entertainment, or the church? All of us spot arrogance on display regularly; on the other hand, it is uncommon to catch someone being truly humble.

Let us pause to consider five contributing factors as to why this may be the case. First, **our fallen human nature rejects humility**. We began this discussion by noting that humility lowers oneself. The problem is that sin has made us climbers, not those who want to submit and lie down. We want to be in charge. We want to be recognized. Humility, therefore, can never be accomplished on our own. Genuine humility can only exist when sinful nature has been acknowledged and confessed.

Second, **our friends and associates reject humility**. Not only do they not practice humility themselves, but they prefer we not do so either. In all honesty, people like to associate with those who are successful. That helps inflate their own self-esteem. Our friends are counting on us to be someone special, which will then elevate their own status in the world. Because very little is gained by hanging around someone of humility, humble servants are not known for having a multitude of admiring friends.

Beyond these personal matters of human nature and our circle of friends, there are larger social factors that impede humility. We will consider two of them. Third, **our educational system rejects humility**. Modern schools and their teachers are designed to prepare students for achievement and success. Humility may have been part of an earlier curriculum, when one learned at the knee of mom or dad, but that curriculum is now considered outdated. Too many more important subjects vie for attention today. No one goes to school to learn humility. No university offers a major in humility. On the contrary, the marks of highly educated individuals are achievement, independent scholarship, an impressive résumé, credentials that hang prominently on an office wall, and elaborate introductions to audiences citing one's accomplishments.

By the way, it seems reasonable to expect a Christian education to have a different goal. The chief mark of a Christian education—beyond the accumulation of requisite knowledge—ought to be the individual's recognition and witness that God is the ultimate authority, the expert on whom we rely within our respective fields of study. An educated Christian minimally should be distinguished by his or her humility.

Fourth, **our artificial intelligence (AI) rejects humility**. We have developed machines that now take the place of human intelligence. Computers and electronic devices hold and dispense a volume of information that once was unimaginable. A vast range of data is at our fingertips and comes to us with lightning speed, giving us a sense of power, control, and invincibility. Knowledge and efficiency have become the new currency; whoever has access to the most useful data and can retrieve it quickly reigns supreme. Jeff Bezos (founder of Amazon), Bill Gates (founder of Microsoft), Mark Zuckerberg (founder of Facebook), Larry Page and Sergey Brin (co-founders of Google), and others have become the gods of this age. Each of these AI authorities, along with being a multi-billionaire, has expanded our virtual world and dictated how the rest of us think and live. Many believe we have only scratched the surface when it comes to AI; future possibilities are tantalizing. Humility is abandoned and seen as a detriment in the race for more innovation, information, and efficiency. Like the ancient Tower of Babel, this modern-day creation known as AI "reaches to the heavens" and its builders have made a great "name for [them]selves" (Gen 11:4).

There is a final important factor that explains why humility is rare. Fifth, **our general lack of familiarity with God's Word leads us to reject humility**. Beyond 2 Chronicles, humility is found and encouraged in the New Testament writings of Luke (14:11; 18:14), Paul (Eph 4:2; Col 3:12; Titus 3:2), James (4:10), and Peter (1 Pet 3:8; 5:5–6). Apparently, humility was never intended to be an unrealistic, ancient characteristic that would one day become obsolete. God's Word admonishes people of all generations to "be completely humble and gentle" (Eph 4:2). Of course, no one illustrated this better than Jesus himself, who "humbled himself and became obedient to death—even death on a cross" (Phil 2:8). The humility Jesus exhibited was selfless, submissive, strenuous, and sacrificial. Nevertheless, Paul called his readers to practice this same extraordinary humility (Phil 2:3).

When I look back over my life for a flesh-and-blood example of someone who took Paul's words seriously, I think of Jake DeShazer. Jake was one of eighty Doolittle Raiders who, in April 1942, set out on a daring World War II mission to bomb Tokyo after the Japanese attack on Pearl Harbor months earlier. Though the military attack was successful, a shortage of fuel resulted in crew members bailing out of their planes. Those who survived were captured. That included Jake, who spent the next forty months as a POW in a Japanese prison camp. While there, he had an encounter with the living, humble Christ that changed his life immediately. Jake dared to believe he should start living like Jesus even while suffering the indignities of prison and torture. Thus, his attitude toward his Japanese captors turned from hatred and spite to love and humility. Though he finally returned to America in 1945 as a war hero, Jake soon went back to Japan, the land of his suffering, and gave the next thirty years of his life to sharing the gospel and love of Christ with those who would listen. Jake DeShazer's inspirational story has been written about by numerous authors (e.g., Watson, 1950; Benge, 2009; Goldstein and Dixon, 2010).

In the 1980s, I was blessed to meet and become friends with Jake in Salem, Oregon. He had retired and attended the Salem Free Methodist Church, where I served on the staff. I never knew a humbler man. Whenever he spoke about his war experiences, gave an interview, or was introduced to a new admirer, humility marked his countenance and thanksgiving to the Lord poured from his lips. Jake consistently acknowledged God's grace and provision. After moving to Illinois to teach in 1995, my family and I traveled back to Oregon in 2007. One of our stops was the retirement home where Jake and his wife, Florence, then lived. Our visit was brief, but I wanted to make sure my twenty-year-old sons had the opportunity to be in the presence of an American hero who embodied humility. Before we left, we stood in a circle and prayed together—Jake, Florence, and the four of us Olneys. It was a holy moment that I shall never forget. Jake died less than a year later, at age ninety-five, the humblest man I ever encountered.

God desires that we all live that way. The book of 2 Chronicles helps us see the importance of humility. Because we sometimes forget, and perhaps because there are so many factors that work against us in this fallen world, God extended an explicit invitation to his people. That invitation is straightforward and speaks of a promise: "If my people . . . will humble themselves . . . I will hear . . . forgive . . . and heal their land" (7:14).

Humility always gets God's attention. Does it have ours?

PRAYER

Our Father in heaven, you have not only called us to humble ourselves, but you sent your son to be our example. Thank you. His humility in enduring the pain and shame of the cross changed the course of history. Help us to follow that example by living in humble obedience as well. May we always honor and recognize you as the supreme authority over all life, all knowledge, all talents, and all relationships. May you become greater; may we become less. We offer this prayer humbly, in Jesus's name. AMEN.

QUESTIONS

1. Read 2 Chronicles 7:14 again. Which word or phrase captures your attention? Why?

2. Who have you known in your lifetime that has exhibited genuine humility? In what ways? What other attributes define that person?

3. What are the signs of false humility? How can you tell when someone is trying to act humble, but it is only for show?

4. Review the five reasons suggested for why humility is rare today. Which of these reasons do you think is most influential in our society? Why? Do other reasons come to mind as to why humility is so uncommon?

SUGGESTED READING

2 Chronicles 1, 6–7, 10–12, 36

15

EZRA: Rebuilding

When they arrived at the house of the LORD in Jerusalem, some of the heads of the families gave freewill offerings toward the rebuilding of the house of God on its site. (Ezra 2:68)

We are the servants of the God of heaven and earth, and we are rebuilding the temple that was built many years ago, one that a great king of Israel built and finished. (Ezra 5:11)

Lest anyone miss the connection between the book of 2 Chronicles and the next biblical book of Ezra, the latter begins exactly as the former ends. The closing and opening two verses of each book, respectively, are identical. This ought not be viewed as mere coincidence. The message of one book is tied to the message of the other: When one generation fails to humble itself before God (2 Chronicles), a future generation will need to rebuild its relationship with God. That is the story that unfolds in Ezra. Remarkably, given the lack of humility that closes 2 Chronicles (36:12), Ezra and his companions humbled themselves before God at the outset of their journey back to Jerusalem (Ezra 8:21).

Ezra, for whom the book is named, was a priest from the line of Aaron (7:1–5). He and his fellow Jews were in exile in Babylon during the height of the Persian Empire. Israel's repeated disobedience, incessant evil, and lack of humility over several hundred years had led to their pitiful condition far from the promised land. Under a series of Persian kings, however, God's people were gradually allowed to return and rebuild their broken-down city of Jerusalem and its temple. The books of Ezra and Nehemiah record the rebuilding efforts, reporting both the challenges and the triumphs.

Rebuilding is neither quick nor easy, regardless of the time period, especially when the destruction that necessitates the work has come from the hands of one's enemies. History is filled with examples (e.g., rebuilding the South after the Civil War; rebuilding Europe and Japan after World War II; rebuilding New York City after the September 11, 2001, terrorist attacks). In addition to the physical labor and materials needed to complete the arduous task, emotional and mental reserves must be drawn upon as well. Rebuilding can be a taxing project when the process entails reflecting on and mourning over the past, all while staying focused on getting the immediate job done.

The rebuilding described in the book of Ezra was physical and literal. After all, the invading Babylonians had burned down the sacred temple and beautiful palaces built during Solomon's reign and had destroyed the walls of Jerusalem (2 Chron 36:19). Those structures demanded attention if the returning exiles were going to inhabit the city once again. Nevertheless, there were other community rebuilding projects also needed. Three of them will be considered here—all three foundational for healthy community life moving forward.

A careful reading of Ezra indicates that the Israelites needed to **rebuild their relationship with God**. These people were in their current trouble (in exile) because they failed to obey God, keep his law, and humble themselves before him. Everything that has come before this in the Old Testament—the preceding fourteen books—helps explain the mess they were then experiencing. The primary issue was a spiritual issue. God's people did not consistently take their relationship with him seriously. Though he chose them as his own, though he warned them repeatedly when they wandered from his plan, though he gave them clear instructions regarding how to live and respond, though he forgave and provided multiple opportunities to return to him, they continued to follow their own ways rather than his. Their relationship with God was broken. The destruction of the temple was symbolic of a deeper spiritual detachment that threatened the fiber of their nation.

The people must have been aware of this problem, for the first physical object they rebuilt was the altar (Ezra 3:1–2). The temple project came next (3:7–11). A logical case could be made for rebuilding the walls of Jerusalem first, as a way of protecting themselves from their enemies who had already done so much harm. However, the walls would not be completed until Nehemiah arrived in Jerusalem several decades later. The people finally seemed to realize that their biggest threat was not external but internal, within themselves. Unless they re-established a proper relationship with God, nothing else mattered. The walls (the focus of the later book, Nehemiah) could wait while the altar and temple were given priority.

I suspect much rebuilding is also needed in our communities and nation. We have recently experienced a pandemic, along with significant social and political unrest. The temptation, of course, is to move quickly to shore up physical, structural, and economic areas. However, maybe one of the lessons of Ezra is that our spiritual relationship with God needs attention first. Is God calling us to rebuild our lives spiritually? If so, how does one do that? Hints are offered by the responses observed in Ezra: First, rebuilding spiritually begins by giving heed to "what is written in the Law of Moses" (3:2). Ezra was described as "a teacher well versed in the Law of Moses" (7:6). Apparently, the first ingredient needed for spiritual rebuilding is becoming more familiar with the Law, the written Word of God. Second, rebuilding spiritually includes celebrating with others God's activity and deliverance (6:19–22). It is very possible that this was the first community Passover celebration in over a century. At best, such celebrations had been irregular and periodic for the past several hundred years (see 2 Chron 35:16–19). We dare not neglect those regular opportunities of pausing to join others in honoring and celebrating God. Third, rebuilding spiritually means sincere repentance of unfaithfulness and detestable practices (9:1–5). Such times will be marked by humility and prayer (9:5–6). Like Ezra and the people of God 2,500 years ago, we would do well to make spiritual rebuilding our top priority today.

Another type of rebuilding is implied throughout this story. God's people had to **rebuild a work ethic**. Rebuilding a temple and a city would take years, even decades. Such a task would not be easy. While the people had certainly endured forced labor in Babylon, this labor was different. Now they would have to motivate themselves, make plans themselves, gather resources themselves, and execute the entire project on their own. No longer responding to or working under foreign masters, anything the returned exiles accomplished would be because they initiated and completed it. Vision, determination, skill, persistence, and hard work would be required. Without a strong work ethic among the people, the job would never get done. A restored relationship with God was foundational, but upon that foundation a determined work ethic would need to follow. The books of Ezra and Nehemiah tell of God's people at work. Ambition, discipline, and tireless effort are recorded there.

Again, this has relevance for us today. Whenever a people emphasize individual rights, as has been true of Americans throughout their history, there is the danger of going too far and establishing a culture of entitlement. Many social historians and analysts suggest we have done just that in our nation. One of the outcomes of such a culture is the loss of a work ethic. Evidence is plentiful. I will provide just one example from my own area of work, the university. I have now been a professor long enough—35 years—to have witnessed many significant changes on college campuses. Reliance on computer technology, mandated accommodations for all types of students, and skyrocketing student debt have all occurred during the past three decades. However, perhaps the single most profound change I have seen is the declining work ethic among a growing segment of the student population. While I want to recognize this is not true of every college student, there are growing numbers who enroll in college and think they can make it without reading a book or taking time to research and write a coherent paper. Somewhere along the line our work ethic has been lost. It needs to be rebuilt—in our homes, communities, schools, and nation—if we expect to stay relevant in the world. Beyond that, however, a work ethic is one of the greatest witnesses we offer to our neighbors that we honor God and his gifts, and that we belong to him. He has called us to steward his gifts—some of which are unique to individuals, others of which are found in creation for all humanity to enjoy. In either case, a work ethic is required if we are to properly develop and employ those divine gifts. May God help us to work hard as a testimony to others of who is our true Master.

If they were to complete all the projects noted above, God's people would also have to **rebuild their courage** in the face of stiff opposition. Raw courage was called for in the middle of Ezra (see chs 4–6). The builders had enemies who tried to "discourage the people" (4:4) and "frustrate their plans" (4:5). When that failed, they "lodged an accusation against" them with the government (4:6). What a daunting task and frightening environment they endured. They had just spent seventy years in captivity because some other enemies had unfairly attacked them; now this. Who could blame them if they lacked backbone and nerve under such circumstances? Yet they persevered. Perhaps remembering the boldness of their forefathers—Moses, Joshua, David, Elijah, and others—they mustered the determination needed to successfully rebuild their temple and city. Their courage helped them prevail when the odds were stacked against them.

We too find ourselves in a cultural moment when courage is needed. There is great antagonism and public hostility to matters of faith and the gospel today. Of course, none of this should surprise us because Jesus repeatedly warned us to expect these things (e.g., Matt 10:22; 24:9; Mark 13:13; John 15:18–19). Our response to opposition and outright hatred is to exhibit humility mixed with courage. We will never achieve anything significant otherwise. Our neighbors and associates will not always approve of our commitments and loyalty to God. Nonetheless, we are called to stand with humble courage and a fixed mindset, following God regardless of adversarial threats that seek to discourage us.

May God help us to rebuild the broken foundations in our generation. The need is too serious to allow further delay.

PRAYER

O Sovereign Lord, there are times we look around and weep. So much destruction, debris, ruin, and pain fill our world. We see it every evening on the news, we read about it daily on our phones and computers, and we experience it all too often in our homes and communities. There is so much rebuilding needed. Forgive us for neglecting our relationship with you. Forgive us for growing lax in our work ethic. Forgive us for failing to stand with courage when opposition comes. Restore our homes, churches, communities, and nation. Grant us the strength, wisdom, and focus needed to rebuild our lives as you will. Help us to start today. AMEN.

QUESTIONS

1. What is the most challenging part of a rebuilding project? Why do you think so? How does one best overcome that challenge?

2. What area of your life most needs rebuilding? Is it one mentioned above, or another? What steps might you take to start the process?

3. How can we encourage and rebuild a work ethic among young people today? Is there a way to effectively communicate its importance? What ideas do you have?

4. How does one stand courageously in the midst of an antagonistic culture? What practical things can be done to avoid compromise while representing God well?

SUGGESTED READING

Ezra 1, 3–7, 9–10

16

NEHEMIAH: Walls

*By night I went out through the Valley Gate . . . examining the walls
of Jerusalem, which had been broken down. (Nehemiah 2:13)*

*Then I said to them, "You see the trouble we are in:
Jerusalem lies in ruins, and its gates have been burned
with fire. Come, let us rebuild the wall of Jerusalem, and
we will no longer be in disgrace." (Nehemiah 2:17)*

I devoted myself to the work on this wall. (Nehemiah 5:16)

Conversations about "walls" today seem to focus on reasons why they
need to come down. Bible students remember Jericho (Josh 6) and
sing that "the walls came tumbling down." Historians point to the Berlin
Wall, erected in 1961 to divide the East from the West, and recall the
immortalized words of President Ronald Reagan who stood at that wall
in 1987 and said, "Mr. Gorbachev, tear down this wall." American politicians today debate completing the wall along our southwest border.

Walls are also spoken of figuratively. Social activists speak of walls
of injustice that divide racial and ethnic groups. Marriage counselors
note walls that keep a husband and wife from communicating effectively. All these allusions share the common theme that walls are detrimental and need to be removed.

The book of Nehemiah counters this position. Its thirty references
to walls—structures that surround, defend, and delineate space—sug-

gest there can be great value in constructing and maintaining them. The rebuilding project that began in Ezra continues in Nehemiah, where the emphasis turns to repairing and rebuilding the walls of Jerusalem that had been destroyed by Nebuchadnezzar and his Babylonian army decades earlier (2 Chron 36:19). The first half of Nehemiah emphasizes work on the walls, while the second half highlights the revival and reforms that follow the walls' completion. One gets the impression that the walls had a bigger and more significant purpose than simply architectural soundness or aesthetic appeal. Walls contribute to security, consistency, and efficiency.

In the discussion that follows we will give attention to several functions of walls, then turn our attention to three types of walls that need rebuilding in our own society today.

First, **walls protect against external threats**. That was certainly the primary reason for the wall around Jerusalem, as well as the walls around most ancient cities. Protection against marauding enemies, or even wild animals, justified building and maintaining a city wall. No community would last long without a wall, or if its wall was in disrepair. No wonder Nehemiah's first words after "examining the walls of Jerusalem" (2:13) spoke of his deep concern: "You see the trouble we are in" (2:17). Walls provided a line of defense to protect homes, families, and communities. Nothing has really changed today. We still look for protection and security behind walls. We seek protection from bad weather and storms, from crooks and thieves, from harmful ideas and influences on our children, and from a variety of other external dangers. Even our computers have firewalls, designed to enhance network security. Walls provide a safe harbor.

Second, **walls preserve internal substance and order**. External threats are not the only reason for walls. Concern about maintaining what is behind walls—both material objects and order—is also why they are erected. In the previous book, Ezra, the temple was rebuilt, and its furnishings restored. If their sacred place of worship was to become operational again, the people of God knew they would need sturdy walls surrounding it. Otherwise, enemies, animals, or winds would find it too easy to enter and disturb what they valued. Walls are designed to preserve what is inside them. We expect a certain level of orderliness every time we enter a room because we know its walls have kept things as we left them. Walls work to keep a home's temperature constant, papers in place on an office desk, and an airplane's cabin filled with sufficient oxygen for its passengers. The walls of a dam hold back and keep water in its proper place, while a retaining wall prevents soil from eroding down a slope. The order of daily life depends, in large part, on sturdy and dependable walls. Things would be much less predictable without them.

Third, **walls provide boundaries**. Definition is given to geography and space when walls are put in place. The very design and purpose of a wall signals boundaries. One can only wonder if those rebuilding the walls around Jerusalem ever thought to themselves, *If our forefathers had taken God's laws and commands—boundaries intended for us—seriously, we would not be in this mess.* Every day they worked and replaced another section of their wall, they were confronted by the importance of boundaries. The Great Wall of China, built across two millennia, serves as another example. Its construction in northern China began in the seventh century BC with the purpose of forming a boundary between China and its Mongolian neighbors. The wall would eventually extend over thirteen thousand miles. It still stands as a testimony to the fact that walls define geography by providing clear boundaries.

Fourth, **walls promote productivity**. They do so by minimizing outside distractions. The challenge of focusing on a task is exacerbated when one always has an eye on others and their activities. The entire Old Testament points out the problem God's people had in this regard. They routinely looked at and wanted to be like their neighbors, though God intended for them to be faithful, attentive, and productive followers who honored him alone. Walls have a way of focusing one's attention. I remember discovering this as a young man while working on a church staff in Salem, Oregon, where I briefly shared an office with another staff member. It only took days to realize I would never be productive given the arrangement; every word and movement of my office mate sent my mind down another proverbial rabbit trail. I needed a room with four walls between my co-workers and me. Though certain types of collaboration and creativity may be enhanced in an open space, completing a task most often needs walls. Behind them is where we focus and produce.

Fifth, **walls proclaim reminders**. Memories are often attached to walls, both literally and figuratively. Family photos, pictures of favorite vacation spots, earned academic degrees, a meaningful and inspirational poem or Scripture verse are examples of items that decorate our walls. These are intentionally placed before us to remind us of what matters. Today walls also serve to commemorate those who have lost their lives in a war or national tragedy, often with names engraved thereupon. In similar fashion, the Jerusalem wall described in Nehemiah brought back memories. The memories were not only of a former glorious structure or an attractive city but also of the Creator God who had called them to be his own. The second half of the book of Nehemiah—once the wall was completed (6:15)—contains numerous reminders of how God wanted his people to live. They were to give attention to the Law (8:1), confess their sins (9:1–3), get their marriages in order (10:30; 13:23–29), keep the Sabbath (10:31–33; 13:15–22), take responsibility for the house of God (10:32–39; 13:1–14), and more. Rebuilding the physical wall around Jerusalem was their reminder that there were other walls and areas—with their roots in Genesis—that needed attention as well.

When all is said and done, talk about the problems and evils inherent in building walls today needs to be evaluated carefully. Like most things in life, balance is required. To be sure, some walls need to come down. However, as we have noted here, walls also have practical value and utility. We know that to be true because no sane person arbitrarily decides to dismantle his or her home walls in their entirety; they have an important purpose. There is universal recognition that walls are needed for protection, preservation, boundaries, productivity, and reminders.

All of this raises several important questions. Have we examined the walls of our lives lately? What structures have we built around us to help us operate efficiently? Are they reliable? Or are threats being allowed to penetrate? Is order sacrificed due to gaps in the walls? Are our boundaries clear and consistent? Do our walls result in optimum productivity? Do they serve to remind us of what really matters in life? Periodically, we would be wise to pause and consider the condition of our walls. They may need repair.

Nehemiah's words still have relevance for us today: "You see the trouble we are in: [our land] lies in ruins . . . Come, let us rebuild the wall . . ." (2:17). If we are to flourish as the people of God in the twenty-first century, we will need to give attention to rebuilding some walls. Here are three for starters.

The first one is *the wall of morality*. At this wall we acknowledge that we are not God. We are not free to pervert marriage, gender, justice, or matters of religious faith and practice to suit our personal desires. These matters are God's prerogative, not ours. Let us build a thick wall of morality that keeps evil out of our lives and declares with Isaiah "O LORD, you are my God; I will exalt you" (Isa 25:1).

The second wall that needs rebuilding is *the wall of civility*. It has been destroyed by our refusal to listen to one another. God calls us to love and forgive our enemies, not to attack and cancel them. Let us build a high wall of civility wherein we are "kind and compassionate to one another" (Eph 4:32), whether we agree on everything or not; civilization itself is at stake.

The third wall is *the wall of tranquility*. We have lost our ability to be quiet and still. Screens bombard us 24/7 with information that makes us anxious and needy. Stress is at an all-time high. We need extended time away from our phones and computers, time to decompress and laugh, time when we see God in a simple flower or in the face of an innocent child. Let us build a long wall of tranquility that restores "the peace of God which transcends all understanding" (Phil 4:7).

Make no mistake about it: thick walls of morality, high walls of civility, and long walls of tranquility need rebuilding in our day every bit as much as the walls of Jerusalem needed rebuilding in the day of Nehemiah. For we too are in trouble. Let us roll up our sleeves and get started.

PRAYER

Lord, as in the days of Ezra and Nehemiah, we look around and see altars, temples, homes, and walls that have been long neglected. Would you point out what needs our attention, and then help us get to work rebuilding and restoring those areas? Would you also show us any rubble or useless walls that need to be removed? Grant us wisdom, strength, and courage to address and complete the task—building what is useful and purposeful in obedience and service to our Lord. Help us to construct strong walls that hold us secure during the storms of life. We pray this in the name of your Son, our Savior, Jesus. AMEN.

QUESTIONS

1. Over time, what specific walls have crumbled or deteriorated in your life? What needs to be done to repair and rebuild those broken walls? How might you start doing so?

2. Why is there such a tendency today to focus on how walls divide and hurt people rather than seeing them positively with prac-

tical use and purpose? What does this tendency tell us about our culture?

3. What are the challenges of building, or rebuilding, walls—whether the walls are literal or figurative?

4. Review the three walls of morality, civility, and tranquility. What factors have led to the breakdown of these walls in society? What practical steps could be taken to rebuild these walls?

SUGGESTED READING
Nehemiah 1–2, 4–6, 8–9, 13

17

ESTHER: Citadels

At that time King Xerxes reigned from his royal
throne in the citadel of Susa. (Esther 1:2)

Now there was in the citadel of Susa a Jew of the tribe of Benjamin,
named Mordecai . . . who had been carried into exile from
Jerusalem by Nebuchadnezzar king of Babylon. (Esther 2:5–6)

Rarely does one hear talk about *citadels* today. The term refers to fortified structures, or entire cities, built to protect against unwanted
intrusions from outsiders. There was a time in history when reference
to a citadel was much more common. For instance, we are repeatedly
reminded that the events found in the book of Esther took place in "the
citadel of Susa" (1:2, 5; 2:3, 5, 8; etc.). The Hebrew word is "birah,"
which most often gets translated as "palace" or "royal city." The picture
is of a guarded, defended, impenetrable area under the rule of one wielding sovereign power. In Esther, the Persian King Xerxes was the ruler
whose authority reigned supreme. Many Jews lived in and around the
citadel of Susa, far from their promised homeland in Canaan. They were
there in exile due to their protracted disobedience to God.

The book of Esther stands out for two primary reasons. First, Esther
and the earlier book of Ruth are the only two books of the Bible—out
of sixty-six—that bear a title referencing a female. Second, the book of
Esther contains no explicit mention of God; his name does not appear

anywhere in the ten chapters. The only other book in the Bible to share this characteristic is Song of Songs. So, here is a book that highlights a woman and her contributions but a book that fails to reference God by name.

What are we to make of these two features? Well, the first point is worthy of note because it reminds us that women have always played an important role in the work of God. This has been true throughout human history. During a time and place where patriarchal lines were dominant in the culture, one could not read Scripture and fail to realize that God valued both males and females and used both for his purposes and glory. Evidence is found in the lives of Sarah, Rebekah, Rachel, Miriam, Deborah, Ruth, Esther, Mary, and others. The Judeo-Christian Scriptures and the faith established upon those Scriptures, properly understood, elevate women. The second point—God's name being entirely absent from the book—is a bit more perplexing. Why would a book even be in the Bible if it did not clearly reference Almighty God? What is going on here? How did God's people end up in a distant citadel under a foreign king, where God was apparently neither honored nor acknowledged? The answer to these questions holds the key to understanding much of the Old Testament as well as understanding the transition to the New Testament.

Perhaps a brief review is in order. God created a perfect world that was soon tarnished by sin (Gen 1–3). Out of that sinful and disobedient world, God called Abraham to father a family (Gen 12:1–3; 15:1–5). The Lord desired a faithful and holy people. Unfortunately, a pattern of disobedience became the norm, as the law and order that God designed for human flourishing were rejected. Nonetheless, God was patient and promised his chosen ones a land of their own. Disaster came upon them, however, when they persisted in ignoring God and doing things their own way. They were more interested in becoming like their neighbors (1 Sam 8:5, 19–22) than becoming like God. Their stubbornness resulted in evil leaders and kings who lacked humility before God. Finally, God removed his hand of protection from Israel and Judah, allowing foreign armies from Assyria and then Babylon to invade the land, control the people, and haul them off into exile. Only after long, lonely decades in exile did some finally return to rebuild Jerusalem and its ruined walls. Others, however, like Esther and Mordecai, remained in the land of their exile which was now under Persian rule. There they found themselves in an environment wherein God was not publicly named. Rather, "at that time King Xerxes reigned from his royal throne in the citadel of Susa" (1:2), a fortified city where apparently even Almighty God was not welcomed.

In a sense, citadels are still constructed today. Perhaps you could name a few—places where God's name is not mentioned or, if it is, it rolls off the tongue as profanity. Brash leaders, like King Xerxes, make it clear that they are in charge in their protected citadels. Any attempt to introduce another ruler is met with ridicule, if not rage. Sound familiar? Sadly, this closely parallels our society today. We have citadels that dominate the landscape. They may come in the form of secular universities, radical community organizations, political offices, a corrupt judicial system, business monopolies, powerful unions, the entertainment industry, social media platforms, and more. Each is a citadel—fortified and elevated to protect its own interests without reference to divine authority. As in Susa, God's name is disdained and not allowed in many of these citadels.

However, one of the central messages from the book of Esther is this: God *was* present, whether his name was spoken or not. God was present in the lives of two cousins, Mordecai and Esther. Just when it looked like the Jews were to be annihilated—an execution date had already been determined (3:13)—God showed up in the lives and influence of these two cousins. Note the pivotal words that describe what happened next: "Now the tables were turned and the Jews got the upper hand over those who hated them" (9:1). Even a foreign, godless citadel could not keep God out of its well-designed fortress. The Jews in Susa ultimately won such a great victory that a national celebration was born in their Persian exile—known as *Purim* (9:18–28)—to commemorate their deliverance from their enemies' plan to slaughter them. Passover and Purim remain today as annual, joyful, Jewish feasts to recognize that God shows up in distant lands and godless citadels to deliver his people.

What often gets missed is that the book of Esther closes the major historical section of the Old Testament. The poetic and prophetic books that follow can almost be understood as appendices. Let me explain. All the poetic writings fit into an earlier period that predates Ezra, Nehemiah, and Esther. The same is true for the major and minor books of prophecy that close the Old Testament. The last twenty-two books of the Old Testament are documents that fit into and expand what is discovered in the first seventeen books. The biblical books that historically, or chronologically, follow Esther are the New Testament gospels.

The four hundred years between the two testaments are often called the intertestamental period. After two hundred years of Persian rule, the Greeks—under Alexander the Great—conquered Persia in 331 BC. The Greeks dominated the entire Mediterranean world for the next three centuries, until Rome ascended to power in the 60s BC under its emperor Julius Caesar. It was Rome that appointed Herod the Great to rule over Judea beginning in 37 BC. Collectively, the four hundred years of Persian, Greek, and Roman influence are sometimes referred to as the "silent" years. Though much was happening on the world scene—with various dynasties rising and falling—for the people of God the divine presence seemed distant, an experience of the past that seemed to have little current relevance. Secular powers prevailed and dominated the world scene. Like noted in the book of Esther, God seemed absent. His name was rare.

Why is this significant? What does any of it have to do with us today? Well, the first thing we should notice is that the gospels reveal that God—who was not named in Esther, and who seemed relatively absent throughout the subsequent four hundred years—came to inhabit the citadel we call Earth. The One who came was named Immanuel, "God with us" (Matt 1:23). He promised never to leave us, but to be "with [us] always, to the very end of the age" (Matt 28:20). He would accomplish this by sending "another Counselor to be with [us] forever—the Spirit of truth" (John 14:16–17). Second, we are correct to call Earth a citadel. In contrast to the citadel of Susa, the fortified palace of King Xerxes (Esther 1:2), Earth is the citadel of our Lord Jesus Christ. He built and now inhabits this world. As the Dutch theologian, Abraham Kuyper (1837–1920), once noted, "There is not a square inch in the whole domain of our human existence over which Christ, who is sovereign over all, does not cry, 'Mine!'" Never again do we need to live in a citadel without God. The whole earth is his.

Though a variety of world leaders, pompous intellectuals, and self-guided activists persist in trying to convince us of their superiority—in hopes that we will follow them—we need to remember that the citadel we occupy belongs to God. He alone rules. This is his world. Perhaps Presbyterian minister Maltbie Babcock (1858–1901) expressed the thought best in the final stanza of his beloved hymn:

This is my Father's world
Oh, let me ne'er forget

That though the wrong seems oft so strong
God is the Ruler yet
This is my Father's world
The battle is not done
Jesus, who died, shall be satisfied
And earth and heav'n be one

Do we really believe that?

When we find ourselves in a place where it seems that God is neither mentioned nor welcomed, let us pause and remember that "the tables [will be] turned" (9:1). For God is here among us, just as he proved to be among his people in the book of Esther. Indeed, Earth—every square inch of it—is his citadel. Let us "celebrate" (9:21).

PRAYER

Lord, we recognize you as the sovereign ruler of this world. Others may attempt to build citadels and structures to keep you out, but your Word teaches that you occupy every space. With David (Ps 139:7–8), we ask, "Where can I go from your Spirit? Where can I flee from your presence?" And with David we conclude, no matter where we go, "You are there." May we live with humility, and yet confidence, knowing that this is your world. May we understand that the citadel of this earth is under your protection and rule. Guide us so that we may rest in you completely. AMEN.

QUESTIONS

1. Have you ever been in a place, or environment, where God seemed absent and not welcomed? What was that like? How did you navigate that experience? What did you learn?

2. Why is it so hard for us, God's people, to really believe the lyrics of the hymn above? What might we do to change our perspective?

3. How would you, in a sentence or two, describe to someone how the magnificence of creation (Gen 1) became the horror of exile (Esther 3:8–15)? What factors led there?

4. The Jewish celebration of deliverance known as Purim reminds us that God's people have always been a celebrating and feasting people. What are appropriate ways for us to celebrate God's deliverance today?

SUGGESTED READING

Esther 1–10

18

JOB: Conversations

The LORD said to Satan, "Where have you come from?" Satan
answered the LORD, "From roaming through the earth . . ." (Job 1:7)

When Job's three friends, Eliphaz the Temanite, Bildad
the Shuhite, and Zophar the Naamathite, heard about all
the troubles that had come upon him, they set out from
their homes and met together by agreement to go and
sympathize with him and comfort him. (Job 2:11)

Then the LORD answered Job out of the storm. (Job 38:1)

Occasionally I have picked up a book and discovered that the appendix is nearly as long, if not longer, than the main content in the earlier chapters of the book. This is particularly true of certain scientific, academic, or legal writings, wherein the appendix contains several supporting documents to strengthen the author's argument. As I indicated in the previous chapter, this is true of the Old Testament. Genesis through Esther—the first seventeen books of the Bible—comprise the chronological history of God's people from creation through their exile and return to Jerusalem in the fifth century BC. The remainder of the Old Testament—the twenty-two books between Job and Malachi—provides supporting documents, analogous to a book's appendix, which clarify, expand, or illustrate further what has come earlier. Five books of poetry (Job through Song of Songs) are followed by sixteen books of prophecy (Isaiah through Malachi). One additional book (Lamentations) is both poetic and prophetic. Together, these books offer a more comprehensive understanding of God and his relationship with his people than we would have by the historical account alone. This appendix ought not be ignored; valuable insights and emphases are contained there without which we would be much poorer.

The book of Job opens this section of Scripture. Whereas I suspect most people would identify "suffering" as the primary emphasis of Job, I want to suggest another theme that may have equal, if not greater, overall significance to our understanding of God. That theme is "conversations." The God of the Bible wants to communicate with his people. The first supporting document after reading centuries of history makes clear that our God is conversational. He talks; and he wants us to listen. Failure to engage him in meaningful conversation has been the source of centuries of human misery.

The Enemy would have us think that the absence of God's name in Esther is the normative pattern of life, that God is distant and inaccessible. Nothing could be further from the truth. The condition we read about in Esther resulted from the repeated sin and rejection of people who chose their own way rather than God's way. The overwhelming evidence of Scripture is that God speaks and communicates with his creation. Perhaps that is why the book of Job—the one that immediately follows Esther—depicts God as one who holds conversations. The fact that God speaks is demonstrated early in Scripture: In Genesis 1 he spoke the world into existence; in Genesis 2 he spoke words of delightful possibility and compassionate warning to Adam; and in Genesis 3 he spoke of the somber consequences of disobedience. God spoke at the beginning of human history and has been speaking ever since.

Therefore, when we come to Job we ought not be surprised at the conversations we notice. Perhaps what is surprising, however, is the nature of them. While there are numerous types of and purposes for conversation in everyday life—more than we have time to address here—three interactions found in Job are worthy of our attention.

First, **there are conversations among heavenly beings to which we are not privy**. Our experiences are limited to what we can see, hear, and feel in this world. However, the Bible tells us there is another realm beyond this familiar physical and material world where conversations occur. The first two chapters of Job reveal that conversations take place between God and his angels (1:6; 2:1) and occasionally between God and Satan (1:7; 2:2). God communicates with his created beings both in this known world and in the world that remains hidden from us. What that means, of course, is that God is active and engaged even when he may appear to be absent and silent (as seemed to be the case in the book of Esther). Conversations occur in the spiritual world that exist beyond this physical world.

Jesus's story of the rich man and the beggar Lazarus (Luke 16:19–31) further illustrates this point. Both men died; the beggar found himself in the presence of Abraham, while the rich man was tormented in hell. In hopes of warning his brothers lest they share his same destiny, the rich man talked with Abraham and tried to convince him to send a special messenger to them. Though the request was not granted, the story is insightful in that it reveals once again that there are conversations beyond this world. If that is true, some of those conversations may be about you and me—just as they were about Job or the rich man's brothers. God, his angels, or those who have gone before us may well be having conversations wherein we are the topic. Commendation, warning, concern, or sympathy may be expressed. A bigger picture is unfolding that we cannot see at this time. Some conversations exist to which we do not have access.

Second, **there are conversations among friends that do not help us**. Job had "three friends" who came alongside him to "sympathize with him and comfort him" (2:11). These three—Eliphaz, Bildad, and Zophar—spoke multiple times between chapters 4 and 31, each time trying to correct what they perceived to be faults with Job and his theology that explained his suffering. After each friend unloaded his version of wisdom and advice, Job responded. Finally, the friends gave up (32:1). Then Elihu, a younger man who had been waiting in the wings and listening to the conversations (32:2–11), approached Job and tried to correct him with a lengthy monologue of his own. Elihu's words cover six long chapters (chs 32–37). The whole point of these middle thirty-four chapters (80% of the book) might be summarized this way: conversations with "friends" often help very little and sometimes do more harm than good. While intended to bring sympathy and comfort, the interactions felt like salt in Job's wounds.

The pattern remains all too common today. We have never had more conversations. Technology and philosophy have combined to crank up the rhetoric in recent years. Thanks to new and advanced forms of electronic communication, we are able to converse 24/7, day and night.

Further, the late American post-modern philosopher, Richard Rorty, suggested we have reached the place wherein ongoing conversations matter more than knowledge or truth. If we just keep talking, goes the argument, we humans eventually will figure things out. However, we are discovering what Job discovered: more talk is not always helpful. Neither the quantity of words, the speed of their delivery, nor access to multiple ongoing conversations appears to be the answer. While we have the capacity to talk more than ever, social chaos seems to multiply.

Discussions may initially appear informative and helpful, but subsequent exchanges often do more harm than good. Self-appointed experts create a social frenzy with their bombastic political or moral claims. Friends post a thought regarding a topic about which they are passionate and seek others' support. Soon others jump into the fray with their varied opinions. If the topic is popular, controversial, and draws enough celebrity attention, the conversation may continue for weeks. However, when all is said and done, many of the conversations are not helpful. Harm too often results. The nonstop stream of chatter not only wears us out and makes us more anxious than ever but also threatens to shut down the more important conversations we really need. In short, conversations alone do not guarantee solutions. A particular type of conversation is demanded, and that leads to a final observation from Job.

Third, **there are conversations with God that we desperately need**. When all the other conversations end, a person is left alone to talk with God. That is how the book of Job closes. The conversation, which begins in chapter 38, is fascinating for several reasons. First, it is the final conversation in Job. Experience tells us that final conversations are often those that matter most and are likely to be remembered the longest. How fitting, then, that the final conversation here is one with God. One day that also will be our final conversation. Second, a quick review indicates that God does most of the talking while Job listens. When the latter speaks, it is brief and respectful. In fact, God's voice is heard here in 123 verses over four chapters (chs 38–41), whereas Job responds twice in a total of only nine verses (40:3–5; 42:1–6). God speaks nearly fourteen times more than Job. What a reminder this is of our need to listen to God rather than always doing the talking. Third, the conversation ends with Job recognizing his own unworthiness (40:4), humility, and need for repentance (42:6). That is how all our conversations with God should end. For there will come a time when, like Job, we too will confess, "Surely I spoke of things I did not understand, things too wonderful for me to know" (42:3).

May God help us to converse with him often. What if we made conversation with the Lord the first and final conversation of every day? What if we listened to him more than we rushed to tell him information? What if we came away from those conversations with a sincere sense of our own unworthiness, humility, and need for repentance? One can only imagine the difference this might make. I suspect it would not only change our relationship with God but also transform all our other conversations and relationships as well.

In closing, it is worth noting that the word *conversation* is used repeatedly in the older King James Version (1611) of the New Testament. The word there takes on the meaning of behavior or conduct in one's social interactions. To converse with another implied proper decorum while growing in familiarity. Paul admonished young Timothy to set "an example of the believers, in word, in conversation, in charity, in spirit, in faith, in purity" (1 Tim 4:12, KJV). The side-by-side placement of "word" and "conversation" is not redundant but is a way to instruct Timothy to set an example in the way he talks and behaves around others. Another time, Peter encouraged early believers to be "holy in all manner of conversation" (1 Pet 1:15, KJV). Again, the meaning is best understood as encompassing the way one conducts his or her entire life, in every social interaction. Translated, conversation is more than just the words one speaks; it is the life one lives. The message here is that we ought to view our words and behavior as connected. Our words—our conversations—only have meaning and legitimacy when we have conduct that matches them. Lips and lives are intended to operate in harmony.

Since conversations are highlighted in this first Old Testament appendix, in the book we call Job, perhaps we ought to ask ourselves: With whom do we regularly converse? The answer to that question will explain a great deal about our lives.

Prayer

Our Father in heaven, we recognize there are an endless number of voices and conversations in our world today. Sometimes the noise is overwhelming and drowns out the one voice we most need to hear: yours. Forgive us. Forgive us for too often valuing conversation with others more than we value conversation with you. Forgive us for talking more than listening. Change our conversational patterns so we become healthier people and better representatives of you—yes, even when life is not going our way, as was true of Job. May our conversation *with* you get lived out in daily conduct that *honors* you. AMEN.

QUESTIONS

1. Are there any current conversations you are participating in that are harmful? Are there any current conversations that would be wise to eliminate?

2. How would you describe your conversations with God? Do you primarily listen, or do you tend to dominate the conversation? How might you strike a better balance?

3. What might be the conversation in heaven about you? Review Job 1:8 and see if the characteristics of Job might be applied to you. How do you suppose God speaks of you?

4. Do your conversations (words) and conduct match? What are some ways you could bring these two into greater harmony?

SUGGESTED READING

Job 1–3, 38–42

19

PSALMS: Songs

But I will sing of your strength, in the morning I will sing
of your love; for you are my fortress, my refuge in times of
trouble. O my Strength, I sing praise to you; you, O God,
are my fortress, my loving God. (Psalm 59:16–17)

Sing to the LORD a new song; sing to the LORD, all the
earth. Sing to the LORD, praise his name; proclaim
his salvation day after day. (Psalm 96:1–2)

Sing to the LORD a new song, for he has done
marvelous things; his right hand and his holy arm
have worked salvation for him. (Psalm 98:1)

Let everything that has breath praise the LORD. (Psalm 150:6)

The second appendix following the Old Testament books of history, coming after Job, is the book of Psalms. If Job teaches us that God engages in conversation, the Psalms teach us that God likes a good song. The Psalms are a collection of songs, expressions of the heart—both prayers and praises—sung by the people of God. Nearly half (73) of the collection is attributed to David. The Psalms mention "singing" or "songs" more than any other book of the Bible, with over one hundred references found in 54 of the 150 chapters. While 39 books of the Bible mention singing, no other book comes close to the emphasis on music found in the Psalms. Of course, the word *psalm* itself comes from a

Greek word suggesting a hymn or sacred song accompanied by a musical (usually stringed) instrument. The fact that right in the middle of the Bible we find a sizeable songbook may indicate that God not only likes a good song but also thinks people of all generations need some music in their lives.

In the original Hebrew language—the dominant language of the Old Testament—there are several synonyms for "singing." Three words are most common: *shir, ranan,* and *zamar.* Each of these terms carries a slightly different emphasis, and all three occur in Psalm 59:16–17 (in the order listed here). *Shir* is the most prevalent of the three words, appearing 160 times in the Old Testament. It refers to making good music; the emphasis seems to be on the appealing sound of gifted musicians. David must have been blessed with such a gift for when he was a young man King Saul found comfort in David's music (1 Sam 16:14–23). In addition to being translated "sing," *ranan* is often rendered "rejoice" or to "shout out joyfully." Thus, the word may be related to the manner of delivery. The emphasis is on the exuberant spirit, or disposition, of the musician. Joy and triumph are communicated. David declared, "in the morning I will sing [*ranan*] of your love" (Ps 59:16), implying he greeted each day with great delight in God. Finally, *zamar* is associated with singing praise, turning the attention to both the object and content of the song. In other words, David is focused on praising God, his Strength (59:17). This suggests that lyrics matter. Songs ought to be more than pleasing melodies from enthusiastic musicians; good songs contain meaningful words.

The songs that are found in the Psalms and, for that matter, throughout Scripture were intended to be musically appealing to the ear (*shir*), delivered with genuine joy (*ranan*), and expressed in lyrics that praised God and commended what was good (*zamar*). Musicianship, presentation, and message all matter when it comes to songs. How music sounds, how it gets expressed, and what it says were all important features of the songs contained in the Psalms. These criteria still define good music today.

Songs, however, also have multiple purposes that extend beyond the music itself. There are other components of music that touch and influence an audience. Every song has meaning that is simultaneously theological, psychological, historical, and sociological. Let me explain.

Songs are theological. In one way or another, songs tell us something about God. The Psalms certainly do that, expanding and enriching our understanding of the sovereign Lord. He is described as our Creator (Ps 139), our Shepherd (Ps 23), our Rock (Ps 18), our Refuge (Ps 46), and more. Favorite songs down through the centuries have enhanced our theological understanding. Consider Martin Luther's "A Mighty Fortress is our God" (1500s), Isaac Watts's "O God, Our Help in Ages Past" (1700s), or Charles Wesley's "And Can It Be?" (1700s). These, and hundreds more like them, speak of God and his nature. In contrast to the above hymns, in 1968 Sammy Davis, Jr., sang "I've Gotta Be Me" and the following year Frank Sinatra popularized the song "I Did it My Way." Both of those songs also carried a strong theological message, suggesting no need for God and promoting oneself as sovereign over life. While the tunes may be appealing, the theological message of those latter two songs is antithetical to the teachings of the Judeo-Christian faith. Unfortunately, some of the newer songs written by, or for, worship bands and sung in churches across America today also have dreadful theology that focuses more on "me" than the sovereign Lord. The point is this: every song contains theology, whether it is intentional or not. We ought to pay attention to what we are singing and listen carefully to what our favorite songs have to say about our holy God.

Songs are psychological. Songs influence how we think and feel. They have the power to lift our spirits and inspire us or to leave us feeling doleful and blue. For centuries, believers have turned to the songs of Scripture for encouragement and comfort. Psalms 23, 40, 42, 91, and 139 have all been favorites, reminding us that God cares and is available during times of distress. Souls have been refreshed by these oft-repeated lyrics. The same is true of other genres of music. Fanny Crosby's music comes to mind. Blind since infancy, Fanny (1820–1915) wrote over eight thousand hymns. Many of those—"Blessed Assurance," "Redeemed, How I Love to Proclaim It," "Praise Him! Praise Him!" and others—have become inspirational favorites. The same might be said of songs not written for use in the church. For example, countless people have been inspired by such songs as "You'll Never Walk Alone," from Rodgers and Hammerstein's Broadway musical *Carousel* (1945), or the Motown favorite, "Ain't No Mountain High Enough" (1967). Songs, by their very nature, have the potential to transport the mind and lift the soul to another realm. Of course, songs can also do the opposite. Some music—either the lyrics, the tune, or both—is music of despair and desolation. Such dirges leave listeners empty or even despondent. Sadly, too much of our music in recent years, both inside and outside the church, might be characterized this way. Written and performed under the banner of honesty and transparency, one can only wonder if these songs are contributing to the widespread rise of psychological pain and anxiety being reported today. The Psalms, though often written in the face of great adversity and anguish (e.g., Ps 40:1–2), routinely point to hope in the sovereign Lord (42:5, 11; 71:5). Songs of hope and victory are needed and welcomed in a fallen world like ours.

Songs are historical. There are two ways in which a song is historical: first, from the perspective of the composer and, second, from the perspective of the listener. Composers tend to write from their own historical experiences. That was true of David. No fewer than thirteen of the psalms (Ps 3, 7, 18, 34, 51, 52, 54, 56, 57, 59, 60, 63, and 142) contain introductory references to events that precipitated the written lyrics. Well-known hymns and patriotic songs have also often been composed after pivotal, if not tragic, life events. Horatio Spafford, a Presbyterian lawyer from Chicago, penned "It is Well with My Soul" in late 1873 after a ship collision in the Atlantic killed his four daughters. Years earlier, in 1847, Henry Lyte wrote "Abide with Me" immediately after preaching the last sermon of his pastoral career in England before dying of tuberculosis. "The Star-Spangled Banner," by Francis Scott Key, was inspired by an attack in Baltimore, Maryland, during the War of 1812; the song would eventually become America's national anthem. We could continue. Songs are routinely written to commemorate significant historical events. However, songs also mark history for the listener. For example, I will always associate "There's a Sweet, Sweet Spirit in this Place" with a revival during my youth. Whenever I hear or sing "And Can it Be?" I am transported back to Asbury College and chapel services in Hughes Auditorium. The 1970s hit, "Bridge over Troubled Waters," sung by Paul Simon and Art Garfunkel, reminds my wife of an emergency landing on her family's return from a vacation in Hawaii, while it reminds me of my high school girlfriend. Songs have historical meaning for all of us, stirring memories of events and people across the years.

Songs are sociological. Songs unite us around shared values and experiences. Singing itself is often a shared activity among community members. Love songs, school songs, patriotic songs, Broadway songs, opera songs, country music, and Christmas carols are all examples of music that has sociological meaning. People connect around their favorite songs. Shared music binds us together in relationships and communities. Public concerts illustrate this social phenomenon. So does the worship hymnal, which emerged in the 1500s, a century after Gutenberg invented the printing press. Christians began printing, distributing, and singing from a standard collection of songs week after week, much like an earlier generation of believers relied on the Psalms. The German sociologist Max Weber (1864–1920) was interested in the process by which music became standardized and had much to say on the sociology of music. Weber believed that society influenced music and that music, in turn, influenced society. Entire communities are formed around musicians and their music. Interestingly, the book of Psalms ends with a clear emphasis on community. The last five Psalms (chs 146–150) all begin with "Praise the Lord;" in the original Hebrew the word is *hallelujah*. A careful reading of these final hallelujah psalms reveals a progression from the individual to the larger community of faith—from "I/my" (146) to "our" (147), to "them" (148), to "the saints" (149), to "everything that has breath" (150). What begins as personal reflection moves to corporate and communal praise. That should not surprise us because songs, by their very nature, are ultimately sociological. They influence, and then become expressions of, entire communities.

In conclusion, all songs—whether they be Psalms from the Bible, hymns written across the centuries, or popular songs enjoyed in the wider culture—share common features. Theological, psychological, historical, and sociological messages are found in music. Much more is contained in the melodies we sing and listen to than we realize. Songs have immense power and influence. Maybe that is why a songbook was placed in the middle of the Bible.

God created music. He is the ultimate composer and has inspired untold numbers of creative individuals to join him in making music. God has given us songs to sing. Sure, some individuals may sing better than others. Some may sing and prompt applause from a crowd, while others may sing alone in a prison cell. Some will sing from the mountain top of victory, while others sing out of the valley of discouragement and difficulty. Regardless of the circumstance, the Psalms make clear that any occasion invites a song.

PRAYER

Lord, we dare believe that music is one of your greatest gifts to the world. Thank you for songs that have encouraged us over the years. You have created us to sing on earth, just as the angels sing in heaven around your throne. So, help us to sing songs that are theologically sound, psychologically uplifting, historically significant, and sociologically expressive. May the music of our lives—that which we sing and that which we enjoy—draw us and others closer to you. We offer this prayer in the name of Jesus, the Song above all other songs. AMEN.

QUESTIONS

1. What is one of your favorite songs? Why? What meaning does it have for you, or what does it do for you?

2. After reviewing the Hebrew synonyms for singing—*shir* (musicianship and sound), *ranan* (joyful presentation), and *zamar* (message and content of praise)—which of these components do you most value in music? Why?

3. What particular hymn contains theology—a word or message about God—that often encourages you? Can you expand on the hymn's lyrics and explain in your own words what the song's message means to you?

4. What song—sacred or secular—almost always seems to lift your spirits? Why? What song—sacred or secular—has the opposite effect and almost always brings you down?

SUGGESTED READING

Psalm 23, 46, 59, 91, 96, 98, 100, 126, 150

20

PROVERBS: Wisdom

The fear of the LORD is the beginning of knowledge, but fools despise wisdom and discipline. Listen, my son, to your father's instruction and do not forsake your mother's teaching. (Proverbs 1:7–8)

Wisdom is supreme; therefore get wisdom. Though it cost all you have, get understanding. (Proverbs 4:7)

Does not wisdom call out? Does not understanding raise her voice? (Proverbs 8:1)

Wisdom—having good sense and judgment—has always been rare. Every generation must seek it anew; it is never automatically inherited. Arguably, however, it has never been so rare as it is today because, in part, we have stopped seeking it and have become blind to our need for it.

King Solomon was lauded for his wisdom and the proverbs associated with that wisdom (see 1 Kgs 4:29–34). Many of those proverbs have been preserved for us, of course, in what we are calling the appendix to the Old Testament. The book of Proverbs speaks of wisdom over 110 times; it is found in every chapter of the book. Ecclesiastes, a companion volume likely also written by Solomon, mentions wisdom another fifty times. Solomon clearly wanted to pass on practical life lessons and instruction to his son—the first ten chapters of Proverbs address "my son" twenty times—perhaps in hopes of sparing future generations the pain of poor decisions that marked so much of Solomon's own life.

Who has not struggled with the enigmatic Solomon? He stands as a biblical character who was far from perfect. Scripture reveals that he had seven hundred wives and three hundred concubines who "led him astray" (1 Kgs 11:3) and "his heart was not fully devoted to the LORD his God" (1 Kgs 11:4). How could someone so out of control and spiritually suspect have anything of value to say to others? Perhaps that is the very nature of wisdom. Could it be that wisdom, in part, is learning from past mistakes, especially one's own, and wanting to steer others clear of those same mistakes? For our purposes, then, I am defining wisdom as practical advice and insight learned from an earlier generation, intended to help an individual avoid the mistakes another has seen or made himself.

Unfortunately, the current cancel culture, at its core, is the rejection of such wisdom. Cancel culture refuses to accept lessons from anyone who is perceived to be less than perfect in the eyes of those wielding power. Solomon would not stand a chance of being heard today. If an individual has a flaw, or even had a distant past flaw, he or she is deemed unworthy and disqualified from having anything worthwhile to offer others. Thus, there is a tendency to act as if nothing can be learned from our imperfect forefathers. They are silenced. Because they did not get everything right, we feel justified in erasing all their ideas, experiences, and influence from our collective memory. What a tragedy such a response creates. What an unfortunate loss of potential wisdom and insight. No wonder so many young people flounder today. They exist as isolated islands where wisdom is absent, trying to make it on their own. Instead of learning from others' experiences—yes, even others' mistakes—too many blindly charge forward, often repeating the same, or worse, mistakes as those who went before them.

How is wisdom obtained? Proverbs indicates that wisdom comes from humbly listening to God and others who are more experienced and mature. Let us briefly consider the four components contained in this statement.

First, wisdom demands *humility*. Proverbs 11:2 is straightforward, noting that "with humility comes wisdom." Humility acknowledges an authority outside oneself; humility opens a person to the possibility of learning from another. Without humility there will be no wisdom.

Second, wisdom is obtained by *listening*. The first word after the prologue of Proverbs is "listen" (1:8). That same word is repeated twenty-six additional times throughout the book. "A wise man listens to advice" (12:15), whereas "plans fail for lack of counsel" (15:22). A person who makes a habit of listening is likely to grow wise.

Third, the primary one to whom a wise person learns to listen is *God*. Solomon makes clear that "the fear of the LORD is the beginning of wisdom" (9:10). He knew this from first-hand experience because God had spoken to him and granted him wisdom as a young king (1 Kgs 3:5–28). God has always been, and remains, the fountain of wisdom.

Fourth, and finally, one obtains wisdom from the *experienced and mature individuals* that God places in our lives. Wisdom is passed from one generation to the next, from the older to the younger. Evidence of this is seen in the fact noted earlier: the phrase "my son" is found twenty times in the first ten chapters of Proverbs. Parents, grandparents, and other mature and trusted people have the privilege of speaking words of wisdom to sons and daughters in their world. The key to gaining wisdom, therefore, is humbly listening to God and those he places in our lives who are more experienced and mature. Wisdom need not be as rare as we humans have made it.

The wisdom highlighted in Proverbs pertains to practical, relational matters. Solomon was concerned that the next generation be discerning about relationships. Perhaps reflecting on how his own relationships had been dysfunctional and destructive (1 Kgs 11:4–9), Solomon wanted his offspring to avoid the same mistakes. We all have much to learn when it comes to respecting and getting along with others. Employers report that the primary problem among ineffective workers is relational rather than task competence. Poor social skills have terminated more jobs than have poor technical skills. The same is true in marriage. Counselors tell us poor communication shipwrecks more relationships than any other single factor. We need wisdom in how to get along with those around us—a spouse, a friend, a neighbor, a colleague at work—and that is the emphasis of Proverbs. I once heard that Billy Graham read from the Psalms daily to maintain his relationship with God and read from Proverbs daily to maintain his relationship with others. That is a good word of wisdom right there.

When one reads the book of Proverbs, he or she will immediately be struck by the wide variety of relationship topics and how wisdom plays a role in all of them. Let us consider here four areas of life that Solomon suggests will require wisdom: one's sexual behaviors, knowing the difference between right and wrong, matters pertaining to wealth, and the value of discipline. Solomon places repeated emphasis on each of these topics.

Wisdom warns against sexual seduction. No one gets too far in the book of Proverbs before encountering multiple warnings pertaining to adultery (e.g., 2:12–19; 5:1–23; 6:20–35; 7:6–27). Solomon's words are unequivocal when it comes to having a sexual relationship outside marriage. Writing to his son about a seductive adulteress, he advises: "Keep to a path far from her" (5:8). Later he warns that "a man who commits adultery lacks judgment [and] destroys himself" (6:32). Sexual indiscretion has brought down far too many individuals in every generation. What initially appears attractive and enticing ultimately disappoints and results in lost potential—both to the individual who succumbs to the temptation and to wider society in the loss of productivity the individual had to offer. Wisdom is needed, for it "will save you from the ways of wicked men" (2:12) and from the untold pain, scars, and baggage that commonly characterize their lives.

Wisdom distinguishes between that which is righteous and that which is wicked. Wisdom discerns between right and wrong. That is the meaning of "righteous" and "wicked." Both words occur over eighty times in Proverbs. We would do well to pay attention when something is repeated so often. The contrast between these choices could not be clearer: "Blessings crown the head of the righteous, but violence overwhelms the mouth of the wicked. The memory of the righteous will be a blessing, but the name of the wicked will rot" (10:6–7). Thus, the distinction between the two not only has meaning today but also continues beyond the grave. Moral and ethical decisions, and the behaviors that flow from them, are needed at every level of society. The stakes are high. Wisdom and boldness are required to make righteous choices. We must become regular and intentional students of God's Word so that we are able to discern clearly between right and wrong. In doing so, let us remember that "the righteous cannot be uprooted" (12:3).

Wisdom approaches wealth with balance and restraint. In addition to the contrast between the righteous and the wicked, wealth and poverty are also repeatedly juxtaposed in Proverbs. Solomon advises to "honor the LORD with your wealth" (3:9). However, he also cautions: "Do not wear yourself out to get rich; have the wisdom to show restraint" (23:4). When Solomon speaks of poverty he notes several possible causes, including laziness (10:4), lacking generosity (11:24), ignoring discipline (13:18), loving sleep (20:13), loving pleasure (21:17), drunkenness and gluttony (23:20–21). The picture provided here is one of balance. Ultimately, both "rich and poor have this in common: The LORD is the Maker of them all" (22:2). No wonder we are told that anyone who "is kind to the needy honors God" (14:31). A wise person desires "neither poverty nor riches" (30:8) but "pursues righteousness and love" toward all and, in the process, "finds life, prosperity and honor" (21:21).

Wisdom promotes discipline and hard work. Solomon does not hide the fact that "fools despise wisdom and discipline" (1:7). Later he returns to the theme, confirming that the one who "loves discipline loves knowledge, but he who hates correction is stupid" (12:1). Solomon does not allow much middle ground. The implication is that the wise practice discipline, whereas fools (or those who are stupid) reject it. "Hard work brings a profit, but mere talk leads only to poverty" (14:23). The virtuous woman described at the end of Proverbs is said to be an individual who "sets about her work vigorously" (31:17). There is no mistaking the fact that the wise know the value of discipline and hard work.

Wisdom is demonstrated in several practical ways. The wise relate well with others by exercising sexual restraint and propriety, having a well-defined awareness of right and wrong, understanding the fleeting nature of wealth, and embracing discipline and hard work. Wisdom makes people attractive, trustworthy, and valued models for others to follow. "Therefore, get wisdom. Though it cost all you have, get understanding" (4:7).

PRAYER

Lord, we need wisdom. Our world is sorely lacking in wisdom because it is sorely lacking in humility. Forgive us for acting as if we are knowledgeable and wise enough on our own to navigate life. We humbly ask for your wisdom to guide us. Help us to find godly, mature counselors and advisors willing to share their wisdom; and help us to be good students in the process. May our relationships give witness to the fact that we fear the Lord and employ wisdom when interacting with others. And may you be honored as a result. AMEN.

QUESTIONS

1. Why is wisdom so often found among imperfect people? Why does our culture increasingly seem to despise and "cancel" such people today? What has led us here?

2. Who have you turned to for wise advice at a critical juncture in your life? What characteristics drew you to that particular individual?

3. What relationship in your life currently needs extra wisdom? Are there steps you might take in pursuing such wisdom (e.g., prayer, seeking forgiveness, talking with a mature and trusted saint, etc.)?

4. Which of the four areas mentioned above—sexual propriety, discerning between right and wrong, your view of wealth, or discipline—most needs wisdom and attention in your life? What might you do to address that need?

SUGGESTED READING

Proverbs 1–5, 12, 17, 22, 31

21

ECCLESIASTES: Vanity

*Vanity of vanities, saith the Preacher, vanity of
vanities; all is vanity. (Ecclesiastes 1:2, KJV)*

*Meaningless! Meaningless! says the Teacher. Utterly
meaningless! Everything is meaningless. (Ecclesiastes 1:2)*

*I have seen all the things that are done under the sun; all of them
are meaningless, a chasing after the wind. (Ecclesiastes 1:14)*

*I denied myself nothing my eyes desired; I refused my heart
no pleasure. My heart took delight in all my work, and this
was the reward for all my labor. Yet when I surveyed all
that my hands had done and what I had toiled to achieve,
everything was meaningless, a chasing after the wind;
nothing was gained under the sun. (Ecclesiastes 2:10–11)*

So much of life is spent pursuing elusive dreams. Sadly, once those
dreams become reality, they never quite seem to fulfill human longing. That, in a nutshell, is the conclusion of the twelve-chapter book
called Ecclesiastes. The author of the book, likely Solomon, repeatedly
refers to this pursuit as "chasing after the wind" (1:14, 17; 2:11, 17, 26;
4:4, 6, 16; 6:9)—a futile exercise sure to disappoint. Those who engage
in such pursuits find their "appetite is never satisfied" (6:7; cf. 5:10).

Vanity is the old-fashioned word used to describe this experience.
Ecclesiastes contains the term over thirty times in the older *King James*

Version of the Bible. The New International Version prefers the word *meaningless.* The idea communicated here is of that which is empty, valueless, and lacking in substance or purpose. Vanity, of course, is often used to describe those who have an inflated sense of importance or who have overblown pride in their appearance. The word brings to mind Carly Simon's 1972 hit recording, "You're So Vain." The song's popular refrain states, "You're so vain, you probably think this song is about you . . . Don't you? Don't you?" Vanity operates like that, with deception and disappointment. It deceives people into thinking everything is about them and their pleasure while ultimately proving to be meaningless and unfulfilling.

Just what is it that Solomon describes as vanity, or as being meaningless? The list is extensive and starts with "everything" (1:2). *Anything* that is out of balance and improperly elevated—even what is inherently good—can become a source of vanity. Anything and everything can become meaningless when it occupies the wrong place in life. Solomon might have stopped there and allowed the reader to define the vanities of his or her own life; the thought is powerful and penetrating enough on its own. However, he continues over the next six chapters to identify some specific areas of caution. For example, vanity and meaninglessness may be found in:

- Study and the increase of knowledge and wisdom (1:12–18).
- Seeking pleasure (2:1).
- Undertaking great projects (2:4).
- Wealth and treasures (2:8; 5:10).
- Hard work (2:17–23).
- Achievements (4:4).
- Advancements and promotions (4:13–16).
- The accumulation of possessions (6:2).
- Honors and recognition (6:2).
- A prolific family (6:3).
- Long life (6:3).
- Speaking many words (6:11).

The list is long and convicting, for I suspect many of us—at one time or another—have placed our hopes in such pursuits.

A reasonable question might be asked here: Are these truly potential sources of vanity? My family and I live in a college community built around study and the gaining of knowledge. Should we not prioritize higher education? We take pride in pointing out some of our great projects. But who does not? Hard work is valued and encouraged everywhere. Achievements, advancements, promotions, and honors are printed in newspapers, posted on Facebook, and highlighted on our résumés. Loving families and long life are standard components of the American dream. Having the ability to speak many words that others love to hear is a gift anyone would cherish. Why in the world is there a book in the Bible that cautions the reader that these things, so many of them good motivators on the surface, may become sources of vanity that result in dead-end disappointments? The answer, of course, is because Solomon was speaking from personal experience and knew the fleeting nature and disillusionment of all these pursuits.

Vanity, along with implying meaninglessness, is typically associated with what consumes a person. In essence, the book of Ecclesiastes repeatedly asks this question: What consumes us? If it is anything other than God, we are acting in vain and heading toward futility. The people of God are to be consumed by God alone. He is to be our passion, our obsession, and our inspiration.

This brings to mind the topic of consumerism, encouraging the acquisition of goods and products, that so dominates our world. What we buy and use often extends far beyond the practical purpose for which a product was made. In 1899, the Norwegian-American sociologist, Thorstein Veblen, coined the term *conspicuous consumption* to describe how we in the West buy products for the purpose of communicating to others a particular social status. Thus, we consume far more than we need in an attempt to make a statement to others. Our vanity is on display. We wear brand-name clothes, drive certain automobiles, live in select neighborhoods, enjoy by-invitation-only events, dine at popular restaurants, and walk around with well-marketed drinks in our hands, in part, to identify ourselves as being people of prestige who are worthy of recognition. We like to be conspicuous about what we consume.

Solomon lived much of his life that way; he was the ultimate consumer. However, his consumption of pleasures, his building projects, his accumulation of wealth and women, and even his reputation for great wisdom eventually all left his soul empty. That is why he opened the book (1:2) with these unnerving words: "Meaningless! Meaningless! . . . Everything is meaningless." It was his way of saying that everything he accomplished and consumed in life was done in vain and had failed to satisfy.

Fortunately, the book does not end the way it begins. Solomon provides us a conclusion that is both insightful and relevant. The Hebrew word at the close of the book that is translated "conclusion" (12:13)—*suph*—carries with it the meaning of "being consumed" and is rendered that way at times in the Old Testament. It is as if Solomon wants the reader to know that what once consumed him—pleasures, projects, position, honors, and more—never truly satisfied the deep longing of his heart. They were driven by vanity, by conspicuous consumption, in a futile attempt to impress others. In contrast, he suggests the reader become consumed with God. He uses three verbs at the end of Ecclesiastes to communicate how this might be accomplished: remember, fear, and keep. Each of these verbs comes as a command, and each is instructive.

Remember. The last chapter of the book begins with Solomon's admonition: "Remember your Creator" (12:1). Everything we have— every possession, every accomplishment, every honor—comes from our Creator, God. Those who fail to acknowledge that will come to the end of life and cry, "Meaningless! Meaningless! . . . Everything is meaningless!" (12:8). There will come a day when people realize everything they have done and worked for has been in vain unless they have remembered to honor the Creator.

Fear. As noted above, the entire book ends with a "conclusion," or consumption (12:13; *suph*). After Solomon has described all the vanities he has seen and experienced, he concludes there is no greater advice he could give than this: "Fear God." Stop chasing experiences. Stop accumulating stuff. Stop consuming people and products for your pleasure. Stop pursuing what ultimately will never satisfy. Instead, fear God. Revere him above all else. Take it from one who had it all—possessions, pleasures, position, and popularity—and yet came to the end of life and labeled it all vanity void of meaning: fearing God is what gives life its ultimate meaning.

Keep. Finally, the reader is encouraged to "keep [God's] commandments" (12:13). To do anything less would be foolishness, considering there will be a future "judgment" wherein one day "every deed . . . every hidden thing, whether it is good or evil" (12:14) will come before God. Therefore, keep his commands. In a consumer-driven world we are encouraged to keep treasures, to keep climbing and advancing, to keep score lest we fall behind our neighbors, to keep young and active, to keep achieving and building our résumés, and to keep experiencing every new product and gadget that is marketed. There is no shortage of commodities that promoters encourage us to keep if we want to enjoy the good life. Solomon counters with the thought that all such consumption is vanity and that what we really need to keep is God's commandments. Nothing else lasts and, therefore, nothing else matters in the long run.

In summary, Solomon urges us to consume, and be consumed by, God the Creator. God alone should be our lifelong passion. Anything else that consumes us—stuff, success, honors, or position—is meaningless vanity.

Solomon's father, David, communicated a similar thought when he wrote: "zeal for your house consumes me" (Ps 69:9). Later, in Psalm 119, a parallel thought is expressed: "My soul is consumed with longing for your laws at all times" (v 20). Consumption itself is not the problem. The issue is what we allow to consume us. The antidote to vanity is to be consumed by God; his commandments, his laws, and his house demand our attention.

In the end, whether we intend it or not, consumption is always conspicuous. We are known by what we consume because ultimately it consumes us. Will it be vanity? Or God, the Creator of this world?

PRAYER

Lord, save us from pursuing that which is meaningless. Save us from vanity that ultimately disappoints. Change our consumption patterns so that we remember you created us and all that we possess. Change our consumption patterns so that we fear you alone, and not those around us who might think we are out of step. Change our consumption patterns so that we focus on keeping your commandments rather than what our neighbors think we ought to keep. May we be wise and humble as we walk with you. AMEN.

QUESTIONS

1. What vanities, or meaningless activities, do you have to guard against? What strategies help you do so?

2. Who do you know that is consumed by a product or pursuit of some kind? How do you know it? What gives it away? On the

other hand, who do you know who is consumed by God? What evidence is there?

3. What really consumes you? Why? Be honest with yourself. (A good way to identify what consumes us is by evaluating how we spend most of our discretionary time and evaluating what occupies our thought life.)

4. If you were writing a book focused on giving practical advice to the next generation, what three verbs might you choose to close the book? Why?

SUGGESTED READING

Ecclesiastes 1–6, 9, 12

22

SONG OF SONGS: Romance

*How beautiful you are my darling! Oh, how
beautiful! (Song of Songs 4:1)*

I belong to my lover, and his desire is for me. (Song of Songs 7:10)

*Love is as strong as death, its jealousy unyielding as the
grave. It burns like blazing fire, like a mighty flame. Many
waters cannot quench love; rivers cannot wash it away.
If one were to give all the wealth of his house for love, it
would be utterly scorned. (Song of Songs 8:6–7)*

The title "Song of Songs" makes a unique and lofty claim intended to grab the reader's attention. Not only is this the only book title of sixty-six in the Bible that consists of more than a single word, but the phrase "song of songs" suggests a level of superiority not communicated in any other book title in the Judeo-Christian Scriptures. Just as King of kings and Lord of lords are ways of referencing the supreme Ruler and Master, respectively, so the label "song of songs" points to the best of all songs ever written or sung. It is a way of saying: pay attention, for this song is at the top of the charts. What is behind such a bold claim? What makes this the best of all songs? Several observations are worth noting.

First, **this is a love song**. The words *love* or *beloved* are found a combined sixty times in the 117 verses that make up the eight-chapter book. Love songs have attracted people down through the ages, and no greater love song has ever been composed than Solomon's Song of Songs (1:1). The love that is described here culminates in a wedding (3:11), with a beautiful bride (4:1, 8–12; 5:1) and the intimacy of sexual expression (4:1–7; 7:1–9). The latter point has resulted in no small discomfort among Bible students and church leaders over the years, causing many to interpret the book's content as allegory. However, given that God created males and females distinctively, gave them the command to reproduce, and called it all "very good" (Gen 1:27–31) makes one wonder if an allegorical approach to the book is warranted. God is neither troubled nor embarrassed by romantic love and sex. We need not be either. He designed us with the capacity for such desire and expression.

Second, **this is a sensuous love song**. One cannot read far in the Song of Songs before discovering multiple references to the human senses. Language describing sights, sounds, smells, tastes, and touches abound. The beauty of the woman is noted early (1:10, 15; 2:14), though the fullness of her beauty (4:1–7; 7:1–9) is not revealed until after the wedding that occurs at the end of chapter 3. Hearing each other speak brings special delight and comfort to the couple (2:10, 14; 8:13). The fragrance that comes from the other's perfumes and breath is satisfying (1:3, 12; 3:6; 4:10; 7:8). References to taste are plentiful and provocative, with allusions to kissing, sweet fruit, honey, and other delicacies (1:2; 2:3; 4:11; 7:9). The touch associated with an embrace is described in some detail (2:6; 7:8; 8:3). Make no mistake about it, this is a very sensuous love song found in the middle of our Bible. That fact has likely contributed to why generations of Bible scholars have interpreted the book allegorically rather than literally. However, doing so risks missing the point that God created us human beings with the capacity to be stimulated by our senses. When we abandon the message of our full humanity, we not only forfeit that which is attractive but unknowingly take what God intended for good and surrender it. Our Enemy, "the father of lies" (John 8:44), then seizes the opportunity to enter the vacuum and distort all human senses. The result of such distortion is evident in a history of sensual licentiousness that has wreaked relational havoc throughout society. We ought not yield this ground. God purposely created us with senses designed to enjoy and maximize healthy relationships from which romance develops. Rather than fear these senses we should harness them for the good the Creator intended.

Part of the sensuous nature of this love song is manifest also in the numerous garden metaphors found therein. The words *garden*

(4:12–16; 5:1; 6:2; 8:13) and *vineyard* (1:6, 14; 2:15; 7:12; 8:11, 12) are plentiful in this written text. While some of the references appear to be literal, others appear to be poetic devices that symbolize the beauty of the human body. This should not surprise us, for few places activate the senses like a well-cultivated garden or vineyard. Over the years, my wife and I have enjoyed visiting gardens—whether it be the National Arboretum outside Washington, D.C., the exquisite rose gardens in Portland, Oregon, the majestic Garden of the Gods in Colorado Springs, or Chicago's beautiful Botanic Garden. Wherever we have lived or visited, we have tended to gravitate toward such places. Something about the sights, sounds, and smells there inspire us. Gardens are sensuous areas. How telling that the Song of Songs, a love song, refers to them so often. Furthermore, it is worth noting that history began in a garden (Gen 2:8) and culminates in a garden-like heaven (Rev 22:1–2). Gardens stimulate our senses and generate pleasure, both of which God designed. The intricacies of God's creation are on full display in gardens. No wonder they are central to both human and divine experience. No wonder their features are drawn upon to write a romantic love song.

Third, **this is a sensuous love song that includes endearing language**. A careful reading of the Song of Songs is revealing in yet another way. Romance is reflected in language that is endearing, tender, and refined. Words like "lover" (1:13, 16), "beloved" (5:9), "darling" (1:15; 2:10), and "my bride" (4:8–12) fill the song. Descriptions of the attraction between the lover and the beloved are courteous and complimentary. The language is never the type that is crass, critical, or disrespectful, such as that found in so many songs about relationships today. How one talks has a great deal to do with romance. Poor conversational habits can be both the cause and effect of a sour relationship. None of that kind of communication occurs here. The language is consistently encouraging and winsome. One can only wish for additional songs like this in our generation. However, even more needed than songs are relationships that model elevated and thoughtful language, thus exhibiting charm and appeal to a watching world. That leads to a final observation.

Fourth, **this is a sensuous love song that includes endearing language while acknowledging the important role of friends**. Three voices are heard throughout the song: the feminine voice is identified as the "beloved;" the masculine voice is identified as the "lover;" and the voice of others is attributed to "friends." These "friends" appear repeatedly along the romantic journey (e.g., 1:4, 8; 5:1; 6:1, 10, 13; 8:5,

8), providing encouragement, accountability, and guidance. The truth of the matter is that friends have a significant role in a budding romantic relationship. This may seem to be a strange or awkward thought initially, but it need not be. Friends are needed to affirm the relationship they see developing. That is why weddings are universally social events. The sanction and support of the community are necessary for healthy relationship development and maintenance. Friends offer support with their words and their actions. Their words of encouragement, instruction, and counsel will be needed at times along the rocky and unpredictable road of life. Their actions often will serve as models of healthy behaviors and patterns from which others can learn. Truth be told, we need each other; we need friends. While elements of marital romance certainly demand privacy, there are critical roles played by friends. They are watching, cheering, and hoping our romantic relationship is pure and enduring, for they seek to achieve the same end.

No wonder this is called the Song of Songs. It is the best song ever produced, the one that continues to sit at the top of the charts centuries after it was composed. It is a love song that is sensuous, endearing, socially situated among friends, and relatable to every generation. This song, or book, closes the collection of poetic writings that form the first part of the Old Testament's appendix. Romance is its unmistakable theme.

Why would God grant a romantic love song such a prominent place in holy Scripture? The question is worth our consideration. Perhaps pointing to the day that we will become his Son's bride, God thought we would benefit from instruction and practice in what it means to be loving and intimate. While I see no need to interpret the Song of Songs as allegory, which would imply the images used here are fictional symbols not to be taken literally, I do think the content is illustrative of that which serves a higher purpose. In other words, God designed us for romance and gave his followers a book rich in romantic appeal to prepare us for the intimacy he desires with us. The divine romance that God desires with us is not sexual, but it is comprehensive, satisfying, and permanent. Centuries later Paul emphasized this same theme of marital romance, noting that it stands as "a profound mystery" that represents Christ and "the church" (Eph 5:32). John alluded to God's romance with his people when he wrote, "the wedding of the Lamb has come, and his bride has made herself ready" (Rev 19:7).

Romance, it turns out, is God's idea. Like so many of his ideas, however, the concept has been hijacked by the Enemy and distorted to where it scarcely is recognizable anymore. For example, today's romance novels or movies too often twist romance so that it looks like inappropriate flirtation that leads to illicit and impermanent adulterous encounters. After a short-lived thrill, those encounters typically dissolve into disappointment and heartbreak. The result is not romance but tragedy.

The 1970s Coca-Cola advertising tagline may be fitting here. The popular soft drink company had this to say about its product: "It's the real thing." The implied caution was to avoid any false substitute. The same is true when it comes to romance. God designed it and the Song of Songs describes it. Let's get the real thing. Why settle for anything less?

PRAYER

Our Father in heaven, we acknowledge you as the Creator of all things, including our senses and our inclinations toward romance. The world around us tries to act like the expert when it comes to relationships, but it peddles what is cheap, false, and fleeting. On the contrary, you have created what is beautiful, satisfying, and lasting. May we find fulfillment both in human relationship here and in divine relationship with you through all eternity. Forgive us for listening to the wrong voices and following the wrong models when it comes to romance. Keep us from that which is artificial, superficial, and harmful. Give us the real thing, we pray. AMEN.

QUESTIONS

1. Besides the Song of Songs, what is your favorite love song? Why? What meaning does the song have for you?

2. Whether you are currently in a romantic relationship or not, how would you describe your language? Do you speak with endearing words and tones? Or is such language strange and foreign to you? What factors cause you to talk as you do? How might you work to elevate your language?

3. What "friends" have spoken into your relationships? What practical advice have they provided? What benefits have resulted?

4. Why has the church historically been reluctant to talk about intimate areas of relationships when Scripture does so? What

has been the result of that reluctance for the church? For society as a whole?

SUGGESTED READING

Song of Songs 1–8

23

ISAIAH: Woes

[T]hey parade their sin like Sodom; they do not hide it. Woe to them! They have brought disaster upon themselves. (Isaiah 3:9)

Woe to those who call evil good and good evil. (Isaiah 5:20)

Woe to those who make unjust laws, to those who issue oppressive decrees. (Isaiah 10:1)

Woe to those who go to great depths to hide their plans from the LORD. (Isaiah 29:15)

Woe to him who quarrels with his Maker. (Isaiah 45:9)

The Old Testament closes with a group of books collectively known as "the prophets." Together these books form the second major division of the Old Testament's appendix. After five books of poetry come seventeen books written by Israel's prophets across several hundred years following the reigns of David and his son, Solomon. The purpose of these writings was largely to warn and instruct God's people—by then divided into the two kingdoms of northern Israel and southern Judah— lest they turn their backs on God and suffer serious consequences. Of course, we know from reading the earlier historical books, particularly beginning with 1 Kings and ending with Esther, that the people did just that. They turned away from God and spent decades under foreign rule, exiled in Babylon. Throughout those turbulent years God kept speaking to his people, primarily through prophets. They warned the people, urged them to repent (to turn back to God), and pointed them to the coming Messiah. We are fortunate to have written records of their words, but the prophets' contemporaries did not feel so fortunate. In fact, the people often despised the prophets for their bold and penetrating declarations.

Isaiah was one of the early prophets. He witnessed the fall of Israel to Assyria in 722 BC and warned that Judah would suffer the same fate under the hand of the Babylonians (ch 39). Three noteworthy features mark the book that bears the prophet's name:

1. Isaiah is often described as a miniature Bible because the first thirty-nine chapters parallel the thirty-nine books of the Old Testament, with a focus on judgment, while the remaining twenty-seven chapters parallel the twenty-seven books of the New Testament, with a focus on comfort (40:1) and hope (40:31).

2. The book offers some of the most vivid Old Testament references to the coming Messiah who will appear in the New Testament. Isaiah speaks of the virgin birth (7:14), the royal son who will reign (9:6), and the suffering servant (53:1–12)—all pointing to the Anointed One, the Christ.

3. It is a book filled with "woes." No single book in the Bible mentions this attention-getting term more than Isaiah. Over twenty times in thirteen chapters the reader is confronted with "woe." This little interjection is a device that makes a big exclamation—expressing grief, sorrow, or distress.

While it would be unreasonable here to attempt a thorough review of every usage of "woe" in Isaiah, much can be gained by noticing a few of the references and how or why they occur. What can we learn about woes, or sorrows, in this book? When is the expression of woe appropriate or fitting? What is the prophet Isaiah trying to communicate to his readers when he interjects the word so frequently? Four observations are worth our attention:

1. Woe is spoken when there is an arrogant affront to God. The first time we encounter woe is immediately after reading that "Jerusalem staggers, Judah is falling . . . they parade their sin like Sodom; they do not hide it" (3:8–9). Remember, this is a description of God's

160

chosen people, those who have known his care and blessing. Yet here we find them haughtily flaunting their sin and unashamedly parading their wickedness. We ought not be surprised, therefore, when Isaiah declares: "Woe to them!" Sorrow, grief, and distress are to be expected whenever people so audaciously and persistently offend God. This is a timeless truth that has yielded devastating consequences throughout history. Though Isaiah sounded the alarm in the eighth century BC, the words continue to reverberate today. Woe to anyone who boastfully continues in sin, thumbs his nose at the Creator, and acts as if God is irrelevant. Unfortunately, the description is all too familiar as we witness such behavior multiple times a day and then watch as new generations of leaders, institutions, and nations stagger and fall.

2. **Woe is spoken when twisted thinking inverts good and evil**. Isaiah offers a clear and practical warning when he writes: "Woe to those who call evil good and good evil, who put darkness for light and light for darkness, who put bitter for sweet and sweet for bitter" (5:20). He saw how truth was being turned upside down and he confronted the problem. Of course, we witness the same inversion in our world. Matters like marriage, gender, and abortion—to name just a few—have been twisted to the point that one is now accused of being evil or bigoted when he or she stands for God's created design and order. What was once considered common sense and decency is now viewed with suspicion and animosity, while formerly unimaginable decadence is elevated and called progressive thought. What has happened? Apparently, the same twisted thinking that distorted Israel and Judah still infects humanity.

Chapter 5 of Isaiah contains more woes than any other chapter in the book, and all the references can be interpreted through the lens of twisted thinking. The prophet declares God's people have distorted views when it comes to the accumulation of property and goods (5:8), lifestyles of revelry (5:11–12), their understanding of sin and the holiness of God (5:18–19), their interpretation of good and evil (5:20), their own elevated self-worth (5:21), and their tendency to be more impressed by how they champion the drinking of wine than they are by being champions of justice (5:22–23). These areas still demand our attention today and still elicit woe when they are misunderstood and turned upside down. May God give us sound minds and discernment lest we, too, be guilty of inverting what is virtuous and noble with what is wicked and corrupt.

3. **Woe is spoken when injustice goes unchecked**. Issues of injustice abound in Isaiah, where the topic is directly addressed in no fewer than seventeen chapters. Those guilty of ignoring or perverting justice are warned of the dire consequences of their actions. The prophet is unequivocal when he writes, "Woe to those who make unjust laws, to those who issue oppressive decrees, to deprive the poor of their rights and withhold justice from the oppressed of my people, making widows their prey and robbing the fatherless" (10:1–2). Injustice toward the vulnerable is no small matter in the eyes of God. The poor, the oppressed, the widowed, and the fatherless deserve compassionate justice. Failure here is a road to disaster (10:3).

God's people are to be guardians and dispensers of justice. Unfortunately, however, we have lost a proper biblical understanding of the matter. While cries for justice and protests against injustice ring out in every generation, the culture rather than God's Word too often dictates the way forward. Biblical justice has to do with righteousness (in fact, the words are sometimes interchangeable in the Old Testament), with getting and doing things right. Today we are inclined to let the end justify the means. We support whatever means are necessary to reach a goal and consider the actions a warranted fight for social justice. If groups of people are harmed in the process of liberating another group, so be it. For example, we see this among some ardent supporters of critical race theory who endorse attacks on police officers, business owners, and intact family units on their way to compensating and elevating racial minorities. This kind of activism, under the guise of social justice, is not biblical justice. The latter is more concerned about *doing right* than *achieving rights*. No, that does not excuse passive acceptance of oppression and injustice; it is rather a call to a higher standard of behavior. God's people never are allowed to overlook injustice, but their pursuit of justice is to focus on the means as well as the end. They are concerned about righteousness—doing things right—at every step along the journey, valuing every individual and social group in the process. Woe to those who do otherwise.

4. **Woe is spoken when disaster is self-inflicted**. The book of Isaiah sadly informs us that God's people "have brought disaster upon themselves" (3:9). Their calamity was preventable. Later we read about those "who go to great depths to hide their plans from the LORD, who do their work in darkness and think, 'Who sees us? Who will know?'" To such people, Isaiah once again cries, "Woe" (29:15). Human audac-

ity to challenge the divine knows no bounds. Do people really think they can "hide their plans from the LORD?" Do they truly think God will not see or know what has been done? A catalog of human catastrophes that could have been avoided down through the years has been assembled in our history books. The catalog points to multiple disasters that have resulted from folly and poor choices. To be fair, not every calamity is self-induced—for example, consider Job or the blind man in John 9:1–3—but too many misfortunes are indeed brought about by human pride and stubbornness.

Isaiah uses the ridiculous illustration of a pot trying to instruct or correct the potter (29:16; 45:9; cf. 64:8). Whenever we—the pots—try to manipulate God—the potter—we risk crashing and falling apart. The shattering that occurs in those instances is due to our own unwillingness to submit to the potter's hands. The result is a tragic loss of potential. Isaiah's last use of the word *woe* occurs in chapter 45, where he says, "Woe to him who quarrels with his Maker" (45:9). It is as if Isaiah issues one final warning: You can quarrel with God and pay the price or you can accept his lordship and know his peace. The choice is yours, but so are the consequences. Woe to anyone who brings disaster upon himself and risks forfeiting divine "joy" and "peace" (55:12).

The behaviors of God's people in the eighth century BC prompted repeated "woes." Woe to those who arrogantly offend God. Woe to those who invert good and evil. Woe to those who pervert justice. Woe to those who bring disaster upon themselves. These were all serious matters. However, perhaps a greater tragedy is that what is described here is still all too familiar today. The lessons of history are recorded as a warning to future generations. Woe to those who will not take heed.

Prayer

Lord, you have called us to be your people and yet we have so often failed you. Forgive us and have mercy on us. We confess that many of our woes are self-inflicted because we have not sought you humbly. Our pride and sense of self-sufficiency have caused us to offend you and hurt our neighbors. Forgive us and have mercy on us. We too often struggle to learn the lessons of history exhibited in your people and, therefore, are prone to repeat the same sins. Forgive us and have mercy on us. May joy and peace—rather than woe—characterize our lives, as you designed. AMEN.

Questions

1. In your opinion, which of the four woes discussed above most needs to be sounded in this generation? Why?

2. How should Christians address issues of social injustice in a world like ours that is torn by deep racial and political divisions? What practical steps might be taken?

3. What are examples of woes (sorrows or distress) you have witnessed in society that have resulted from disobedience to God?

4. Who has been most like Isaiah in your lifetime? Are you able to identify a "prophet" in your world who has boldly spoken warnings while compassionately pointing to Christ? Why are such prophets rare?

Suggested Reading

Isaiah 3, 5, 6, 40, 53, 55, 66

24

JEREMIAH: Listening

To whom can I speak and give warning? Who will listen to me?
Their ears are closed so they cannot hear. The word of the LORD
is offensive to them; they find no pleasure in it. (Jeremiah 6:10)

I spoke to you again and again, but you did not listen; I
called you, but you did not answer. (Jeremiah 7:13)

Therefore the LORD Almighty says this: "Because you
have not listened to my words . . . This whole country will
become a desolate wasteland, and these nations will serve
the king of Babylon seventy years." (Jeremiah 25:8, 11)

Listening is often considered a lost art these days, implying that there was a time when people were much better at the task than we are in the twenty-first century. Ample evidence exists, however, that suggests we humans have always struggled with listening. The first problem between God and man was a listening problem. God spoke (Gen 2:16–17), man did not take him seriously (Gen 3), and centuries later we are still living with the consequences. Listening, or the lack thereof, is emphasized in the book of Jeremiah where the words *listen* or *hear* are mentioned in some form nearly 150 times.

Every parent knows the frustration of children who will not listen. How many times have parents sent a child to time out for his or her repeated failure to listen? The hope, of course, is that during the time out the child will think about his uncooperative ways and reform. Well, parents ought to take heart for they are not alone. God told his children to listen over and over again. When they stubbornly refused to do so he sent them to time out—seventy years in far-away Babylon (25:8–11). That was a long time to think about the error of their ways!

Jeremiah is sometimes known as "the weeping prophet," with references to weeping dotting the book that bears his name (e.g., 9:1, 10; 13:17; 31:15–16; 48:32). We ought not be surprised that Jeremiah wept, for he endured heartless persecution (e.g., 20:2, 7–8; 37:14–20; 38:6–13) as he dared speak on behalf of God to the inhabitants of the southern kingdom of Judah. The prophet was despised for declaring that God's judgment soon would be unleashed on Judah from the hands of the Babylonians (20:4–5). It is worth noting that no book in the Bible comes close to mentioning Babylon as often as the two hundred times that Jeremiah does. Nonetheless, Judah refused to pay attention to Jeremiah's warning that Babylon's attack and captivity were looming. Jeremiah wept because the people ignored the message and reaped the bitter consequences. Their refusal to listen resulted in a brokenhearted prophet.

Why has listening historically been so difficult? From Adam and Eve to God's chosen people during Jeremiah's day, to our own friends and family members, the pattern has been universally predictable. Listening is hard work, and few do it well. Whether expected to listen to God, to a spouse, or to a friend, the struggle is an all-too-common human experience. Forming and expressing an opinion is preferred to listening. Jeremiah highlights several hindrances that interfered with listening to God. I suspect the same hindrances exist today.

Arrogance. Having an inflated view of one's own ability to handle life always will impede listening. The arrogant individual asks: Why listen to another who is deemed inferior in knowledge, wisdom, and decision-making? We began these thoughts by noting that man had a listening problem soon after he was created; that listening problem was the result of pride and arrogance, wherein Adam and Eve became convinced that they knew better than God (Gen 3). Though centuries had passed by the time Jeremiah was written and though human history contained several warnings along the way, one thing remained constant: man's inclination to decide things himself without consulting God. Thus, the repeated refrain throughout Jeremiah is that the people "did not listen" to God (e.g., 25:3, 4, 7, 8). No wonder God sent them into exile for seventy years (25:11). Tragically, even then—while in exile—the people still did not listen (29:19). Arrogance is a stubborn trait with deep roots that are hard to extract. One would think that disasters such as exile, pandemics, plagues, storms, floods, fires, and wars might get people's attention and cause them to listen. History has not proven that to be the case. Fallen humanity is infected with arrogance, which, regardless of the generation, still hinders people from listening to God and to those through whom he speaks.

Alternatives. If arrogance (one's pride) does not impede listening, the Enemy has devised another clever approach in the voices of others. The competing voices of those around us often prevent us from hearing the singular voice most deserving of our attention. The people of Israel and Judah had a long history of comparing themselves to and listening to their neighbors. Therefore, much of the Old Testament consists of warning God's people not to listen to their neighbors and not to follow their neighbors' gods. If the problem of competing, or alternative, voices was a concern then, how much bigger is the concern today with our smartphones and computers keeping us connected to our social networks 24/7? As distractions have proliferated, focused listening has become more challenging than ever. Multiple voices vie for our attention. Furthermore, those alternative voices now come in tantalizing packages, marketed with appealing background music, attractive images, and catchy lyrics. There are a myriad of enticing choices calling our names and stirring our emotions. It is nearly impossible to single out just one voice in an environment such as this. Incredible determination and discipline are required to sort through the noise and distractions. Rare is the person able to "be still" (Ps 46:10) and listen to God's voice when so many alternatives beckon.

Activity. Humans of every generation have found ample work to keep themselves busy. Such activity, if one is not careful, can consume an individual and become a barrier to listening. Sometimes the pursuits demanding our focus and attention are noble and worthwhile; they may even come under the label of ministry or service. Religious activity—making sacrifices, keeping the Sabbath, celebrating holy days and festivals, and observing the law—marked the people of God and signified their devotion. The Israelites were not people known for sedentary and slothful lifestyles; they had busy lives focused on the dual tasks of daily survival and religious observance. Yet Jeremiah repeatedly noted that they did not listen. Centuries later Jesus observed a similar phenomenon when he visited the home of Martha and Mary. Here is how Luke described the visit: "Mary . . . sat at the Lord's feet listening to what he said. But Martha was distracted by all the preparations that had to be made" (10:39–40). Mary listened, while Martha was busy with what she perceived to be necessary activity. Not much has changed over the years. There are always those who see a job to be done and jump into action, like Martha; they are responders who are applauded for their initiative and work ethic. Others, like Mary, take time to listen lest they miss important information or a subtle nuance; they, however, tend to be viewed more negatively and may even be seen as freeloaders. The truth is a balance of both action and listening is needed. God's people too easily lose that balance. They go through their familiar rituals, but careful listening has ceased. Every generation faces the same risk, resulting in the same ominous consequences of a broken relationship with God.

Authorities. Listening can also be hindered by leaders who inappropriately model or misguide their people. When "priests . . . leaders . . . [and] prophets" (2:8) fail to listen, we should not be surprised to see community members experience the same failure. Authorities who do not listen themselves cannot inspire others to do so. Jeremiah repeatedly groups together kings and officials, and prophets and priests (e.g., 2:26; 4:9; 8:1; 32:32)—noting how they, along with their people, have become "corrupt" (2:21) and "disgraced" (2:26). The nation's authorities, rather than listening to the sovereign God, were spreading lies and falsehoods (14:14; 23:16, 32); the people were following in their steps and suffering severe consequences. Leaders—whether civic or religious—have an obligation to pay attention to God, the divine authority. When they do, they provide a powerful model for others. However, when they fail to listen and try to usurp authority that is not rightfully theirs, the art of listening becomes a casualty at every level of society. Once that happens, social chaos follows, and authority ultimately gets upended. Both Israel and Judah experienced this firsthand.

The message of Jeremiah is captured in the repeated refrain: "but you did not listen" (7:13; 25:7). Arrogance, alternatives, activities, and authorities made it difficult for God's people to tune in to his voice. The same obstacles exist today. If we are to become good listeners, we need to meet these hindrances head on and respond with boldness. Arrogance needs to be replaced with humility that is willing to learn from others. The alternative voices that bombard us today via our phones and screens need to be turned off long enough so we can quiet ourselves and hear from God. Our activities and calendars need to be honestly assessed so we can create periods of silence and quietness that allow us to listen. Discernment of authorities, whether they be kings and officials or prophets and priests, is needed to determine if they are trustworthy representatives who are drawing us closer to God or driving us farther from him. Listening demands a herculean effort.

Three final observations may be helpful here. First, the book of Jeremiah ironically opens with an emphasis on how the prophet heard "the word of the LORD" (1:2, 4, 11, 13; 2:1). Jeremiah was not only the weeping prophet but also the listening prophet. What a contrast is painted in the rest of the book as God's people repeatedly failed to listen. The scene begs the question: Will we dare to listen, like Jeremiah, even when so many around us do not?

Second, the Hebrew word that is translated "listen" or "hear" is the same word that often gets translated "obey." For example, at one point in Jeremiah we read: "I warned them again and again, saying, 'Obey me.' But they did not listen or pay attention" (11:7–8). In this passage, the exact same Hebrew word is translated "obey" the first time and "listen" the second time. To listen is to obey; these two words are used as synonyms throughout the Old Testament. When a frustrated parent says to a child, "you are not listening to me," a failure to obey is implied. Again, this raises an important question: When God speaks, do we listen with the intent of obeying?

Third, Jesus underscored the significance of listening and obeying when he often said, "He who has ears, let him hear" (Matt 11:15; 13:9, 43; Mark 4:9, 23; etc.). The emphasis is on more than physical hearing and the measurement of sound via decibels. The intent is that those who hear will also do the will of God. Does our listening result in our doing God's will?

Let us listen well. It may be the most important thing we ever do.

PRAYER

Lord, we confess that we suffer from the same problem that has inflicted your people for centuries. We are not very good listeners. We have let too many hindrances distract us from paying attention to you. Forgive us. Quiet us. And give us ears to hear. May we obey you and, thus, honor you through our witness all the days of our lives. AMEN.

QUESTIONS

1. What have you found to be the greatest hindrance to listening to God? Is it one of those issues mentioned above or another issue? How might you address the problem so that you become a better listener?

2. Can you think of a time when you tried to communicate with someone, but felt the person was not really tuned in and listening? What was your response?

3. Have you ever felt misunderstood, persecuted, or marginalized—like Jeremiah—because you dared speak for God? Describe the situation and how it made you feel.

4. When have you unmistakably heard from God? What were the circumstances? What made it possible, and perhaps even easy, to listen to him at that moment in time?

SUGGESTED READING

Jeremiah 1, 2, 7, 11, 23, 25, 29

25

LAMENTATIONS: Mourning

The roads to Zion mourn, for no one comes to her appointed feasts. All her gateways are desolate . . . (Lamentations 1:4)

The Lord is like an enemy; he has swallowed up Israel. . . . He has multiplied mourning and lamentation for the Daughter of Judah. (Lamentations 2:5)

Joy is gone from our hearts; our dancing has turned to mourning. (Lamentations 5:15)

Mourning is a timeless and universal human response to loss. The book of Lamentations describes the sorrow and grief experienced by God's people when Jerusalem was destroyed and its inhabitants were exiled to Babylon. The loss of their holy city, their promised land, and their sense of dignity resulted in bereavement and mourning. Meaningful loss always leads to mourning. We are probably most accustomed to experiencing or witnessing mourning when confronted with death. Funerals are occasions for mourning as people say good-bye to a loved one. However, any loss can result in mourning. The loss might indeed be a spouse or family member who has died. But the loss might also be a miscarriage during pregnancy, a job or position that has vanished, a home destroyed by a storm, a parent who has left due to divorce, a dream or aspiration that has evaporated, being deprived of access to power and decision-making, a rapid decline in one's health or income, or an endless number of other possibilities. What these losses all have in common is the emotional response they elicit. People do not mourn their gains but their losses.

Though other Old Testament books contain laments (e.g., certain Psalms and several of the prophets), Lamentations is the only book given totally to laments. The mournful cries of God's people fill its pages as they respond to destruction and exile (2:9) at the hands of the Babylonians. Written by the prophet Jeremiah, Lamentations qualifies as being both prophetic and poetic. The book's message corresponds with the preceding book of Jeremiah, while its poetic form makes it stand out as one of the most unique writings of all Scripture. The first four chapters of this five-chapter book were written as Hebrew acrostics. There are twenty-two letters in the Hebrew alphabet, and each letter begins a new verse or thought. The same poetic device—the Hebrew acrostic—is also found in Psalm 119 and Proverbs 31:10–31. Its use is intentional and thoughtful, creatively attempting to engage and focus the mind of the reader.

A helpful description, or outline, of mourning is provided in Lamentations. Jeremiah suggests that mourning is composed of various elements. Each chapter—or each new acrostic—presents another component. The elements noted here offer aid in understanding the mourning process.

Chapter 1 reveals that mourning (1:4) is indeed *precipitated by loss* (1:6). The city of Jerusalem, "once so full of people," lies "deserted" (1:1). "Her children have gone into exile" (1:5) and "all the splendor has departed" (1:6). The grandeur of Jerusalem had been lost. The Hebrew word (*hadar*) that gets translated "splendor" is sometimes translated honor, glory, beauty, or majesty. All that was magnificent about Jerusalem had faded. The heyday, or zenith, of cultural life and prominence was now history. The people mourned what once was but was no more. Their dreams for their children and grandchildren, their hopes for a secure and comfortable future, and their cherished religious patterns of life were all destroyed. The splendor had given way to repeated "groans" (1:8, 11, 21, 22). Such serious loss can be expressed only through groans and mourning. Mourning is a mechanism that releases grief and anguish. We tend to pity those who mourn; however, we ought to pity those who do *not* mourn when there has been significant loss. In a sense, mourning is a gift necessary to the restoration of health.

Chapter 2 notes that *the Lord has done this* (2:1, 2, 5, 6, 7, 8, 9, 17); he is behind all that has happened. "The LORD has done what he planned; he has fulfilled his word, which he decreed long ago" (2:17). His warnings were ignored; as we noted in Jeremiah, the people did not listen (see Jer 7:13; 25:3–11). So, the Lord allowed the events that resulted in the mourning found in this book. The author states it this way: "He has multiplied mourning and lamentation for the Daughter of Judah" (2:5). This is a foreign thought to most American Christians. We have remade God into a soft, loving grandfather and convinced ourselves that he would never cause us to mourn. How different the picture provided by Lamentations, where the Jewish writer acknowledges that God metes out consequences that sometimes result in mourning. Even God's chosen people are not exempt. Mourning helps us realize our utter dependence on God. Loss reminds us that the things we value here on earth—positions, relationships, possessions—are fleeting. There is a bigger picture. Painful though our experiences may be, the sovereign God is actively bringing about his purposes even when our vision is clouded by suffering and mourning. So maybe the problem is not that God allows mourning but that our understanding of its purpose is incomplete.

Chapter 3 indicates this is all *very personal*. Reading through this third acrostic, one is struck by the number of first-person pronouns (I, me, my, we, us, our). Make no mistake about it, what is described here hits close to home. This is not about my enemy or even my neighbor. This is about my community, my family, and me. Over eighty times the reader encounters first-person pronouns in Lamentations 3. Over eighty percent of those pronouns are first-person *singular*, most of which are found in the first twenty-one verses. Indeed, what is described here strikes the author personally; he is intimately acquainted with "affliction" (3:1, 19). Stated another way, *I* am the subject here; *my* painful experiences are under the microscope. That, of course, is the very nature of mourning. It is always personal. Something touches me and then leaves a hole in my heart. The loss and its emotional response are very personal, private, and subjective. No one else can quite fully understand it and that amplifies the problem.

Chapter 4 records how *the unthinkable has happened*. Here is the description we read: "The kings of the earth did not believe, nor did any of the world's people, that enemies and foes could enter the gates of Jerusalem" (4:12). No one saw this coming. This is a tragedy that caught everyone by surprise. What was once unimaginable has come to be. The chapter catalogs a list of once-unthinkable events:

- "Gold has lost its luster" and value (4:1).
- God's "people have become heartless" (4:3).
- The wealthy are now "destitute in the streets" (4:5).
- Royal princes are no longer "recognized in the streets" (4:8).
- Famine has resulted in "compassionate women [who] have cooked their own children" (4:10).
- Prophets and priests sin (4:13).
- "The LORD's anointed" (the king) has fallen into the enemies' "traps" (4:20).

Everything described here was once inconceivable. That, too, is a common feature associated with mourning. When an unthinkable tragedy happens, we are left to mourn.

Chapter 5 is a plea for the Lord to "remember" his people and their "disgrace" (5:1). There is recognition here that the only way to move beyond their mourning is for God to "restore" and "renew" (5:21) his people. The plea is made directly to the Lord; this is not talk *about* him but talk *to* him. Those who mourn do not need more information about God during their time of sorrow, but they do need access to God. They do not need rules or guidelines for effectively dealing with loss, but they do need a relationship with the sovereign Lord. The book of Lamentations ends with an earnest plea for God to respond to his people's unbearable sorrow.

In summary, this little Old Testament book provides practical and timeless principles pertaining to mourning. We learn here that mourning is precipitated by loss, attributed to the hand of the Lord, is very personal, is a response to what was once unthinkable, and demands that we turn to God for recovery. We owe a debt of gratitude to Jeremiah for leaving us this written treasure regarding the anatomy of mourning.

We are now three books into the prophets and the cumulative message is sobering. Isaiah sounds the warning of woe. Jeremiah follows by pointing out that God's people have not been listening. The book of Lamentations emphasizes great mourning. No wonder we would rather skip over the prophets and jump to the New Testament. Unfortunately, when we do that—when we choose to be uninformed or ignorant of God's entire Word—we do so at our own peril. Such a choice prompts a modern-day woe, for it is another way of choosing not to listen. That decision always ends in mourning as we lose God's design and the sweet fellowship that we otherwise would enjoy with him.

Look around. There are many people mourning today. Some are close by, perhaps people in our own family or community. Some are mourning the loss of a loved one. Others are mourning the loss of an opportunity. Still others are mourning the loss of security and promise. Maybe you are one of those who is currently mourning. Or maybe you are one who needs to be given permission to mourn. One thing is clear: God's people have a history of mourning loss. Even Jesus wept (John 11:35). Mourning is a healthy outlet for our bottled-up grief and pain. Jesus went so far as to pronounce a blessing on those who mourn (Matt 5:4). Perhaps if we would freely and honestly mourn our losses, we would enjoy better health and experience less depression, anger, and bitterness. Mourning need be neither feared nor avoided.

The older I get, the more I feel free to mourn and the more I observe others who mourn. We will never escape the experience this side of heaven. Loss is part of the fallen condition of humanity. As long as we live in this world, therefore, we will have seasons when we need to mourn. However, there is hope. One day all mourning shall cease. Isaiah anticipated that day (51:11; 60:20), as did John when he penned this promise at the end of the Bible: "He will wipe every tear from their eyes. There will be no more death or mourning or crying or pain, for the old order of things has passed away" (Rev 21:4).

Heaven, you see, is not a place of loss. When we awaken on that grand *morning* there, the *mourning* we have known here will be no more.

PRAYER

Lord, we acknowledge that we are a sinful and fallen people who have experienced our share of loss and sorrow. Consequently, we often mourn. Some of us find ourselves doing so even now. We admit that our broken hearts sometimes make it hard to find words to pray. The future looks so uncertain. Please come and restore us, Lord. Renew us. Revive us. Give us hope, joy, and encouragement once again. Turn our mourning into dancing, we pray. AMEN.

QUESTIONS

1. When have you experienced deep mourning in your life? How did you make it through to the other side? What (or who) helped you along the way?

2. Can you think of recent losses that have resulted in mourning for either you or others you know? What were those losses?

3. Why do some people struggle to mourn when they experience significant loss? How might we help them do so in a healthy manner?

4. When Jeremiah mourned, he wrote a poem using several acrostics. What sorts of things do you turn to when you mourn? What have you seen others do during seasons of mourning (e.g., music, poetry, woodwork, yardwork, serving others, baking)?

SUGGESTED READING

Lamentations 1–5

26

EZEKIEL: Sovereignty

*"The people to whom I am sending you are obstinate and stubborn.
Say to them, 'This is what the Sovereign LORD says.'" (Ezekiel 2:4)*

*"Go now to your countrymen in exile and speak to them.
Say to them, 'This is what the Sovereign LORD says,'
whether they listen or fail to listen." (Ezekiel 3:11)*

*"You will suffer the penalty for your lewdness and bear
the consequences of your sins of idolatry. Then you will
know that I am the Sovereign LORD." (Ezekiel 23:49)*

The book of Ezekiel emphasizes the sovereignty of God. To say one
is sovereign is to acknowledge one's supreme power and authority.
Sovereignty implies having control and being in charge. The term is
descriptive of one who has absolute rule. Interestingly, the actual word
"sovereign" does not appear anywhere in the older *King James Version
of the Bible* (1611), though the idea is found throughout Scripture and
has long been considered an attribute of God. When it comes to more
recent translations of the Bible, however, such as the *New International
Version of the Bible* (1978), the word *sovereign* occurs numerous times.
For example, in the NIV translation of Ezekiel there are over two hundred distinct references to "the Sovereign LORD." This English phrase
is used to capture the meaning of the compound Hebrew name for God,
Adonai Yahweh. Older versions like the KJV preferred the more literal

designation, *Lord God*, signifying the supreme God who ruled over all. Ezekiel stands out in that no other book of the Bible speaks of sovereignty more than twenty times. In other words, Ezekiel mentions the sovereignty of God ten times more than any other single book in the Bible.

Who was Ezekiel and just what was his message and purpose? We know very little about this Old Testament writer except for what we read in the book that bears his name. There Ezekiel is described as a Jewish priest in Babylonian exile along with his fellow Jews (1:1–3). He was both priest and prophet, declaring a penetrating message that had three connected themes. First, as noted above, he wanted it known that *God is sovereign*. Thus, he applied that label to God boldly and repeatedly. Second, Ezekiel wanted people to know that *this sovereign God speaks*. The vast majority (95%) of the two-hundred-plus references to "the Sovereign LORD" describe him as speaking. Again and again we read these words: "This is what the Sovereign LORD says" (e.g., 2:4; 3:11; 5:5, 7, 8; etc.). God is neither distant nor detached. Rather, he is engaged and desires to communicate with his people. Third, Ezekiel wanted to make clear that *the sovereign God wants everyone to know he is sovereign*. The statement "then they will know that I am the LORD" (e.g., 12:16, 20; 13:23; 14:8) occurs nearly sixty times in Ezekiel. Numerous times the wording is even more specific, expressing the desire that people "know that I am the Sovereign LORD" (e.g., 13:9; 23:49; 24:24; 28:24; 29:16). Clearly, God wanted people to recognize his absolute sovereignty; he still does. The message of the book, then, is this: God is sovereign, he speaks, and he wants people to know he is in charge. Ezekiel's purpose was to make this message known.

There are two common problems, or obstacles, we humans have when we consider God's sovereignty. The first problem is that we do not like surrendering sovereignty to another. We are not fans of God being sovereign because, quite frankly, *we* want to be in charge ourselves. American Christianity has a strong independent streak. We feel comfortable, confident, and competent. Therefore, we bristle at the thought of yielding control to another. Though we claim to serve God, we much prefer it when God serves us and our needs. The second problem is we do not really believe God is sovereign. We may never forthrightly say so, but when we look at our world we struggle to believe in divine sovereignty. There are too many serious problems everywhere we look. How can one say there is a sovereign God—one who is in charge and rules over all—when racial tensions, riots, poverty, terrorism, homicides, pandemics, child sexual abuse, painful divorce, educational disparities, drug addictions, political distrust, abortion, cancer, childhood diseases and a host of other ailments afflict society and threaten our stability? If there is a sovereign God allowing these conditions to exist, he must be either cruel, sick, or not as powerful as some claim. Therefore, almost as a way of protecting God, we find it preferable to minimize any meaningful discussion of his sovereignty. It is much more courteous and comfortable to focus on God's other attributes such as his love, patience, and desire to console the downcast. At least those better fit the context of our present world. Sovereignty no longer suits the narrative and is best ignored. Perhaps that is one reason we rarely hear from Ezekiel these days in our churches. The silence is certainly understandable.

The reader should know, however, that Ezekiel was written in a social climate not that different from our own. Trouble, discouragement, and national crises grabbed the headlines then as they do now. Those things once considered firm and inviolable—the temple and centuries of religious rituals—had been attacked by enemies, mocked, and discarded as useless relics of the past. The stress of uncertainty and change dominated life. Out of that social environment, a relatively unknown priest named Ezekiel had the audacity to point people to the sovereignty of God. It was his way of saying: *Stop paying attention to the headlines. Stop worrying about what has been lost. Stop the obsession with all that has changed. Put your focus on God. For, yes, he is still the sovereign Lord. Let me repeat that—in fact, I think I will do so about two hundred times—our God is sovereign over everything.* That, in a nutshell, summarizes Ezekiel.

The book opens with three messages, or themes, that help define the scope of God's sovereignty. The themes are found in the first three verses of the forty-eight-chapter book.

First, **God is sovereign everywhere, even in exile** (1:1). Ezekiel was living "among the exiles" when he "saw visions of God." God had not abandoned his people after all. The divine presence was accessible even in far-off Babylon. God's sovereignty is not limited by man-made borders. He can be encountered wherever one finds himself and whatever the experience. God still reigns even when the place we find ourselves feels distant and forsaken. Peter (Acts 12:5–19) and then Paul (Acts 16:23–40) discovered God was present and sovereign in prison.

John experienced God's sovereignty on the remote island of Patmos (Rev 1:9). He reigns everywhere.

Second, **God is sovereign over everyone, even kings and priests** (1:2–3). Judah's "King Jehoiachin" and "Ezekiel the priest" are both described as being in exile. Though they were important civic and religious leaders, they did not operate independently; both were under the sovereign rule of God. Position or rank never exempts one from God's control. Leaders may temporarily act as if they are exceptions, but in the end God's authority is extended over every individual regardless of his or her earthly status. God's sovereignty is universal over every man, woman, boy, and girl. Autonomy is an illusion.

Third, **God is sovereign in directing the affairs of life** (1:3). We are told that "the hand of the LORD was upon" Ezekiel. The phrase— "the hand of the LORD"—which is repeated multiple times throughout the book (1:3; 3:14, 22; 8:1; 33:22; 37:1; 40:1)—is a way of saying that God directed the events of the prophet's life. That is what God does, for he is sovereign. He is in charge even when the circumstances may not seem to make sense at the time. Dennis Kinlaw notes that the people "wanted [God] to change their circumstances, not to change them;" but his way of working was to "change them so He could [then] change the circumstances of other people" (*This Day with the Master*, June 24). The sovereign God still works that way. Though he does not always promise favorable circumstances, he is still sovereign over the circumstances.

God directs and orchestrates what we cannot possibly understand in the moment. He is sovereign over place, people, and problems we may face. His hand will guide us through all circumstances to accomplish his purposes. Let me illustrate with a personal story.

Back in 1999, while on the faculty at Olivet Nazarene University, I flew out to defend my doctoral dissertation at the University of Oregon. Having struggled to get admitted to the university's sociology program in the first place due to affirmative action policies, having then sat through classes on Marxism, and having already failed (and then retaken) one major doctoral exam, I was a bit apprehensive as I approached the daunting task of my oral defense. The four committee members who formed my dissertation panel had earned doctorate degrees from Harvard University, the University of Chicago, the University of Wisconsin, and Syracuse University, respectively. This intimidating group of erudite individuals would evaluate my work and determine my future career path.

The chair of my dissertation committee suggested ahead of time that I begin my defense by demonstrating a bit of sign language. After all, my dissertation focused on religion's role in shaping the American Deaf Community. Because I had grown up using sign language with my deaf siblings, because my research had focused on the life and work of a deaf minister in the Chicago area, and becase my printed dissertation included a sketch drawing of that same minister signing the Lord's Prayer, I complied and decided I too would sign the Lord's Prayer to open my oral defense. The day came, I flew from Chicago to Oregon, stood before my imposing committee, and began as planned. As I prayed the Lord's Prayer—both speaking and signing simultaneously—God's presence unexpectedly filled the exam room. It was unmistakable. By the time I came to the final "amen" I noticed my committee members were fighting back tears, and I clearly heard God whisper: *They are not in charge; I am.* The sovereign God had shown up and made his presence known. With a quiet inner confidence and peace, I proceeded to sail through the hour before me. I have often reflected on that rare experience. I suspect few, if any, doctoral candidates have opened their oral defense with a public recitation of the Lord's Prayer—especially in a secular, Marxist-influenced sociology program. The collective brain power of highly educated committee members was reduced to tears when the sovereign Lord entered the room that day. The sovereignty of God ought never be underestimated.

God is in control, even when appearances may tempt us to think otherwise. He is Lord, the one in charge whether or not:

- We find ourselves in a pleasant place.
- The right people are in positions of leadership.
- We see his hand at work.
- We like it.
- We believe it.

God is sovereign over all—he always has been and always will be.

PRAYER

O Sovereign Lord, we confess that there are places, people, and problems that disturb us and make us wonder if you are active and in control in our world. Help us to understand that you are indeed the Sovereign One—who rules over all—even when the circumstances are not what we wish. We acknowledge that you are in ultimate control even when things do not go our way. Grant us faith and hope, so that we may know you are accomplishing your purposes in our lives and in this world. We pray this in Jesus's name. AMEN.

Questions

1. Has there been an event or circumstance that recently has caused you to question the sovereignty of God? What was it? How did you resolve it in your mind or heart?

2. Two common problems pertaining to God's sovereignty were noted above—the problem of surrender and the problem of belief. Which of these presents the biggest challenge to you? Why? How might you address the problem?

3. Why does a clear understanding of God's sovereignty matter so much? How does it influence how we live in the world today?

4. When have you witnessed clear evidence of the sovereignty of God? What led you to recognize it as God's sovereignty? What difference did it make in your life?

Suggested Reading

Ezekiel 1–3, 7, 11, 22, 33, 37

27

DANIEL: Courage

But Daniel resolved not to defile himself with the
royal food and wine, and he asked the chief official for
permission not to defile himself this way. (Daniel 1:8)

"If we are thrown into the blazing furnace, the God we
serve is able to save us from it, and he will rescue us from
your hand, O king. But even if he does not, we want you to
know, O king, that we will not serve your gods or worship
the image of gold you have set up." (Daniel 3:17–18)

Now when Daniel learned that the decree had been published, he
went home to his upstairs room where the windows opened toward
Jerusalem. Three times a day he got down on his knees and prayed,
giving thanks to his God, just as he had done before. (Daniel 6:10)

Courage is rare in every generation. *Webster's Dictionary* (2011) defines courage as having the "mental or moral strength to venture, persevere, and withstand danger, fear, or difficulty." Few people exhibit this kind of strength, or fortitude, during a time of crisis; fewer still make it the pattern of their life. That is what made the prophets stand out among their contemporaries. They were individuals of courage, perhaps none more so than Daniel, who repeatedly demonstrated resolve when the odds were stacked against him. The first half of the twelve-chapter book that bears his name contains several instances wherein courage was on display.

Daniel was one of the young men ripped from their homes in Judah and carted off hundreds of miles to Babylon under King Nebuchadnezzar (Dan 1:1–7). What personal torment and turmoil Daniel experienced! Fears and uncertainties regarding the future must have been daily companions. Yet Daniel is remembered centuries later for his raw courage in the face of adversity. He long has stood as a model for others.

In 1993, author William Bennett wrote *The Book of Virtues*, a call to restore our country's moral footing. In that volume Bennett identifies courage as one of the central virtues needed for the proper development of character. Interestingly, he notes, "The brave person is not one who is never afraid. That is rather the description of a rash or reckless person, someone who may be more harm than help in an emergency" (p 441). The courageous person, on the other hand, "know[s] what the right thing to do is" (p 442) and does it despite overwhelming obstacles.

Bennett's thoughts are consistent with what we find in the book of Daniel. Several demonstrations of courage are recorded there, all serving to inspire future generations of readers. Some of those courageous acts, along with the corresponding book chapters that highlight them, are worth our consideration:

The courage to be different from one's peers (ch 1). After being hauled off to Babylon, Daniel and his Jewish friends were sent to a three-year training camp where they were to learn the culture and customs needed to serve in the king's palace. "But Daniel resolved not to defile himself with the royal food and wine, and he asked the chief official for permission not to defile himself this way" (1:8). Daniel's audacity initially failed to move the official, but that did not stop him. Daniel persisted and finally negotiated a ten-day trial, after which the king found these young Jewish men to be "ten times better than all" the others in the camp (1:18–20). It takes courage to be different. Those without courage make up the mediocre masses of society; those with it influence kings and officials and, ultimately, change the world.

The courage to honor God in a foreign land (ch 2). In addition to having the courage to be different, Daniel also had the courage to exalt God among a people who dismissed him as irrelevant. The Babylonians did not honor Yahweh, the God of Israel; they had their own gods. Yet when King Nebuchadnezzar had a dream that needed interpreting and all the king's assistants and their gods (2:10–11) were incapable of the task, it was Daniel who stepped forward and saved the day. The amazing thing here, however, is that Daniel refused to take credit for his ability to interpret the king's dream (2:26–27). Rather, he immediately pointed to the "God in heaven who reveals mysteries" (2:28). Daniel exhibited rare boldness. Though surrounded by people who did not worship or respect his God, he refused to do anything less than give full credit to God. By the end of the chapter, King Nebuchadnezzar said to Daniel, "Surely your God is the God of gods and the Lord of kings and a revealer of mysteries" (2:47), and then the king put Daniel "in charge of all [Babylon's] wise men" (2:48). When God is honored with human courage, doors of opportunity often open unexpectedly.

The courage to stand against the crowd and culture (ch 3). The book of Daniel contains one of the best-known of all Bible stories: Shadrach, Meshach, and Abednego in the fiery furnace. Unfortunately, the story too often gets relegated to children's books and Sunday school classes. The incident underscores what can happen as the result of persistent raw courage. The three Hebrew men refused to bow to the popular image, or icon, of their day. Thus, their fate was sealed; they would be burned alive in the fiery furnace reserved for such noncompliant, recalcitrant types who did not embrace the culture. Of course, we know how the story ends and smile at the thought that God rescued them. Whenever we hear this childhood story again, however, I fear that we fail to reflect adequately on the depth of courage required to choose a path that deviates from the dominant culture. Only those with an unusual combination of conviction and determination ever demonstrate that kind of courage.

The courage to speak hard truth that is not politically correct (chs 4, 5). Daniel routinely rubbed shoulders with the kings of Babylon, the most powerful rulers in the world during his day. On three different occasions Daniel was called to interpret for the king. The first two occasions involved dreams (chs 2, 4), the last one involved mysterious handwriting on the wall of the palace (ch 5). While the details of each are unique and fascinating, a common thread ties them all together: what Daniel interpreted and declared to the king was consistently a hard truth with serious political consequences, both for himself and the king. The first hard truth was that Nebuchadnezzar's kingdom would not last (2:39). The second bold truth was that God is sovereign and arrogant Nebuchadnezzar was about to be driven from his throne until he acknowledged that fact (4:24–27). Daniel's words were soon fulfilled, as the king lost his throne (4:28–37). The third forceful truth was delivered to Nebuchadnezzar's son, Belshazzar, warning him that, because he failed to honor God, Belshazzar's kingdom, too, would come to a screeching and ignoble end (5:22–28). Indeed, the king died later that same night (5:30). None of these messages could have been easy to deliver. None would have been welcomed. None was politically wise or advantageous in any way. Yet all of them were true; and all of them required courage. It is always a daring and courageous act when one listens to God carefully and then speaks his truth clearly.

The courage to do right even when the circumstances suggest otherwise (ch 6). The story of Daniel in the lion's den is as popular as the story of the three Hebrew men in the fiery furnace mentioned earlier. Both illustrate uncompromised courage. The legal ban on prayer to anyone except King Darius did not derail Daniel (6:6–10). Changing circumstances and risky conditions did not deter Daniel from doing what he knew was right. Prayer to God was his lifeline and he intended to maintain his pattern regardless of the potential consequences. Daniel's courage of conviction resulted in the inconvenience of spending a night in the lion's den, whereas the king's lack of courage to change his poor decision resulted in distress (6:14) that culminated in an entirely miserable, sleepless night (6:18). The contrast between Daniel and the king—and their respective responses—could not be more obvious. Perhaps the lesson here is this: the best way to ensure a good night of sleep is to have the courage to do what is right, regardless of circumstances that might tempt us to follow an alternate course of action.

Dennis Kinlaw, in his devotional book *This Day with the Master* (2002, June 19), reflects on how Daniel and an earlier Bible hero, Joseph, exhibited courage, integrity, and victory while enduring unpleasant circumstances. Kinlaw's words are illuminating:

> There is something remarkable about Joseph and Daniel.
> Both of them were able to live in a world that was alien to
> them. Joseph lived in Egypt and Daniel in Babylon, centers of
> worldly power. Separated from God's people, they were able
> to live victoriously in the midst of idolatry and paganism. One
> of the reasons for their triumph was that they came to grips
> with a truth that many people struggle to accept: life includes
> many factors outside of our immediate control. There is
> nothing harder to accept than things that happen to you that
> you cannot control or change.

Joseph was sold by his own brothers, put in chains, taken to Egypt, and sold into slavery. Then because of his purity and integrity, he was unjustly thrown into prison and forgotten.

Daniel was taken captive to a foreign land and put under the control of a king who did not believe in Daniel's God. The people around Daniel attempted to make him suffer for his faith in God and his success at court. Both Joseph and Daniel knew what it meant to live in circumstances they did not control. They were able to remain victorious when life was out of their control because they trusted that their God remained in control.

Ultimately, the source of courage for both Joseph and Daniel was their determination as young men that God, not circumstances, would control their lives. The principle is universal and timeless. When the matter of control is settled and surrendered to God, one is free to act with extraordinary courage.

Heroes like Daniel are still needed in our generation—people with courage to be different, courage to honor God where he is not welcomed, courage to stand against the culture, courage to speak truth in an antagonistic environment, and courage to do right regardless of the consequences. It is that kind of courage that produced the prophets, later leaders like Luther and the Wesleys, and many of our own nation's forefathers and foremothers on whose shoulders we now stand. All of them courageously faced their fears and overcame hardships so that others might know "the living God" who "rescues and . . . saves" (6:26–27).

There is no telling what God will do with one courageous man or woman at his disposal. Will you be that one in your generation?

PRAYER

Our Father in heaven, we confess our need of you. We live in a world that is increasingly hostile to you and your ways. In such a world, we often find ourselves gripped with paralyzing fear and lose heart. Forgive us, strengthen us, and lead us. Help us to adopt the character and patterns that defined Daniel. His social environment and ours are not all that different. So do for us what you did for him. Grant us strength and courage to stand as your representatives in this world that so desperately needs a courageous witness. AMEN.

QUESTIONS

1. Who is one of the most courageous people you know? Why? What has that person done that makes you think of him or her as courageous?

2. What does it take to be a person of courage? What are the factors, or ingredients, that define such a person?

3. How does one differentiate between godly courage and self-driven foolishness? What are the distinguishing marks of each?

4. After reviewing the five types of courage exhibited by Daniel, which one would you say is most needed in the church today? Which one most needs attention in your own life? How might you address that need?

SUGGESTED READING

Daniel 1–6, 12

28

HOSEA: Prostitution

Then I told her, "You are to live with me many days;
you must not be a prostitute or be intimate with any
man, and I will live with you. (Hosea 3:3)

They consult a wooden idol and are answered by a stick
of wood. A spirit of prostitution leads them astray;
they are unfaithful to their God. (Hosea 4:12)

Their deeds do not permit them to return to their
God. A spirit of prostitution is in their heart; they
do not acknowledge the LORD. (Hosea 5:4)

Prostitution is rarely a topic of discussion anywhere, least of all among God's people. If you are like me, you have probably never heard a sermon on the subject. Nonetheless, the theme appears frequently across the pages of the Old Testament, especially among the prophets. The word *prostitution* and its older synonyms, *whoredom* and *harlotry*, are found well over one hundred times in the Old Testament. Half of those references occur in the books of the prophets, primarily in Ezekiel and Hosea. Apparently, God had something to say on the matter whether we are comfortable with the discussion or not.

The practice of prostitution has a long history. The Bible reader will not advance past the first book of Genesis without encountering it (e.g., Gen 34:31; 38:15). Prostitution is commonly defined as offering sex in exchange for goods or money. While that is indeed the general understanding of the term, an expanded interpretation includes any corruption or debasement of an individual that results from some sort of exchange which then leads to diminishing one's value, character, or purpose in the process. Therefore, while a sex worker may engage in prostitution, a person who compromises his character to curry favor with another may also figuratively be described as prostituting himself.

Hosea was not the only person to write extensively about prostitution. While I was a graduate student at the University of Oregon in the 1990s, my doctoral advisor was sociologist Marion Goldman. She, too, had written a great deal on the topic. Back in the 1970s, Goldman wrote her doctoral dissertation at the University of Chicago on the social and historical factors associated with the behavior. Her work, entitled "Gold Diggers and Silver Miners: Prostitution and the Fabric of Social Life on the Comstock Lode" (1977), focused on a community of miners and prostitutes in Nevada in the late 1800s. Goldman proceeded to write several other articles and chapters on prostitution and became recognized as an authority for her perceptive analysis. Unlike Goldman, however, we will not concern ourselves here with trying to understand and analyze the myriad social conditions related to prostitution's development. Rather, our aim is to understand how and why God's people engaged in the practice in the eighth century BC and then determine what implications there might be for us today.

The prophet Hosea was not an objective social scientist like my University of Oregon advisor. His interest in the topic of prostitution grew out of his personal experience and his willingness to be God's messenger. The book that bears his name, Hosea, begins with the story of Hosea marrying an unfaithful wife (1:2–3). Time and again she committed adultery, prostituting herself to other lovers. Despite his wife's waywardness, the Lord instructed Hosea to pursue and love her (3:1). As the painful experience unfolded over time, God told Hosea that he was not alone in having a wife who had abandoned him and prostituted herself to others. In fact, this is what the Israelites—God's chosen people—had done to God himself. Collectively, they had chased after other "lovers" (2:5, 13), "deserted" their Lord (4:10), and been "unfaithful to their God" (4:12). While it was bad enough that Israel, the northern kingdom, had taken this route, the fear was that Judah, the southern kingdom, would do the same thing (4:15). Of course, we know from history that is exactly what happened: both Israel and Judah were unfaithful and suffered the devastating consequences of their prostitution. The allure of the nations around them was too much for them to resist, and unfaithfulness followed. Alarmingly, even the priests—those charged with spiritual leadership in their community—were guilty of the same moral corruption and adulterous behavior (4:9; 5:1; 6:9; 10:5). God's chosen community was in shambles and disgrace.

Though he had long made clear that he was a "jealous God" (Ex 20:5; 34:14; Deut 4:24; 5:9; 6:15), his people ignored his word and did the unthinkable by turning from him and prostituting themselves to other gods. Sarah Young, in her devotional *Jesus Calling* (2014, p 202), offers the following insight:

> Idolatry has always been the downfall of [God's] people. [He] make[s] no secrets about being a *jealous God*. Current idols are more subtle than ancient ones because today's false gods are often outside the field of religion. People, possessions, status, and self-aggrandizement are some of the most popular deities today.

Unfortunately, prostitution knows no boundaries.

There are a total of twenty-five instances in Hosea that reference the problem we are discussing. English words like "prostitution," "adultery," and "unfaithfulness" are used in the text—all describing the same troubling behavior. In the older *King James Version of the Bible*, the words of choice are "whoredom," "adultery," and "harlotry." More important than the words and their synonyms, however, is understanding the meaning of what was taking place in Israel at the time. Two realities are particularly noteworthy. First, *a wedding vow was violated*. The vow, or covenant, between God and his people had been broken. God's wife—Israel, his chosen ones—had walked out on him. This fact is emphasized throughout Hosea in descriptive phrases such as these: "there is no faithfulness, no love, no acknowledgment of God in the land" (4:1); "they have deserted the LORD" (4:10); "they have rebelled against me" (7:13); "Israel has rejected what is good" (8:3); and "they forgot me" (13:6).

Second, the adultery that is repeatedly described here is *a figurative way to speak of idolatry*. Just as adultery is cheating on a spouse, idolatry is cheating on God; adultery and idolatry are both forms of unfaithfulness that result in finding another lover. In summary, then, the picture we get in Hosea is of a people who have broken their promise to God and sought fulfillment in a variety of substitutes.

Consequently, Hosea's message is clear and to the point. God, speaking through the prophet, charged his people with prostitution. This was a serious charge. In fact, it got worse. Twice we read that the people were controlled by "a spirit of prostitution" that "leads them astray" (4:12) and occupies "their heart" (5:4). Prostitution had come to define them. Minimally, what that meant was that their sense of intimacy, pleasure, purpose, and affection had all been corrupted and redirected:

- God's people were becoming intimate with something or someone (3:3) other than God himself. Their knowledge of and familiarity with the surrounding culture was deepening, while their knowledge of and familiarity with God was diminishing. They were prostituting themselves to another.
- God's people were seeking pleasure and satisfaction in what would not last rather than finding pleasure in God. The pleasures they found were temporary, fleeting, and ultimately unfulfilling. They were chasing a fantasy that would disappoint in the end. They were prostituting themselves to an illusion.
- God's people were corrupting the purpose for which they were created. God designed them for meaningful and lasting relationships, the primary relationship being with himself. His plan was that his people would enjoy close communion with him. They were prostituting themselves to an alternate vision that rejected his divine plan.
- God's people were giving their affection to another. At times they were even buying affection from another. The affection once directed to God—their "forsaken ... first love" (Rev 2:4)— was being directed elsewhere. They were prostituting themselves to other "lovers" (2:5, 13).

Hosea's message makes us feel uncomfortable. Not only is the topic of prostitution, by its very nature, sordid and decadent, but the discussion here is all too relevant to the modern reader. Like all books of the Bible, these words appear to be timeless and aimed right at us. Though Hosea dates back to the eighth century BC, we realize that we, too, are the intended audience. God chose and redeemed us to be his bride and yet we sometimes prostitute ourselves before other gods and loyalties.

Too often our decisions and choices reveal our unfaithfulness. We seek intimacy, pleasure, purpose, and affection in the wrong places. God intended that we find fulfillment of these desires in a relationship with him. Anything else is prostitution and an affront to the bridegroom, our holy God.

Because the act of prostitution and its repercussions are so serious, maybe we should talk about it more than we do. Hosea certainly did not shy away from the topic. The book is positioned first in the collection known as the twelve minor prophets, immediately grabbing the reader's attention by tackling the sensitive subject head on and then making known that prostitution can make its way into the community of God in any generation.

Reader, take warning: wisdom and discernment are needed to stand against such unfaithfulness. That is probably why Hosea closes with these words of caution and reflection: "Who is wise? Let them realize these things. Who is discerning? Let them understand" (14:9).

We would do well to listen carefully to "[t]he word of the LORD that came to Hosea" (1:1). The message is timeless and needed. Every generation is called again to battle the subtle "spirit of prostitution" (4:12; 5:4) that seductively draws God's people into its trap and away from the Creator and Lover of their souls.

PRAYER

Dear God, you have invited us to enjoy an intimate relationship with you. You want us to find our deepest pleasure and purpose in you. You desire that we respond with faithfulness and affection. But if we are honest, we must admit that too often we have prostituted ourselves before alternatives and competitors. Unfaithfulness has marked too many days and years. "[O]ur sins have been [o]ur downfall" (14:1). Forgive us. "Heal [our] waywardness" (14:4). Help us always to understand that "the ways of the LORD are right" (14:9), and then give us strength and courage to walk in those ways. AMEN.

QUESTIONS

1. Why is unfaithfulness to the Lord such a common problem, one that emerges in every new generation? How might we address that potential problem in our own lives?

2. Focus on one of the features of prostitution—intimacy, pleasure, purpose, or affection—and be honest with yourself. Where do you turn to seek fulfillment in that area? How does that fit with the message of Hosea? Is what you are doing an act of prostitution?

3. What comes to your mind when you think of "a spirit of prostitution" (4:12; 5:4)? How do you interpret this phrase? What example might you provide to illustrate it?

4. What would you describe as the biggest tragedy associated with prostitution? Why?

SUGGESTED READING

Hosea 1–7, 14

29

JOEL: Invasion

*A nation has invaded my land, powerful
and without number . . . (Joel 1:6)*

And afterward, I will pour out my Spirit on all people. (Joel 2:28)

*Then you will know that I, the LORD your God, dwell
in Zion, my holy hill. Jerusalem will be holy; never
again will foreigners invade her. (Joel 3:17)*

Have you ever felt invaded by that which was unexpected or threatening? If so, you will relate to Joel. This rather obscure, three-chapter book draws attention to such experiences in Israel's history and foretells what future generations also might encounter. Of course, no one wants to be invaded for the two reasons already noted. Invasions, by definition, are likely to be both unexpected and threatening—invaders tend to operate using the element of surprise and are certain to bring about forceful and significant change that jeopardizes social stability. Few people, if any, yearn for such an experience.

Little is known about the prophet Joel other than his concern for Judah and Jerusalem (2:32; 3:1, 6, 8, 16–20) and the fact that Peter later quotes from him in Acts 2:16–21. Joel stands as a reminder that when God has a word for his people, he will use whomever he chooses. One need not be well-known or highly credentialed to speak for God. "The word of the LORD . . . came to Joel" (1:1) and a warning was sounded to both the "elders" and common people "in the land" (1:2) regarding an invasion (1:6). Widespread mourning, grieving, and despair was the result (1:8–13). Only at the end of the book—after much upheaval, terror and devastation—did God promise "never again will foreigners invade" Jerusalem (3:17).

Joel's message is clear: invasions occur and are rarely pleasant. Unfortunately, they still happen today with regularity, wreaking havoc among those victims who are left in their wake. Several types of invasions are alluded to in Joel. A look at some of them may be helpful as we consider similar intrusions and the disruption they bring to both individuals and entire communities. I suspect many of us have already experienced one or more of these at some point in our lives.

An invasion of our space occurs when foreigners invade the land. That is what Joel described when he said, "a nation has invaded my land, powerful and without number" (1:6). The nation referenced here consisted of non-Jewish foreigners—Gentiles who were oppressive, different, and numerous. The threat is not hard to understand; people stake a claim to their space, their turf, and want to protect it. History is replete with territorial battles. The Nazi invasion of European countries during the 1930s and the influx of immigrants along America's southern border today are just two of many familiar examples. Whether it is an invasion of enemy soldiers, foreign immigrants, or uninvited guests at a party, the response is predictable. People value their private space and resent it when others violate boundaries and invade that space. God's chosen people, living in their promised and cherished holy land, never dreamed an invasion would rip them from their comfortable and sacred home. Human nature has not changed across the years; no one wants his or her space invaded.

An invasion of our security occurs when problems arise that appear beyond our control. Poor Judah was overwhelmed. Swarms of locusts descended upon the crops and devastated the land (1:4; 2:25). Whether the language is to be taken literally or figuratively (some suggest the reference to locusts may speak of invading soldiers) is not what matters most here. The fact is that security had been diminished, the threats were real, and there was little that could be done to stem the tide. The result was a feeling of helplessness. I do not think it a stretch to suppose their experience parallels ours. We, too, have had our security shaken over the past few years by an extended pandemic, an economic downturn, heightened racial tensions, riots and looting in the streets, and an endless string of homicides in our cities. The invasion of these problems appears beyond our control and has crippled our communities. Security has given way to vulnerability. Life feels more uncertain than it once did.

An invasion of our spirit occurs when misery and despair come to define a group of people. Joel referenced a day of "darkness and gloom" (2:2, 31) when the spirits of the people would be crushed. Their world was about to be turned upside down. In fact, it already had begun. We read that even their religious practices and symbols had become useless and hollow (see 1:9, 13–14), and the "joy and gladness" once associated with "the house of [their] God" (1:16) was but a distant memory. A spirit of depression and anxiety had invaded their land. This sounds strangely familiar, does it not? The National Institute of Mental Health estimates that 40 million adult Americans (15% of the adult population) now suffer from anxiety disorders, while 16 million adults (6%) experience major depression. The need for mental health counseling is expected to increase by nearly 25% over the coming decade. Who can deny that we, like Judah during Joel's day, are witnessing an invasion of our spirits that has stripped us of joy and left us in darkness and despair? This explosion of gloom is heard in today's music, emblazoned on T-shirts, and witnessed on the faces of growing numbers of youth in schools and universities across the country. The optimistic spirit that once dominated homes, communities, and the nation has been invaded by a foreboding darkness.

An invasion of our sanity occurs when the human mind is overwhelmed by information and decisions. An interesting description is found near the end of Joel, where we read, "Multitudes, multitudes in the valley of decision! For the day of the LORD is near in the valley of decision" (3:14). The repetition here is likely intentional, serving in the Hebrew language to emphasize a point. Twice we read "multitudes" and twice we encounter "the valley of decision." Scores of people were apparently facing choices that would determine their future destiny. When so many decisions must be made in a short period of time—think "information overload"—the trajectory of an entire community is at risk. We, too, might describe ourselves as living in a "valley of decision." Has there ever been a time when we face more consequential decisions? What will we choose when it comes to how we use artificial intelligence, views regarding transgenderism, sex education for our children, family structure, law enforcement standards, religious liberties, and a host of other concerns? Our collective sanity is being tested. Not only are multitudes of people faced with key decisions but also there are multitudes of key decisions that people need to make. Individual and national sanity is being invaded by forces that threaten biblical standards, common decency, and public civility. Like our spiritual ancestors described in Joel, we stand at a crossroads today in "the valley of decision."

One of the lessons we discover as we read Scripture is how timeless and universal is its message. The words of the prophets, included in an appendix that is too often neglected at the end of the Old Testament, continue to have relevance today. We dare not hurry past these treasures that have so much insight to offer.

An invasion of our souls occurs when dark times give way to renewal and hope. Joel spoke of another type of invasion that stood in contrast to all those above. He pointed ahead to a refreshing invasion of the human soul. God looked at the sad condition of his people and announced, "afterward, I will pour out my Spirit on all people. Your sons and daughters will prophesy, your old men will dream dreams, your young men will see visions. Even on my servants, both men and women, I will pour out my Spirit in those days" (2:28–29). Note the extent and reach of this hope. It is for all family members, all ages, all socio-economic classes, and both genders. This invasion by God would leave no one untouched. No wonder Peter referenced this passage centuries later, on the day of Pentecost (see Acts 2:16). The first followers of Jesus saw Joel's words fulfilled during their lifetime. However, they were not the only ones to have their souls invaded by the Holy Spirit. The book of Acts indicates such an invasion occurred more than once (e.g., Acts 8:15–17; 10:44; 19:6).

And over the years God has continued to invade the souls of his people by pouring out the Holy Spirit on groups of unexpectant people. Revivals across the centuries have borne witness to this fact. Let me tell you briefly about a revival that invaded the souls of numerous individuals in a span of less than two years back in the early 1970s. The event was an extension of the 1970 Asbury College revival in Wilmore, Kentucky. After a nineteen-year-old Asbury College student came to my home church in Michigan to describe God's invasion of the college campus, I witnessed a remarkable movement of God. My mother had a powerful encounter with God at this time wherein she repented of her sins and recommitted her life to the Lord, from whom she had wandered. Mr. Wheatly, a seventy-two-year-old neighbor of the church, who for years had intentionally kept his distance from its doors, came one Sunday, knelt at the church altar, and experienced a startling and radical conversion. A young man nicknamed "Dash" gave his heart to Christ, gave up drinking with his friends, led several of them to Christ, later became my college roommate, and spent his life thereafter as a minister of the gospel. Jim Robinson, my high school football coach and a highly respected man in Michigan athletic circles, was convicted of his life of hypocrisy and began using his influence to point people to Christ. And I myself, as a young teenager, was called into ministry through a life-changing encounter with the living Christ. The invasion of God's Spirit—whether described by an obscure prophet in Bible times or by an obscure nineteen-year-old college student—always brings hope and changes souls.

Joel reminds us of the power of invasions. They still happen with frequency in our world. Rather than get sidetracked or discouraged, let us watch and pray for God to "pour out [his] Spirit on all people" once again (2:28). We need that kind of invasion—an invasion of the soul—in our communities today.

When God invades, all other invasions are diminished.

PRAYER

Dear Lord, we ask you to pour out your Spirit upon us. We have been invaded by so many forces and ideas in recent days that at times we grow dizzy, weary, and disoriented. Save us from that which seeks to distract and harm us. Keep us steady, strong, and courageous when we face threatening winds of uncertainty. We ask you to come and invade our homes, our churches, and our communities. Grant our souls a fresh new touch, lest we lose our way. Invade us once again with your Spirit, so that all other invasions are put in proper perspective. AMEN.

QUESTIONS

1. Joel is a rather obscure prophet of whom little is known, yet he had an important message that found its fulfillment and played a big role in the book of Acts. What little-known person has played a big role in your life? Describe that person's influence.

2. Do you remember a time when someone invaded your space or security? How did you respond? If the same scenario happened again, how would you like to respond?

3. Take a few minutes to reflect on your life over the past few years. What invasion has most affected you during this time? Has the invasion been helpful or harmful? Why?

4. When have you been most aware of the Holy Spirit invading your life, church, or community? What was that like? What has been the lasting outcome?

SUGGESTED READING

Joel 1–3

30

AMOS: Judgment

*But let justice roll on like a river, righteousness
like a never-failing stream! (Amos 5:24)*

*Woe to you who are complacent in Zion, and to you
who feel secure on Mount Samaria ... (Amos 6:1)*

*This is what the Sovereign LORD showed me: The Sovereign
LORD was calling for judgment by fire; it dried up the
great deep and devoured the land. (Amos 7:4)*

*Surely the eyes of the Sovereign LORD are on the sinful kingdom.
I will destroy it from the face of the earth ... (Amos 9:8)*

Two things are currently true when it comes to *judgment*; one has to do with silence and the other has to do with confusion. First, the word has nearly disappeared from the Church's twenty-first-century vocabulary. Though the final judgment of God may still be printed as a tenet in a church's dusty statement of faith somewhere, discussion of it in any meaningful or practical way seldom occurs. Long gone are the days of Jonathan Edwards, who in the eighteenth century preached his well-known sermon, "Sinners in the Hands of an Angry God," forewarning his hearers of the coming judgment, the wrath of God, and the torment of hell. Times have changed and we much prefer friendlier topics and tones from our preachers and teachers. Emphasizing judgment is no way to attract a crowd or build a church. Thus, we have grown relatively silent on the topic in our religious gatherings and literature.

A second truth is that society demonstrates confusion and contradiction surrounding the topic of judgment. Two conflicting statements are often heard these days: "don't judge me" and "we demand justice." Stop and think about these two statements. On the one hand, we personally want nothing to do with anyone who dares to make an evaluative judgment regarding our opinions, habits, or lifestyle. We quickly quote Jesus when he said, "Do not judge" (Matt 7:1), and then dismiss the offender as either a fanatical extremist or socially incompetent. However, we have no problem turning around and enthusiastically raising placards that read "Justice Now!" The latter action, of course, is a call for some authority figure to make a judgment that supports a position we favor. While we do not want a judgment made *against* us, we do want a judgment made *for* us and for any cause that we represent. I suspect many, if not most, people do not even see the contradiction in these opposing positions. Confusion exists, but we prefer that to uncomfortable coherence and logic.

The book of Amos challenges both the contemporary silence and confusion surrounding judgment. However, let me quickly add that this book does not stand alone in this regard. The topic of judgment is referenced in 30 of the 39 Old Testament books (77%) and in 19 of the 27 New Testament books (70%). One would be hard-pressed to miss the theme when opening the Bible. Furthermore, the popular idea that judgment is restricted to the Old Testament simply is not accurate. Jesus and the apostles also took up the theme of judgment, repeatedly warning people of the coming day when God will judge all people (e.g., Matt 5:21–22; 11:22; Rom 2:3; 14:10; Heb 9:27; 1 Pet 4:17; Rev 20:12). Therefore, it is only reasonable to acknowledge that the judgment of God deserves our attention today as well.

Judgment is not the only word or topic that is neglected by the church today; sin fits that same category. The word is too harsh for modern sensibilities. We may speak of failures, disappointments, poor choices, or having a bad day, but rarely do we identify anything as sin. To do so, of course, sounds too . . . well, judgmental.

Because we want to avoid offending anyone or indicting ourselves, we have cleaned up our language. However, in the process I fear we have lost more than a word or two. I suspect we have also lost, or at least marginalized, the truths behind those terms. Scripture teaches that God's *judgment* will respond to human *sin*, whether we avoid those dual topics or not. In a sense, that is the message of Amos.

The reader should be aware that Amos is a tough book with a hard message. The fragile person will not like wading through its waters. Even the way the book begins will scare some away. After briefly introducing himself (1:1), Amos informs the reader that "the LORD roars . . . and thunders from Jerusalem" (1:2). Though this hardly seems like an effective way to engage an audience, it does capture the reader's attention and raises the question: Why is God doing that? Why is he roaring and thundering? The answer is because sin is rampant everywhere—among every nation, even among God's people in Judah (2:4) and Israel (2:6). There are over fifty references to sin in the nine chapters of Amos; nine of those references are in the first chapter alone. The book begins with God roaring because sin was soaring. No wonder we later read: "The Sovereign LORD was calling for judgment by fire" (7:4).

Amos, who many scholars consider to be one of the earliest of the writing prophets, was an unlikely spokesman for God. He was a poor shepherd (1:1) who apparently supplemented his earnings by tending "sycamore-fig trees" (7:14). He claimed no credentials or polish as a prophet (7:14). However, perhaps like the shepherds Moses and David before him, his background prepared him for the tough task of speaking unpopular truth regarding sin and judgment. Is it possible that our backgrounds, some of which seem so ordinary or unimpressive, also may be just what God wants to use to speak a word to someone today? What we know is that Amos stepped forward and called out sin where he saw it and warned of the coming judgment of God.

Three manifestations of the people's sin are particularly striking. These three sins not only led to God's judgment being poured out during the eighth century BC but also are categories that have continued to define sin and bring God's judgment in every generation: rejecting God, mistreating others, and indulging oneself.

Rejecting God (2:4). The book of Amos informs the reader over fifty times that God speaks. He has something to say. Every chapter provides the same reminder. God was talking, but his people turned a deaf ear and "rejected the law of the LORD" (2:4). Multiple times God provided community and national warnings—such as food shortages, strange weather and climate patterns, ruined crops, plagues, and more—and yet five times we read that the people "have not returned to me" (4:6, 8, 9, 10, 11). The people repeatedly ignored God when he was trying to get their attention. No wonder God responded with judgment. He spoke, but the people did not take him seriously. Rejecting the word, voice, or instruction of God still results in trouble and judgment for humanity. The sovereign Lord wants our attention.

Mistreating others (2:6–7). Oppression of the poor and needy is a common refrain in Amos (2:7; 3:9; 4:1; 5:12). When God's judgment was poured out on six of Israel's neighboring nations (see Amos 1:3–2:3), each time it was "because" the nation disrespected and mistreated someone. A particularly strong word was leveled against those who continued celebrating "religious feasts" (5:21) and making "noise" and "music" (5:23) while not "let[ting] justice roll on like a river, righteousness like a never-failing stream" (5:24). Martin Luther King, Jr., aware of the prophet's powerful words, quoted this passage from Amos 5:24 in his well-known "I Have a Dream Speech," delivered in 1963 from the steps of the Lincoln Memorial in Washington, D.C. Justice and righteousness—treating others with impartiality, honesty, and decency—are what God always expects of his people, in every generation. Repeated failure to do so surely will reap bitter consequences.

Indulging oneself (6:1–7). Complacency, security, lounging, and entertainment had become the standard among God's people. The description in the first part of chapter 6 sounds so familiar that it could have been written last week rather than twenty-nine centuries ago. Physical, social, and psychological comforts dominated life. Pampering oneself with choice foods (6:4), beautiful music (6:5), abundant wine (6:6), and fine lotions (6:6) was the common pattern of the day. God had seen enough and was about to bring the party to an "end" (6:7). Prioritizing the pampering of oneself above the sincere praise of God is always a formula for judgment. We would do well to take heed.

As noted earlier, these categories continue to define much human behavior today. Rejecting God, callously harming others, and seeking one's own pleasures are the root of most sinful activities. When these patterns persist and unrepentant sin prevails, God's judgment can be expected.

A curious allusion to a plumb line is made in Amos, chapter 7. A plumb line is used by builders as a standard for ensuring that a wall is built vertically straight. God was building a community of people who would honor and follow him, but they were out of plumb. Their vertical relationship (with God) was bent, deformed. Therefore, "the Lord said, 'Look, I am setting a plumb line among my people Israel: I will spare them no longer'" (7:8). The judgment that God delivered to others (see ch 1) was now coming upon God's own people. No one would escape (9:1); all sinners would die—even those "among [God's] people" and those who say, "disaster will not overtake or meet us" (9:10). Neither heritage nor optimism could save them from the judgment of God.

If that was true then, why would we expect anything different today? Is it possible that God has sent warning after warning to us by letting us experience natural disasters, famines, diseases of all kinds, a worldwide pandemic, unimaginable perversions of his divine design for family and gender, chaos in our cities and streets, political upheaval, and widespread animosity between groups of people? Is it possible these events and more are intended to point to God and prepare us for the judgment? Oh, I know, in a day like ours—with our highly-educated minds, resourcefulness, and prosperity—many think even suggesting something like this borders on lunacy. Amos endured a similar charge, being accused of "raising a conspiracy" (7:10) and then being kicked out of town (7:12–13). However, eventually the prophet's words were fulfilled, and God's judgment was poured out on his people.

History reveals that people ignore God's word at their own peril. We ought not presume that God's mercy and patience have canceled our appointment with God's judgment (Heb 9:27). It would be foolish to disregard history's lessons today.

Perhaps there is a reason these books written by the prophets are included in an appendix at the end of the Old Testament rather than interspersed chronologically among earlier books. Few people read the appendix of a book. Amos provides one of the reasons why: his is a difficult message that leaves us uncomfortable. Nonetheless, this is a message we ought to hear.

Is there hope? Yes. God has provided a way out of the dilemma of judgment. That way is found in a short statement in the middle of the book: "Seek the LORD and live" (5:6). Let us do so before it is too late.

PRAYER

O Sovereign Lord, just as you showed Amos that you were calling for judgment (7:4), so you have shown us. Give us eyes to see, ears to hear, and hearts to respond. Forgive us for our indolence and casualness when it comes to your word. Forgive our sins. We confess that we have too often rejected you, mistreated others, and indulged ourselves when we should have been looking to you for guidance. Hear our prayer. Have mercy upon us. And help us to "seek" you so we can "live" (5:6). AMEN.

QUESTIONS

1. What thoughts come to mind when you consider the judgment of God? Are those thoughts supported by Scripture? If so, where?

2. Which category of sin mentioned here—rejecting God, mistreating others, indulging self—most needs attention in your community today? Why? What is the evidence?

3. Though we prefer to think of God as caring and compassionate—which he is—Amos notes he sometimes "roars" and "thunders" (1:2). Has there ever been a time when you have heard God roar and thunder? When? What was the occasion?

4. How can the Church present a clear and accurate message regarding sin and judgment in a world like ours that is not inclined to listen to hard, uncomfortable truths?

SUGGESTED READING

Amos 1–9

31

OBADIAH: Deception

The pride of your heart has deceived you. (Obadiah 3)

All your allies will force you to the border; your friends will deceive and overpower you; those who eat your bread will set a trap for you, but you will not detect it. (Obadiah 7)

The day of the LORD is near for all nations. As you have done, it will be done to you; your deeds will return upon your own head. (Obadiah 15)

Have you ever deceived someone or been deceived by another? I suspect we all have a story or two we could tell. Some of those stories would likely involve a combination of pain, shame, and regret. The nature of deception is such that someone is bound to get hurt. I learned that lesson at a young age.

The only time I remember being spanked by my father was in response to a deceptive act on my part. I grew up between two deaf siblings, an older sister and a younger brother. When I was nine years old, we lived down the street from a family who had three boys, all of whom were a little older than I. One day they planned to head to the nearby city park on their bicycles where there was a steep and daring hill to ride down—an adventure sure to thrill any child. The three brothers invited me, their younger neighbor, to join them. I was flattered and could think of no better way to spend a summer afternoon. However, I had a minor problem in that, if I was to go with them, I had to figure out a way to ditch my five-year-old deaf brother. An idea came to me all too quickly. I can remember it as if it were yesterday. Straddling my bike there on the sidewalk in front of our house, I leaned my ear toward the open window and pretended I heard our mom calling. I then turned to my brother and in sign language said, "Mom wants you." As my brother scampered off into the house to check with mom, I felt like a bird released from its cage. My renegade spirit had triumphed, and I rode down the street to join the brothers who were waiting. Together the four of us pedaled our way through a few streets, until we reached the park and its beckoning hill. What a delightful afternoon we had, each of us making several trips up and then gliding down that monstrous hill, hooting and hollering all the way. It was a boy's dream.

However, the fun ended once I returned home later that day. My dad was waiting and called me into the small office he used when he was home. I remember that he did not beat around the bush, but asked me in a straightforward manner, "Did you lie to your brother by telling him that Mom wanted to talk to him?" I am quite sure I dropped my head as I sheepishly replied, "Yes." The spanking followed. I had deceived my brother and there were consequences. My parents wanted to make sure I knew that deception was never acceptable and always carried a serious penalty. Decades later I can testify that their plan worked. I despise deception and often have advised both my sons and my students: Be honest and truthful at any cost. Take the consequences that might come from honesty rather than those that will certainly come later from lying and deception.

Obadiah, the shortest book in the Old Testament, speaks of deception. The book consists of only one chapter, with twenty-one verses. Though it is small, the book carries a big message: unchecked deceit ruins people. Interestingly, rather than addressing God's chosen people directly, the prophet's message here addressed Edom, Israel's southern neighbor and relative. Edom was another name for Esau (see Gen 25:30; 36:1). The Edomites, therefore, were descendants of Esau, the older twin brother of Jacob whose name was changed to Israel. In other words, when traced back through history we discover that Israel and Edom were originally twin brothers, Jacob and Esau. It was to the latter— the Edomites—that the prophet Obadiah voiced his warning regarding deceit. There is a certain irony in this, of course, since Jacob is the one whose name meant "deceiver" (Gen 25:26; 27:36). A careful reading of Genesis reveals that the entire family of Jacob and Esau, beginning with their grandfather Abraham, had a problem with deception. It was a family trait that kept showing up in each new generation. Obadiah, another relatively obscure prophet, had the courage to name the problem here twice (vv 3, 7). Family sins, such as this one, are stubborn and destructive.

Edom was feeling rather smug over Israel's troubles and the devastation the Israelites suffered at the hands of foreign powers. The two brothers had a long history of rivalry, tension, and distrust. Consequently, when Israel fell—first to Assyrian and then Babylonian invaders—Edom took some pleasure in the fact and assumed they were exempt and secure in their remote location south of the Dead Sea. However, they were wrong. They were deceiving themselves. In fact, deceit presents itself in four different ways in Obadiah. Each of them is worthy of attention because deceit continues to operate much the same way today.

The deception of pride. Obadiah is forthright: "The pride of your heart has deceived you" (v 3). Pride always leads to self-deception, promoting the belief that one is far superior to another or more secure than is true. Edom's pride resulted in the question, "Who can bring me down to the ground?" The question reminds us of Solomon's warning that "Pride goes before destruction, a haughty spirit before a fall" (Prov 16:18). The Lord answered the Edomites' question by saying: "I will bring you down" (v 4). We deceive ourselves when we let pride ascend to the throne of our lives. Pride makes us think we cannot be touched by calamity and deludes us into believing we are in control. The truth is that the sovereign God still reigns (see the chapter on Ezekiel), whether we believe it or not. Pride blinds us to that timeless fact, deluding us into thinking we are in charge when we are not.

The deception of friends. Another way that deception comes to us is through others in whom we have placed our trust. Obadiah warns that "your friends will deceive and overpower you" (v 7). Therefore, beware. Those you consider "your allies" and "your friends" (v 7) may not be the people to trust for wisdom and guidance. Betrayal has a long and colorful past. Friends—whether flesh-and-blood or the virtual variety—are not always the best source of information and advice. Sadly, history is littered with those who have taken their marching orders from friends and associates rather than from God himself. Sometimes the deception and its consequences are not evident for years or even decades when sorrow and regret come calling with compound interest.

The deception of silence. Silence, or inactivity, also can deceive us. Failure to commit one way or another gives the illusion of neutrality. We see that often during our national election cycles. Far too many people choose to be silent—by not voting at all—thinking their action (or their inaction) will keep them from being culpable should things go wrong. Obadiah said to the Edomites: "you stood aloof" (v 11). Earlier KJV translators described things this way, "you stood on the other side." You stood by and watched, but said or did nothing while "the violence [occurred] against your brother" (v 10). This is another form of deception. To stand by and watch while refusing to speak up or act makes one complicit in the behavior. We dare not be deceived in this way. The Lord calls us to engagement, not passivity. Idle observation of another's suffering does not excuse us from responsibility. We are misled when we think otherwise.

The deception of revenge. While it is never stated explicitly, the idea of retribution is apparent in Obadiah 12–14. The Edomites were happy to see the "misfortune" (v 12) and "disaster" (v 13) that had befallen their brother to the north and were eager to loot and "seize their wealth." There is an attitude—repeated today and in every generation—that assumes taking revenge against an enemy will right past wrongs and hurts. Unfortunately, it too is a form of deception that leads to a disappointing dead end. Gloating in the troubles endured by others—even one's oppressors—brings no lasting satisfaction or resolution. Near the end of Obadiah, we read "there will be no survivors from the house of Esau" (v 18). This should not surprise us. Any who fall prey to the deception of revenge are doomed to their own destruction. I find it interesting that no one on the international scene today talks about Edom anymore, whereas Israel—despite a history of struggles—continues to be a major force in the world. Do not be deceived. Revenge never pays and ultimately hurts those who seek it.

Deception is more than dishonesty. Whereas the latter is the distortion of truth, the former adds the element of willful intent. To deceive means to lead another astray intentionally and therein lies its greatest harm. Not only is truth misrepresented but also trust is broken. When both truth and trust are lost, an orderly society can no longer exist. Translated, whenever a country and its leaders follow Edom's pattern and succumb to flagrant and repeated deception, that country's very existence is at stake. There are no exceptions—whether that country is named Israel, Edom, America, or any other that comes to mind. The warning of Obadiah is that unchecked deception always spells downfall.

I began this reflection with a personal story. Let me conclude with another. This one involves my father and one of his closest friends, Edsel Bedell. Edsel may have been the most honest man I have ever known. He periodically helped my dad with his auto business in Flint, Michigan. Dad needed cars driven to auctions, dealerships, and elsewhere and often asked his retired friend, Edsel, to help with the operation. It was not uncommon for my dad to hand Edsel a $10 or $20 bill and ask him to stop and put gas in the car he was delivering. Late one evening, just prior to turning out the lights and heading to bed, my dad heard a knock on the door. It was dark outside, and Dad wondered who could possibly be at the door at such a late hour. It was Edsel. He had completed his day's mission and delivered an automobile as requested, but when he got home he realized he still had a nickel left in his pocket after filling the tank with gas. Not wanting to go to bed until he had settled the account, he headed out to return the nickel to my dad. That was the kind of man Edsel was. Integrity mattered to him.

Edsel preceded my dad in death by a few years, but Dad never stopped talking about him. In fact, Dad had so much love and respect for Edsel that he wanted to be buried next to him. Today my father's grave is only a few feet from the grave of his friend Edsel. Every time I visit the cemetery, I smile as I remember these two friends, the nickel, and the integrity that defined their relationship.

The absence of deception is a powerful witness. Let us commit to lives of complete integrity. Jesus was described as one who had no "deceit in his mouth" (Isa 53:9). He would later tell his followers, "Simply let your 'Yes' be 'Yes,' and your 'No,' 'No'" (Matt 5:37).

May we be so trustworthy—even when it only involves a nickel.

PRAYER

Lord, forgive us. Too often we observe or participate in deception to get our own way. At other times we stand aloof and deceive ourselves into thinking there is nothing we can do. We confess our sin. Make us people of integrity in every way, on every platform, in matters big and small. Keep us from Edom's sin described in this brief but important book. May we live like your Son, Jesus Christ, always trustworthy in conversation and conduct. AMEN.

QUESTIONS

1. Why is deception so tempting and common in every generation? Why has it become so widespread at so many levels in our current world? What factors contribute to deceit?

2. Review the thoughts on "silence" and "revenge" above. Can you think of examples in your world when either of these responses have been forms of deceit? Explain.

3. Why is it so painful when you discover you have been deceived? Can you remember a time when someone deceived you? How did that feel? What was your response?

4. Who is one of the most honest people you have ever known? What makes you identify the person this way? Is there a particular example of his or her honesty that you recall?

SUGGESTED READING

Obadiah

32

JONAH: Down

*But Jonah ran away from the LORD and headed for
Tarshish. He went down to Joppa . . . (Jonah 1:3)*

*To the roots of the mountains I sank down; the earth
beneath barred me in forever. (Jonah 2:6)*

Jonah went out and sat down at a place east of the city. (Jonah 4:5)

Anyone who has enjoyed the musical *Les Misérables*—depicting the
Paris Uprising of 1832—will remember the opening song, "Look
Down." The unnerving tune is sung by dejected, worn, pitiful convicts
under the watchful eye of merciless French guards. The lyrics set the
stage for the unfolding drama that follows:

> *Look down, look down*
> *Don't look them in the eye*
> *Look down, look down*
> *You're here until you die*

The song goes on to introduce the two main characters, the protago-
nist Jean Valjean and the antagonist Javert. The doleful conclusion of
the refrain casts a pall over the audience:

> *Look down, look down*
> *You'll always be a slave*

Look down, look down
You're standing in your grave

Now I must confess that these lyrics often come to mind when I walk across a university campus today. It seems that everyone there is looking down. I pass by scores of young people looking down at their phones, rarely looking anyone in the eye. They are mesmerized by the device they hold in their hands and give the impression it is their lifeline to the world and its possibilities. However, these same young people too often appear like slaves, missing opportunities in their world here-and-now—opportunities to greet a fellow human on the sidewalk, to smile at someone who needs encouragement, or to marvel at two butterflies chasing each other around a nearby bush. Instead, they look down, oblivious to what is going on around them. In effect, they are standing in the grave of their own isolation and self-absorption. The tragedy plays out day after day and parallels the opening scene of *Les Mis.*

The phenomenon being described here, however, has a long history. Long before phones were imagined and long before *Les Mis* premiered on Broadway in 1987, Jonah also knew the experience of looking down. He looked down when God called him. He looked down at the deep, dark sea and thought it would serve as his eternal grave. He looked down at his despised enemies, the Ninevites. He even looked down at how God responded to that same enemy. Indeed, Jonah's tendency—or posture—was to look down.

Everyone is familiar with Jonah. The book that bears his name tells his story in four movements:

1. Jonah ran away from the Lord (Jonah 1:3), wanting nothing to do with the mission in Nineveh.

2. Jonah was then swallowed by "a great fish" (1:17), where he spent the next three days and nights before being "vomited . . . onto dry land" (2:10).

3. Given a second chance, Jonah obeyed and eventually went to preach in Nineveh (3:1–3).

4. When the Ninevites repented, Jonah was "displeased and became angry" (4:1) that God would extend compassion to Israel's heartless enemies.

Yes, most of us have been well acquainted with Jonah since our childhood. However, familiarity can sometimes cloud one's vision to important details. Our fascination with the improbability of being swallowed by a whale may have caused us to miss a key, overarching theme that ties together the book of Jonah. A careful reading reveals that Jonah was a person with a downward look and a downward trajectory.

Four times, once in each chapter of the book, Jonah acted in a way that took him down—down in *direction, defeat, decree,* and *despondency.* Each label is descriptive of Jonah's experiences, and each identifies similar trends we witness in the world today. Let me explain.

Direction. "He went down to Joppa" (1:3). God called Jonah to Nineveh, the capital of ancient Assyria (located in modern-day Iraq). The six-hundred-mile trip would have taken a person over land to the northeast. However, Jonah went down to Joppa, a seaport to the west; his ultimate destination was Tarshish, even further west (some speculate as far as Spain). Jonah attempted to get as far from God's call as possible. Any time an individual runs away from God, he is headed on the wrong path and headed downward. Jonah knew it and confessed it to his shipmates (1:10). Scores of people since Jonah have done the same thing. They have gone "down to Joppa" figuratively, hoping to escape God's call. Anyone not seeking and following God's plan is headed down a path that ultimately will lead to disappointment and disaster.

Defeat. "I sank down" (2:6). In order to save the ship and its crew, Jonah was thrown overboard, where he sank down into what he believed would be his watery grave. He had gambled by trying to run away from God and had lost. Defeat slapped him in the face when his body hit the sea. Some of us know that feeling for we, too, have encountered defeat through the loss of a relationship, reputation, or responsibility. We may have sunk down, like Jonah, to the lowest "pit" (2:6) and felt life "ebbing away" (2:7). To his credit, however, Jonah "remembered" the Lord while he was sinking and prayed (2:7). God spared his life—we are told "the fish . . . vomited Jonah onto dry land" (2:10)—and gave him another chance. What takes us down and looks like defeat and failure need not be final. God has a way up and out of the pit when we remember to turn to him.

Decree. "Forty more days and Nineveh will be destroyed" (3:4). Those were the words Jonah decreed when he finally arrived in Nineveh. It was his way of saying, "You Ninevites are going down!" Though Jonah had tried to abort the mission earlier, it must have brought him great joy to make such a declaration. After all, Nineveh was the leading city of Assyria, and the Assyrians were the despised enemies of God's people.

Their strength and brutality endlessly terrorized all their weaker neighbors. Reluctant Jonah must have felt a degree of personal satisfaction to be the voice that foretold Assyria's doom. This rogue nation was finally getting what it deserved. They were going down. Justified punishment awaited them for the atrocities they inflicted on others.

Despondency. "Jonah went out and sat down" (4:5). As he did so, he was "greatly displeased and . . . angry" (4:1). God—who ironically had given Jonah himself a second chance (3:1)—also gave Nineveh a second chance. The despised Ninevites repented (3:5–10) and God, acting out of compassion and love, held back the calamity he intended for them. Jonah then sat down and pouted. It was as if he said: *I knew it, God! I knew you would allow this to happen. First, you pursue and recruit me to do a tough job. Then you disappoint and embarrass me by honoring my enemies.* Despondency and despair overwhelmed Jonah. The wrong people were receiving God's "gracious" (4:2) blessings, while Jonah—who had "obeyed the word of the LORD" (3:3), even if it was delayed obedience—suffered misery and humiliation. Make no mistake about it, Jonah had good reason to be down. The same is true for many of us.

We can easily relate to Jonah. Who among us has not been down at one time or another, perhaps even now? The entire direction of life may feel like it is spiraling *down*. Crumbling circumstances may have us sinking *down* in defeat. In frustration, we may be looking at our adversaries, decreeing—whether publicly or privately—that they are going *down* due to their despicable actions. Our emotional state may be such that we are feeling *down* and despondent. All these descriptions were true of Jonah, to whom God had given his "word" (1:1; 3:1). Apparently, even God's spokesperson was not exempt from the possibility of being down.

If all that is true, is there a word of hope for us? Yes. The writings of Luke, in the New Testament, offer an alternative. If the book of Jonah points downward, the books of Luke and Acts, both authored by Luke, point upward. For example, looking ahead to a time of great "anguish and perplexity" and "terror" (Luke 21:25–26), Luke records these words from Jesus: "stand *up* and lift *up* your heads, because your redemption is drawing near" (Luke 21:28, emphasis added). This is not an isolated reference, for Luke repeatedly emphasizes the value of an upward gaze or movement. Consider that the prodigal son got *up* to go to his father (Luke 15:20); Jesus was taken *up* into heaven (Luke 24:51; Acts 1:9); the disciples looked *up* as Jesus ascended (Acts 1:10); they returned to

Jerusalem and went *up* to a room where they gathered and prayed (Acts 1:13); and Peter stood *up* to address the crowd on the day of Pentecost (Acts 2:14). Luke repeatedly draws his readers' attention upward, away from the clamor and agitations that too easily entangle and distract down here.

Les Misérables ends by raising the sights and aspirations of its audience. One of the musical's major songs is repeated in both the opening and closing acts. It is a song of hope—ensuring the audience that defeat, despair, and despondency are not inevitable. In the finale, the entire cast joins in the crescendo, their voices bursting forth with these lyrics:

Do you hear the people sing
Lost in the valley of the night
It is the music of a people
Who are climbing to the light
For the wretched of the earth
There is a flame that never dies
Even the darkest night will end
And the sun will rise

The meaning is clear; the picture that gets painted is unmistakable. Night and darkness will give way to light and sunrise. No one is destined to spend life looking down; we were designed to climb and soar. Darkness need not be permanent; light is available to those who seek it. Of course, the message appeals to believers who remember that Jesus claimed to be that light. He called himself "the light of the world" (John 8:12; 9:5; 12:46). Our hope is in him.

Jonah is more than a tale of a whale swallowing a man. It is a tale of the tragedy created when someone goes down who could have gone up. What direction are we headed?

PRAYER

Almighty God, we acknowledge our need of you. Left on our own, we are prone to look down. Help us instead to look up and reach up to what you have for us. We are not praying for an emotional "high," but we are praying that you will help us establish a trajectory that represents and honors you, the triumphant Lord. Lift our eyes so we see more of you. Lift our lives so we act more like you. We pray in the name of your Son, Jesus Christ, the light of the world. AMEN.

QUESTIONS

1. What is it that gets you down? What do you do when you are feeling down? What strategies have you found helpful?

2. Do you know people in your circle who are down and discouraged today? How might you encourage them?

3. Why are so many people—even Christians—defeated and despondent today when God promises peace, victory, and abundant life? Is there a way to change that trend? How?

4. If even Jonah, one to whom God spoke and gave his word (1:1; 3:1), knew the experience of being "down," what does that tell us about his chosen servants today?

SUGGESTED READING

Jonah 1–4

33

Mɪᴄᴀʜ: Mercy

He has showed you, O man, what is good. And what does the LORD require of you? To act justly and to love mercy and to walk humbly with your God. (Micah 6:8)

Who is a God like you, who pardons sin and forgives the transgression of the remnant of his inheritance? You do not stay angry forever but delight to show mercy. (Micah 7:18)

You will be true to Jacob, and show mercy to Abraham, as you pledged on oath to our fathers in days long ago. (Micah 7:20)

Everyone wants mercy, but few want to give it. Surprisingly, the book of Micah puts the emphasis on the latter and speaks of the "delight" that comes from "show[ing] mercy" (7:18). Perhaps this explains, in part, why this particular Old Testament book has never been a widely read piece of Christian literature. We like it when others overlook our irritating habits and show us kindness, but we find it difficult to extend the same level of kindness to others. Thus, mercy is hard to give but a joy to receive.

Mercy, by its very nature, has three features. First, *mercy requires a recipient.* An act of mercy must be directed to another person, who is incapable of earning the courteous gesture. It is never directed inward, only outward. Second, *mercy is an act of compassion initiated by the giver.* Kindheartedness and consideration mark the one who offers the gift of mercy. Third, *mercy is undeserved.* It entails granting a blessing to the individual who does not warrant the gracious response and can do nothing to earn it. In summary, mercy includes a recipient, an act of compassion, and a response that is totally unmerited. Mercy is compassion directed to another who does not deserve it and who is often powerless and in distress.

Micah 6:8 is one of the best-known texts in all Scripture on the topic of mercy. It reads as follows:

> He has showed you, O man, what is good. And what does the LORD require of you? To act justly and to love mercy and to walk humbly with your God.

The verse is worth our attention. Our understanding is enhanced by reflecting on some of the key words found here. For example, two words in the first line are insightful, both with roots in Genesis 1. First, the Hebrew word translated "man" is *adam*, which refers to human beings that God created from the ground or earth. Fittingly, of course, the first created human was named Adam. The second word, "good," also is initially found in Genesis 1, where the descriptor was used repeatedly of God's created world. The reader of Micah 6:8 is immediately taken back to creation and reminded of the fact that God had a design for Adam—and for all subsequent human beings—that would result in much good. Just what was that good design or plan? Micah asked the question this way: "And what does the LORD require of you?" The prophet proceeds to answer the question by highlighting three requirements: "to act justly;" "to love mercy;" and "to walk humbly." The first of these is a legal reference to being honest and trustworthy. The second term has to do with the affections of the heart expressed toward another. The third references one's posture or status in the world. A final observation pertains to the Hebrew word for God that comes at the end of the sentence. The term that appears here is *Elohim*, the same name used to describe the Creator in Genesis 1–2. Therefore, we might paraphrase the last sentence this way: *Be honest and trustworthy, prioritize compassion, and live submissively before your Creator, God.*

Every verse of Scripture, of course, exists in a larger context. Micah 6:8 is no different. The reason this verse is so meaningful is because God's people had not been practicing what he intended. Micah was a contemporary of the better-known prophet, Isaiah. Both prophets, writing around 700 BC, warned Israel of God's impending judgment.

Israel's behavior had become abhorrent to God. While attempting to maintain a religious appearance (5:13–14; 6:6–7), God's people were guilty of mistreating their neighbors (2:1–2, 8–9); putting up with corrupt leaders, rulers, priests, and prophets (3:1–3, 11); and employing "dishonest scales," violence, and deceit (6:11–12) when it worked to their benefit. Frankly, they were a mess. Their condition sounds all too familiar, paralleling much of what we experience in our world today. It was out of that wretched and depraved environment that Micah dared declare what God expected from his people: Be honest and just, love mercy, and walk humbly with God.

While all three of these admonitions are worthy of attention, it is the middle declaration—*love mercy*—that is our focus here. The implication is that we should love extending mercy every bit as much as we love receiving it. What might that look like today? Or perhaps, asked another way, who needs mercy in our lives? While we could undoubtedly answer those two questions in several ways, let me suggest three responses:

1. **Show mercy to the one who annoys you.** That person likely annoys others as well. Consequently, he or she is probably rarely on the receiving end when it comes to mercy. What an opportunity to make a difference in that person's life. Someone who loves mercy delights in extending it to the undeserving and unexpecting. What if we determined to be dispensers of mercy to such people?

2. **Show mercy to the one who is painfully insecure.** Insecurity often results from having been harshly criticized or rebuked by significant people at an early and critical juncture in life. Rather than experiencing mercy and encouragement, cruelty and disapproval were probably the normal treatment. Someone who loves mercy looks for ways to offer it to the hurting, wounded, and insecure individual. Is there anyone who needs mercy more than one who is insecure?

3. **Show mercy to the one closest to you.** Most of us dump our own pain, anger, and frustration onto the one closest to us. That person may be a spouse, a child, a sibling, a friend, or a co-worker who listens and shares our burden as his or her own. At times the extra weight—added to one's own personal concerns—feels heavy and unbearable. Someone who loves mercy looks for ways to demonstrate it to the distressed person within

his or her intimate circle of family and friends. When was the last time we extended mercy to, rather than made a request of, that one who is so close to us?

In summary, those who love mercy find pleasure in extending it as well as receiving it. They look for opportunities to brighten another's day or help lift a heavy load. Lovers of mercy serve as angels who pour soothing oil on unsuspecting, vulnerable, worried people. The problem—as was also true in Micah's day—is that there are far too few lovers of mercy, those eager to give it as well as receive it.

I had the fortune during my formative years of living with one who loved mercy: my father. When I was in high school in the early 1970s, my dad worked for an auto dealer in Flint, Michigan. Thus, cars of all kinds—new and used—appeared in our driveway. One day a brand new 1972 Monte Carlo was parked behind the car I was planning to drive to school that morning. I secured the keys to the red Monte Carlo with its striking white leather interior so that I could move it and gain access to the other vehicle. Because I had injured my left leg in a recent high school baseball game, it was difficult to bend my knee. Undeterred and feeling much more competent than I really was, I swung wide the car door and let my left leg hang out the side of the car while backing up. The sickening sound of stressed and scraping metal told me I had made a bad decision. The open door had caught the metal basketball pole encased in concrete next to our driveway, and before I could hit the brakes the door was wrapped around the left front fender of the new car. My dad came running out of the house only to see the auto dealer's Monte Carlo with a new design. I was both humiliated and sickened by what I had done. Though my dad grimaced at the sight, he held his tongue and handed me the keys to the other car lest I be late for school. He responded with mercy.

A few months later I cracked up a 1969 Buick Skylark when I pulled in front of oncoming traffic while making a left turn. The accident was my fault. This time in addition to the ugly sound of metal colliding, the episode included shattered glass spraying my sister and brother who were both passengers in the car, a detailed police report, and a fortunate-to-be-alive outcome. My dad would have been justified in never handing me the keys to another car while living under his roof. However, that was not his response. He once again gave me the gift of mercy. It was totally undeserved, compassionate, and forward-looking.

He knew that a young man was in the making—one who would need to learn from his painful mistakes.

God did the same. Disappointed though he was with Israel's behavior that kept making a mess of things, God's final act is described as one of mercy. At the conclustion of Micah, the last picture a reader has is of God extending mercy to an undeserving, annoying, insecure people who have abandoned him and his covenant. Despite the rejection and failure, the last three verses of the book reveal God's "delight to show mercy" (7:18). It is a mercy that "pardons . . . and forgives" (7:18), offers "compassion" (7:19), and keeps its promise (7:20).

Come to think of it, that pretty much defines mercy for all of us—whether we are on the giving or receiving end. Forgiveness, compassion, and faithfulness are always the central ingredients of mercy.

PRAYER

Our Father in heaven, thank you for your mercy. We are undeserving. At times we are the ones who are annoying and insecure. Yet the nature of mercy is that you still choose to extend it to us under those circumstances. We are grateful for your forgiveness, compassion, and faithfulness. Now help us to love mercy so much that we find delight in extending the same to others. May forgiveness, compassion, and faithfulness—even when it is unwarranted—become our primary response to those around us. Make us more like Jesus, who exhibited all these qualities. We offer this prayer in his name. AMEN.

QUESTIONS

1. What example comes to mind of someone who has shown you mercy? How did that extension of mercy feel at the time? What was your reaction?

2. Who do you know—perhaps an individual or an entire group—that needs mercy right now? How might you demonstrate mercy to that individual or group?

3. Why is it so hard to extend mercy to someone who is annoying? To someone who is insecure? To someone who is close to you?

4. When have you most been aware of the mercy of God in your own life? What were the circumstances? Have you adequately thanked him?

Suggested Reading

Micah 1–7

34

NAHUM: Anger

*The LORD is slow to anger and great in power; he will
not leave the guilty unpunished. (Nahum 1:3)*

*Who can withstand his indignation? Who can endure
his fierce anger? His wrath is poured out like fire; the
rocks are shattered before him. (Nahum 1:6)*

We need to correct our faulty view of God. Too often God's people develop a caricature of him that is inaccurate. J. B. Phillips thought so in 1952 when he wrote the helpful little book, *Your God Is Too Small*. I have read the volume multiple times over the years to adjust my own understanding of God. Today a sequel is needed, entitled *Your God Is Too Soft*. We have largely remade God into a doting grandpa or jolly ole St. Nick, void of any backbone or conviction. Thus, we are stunned or offended when anyone suggests God may be angry. If that describes you, Nahum probably should not be added to your reading list any time soon.

Nahum is another short book tucked away in what we are calling the appendix of the Old Testament. The book cannot be understood properly without reference to the two books that precede it, Jonah and Micah. The book of Jonah provides important information and context regarding Nineveh, which is also the subject of Nahum. In fact, no two books in all Scripture mention Nineveh, the capital of Assyria in the seventh and eighth centuries BC, more than these two small books of prophecy. Jonah, against his will, went to Nineveh along the Tigris River and warned the people there of God's plan to destroy the city (Jon 3). To Jonah's dismay, the Ninevites repented; God withheld his judgment (Jon 4). However, after Assyria returned to its wicked and cruel ways (see Nah 3:19), invaded the land of Israel, and took its people captive in the early 700s BC, it too was destroyed. The anger and wrath of God were poured out on Nineveh, paving the way for Babylon to become the region's new power.

Micah provides further context for understanding Nahum's message. As noted last time, Micah ends with God's promise of mercy. There is a tendency, then, to assume that God responds with mercy to his people Israel, while responding with anger to his enemies—whether they be the Assyrians, the Babylonians, the Philistines, or any other group. The problem with such thinking is that it is not supported by the rest of Scripture. God's anger is witnessed multiple times throughout both the Old and New Testaments, and it is not restricted to his enemies. More often than not, God's people are the ones who provoke him to anger. Thus, a better interpretation of the apparent contradiction between Micah's picture of mercy and Nahum's portrayal of anger is this: it is possible to hold both characteristics simultaneously. Both are descriptive of God (see Hab 3:2). Just as God's mercy is a repeated theme of Scripture, so is his anger. We misrepresent God when we fail to recognize either of these characteristics. Any parent knows that both mercy and anger can co-exist.

What does Nahum teach us? Why is this three-chapter book that references an ancient, long-lost, foreign city surrounded by a barren desert even preserved in Scripture? What value does it hold for future generations? What lessons ought we learn? Several observations are worthy of our attention.

God gets angry (1:2). Though this book is primarily about the Assyrians who inhabit Nineveh, the prophet makes clear it is Israel's God—not an Assyrian god—who is angry. The anger and wrath noted here come from the LORD. The Hebrew word is "Yahweh," the great "I am" of Exodus 3:14, who was distinguished from all other gods. Lest anyone miss this point, Yahweh is mentioned ten times in chapter one alone; five of those references occur in the first three verses of the book. Nahum wants it known far and wide: the Judeo-Christian God, Yahweh, *does* get angry.

God is slow to get angry (1:3). Equally important, however, is the fact that God is "slow to anger." God does not suddenly fly into a fit of rage when he witnesses an offense. He does not throw a temper tantrum. Peter would later write: "The Lord is . . . patient with you, not wanting anyone to perish, but everyone to come to repentance" (2 Pet 3:9). God's anger does not get roused easily. He does not have a short fuse. Those who see God this way have made the mistake of attributing a human tendency to Almighty God.

God has power to act on his anger (1:3). Not only does Nahum report that Yahweh is "great in power," but the Hebrew word that gets translated "God" (1:2) is *el*, meaning "the mighty one." There is good reason to fear the anger and wrath of God. He is not a wimp whose weakness leaves him impotent and merely shaking his head in disgust. God is mighty, capable of acting when he is angry. The Hebrew word for anger, *aph*, is the same term used for nose or nostrils. The picture that emerges here, then, is of a God who flares his nostrils and unleashes his power when he is angry.

God's anger is often witnessed in nature (1:3–6). We ought not miss the multiple allusions to nature in these opening verses. God's anger—or "his way" (1:3)—is found in "the whirlwind," "the storm," "clouds" (1:3), "the sea," "the rivers" (1:4), "the mountains [that] quake," "the hills [that] melt away," "the earth [that] trembles" (1:5), and "the rocks [that] are shattered before him" (1:6). Of course, when God is ignored all these events are explained away as mere coincidence or as predictable outcomes of natural forces. Nahum suggests there may be a supernatural explanation resulting from the anger of a sovereign God. Centuries later Jesus himself taught his followers to look for signs of God's activity in nature all around them (see Matt 16:1–4; Luke 21:25).

God's anger is fierce (1:6). God's anger ought not be taken lightly. It is described here as "fierce anger," meaning a burning anger. The same description occurs back in Jonah (3:9). However, lest one assume God's fierce anger is reserved only for the Assyrians and other loathsome enemies, Scripture repeatedly uses the phrase to refer to how God feels toward his own people when they continually disobey him and sin (e.g., Ex 32:12; Num 25:4; Deut 13:17; 2 Chron 28:11; Jer 4:8; Zeph 2:2). God's anger, though slowly roused, is severe.

God's anger does not negate his goodness and mercy (1:7). After beginning his prophetic word by warning of God's anger, Nahum reminds the reader that God is "good" and "cares for those who trust in him." Given how contemporary culture has distorted so much of our thinking and made us all paranoid and fragile, this may seem like a contradiction. How can anyone who is angry be good? The problem is our flawed understanding of the nature of anger, goodness, and God. As we noted earlier, anger does not cancel his mercy. God's nature is good. In fact, it is *because* God is good that he responds in anger to that which is not good, which leads to the final observation.

God's anger is the result of nonstop wickedness (3:19). Nahum concludes by pointing out the Ninevites' "endless cruelty." The older *King James Version of the Bible* renders this "wickedness . . . continually." The people were guilty of perpetual evil. God withheld his anger and punishment once (see Jon 3–4), but a century later the Ninevites returned to their evil ways and provoked the anger and wrath of God. Their wickedness took the form of plotting against God (1:9–11), serving other gods (1:14), lying (3:1), mistreating others (3:1–3), prostitution and witchcraft (3:4). God is slow to anger, but nonstop wickedness eventually will be met by his fierce wrath.

Let us consider once again our view, or understanding, of God. When we erroneously make God too soft on sin, at least two problems arise—one is theological, the other is sociological. God's anger at persistent sin is always appropriate and has a theological basis. To think otherwise—to assume that God tolerates what is unholy and accepts sinful behavior because he is benevolent and sympathetic—does harm to the entire gospel message. If sin is irrelevant and getting angry over it is nothing but misguided legalism or emotionalism, then it brings into question the cross that stands at the center of our faith. Implied here is that God the Father made a mistake by sending his Son to be crucified; Jesus need not have died on the cross for the sins of the world. Going soft on sin leads to this conclusion. No wonder Scripture emphasizes repeatedly that persistent sin does indeed anger God. A heavy price was paid for sin. God's people dare not presume his mercy is without limits. Yes, God is slow to anger (1:3), but he does exhibit "fierce anger" (1:6) when "endless cruelty," wickedness, and sin prevail (3:19). God's anger toward sin demanded the cross for our redemption.

There are also sociological ramifications for going soft on sin and the anger it produces. William Bennett, whose 1993 *Book of Virtues* was referenced when we took up the theme of "courage" as we looked at Daniel, wrote another book entitled *The Death of Outrage* (1998). Though the book was written in response to a White House scandal in the mid-1990s, it focused a spotlight on the fact that no one seems to get upset or angry anymore when our leaders engage in immoral failure and then lie attempting to cover up the failure. Instead, there is a collective yawn. Bennett's thesis was that there are certain things that should anger us. This may seem counterintuitive in a world where anger is routinely expressed. Our streets, schools, political rallies, and social media are filled with anger today. We do not need more anger, do we? A case could be made that we already have too much anger threatening civility and destroying communities. Outrage has not died but exploded everywhere.

While anger does indeed seem to be intensifying and ruining our social fabric, it raises an important question: *Why* are so many people angry? What are its roots? Anger is rarely aimed at sin and moral corruption that shakes a fist in the face of God. Rather, what angers us today is someone having the audacity to question, criticize, or tell us what we are doing is harmful and wrong. We become angry when our rights get violated or even threatened. No longer do we share a common sense of propriety, morality, and decency. No longer do we get angry at sin that offends God. No longer do we respond with indignation when wickedness flourishes and self-centered desires reject his sovereignty. Ironically, our outrage is aimed not at sin but at the one who offends us by telling us we ought not sin.

Know this: God does get angry. Nahum reminds us of that fact. We, too, ought to get angry at times. Paul offered a caution, however, when he addressed the Ephesians (4:26): "'In your anger do not sin': Do not let the sun go down while you are still angry." Anger itself is not the problem. The problem is how we respond and our tendency to let anger fester rather than taking action to resolve it. To be Godlike is to know anger, its cause, and how to respond appropriately.

PRAYER

Our Father, forgive us for growing too soft on sin. And forgive us for getting angry, but for the wrong reasons. Help us to get angry at what offends you, not at what offends us or seems to limit our rights and privileges. Make us more like you—good and merciful while slow to anger. We pray all this in the name of your Son, and our Model and Savior, Jesus Christ. AMEN.

QUESTIONS

1. What makes you angry? Why? What do you do with anger when it rises within you?

2. Who have you witnessed become angry and then respond in an appropriate and healthy way? What did you learn from that experience?

3. Why does the Church rarely acknowledge the anger of God these days? What factors have led to ignoring this characteristic of God?

4. Are there other theological problems that result when we make God too soft? If so, what are they? Do other social problems emerge when we make God too soft?

SUGGESTED READING

Nahum 1–3

35

HABAKKUK: Waiting

How long, O LORD, must I call for help, but
you do not listen? (Habakkuk 1:2)

For the revelation awaits an appointed time; it speaks of the
end and will not prove false. Though it linger, wait for it; it
will certainly come and will not delay. (Habakkuk 2:3)

Yet I will wait patiently for the day of calamity to come on
the nations invading us. Though the fig tree does not bud and
there are no grapes on the vines, though the olive crop fails
and the fields produce no food, though there are no sheep in the
pen and no cattle in the stalls, yet I will rejoice in the LORD,
I will be joyful in God my Savior. (Habakkuk 3:16–18)

H ow long? How long will this continue? How long until we get there?
Some form of this question has been asked countless times over the
years. The question is asked frequently by children traveling with their
parents. However, its origins are ancient and not limited to children.
The question was asked here by Habakkuk as he began his prophecy
(1:2; also 2:6). It was asked by Moses and Aaron when they stood before
Pharaoh (Ex 10:3). Joshua asked it of the Israelites in the promised land
(Josh 18:3). Job asked the question when suffering under the weight of
his burdens (Job 7:4; 19:2). It was asked by David the psalmist (Ps 6:3;
13:1). The prophet Isaiah raised the question (Isa 6:11), as did Jeremiah
(4:14, 21; 13:27). God himself even asked the question of his rebellious

people (Num 14:11), as did Jesus in the New Testament (Matt 17:17). Yes, the question is familiar and usually indicates some degree of frustration. No one wants to wait.

Becky and Chad, my niece and nephew, did not want to wait on Christmas morning nearly forty years ago. Like all young children, their hearts raced when they went to bed on Christmas Eve. Though their parents coached them to get good sleep and wait for the family to gather around the tree in the morning, their excitement made sleep nearly impossible. In the early morning hours, while it was still pitch dark and before anyone else stirred, young Becky and Chad rose and together quietly approached the family Christmas tree surrounded by its beautifully wrapped presents. The temptation was strong, and soon they sat down and began opening presents. They had the distinct advantage of having deaf parents (my sister and her husband), so noise and squeals went unheard during those early morning hours that Christmas. Too young to practice restraint on their own or to know which presents were for whom, they proceeded to open every single present that had been so neatly wrapped and stacked against the tree—even those intended for their mom, dad, and relatives who would be joining them later in the day. When the parents finally awakened sometime later and made their way to the living room, they were stunned. Every gift was opened, many had already been examined and used, and wrapping paper littered the floor. Needless to say, the parents, who had missed it all, were not very happy with their children and their inability to wait.

Habakkuk wrote about some of the challenges associated with waiting. Another relatively unknown prophet who was a contemporary of Jeremiah, Habakkuk lived during the time when the Babylonians invaded the promised land (Hab 1:6). God's people were under siege when the prophet cried out in desperation (1:2), "How long, LORD, must I call for help, but you do not listen?" Later, the abuse suffered at the hands of the enemy elicited a follow-up question (2:6): "How long must this go on?" Waiting for relief—whether it was God's people who were oppressed under the cruel hands of the Babylonians, the Israelites who experienced earlier mistreatment and needed a deliverer in Egypt, or poor Job who called out to God after he suffered devastating personal loss—is a common theme found across the pages of the Old Testament. The New Testament also highlights waiting, perhaps nowhere more clearly than when Jesus instructed his followers to "stay in the city" of Jerusalem (Luke 24:49) and "wait for the gift my Father promised" (Acts 1:4)—a reference, of course, to the gift of the Holy Spirit. The message was to stay put and not hurry on until God had accomplished his purpose.

Waiting has always been difficult, but arguably never so much as in recent times when we have grown accustomed to instant gratification. Today we have instant coffee, instant meals in our microwaves, instant communication via texting, instant credit, instant divorce, instant delivery thanks to Amazon, and more. Waiting has gone the way of the transistor radio, a relic of the past that produces a great deal of static and is uncommon to our daily experience.

Furthermore, waiting is hard because it is so passive. We are doers and problem-solvers. We do not have time to sit down and wait while golden opportunities bypass us. If only Jesus had instructed his disciples to do more than "watch and pray" (Matt 26:41) in Gethsemane. Those poor guys needed a project to occupy them. They needed a puzzle to solve, a building to construct, or an escape plan to design. Anything would have been helpful in passing the time. Jesus told them just to sit there and "watch and pray." Are you kidding me? That was one of the most impossible requests ever made of mortal man!

And yet the message of Habakkuk is that there are times when God's people must wait. Two specific scenarios are noted here. First, Habakkuk was instructed to wait for the full "revelation" of God to come at its "appointed time" (2:3). At such times, "the righteous will live by his faith" (2:4), not knowing all that God has in store in the days ahead. The unfolding plan of God is rarely revealed quickly or all at once for an individual or nation; resolve and steadfastness are needed.

Second, Habakkuk also declared his intention to "wait patiently for the day of calamity to come on" those determined to bring them harm (3:16), choosing to keep his eyes fixed on "the Sovereign LORD," his "strength" (3:19). God is to be trusted to deal with those who oppose us when he deems it appropriate. We are not to take these matters into our own hands. Both scenarios, of course, are instructive and call us to do the same.

Unfortunately, the human struggle or unwillingness to wait comes with a price tag. There are valuable lessons lost when we do not recognize the need to linger. On the other hand, those who learn the secret of waiting discover its shaping potential and positive influence on our posture toward God, our prayer life, our preparation for important events, and our perspective during adversity.

Our posture toward God. Waiting communicates that we are not in charge; God is. The timing of events is under his control, not ours. Thus, when we wait, we signal to those around us—as well as to ourselves—that we have surrendered decision-making power to Almighty God. Our waiting is an act of submission, positioning ourselves under divine lordship and accepting God's will for our use of time. Those who have learned to wait have a posture of humility.

Our prayer life. How often do we stop to think that every time we are forced to wait we are being offered a gift? That gift is time—time to reflect and pray to, or communicate with, the sovereign Lord. Over the years I have heard many Christians remark that they wish they had more time to pray. What if we began disciplining ourselves to turn our waiting moments and hours every day, or our sleepless moments and hours every night, into prayer time? Imagine how different life might become. We probably have more time to pray than we realize if we would just take advantage of our waiting moments.

Our preparation for important events. In a world of speed and efficiency, fewer and fewer people take time to prepare well. The lack of sufficient preparation is evident in public presentations, written assignments, musical performances, athletic contests, remodeling projects, financial planning, and more. It takes a lot of hard work to do something well; the preparation required to create a prized final product may take hours, days, or even months. The reality is much preparation can occur in the down time wherein we are waiting for something else. Our inability to harness waiting time and transform it into preparation time results in a tragic loss of potential never to be regained.

Our perspective during adversity. Waiting offers us a chance to check our attitude. Habakkuk confessed he was waiting for calamity to befall Babylon because the latter was invading his homeland (3:16). He anticipated personal deprivation, shortages, loss of income, and a bleak future (3:17). Despite the gloomy forecast, however, he came to this conclusion: "yet I will rejoice in the LORD, I will be joyful in God my Savior" (3:18). Though he waited for God to deal with his enemies and for the conditions of life to improve, Habakkuk determined that the waiting would not conquer his spirit. His outlook would still be marked by optimism, joy, and trust in the sovereign Lord. Whereas some people grumble when they wait, Habakkuk chose to rejoice. Every time we wait, we have a choice to make.

While waiting is universally disliked, it is often God's tool to help us mature. It is an instrument by which we learn to surrender control, increase our communication with God, find time to revise or improve a piece of work, or demonstrate a winsome and victorious spirit even when life is not going as we planned. Few of us see waiting through this lens, however, and our disdain for delay ends up hurting us all. Drivers elicit honks, gestures, scowls, and rage from those who are in a hurry. Neighbors know the contempt of an icy glare for not having manicured a lawn up to community standards. Family members hear the criticism and disgust when they are the ones perceived to keep others waiting for a meal or outing. No one wants to be inconvenienced in the least by having to wait. Because we want to control our use of time, we feel justified in letting others know of our displeasure at the slightest delay.

What if we changed our view on waiting? A careful reading of Scripture indicates God's people have always been asked to do a lot of waiting, learning valuable lessons in the process. In fact, his people still wait—in anticipation of the Lord's glorious return.

Wait and *waste* ought not to be viewed as synonyms. We are admonished to "redeem the time" (Eph 5:16, KJV)—yes, even while we wait.

PRAYER

O Sovereign Lord, we confess how hard it is to wait. We have needs and desires that we bring to you—because you invite us to do so—and yet sometimes we feel as though the response is slow in coming our way. We wait, but not always with good attitudes. Forgive us. We humbly ask you to speak to us, sustain us, and send your Spirit to us as our constant counselor and comforter. Help us to maintain our uncompromising devotion to you, even when it feels like the waiting is long. May we use those periods of delay to draw closer to you. May our posture, our prayers, our preparation, and our perspective all demonstrate that we have not wasted the time you have given us. We offer this prayer in Jesus's name. AMEN.

Questions

1. What is one of the hardest things for which you have ever had to wait? How did you handle the experience of waiting? Looking back, what might you have done differently?

2. How does contemporary culture add to the difficulty of waiting? What factors make waiting so hard today? What practical things can be done to help us overcome these challenges?

3. What are some examples of God's people waiting in the pages of Scripture? Why do you think God, who is all-powerful and capable of the instantaneous miracle, so often calls upon his people to wait? What is his purpose in having people wait?

4. Four possible benefits of waiting were noted: improved posture, prayer, preparation, and perspective. Which of these benefits have you witnessed in your own life? Are there other advantages, or lessons, that result from having to wait?

Suggested Reading

Habakkuk 1–3

36

ZEPHANIAH: Day

Be silent before the Sovereign LORD, for the day
of the LORD is near. (Zephaniah 1:7)

The great day of the LORD is near—near and coming quickly. Listen!
The cry on the day of the LORD will be bitter . . . (Zephaniah 1:14)

The LORD . . . does no wrong. Morning by morning he dispenses
his justice, and every new day he does not fail . . . (Zephaniah 3:5)

On that day they will say to Jerusalem, "Do not fear, O Zion;
do not let your hands hang limp. The LORD your God is
with you, he is mighty to save." (Zephaniah 3:16–17)

Do you have a day that is etched in your memory? If so, what is it? Why do you remember that day? As a child I often heard my elders speak of December 7, 1941. The day—President Roosevelt called it "a date which will live in infamy"—marked the Japanese attack on Pearl Harbor that drew the United States into World War II. Sixty years later, a new generation carried memories of September 11, 2001, when terrorists hijacked airplanes and flew them into buildings in New York City and Washington, D.C. Who could forget that day? Others refer to the day President John F. Kennedy was assassinated—November 22, 1963. Diehard Chicago Cub fans will never forget November 2, 2016, the day the team ended over one hundred years of futility by winning the World Series. The series ended with a dramatic extra-inning win in the seventh and final game. My extended family will never forget March 28, 2006, the day my fifty-two-year-old sister died of multiple myeloma; ironically, it also marked the day that her first grandchild—a little girl—was born. For us Olneys it was a time of conflicting emotions, a day never to be forgotten.

Most of us can point to certain days that hold special meaning in our lives, both good and bad. In fact, sometimes the good and bad both occur on the same day, as was true for my family when my sister died and her first grandchild was born within hours of each other. Zephaniah described such a day in his short book near the end of the Old Testament. The day he described—"the day of the LORD" (1:7, 14)—would come as both a day of judgment and a day of salvation. The longer I live the more I realize every day holds the potential for good or bad, virtue or evil. Furthermore, the opportunities we have each day are unique to that day, likely never to be repeated. The book of Zephaniah, while pointing forward to a particular day, reminds us of the value contained in every day.

Zephaniah is the only prophet in the Bible identified as being born of royal blood. He opens his book by describing himself as a descendant of King Hezekiah (1:1). Perhaps it was his family background—concerned with royal ceremonies, decrees, and a calendar of important events—that caused Zephaniah to focus on the potential found in a day. All we know for sure is that he referenced the word *day* twenty-one times in his three chapters—fourteen of those references occur in the opening chapter, and six of the references are found in verse 15 alone. Zephaniah's focus was not on a century, decade, year, month, or even a week; he spoke of a single day. Of course, that is how life unfolds: one day at a time. For Zephaniah, a day could bring judgment, salvation, or a new opportunity. Let us consider all three of these possibilities.

Day of judgment. Most of the references to "day" found in Zephaniah are associated with God's judgment against his people. In other words, there was coming a day of punishment (1:8, 9, 12), wailing (1:10), and bitterness (1:14). Wrath, distress, anguish, trouble, ruin, darkness, gloom, clouds, and blackness were also descriptive of that coming day (1:15). Many Bible scholars date that day of judgment against the Israelites as the time when they suffered attack, defeat, and captivity under the hands of the Babylonians. Interestingly, however, New Testament writers Paul (Rom 2:16), Peter (2 Pet 2:9; 3:7), John (1 John 4:17), and Jude (6) all talked about another "day of judgment." Jesus also referenced such a day (Matt 10:15; 11:22, 24; John 12:48). One cannot escape the fact that a day of judgment is central to the Bible's message. The theme of judgment was considered earlier, when reflecting on the book of Amos. The prophets recognized there was coming a day when accounts would be settled, and God would punish those who had turned from him in disobedience. A day of judgment is in our future; no one is exempt.

Day of salvation. While most of Zephaniah's three chapters speak of that future day in terms of judgment, the book also speaks of it as a day of salvation and restoration for those who "trust in the name of the LORD" (3:12). There will be a "remnant" (3:13) "on that day" (3:16) who will find God "is mighty to save" (3:17). Consequently, that coming day will bring both good and bad, hope and despair. For some it will mean judgment for rejecting God; for others it will mean salvation for turning to God. The dual possibilities of good and bad noted earlier will mark this day as well. Those who have placed their trust in God will "sing" and "rejoice," knowing that "the LORD has taken away [their] punishment" (3:14–15) and restored their "fortunes" (3:20). What a celebration will occur on that day of salvation!

In 1955, Jim Hill wrote a song that described Zephaniah's hope. The tune quickly grew in popularity and was sung by several quartets and other artists in subsequent years. Eventually Hill's song was even included in a few hymnbooks. Many will recognize the lyrics:

> *What a day that will be*
> *When my Jesus I shall see*
> *And I look upon his face*
> *The one who saved me by his grace*
> *When he takes me by the hand*
> *And leads me through the Promised Land*
> *What a day, glorious day, that will be*

Indeed, a glorious day of salvation awaits those whose trust is in the Lord. It will be a day like no other, filled with singing and rejoicing in gratitude for eternal salvation.

Day of opportunity. A third type of day is implied in the book of Zephaniah. We might call it a day of opportunity. The prophet writes: "The LORD . . . is righteous; he does no wrong. Morning by morning he dispenses his justice, and every new day he does not fail . . ." (3:5). It is as if Zephaniah wants to communicate to his readers not to focus so exclusively on a future day of judgment and salvation that today and its opportunities are missed. God is at work every day. "Morning by morning" he engages his created world and generously bestows justice (i.e., "he does no wrong"). "Every new day" the Lord proves himself reliable (i.e., "he does not fail"). What a shame it would be to miss an encounter with him today. Every morning we awaken to another opportunity to embrace and enjoy the goodness of God. We are required neither to be in a certain place, nor to be part of a designated crowd, nor are we limited to special holy days on the calendar. *Every* new day presents opportunities to see God at work and to join him in that work. The possibilities that fill a day are limitless.

"The day of the Lord" is a repeated theme that extends far beyond Zephaniah. The phrase is found in nine of the sixteen prophets, from Isaiah to Malachi. Even the prophets who do not use the phrase verbatim still reference the day in some fashion. Any time something occurs so frequently in God's Word, we ought to pay close attention to it. The message is clear: a day is coming when we will meet God and give a full account of our life here on earth. Both Old and New Testament writers pointed to such a day. We dare not minimize and miss this important scriptural truth. Those who are wise will prepare and be ready for that day—the day of judgment and salvation.

However, careful Bible readers soon realize that its authors also use a similar reference to "day" in other contexts. For example, after the resurrection of Jesus, "the day of the Lord" came to carry another important connotation. "The Lord's Day" (Rev 1:10) signified the day the church gathered to celebrate and worship the risen Christ. Following the pattern of God at the time of creation, one day a week was set aside to rest, worship the Lord, and fellowship with other believers. This became the universal practice for all believers, reflecting their shared desire to follow God's example by taking one day in seven for rest, to commemorate the resurrection that occurred on the first day of the week, and to honor Christ as supreme by giving him that same first day of each week.

There is yet another sense wherein biblical writers emphasize *every* day as being the day of the Lord. God is the Creator of all our days. The psalmist (118:24) penned these words: "This is the day the LORD has made; let us rejoice and be glad in it." While acknowledging the coming great day of the Lord—to judge and to save eternally—and while pausing on the first day of every week to express gratitude for the resurrection, believers see every day as God's gift. The gift is ripe with potential and opportunities. Though circumstances may enter the day that are beyond our control, we have a choice when it comes to how we respond to each day. We can do what is virtuous and helpful or what is wicked and harmful. Paul recognized this fact when he wrote the following: "Be very careful, then, how you live—not as unwise but as wise, making the most of every opportunity, because the days are evil" (Eph 5:15–16). The apostle Paul acknowledged the existence of evil in our fallen world but believed wise people could still live their days virtuously and victoriously.

Whatever a day brings, we have a choice in how we will respond and live within its parameters. In truth, every day is filled with opportunities for judgment or salvation, birth or death, encouragement or despair. What choice will we make today?

I will never forget March 28, 2006. Not only was that the day my loving sister died just after her first grandchild was born, but it was the day that I learned firsthand that the seeds for birth and death exist in *all* our days. "Morning by morning" we get to decide how to live each "new day." May God, the one who "does no wrong" and "does not fail," help us choose wisely (3:5).

This day is God's singular, never-to-be-repeated gift. May we not squander it.

Prayer

Lord, we thank you for the days of our lives. Through them you have given us meaning and purpose. You have granted us relationships and commitments to keep us steady. You have bestowed on us the favors of health and resources. Indeed, our days are filled with your bountiful blessings. Therefore, with the psalmist we pray that you, O Lord, would "teach us to number [and use] our days aright, that we may gain a heart of wisdom" (Ps 90:12), be a winsome witness to others, and please and honor you in all that we do. May our days count for your glory and lead us to eternity with you. AMEN.

QUESTIONS

1. Some biblical themes are popular in one era but not in another. Why do you think we hear so little about the coming "day of the Lord" in this generation?

2. What particular day is etched into your memory? Why? What makes that day so memorable? What lifelong lessons did it teach you?

3. What new opportunities might this very day hold for you? Are you able to enumerate some of them? What evidence is there in this day that God "does not fail?"

4. Can a person really choose how he or she approaches a new day? How does that happen? How can one experience and exude life rather than death in his or her days? What advice might you offer to help make that a reality for someone else?

SUGGESTED READING

Zephaniah 1–3

37

HAGGAI: Thoughts

*Now this is what the LORD Almighty says: "Give
careful thought to your ways." (Haggai 1:5, 7)*

*Now give careful thought to this from this day on—
consider how things were before one stone was laid
on another in the LORD's temple. (Haggai 2:15)*

*From this day on . . . give careful thought to the
day when the foundation of the LORD's temple was
laid. Give careful thought . . . (Haggai 2:18)*

A *Christmas Carol*, written by English novelist Charles Dickens in
1843, is a universally loved story. The main character, Ebenezer
Scrooge, is forced to think about his life when the spirits of Christmas
past, present, and yet-to-come visit him. Though each visit is unsettling,
they eventually combine to transform Scrooge from a miserable miser to
a gentler and more benevolent man. The story has become an annual reminder that there is hope if one changes his outlook, the way he thinks.

Dickens was not alone in his concern regarding how people approach, or think about, life. Apparently, the Lord shared that same
concern. For in the book of Haggai, the second shortest of the Old Testament books (only Obadiah is shorter), on five different occasions the
Lord mentions giving "careful thought" (1:5, 7; 2:15, 18, 18) to important issues. The King James Version uses the word *consider*, translat-

ing a Hebrew phrase that includes the word *heart*. Careful thinking comes from deep within a person, from the heart. In English we have expressions that encourage people to "put their heart into a matter" or to "take a matter to heart." The meaning in either case implies seriousness. Giving careful thought requires an intentional and sober focus. That is the implication behind Haggai's repeated admonition.

We have at least two problems, however, when it comes to our thought life today. First, our busy and materialistic lifestyles distract us from too much careful thinking. We have become doers and responders rather than thinkers. The latter requires too much time; we prefer simply to get the job done. There is personal satisfaction when we act quickly, even if that action—ironically—is nothing more than posting a random thought. We have grown accustomed to responding without much deep thought and without seeking godly counsel. Second, the content of our thought life is influenced by the constant stream of news, pictures, and social media posts that fill our days. What we feed our minds influences our thought life. Let me illustrate.

Several year ago, when both of my sons went off to college, I went on a forty-day fast from TV. I unplugged it and ended up leaving it that way beyond the forty days. I also had no cell phone at the time and limited computer access. That experience changed how I spent my time (I became an avid reader), how I viewed my wife (she became more beautiful in my eyes), and renewed my relationship with the Lord (there was more space for me to listen to him). Our eyes and ears are the doorways to our minds. It is nearly impossible to have the "noble" thoughts that Paul advised (see Phil 4:8) when we are regularly bombarded with pornographic-like images, sensational and malicious news reports, and posts from friends and associates that make us either envious or angry. Careful thought takes time and discipline, both of which seem to be in short supply in twenty-first-century America.

The message of Haggai, like messages from most Old Testament prophets, is countercultural. We are not asked to do what is easy but what is beneficial. Pausing to "give careful thought" to what God may be saying and doing is as needed today when Afghanistan, Iran, and Iraq are making headlines as it was during Haggai's day when God's people were dealing with Assyria and Babylon in the same part of the world. Think about it.

We have been calling the last twenty-two books of the Old Testament (Job through Malachi) an appendix that supplements and supports the first seventeen books (Genesis through Esther). Haggai is a small book that fits into the story that unfolds in Ezra (see Ezra 4:24; 5:1; 6:14). The prophet Haggai, in 520 BC, had a word from God for those who had returned to Jerusalem from their Babylonian exile. His message—like the one that came to the character Scrooge—had three parts that called for carefully thinking about the present, the past, and the future. Haggai's two-chapter book might be outlined using these three categories.

Give careful thought to your present ways (1:5, 7). The first chapter of Haggai focuses on present circumstances. Though many of God's people were back home in Jerusalem, rather than stuck in distant Babylon, life was still not what they—or God—hoped it would be. Consequently, God spoke to them through his prophet Haggai, calling them to give careful thought to three significant areas of their lives. First, their *priorities* needed attention. The people were more concerned about their own "paneled houses" than they were about God's house that "remain[ed] a ruin" (1:4). Anytime our comforts take precedence over God's work it is time to "give careful thought to [our] ways" (1:5).

Second, their *practices* were benefitting no one (1:6). Nothing they did led to satisfaction or lasting gain. God made clear that he was not about to bless them and their practices until they made *him* their uncontested priority (1:9–11). Giving careful thought to practices, habits, and patterns is needed in every generation. The process helps us see where change is needed in our lives.

Adjusting priorities and practices may have been the easy part. The third area that needed attention had to do with listening to and obeying their *prophets*. God had "sent" Haggai with a message and "the people obeyed" (1:12). While that sounds good, the truth of the matter is God had been raising up and sending numerous prophets over the years— Isaiah, Jeremiah, Amos, Micah, and Zephaniah, just to name a few—and God's people had largely ignored them. That is why the Israelites landed in exile; their trouble was a result of their defiance. Dare I say it? That is why God's people across the years have often found themselves in trouble. They ignore the prophets' message; they ignore the word of God. May God help us give careful thought regarding how we treat the prophets today (i.e., God's word that comes through his messengers). The written word of the ancient prophets and the spoken word of those God raises up in our times are intended for our instruction and guidance. Let us "give careful thought" to what they say. Priorities, practices, and prophets still need attention. What was true in the sixth century BC is no less true in this century

Give careful thought to your past days (2:1–5). Whereas Haggai 1 focuses on the present, Haggai 2 invites the reader to consider both the past and the future. The second chapter begins by drawing attention to Israel's past. Three emphases are made: the glory of the former temple (2:3), the repeated admonition to "be strong" (2:4), and a reminder of their Egyptian experience (2:5). These were reminders of past glory, past courage, and past deliverance. There was a time when the magnificent temple in Jerusalem, built by Solomon (1 Kgs 6–8), was the talk of the land. God's glory was known to inhabit the place. That was worth remembering. Then three times Haggai encouraged Zerubbabel, Joshua, and the people, respectively, to "be strong." In doing so, he takes the reader back to an earlier time in Israel's history when another Joshua was told the same thing: "Be strong and courageous" (Josh 1:6–9). Such a reminder is fitting in every generation. Finally, a reference is made to when the Israelites came out of Egypt, a clear allusion to God's deliverance from the hand of Pharaoh and his army (Ex 14).

There is benefit in pausing and carefully considering the past. Remembering past glory, exhibitions of courage, and times of miraculous deliverance offer inspiration and encouragement in times of struggle. We do ourselves a favor when we give careful thought to God's work in past days. On the flip side, we hurt ourselves immeasurably when we forget the long history of God's activity. Let us remember what he has done across the pages of time.

Give careful thought to your future possibilities (2:6–23). The end of the book pivots and looks toward the future. In this final section, the Lord reminds his people, "In a little while I will once more shake the heavens and the earth . . . and the desired of all nations will come" (2:6–7). Most scholars agree this latter description is a Messianic reference pointing to the future coming of Christ. The repetition of the phrase "From this day on" (2:15, 18, 19) is yet another way to underscore the emphasis on what lies ahead. God promises future blessing to his people (2:19). How often do we stop to give careful thought to the future promises of God, especially to that day when "the desired of all nations will come" (2:7)? Those who carefully keep that future in mind find that they are shaped by it. We will live differently today if we know where we are going tomorrow. The wise will give careful thought to God's plans for the future.

Thoughts have great power. Decisions that we make, words that we speak, and actions that we take have their roots in a thought. Jesus acknowledged as much when he said murder, adultery, theft, slander, and a host of other sins begin long before the acts themselves—in one's thought life (Matt 5:21–30; 15:16–20; Mark 7:17–23). The power of the mind is why Paul emphasized the importance of taking "captive every thought to make it obedient to Christ" (2 Cor 10:5). On another occasion, Paul encouraged believers to think about "whatever is true, whatever is noble, whatever is right, whatever is pure, whatever is lovely, whatever is admirable . . . excellent or praiseworthy" (Phil 4:8). The reality is that what we think will define who we are and what we do. No wonder Haggai wrote "give careful thought to your ways" (1:5) and repeated it so often (1:7; 2:15, 18).

When was the last time we paused to take inventory of our thoughts? What are we thinking? Are we careful, intentional, and disciplined? The LORD Almighty considered this such an important matter that he "sent" Haggai to talk to his people about it (1:12).

Haggai, like every other book of prophecy, is incredibly relevant. It has a word that still needs to be heard today. If the work of Charles Dickens is deemed valuable enough to get performed multiple times every year, one can only wonder why we do not hear "the word of the LORD [that] came through the prophet Haggai" (1:1) more often. Dickens and Haggai share a similar theme and purpose in their literature—encouraging others to give careful thought to life's decisions and behaviors. One piece of literature originated in the mind of a novelist from England. The other originated in the mind of Almighty God, who once told Isaiah (55:9): "my thoughts [are higher] than your thoughts." It seems reasonable to think we ought to pay attention to the One with higher thoughts.

PRAYER

Lord, in accordance with the prophet Haggai, we ask you to help us give careful thought to our ways. And in accordance with the apostle Paul, we ask that you transform us and renew our minds (Rom 12:2). Forgive us for allowing our thought life to be less than you desire and designed. Elevate our thoughts. Indeed, may we "fix [our] thoughts on Jesus" (Heb 3:1), this day and every day, as a demonstration and witness of your lordship. AMEN.

QUESTIONS

1. In addition to what was mentioned above—lack of time and discipline—what are other common barriers, or challenges, to demonstrating "careful thought" today? Why is it so hard to engage in such activity in our generation?

2. Which of the three time periods mentioned—present, past, or future—do you find most difficult to carefully consider? Why do you suppose that is the case?

3. What past glory, past act of courage, or past deliverance do you occasionally think about when you need inspiration and hope? Why does this memory help inspire you? What were the details of that past event?

4. When are you most apt to struggle with your thoughts? What helps you overcome and get back on track with a healthy thought life?

SUGGESTED READING

Haggai 1–2

38

ZECHARIAH: Future

*This is what the LORD Almighty says: "My towns will
again overflow with prosperity, and the LORD will again
comfort Zion and choose Jerusalem." (Zechariah 1:17)*

*This is what the LORD says: "I will return to Zion and
dwell in Jerusalem. Then Jerusalem will be called the
City of Truth, and the mountain of the LORD Almighty
will be called the Holy Mountain." (Zechariah 8:3)*

*The LORD will be king over the whole earth. On that day there
will be one LORD, and his name the only name. (Zechariah 14:9)*

God's people have always been forward-looking. While in Egypt,
they looked forward to returning to their promised land. While in
Babylonian exile they looked forward to the restoration and rebuilding
of their temple back in Jerusalem. Century after century they awaited
the coming of the Messiah. One of the major threads of the Old Testament is anticipating what is yet to come. When we turn the page to the
New Testament, we find the same pattern. Its writers were expecting the
second coming of the Messiah (Christ). Paul would go so far as to write,
"For to me, to live is Christ and to die is gain" (Phil 1:21). This was his
way of saying the present is good, but the future is better. John referenced that future when he spoke of "the Holy City, the new Jerusalem"

(Rev 21:2). Regardless of circumstance or generation, the future has always beckoned God's people.

Zechariah, the next to last book in the Old Testament, was written through that futuristic lens. A contemporary of Haggai, Zechariah was a product of the exile in Babylon. His very name means "the Lord remembers," presumably serving to remind the prophet and those who came after him that God does not forget his promises. The future is filled with hope.

Nonetheless, few writers today draw inspiration from Zechariah and its message. I find that interesting, given that back in the eighteenth century, writers such as John Wesley and William Cowper both found great value in the book. Let me explain. Early in the century, five-year-old Wesley had to leap from an upstairs window to escape a fire that destroyed his family's home. During his adult years he would look back and use Zechariah's words to describe the experience, frequently referring to himself as "a brand plucked out of the fire" (3:2 KJV). Later in the eighteenth century, the poet and songwriter William Cowper was inspired to write "There is a Fountain Filled with Blood" after reading Zechariah 13:1, wherein Zechariah declared, "On that day a fountain will be opened . . . to cleanse them from sin and impurity." Clearly, the book of Zechariah, pointing as it does to a promising future, played an important historical role by inspiring significant writers of the Christian faith.

Zechariah's fourteen chapters match the length of Hosea. These two books are the longest of the twelve minor prophets. Several intriguing features are found in Zechariah. For example, the first half of the book includes several visions, along with conversations with an angel. The latter observation is particularly noteworthy because only three other prophets—Isaiah, Daniel, and Hosea—even mention an angel; and throughout the entire Old Testament only the book of Judges refers to angels as often as the twenty references found in Zechariah. What we have here is a prophet who was in touch with heaven. The second half of the book focuses on the future. That focus is not subtle. The word *will*, indicating future tense, occurs over two hundred times in Zechariah, the majority (80%) of which appear in the final seven chapters of the book. Clearly, this prophet who communicated with heaven had a message about the future. He anticipated what lay ahead for the people of God.

I suspect few of us today spend much time contemplating the future. We are a present-oriented people, concerned about our pleasures and feelings right now. We make decisions that give us a thrill in the moment and put off serious thought of any possible consequences down the road. Perhaps nowhere is this more evident than in our buying habits. The use of credit allows us to enjoy a product today while postponing any worry about how we will pay for the item. Amazon makes billions of dollars annually because it recognizes the dual tendency of present-oriented desire and a willingness to use credit. The promotion of the idea to seek enjoyment now and pay for it later has allowed Amazon's online retail business to flourish. We want consumer products on our doorstep in the morning. Tomorrow has become the outer boundary of our future; beyond that is an abyss we cannot fathom or tolerate. Furthermore, in a world of despair and hopelessness like ours—filled with terrorism, hatred, and anxiety—we are not even sure there will be a future beyond the end of the week. So, like the description provided by both Isaiah (22:13) and Paul (1 Cor 15:32), many people today live by the philosophy, "Let us eat and drink, for tomorrow we die."

In contrast to that immediate-gratification philosophy, to be a forward-looking, future-oriented people requires four qualities that are increasingly in short supply: patience, perseverance, contentment, and faith. *Patience* has to do with being willing to wait. Patient people do not demand their way, nor do they throw tantrums when inconvenienced by delays. *Perseverance*, by definition, implies adverse circumstances. To persevere means to keep focused on a goal and move forward gradually, even when the conditions are unfavorable. *Contentment* refers to the inner peace some people exude regardless of life's conditions and the perception of things being unfair. People who are content understand there is a bigger picture unfolding beyond themselves. *Faith* points upward and forward. Those with faith look upward and embrace the sovereign Lord who controls the affairs of their life and the wider world. The writer of Hebrews (11:16) reminds us that faith also looks forward and describes those who are "longing for a better country—a heavenly one." People with faith know that "God ha[s] planned something better for us" (Heb 11:40). That was the audience—people of patience, perseverance, contentment, and faith—Zechariah had in mind when "the word of the LORD came to" him (1:1) and compelled him to write.

Though written some twenty-five-hundred years ago, Zechariah, like the other prophets whose themes we have been considering, had a message that still rings true today. "The word of the LORD" that stirred him—and that was acknowledged another twelve times throughout his book (e.g., 4:6, 8; 6:9; 7:1; 8:1, 18; 9:1; 12:1)—described a future wherein light would be shed on shepherds, Jerusalem, impurity, and sovereignty. Let us pause to notice the prophet's message as it pertains to each of these topics.

Shepherds will be rebuked. Israel's shepherds—the community's spiritual leaders—are mentioned a combined ten times in chapters 10, 11, and 13. Zechariah noted that God's "anger burns against the shepherds" (10:3). Later, they were called "foolish" (11:15) and "worthless" (11:17) because they deserted the ones for whom they were supposed to be providing care. Future punishment awaited those shepherds (10:3). They were preoccupied with "their rich pastures" (11:3), but God would hold them responsible for neglecting to safeguard their flocks. The message was chilling, the consequences severe, and the future ominous for spiritual leaders who failed to heed God's word and instruct their people in it. That was the future about which Zechariah spoke.

Jerusalem will be restored. Zechariah, far more than any of the twelve books that collectively form the minor prophets, highlighted Jerusalem. The city is mentioned forty times throughout Zechariah; most of those references occurring in the last half of the book. Jerusalem, the Israelites' cherished and sacred city, had been attacked and plundered by the invading Babylonians (see 2 Kgs 25:1–15). Vandalism and looting took place, resulting in fear and humiliation among God's people. Zechariah pointed to a day, however, when Jerusalem will be inhabited by God and his people once again (8:3–8). The city will become "an immovable rock for all the nations" (12:3). God himself will defend her (14:3–5). That was the future about which Zechariah spoke.

Impurity will be removed. The prophet described a day when "a fountain will be opened . . . to cleanse [the people] from sin and impurity" (13:1). As noted earlier, William Cowper captured this thought in his popular eighteenth-century hymn. A line from that hymn reminds us that "sinners, plunged beneath that flood, lose all their guilty stains." Zechariah pointed to a day when all such stains would be washed away. All idols and impurities will be eliminated (13:2). All that is filthy and defiled will be expunged from the earth. We would do well to remember this when we are tempted to grow discouraged and overwhelmed by the depths of sin, corruption, and perversion in our culture today. Sin and impurity will not always have the upper hand. A day is coming when our world will be "cleansed" (13:1)—washed clean—of all such filth. The book closes with a unique and fascinating picture: widespread signs of holiness will mark the everyday life and activities of God's people in and around Jerusalem (14:20–21). That was the future about which Zechariah spoke.

Sovereignty will be revealed. There is coming a day when there will be no mistake about who is in charge. History tells us of those who have risen to such heights of power that they think themselves invincible and sovereign. Caesar, Hitler, Stalin, Mao Zedong, and bin Laden are all examples of familiar tyrants who thought they could control the world. Zechariah sets the record straight near the end of his book when he assures us with these words: "The LORD will be king over the whole earth. On that day there will be one LORD, and his name the only name" (14:9). All others who have tried to rule the world—regardless of their position, power, credentials, era, or geographical location—have been imposters. One day the Lord (the Hebrew word is *Yahweh*, the great "I am") will make known to the entire world that he alone is the supreme king over all that exists. There will be no competitor. God alone will be exalted. That was the future about which Zechariah spoke.

If Zechariah is correct, here is what we ought to know and how we ought to respond:

- We have a future. *Remember that!*
- That future will see wrongs made right. *Relax!*
- The best is yet to come. *Rejoice!*
- The Lord will be king. *Repeat it!*

Prayer

Lord, the future calls us upward and forward. Help us to listen to you and then walk boldly into that future. Remind us that to be the people of God means that what lies ahead is always promising, regardless of the conditions we face today. Give us balance in this area of life. Save us from being so focused on today that we neglect to prepare for our future. But also keep us from being so future-minded that we are of no use today. Guide us into our future with confidence. Wherever we find ourselves in this moment—at whatever stage of life—remind us that "the Lord will be king over the whole earth" (14:9). We declare our trust is in that Lord today. AMEN.

QUESTIONS

1. Why does every group or organization need someone in it who is thinking about the future? Can one be too future-oriented? How does an organization, or individual, balance the present and the future?

2. Which quality of a forward-looking person mentioned above—patience, perseverance, contentment, or faith—most needs attention in your life? What factors make that particular quality difficult?

3. What inspires or encourages you as you think about the future? What concerns you about the future?

4. What primary message from Zechariah do you most need to hear right now? Why? How might you respond to that message today?

SUGGESTED READING

Zechariah 1, 4, 7, 8, 10, 11, 13, 14

39

MALACHI: Change

Great is the LORD—even beyond the borders of Israel! (Malachi 1:5)

I the LORD do not change. (Malachi 3:6)

"They will be mine," says the LORD Almighty, "in the day when I make up my treasured possession. I will spare them, just as in compassion a man spares his son who serves him." (Malachi 3:17)

To say we live during a time of unprecedented and rapid change is to state the obvious. Social change has become as predictable as death and taxes. I suppose no one who knows me would be surprised by my interest in the topic of social change. After all, I am a sociologist and that is the substance of most sociological investigation: the observation and analysis of social change. However, there is more to the story. The very emergence of sociology is the result of significant social change. Sociology traces its roots back to the early 1800s and the Industrial Revolution that was beginning to transform life in Europe. Until society began changing at such a rapid pace—moving from a rural to an urban economy, experiencing changes in travel and communication, and witnessing large-scale political and economic revolutions—there was not much for a social analyst to observe or say. All that began to change some two hundred years ago, accelerating in recent decades to a speed that often leaves us dizzy and disoriented. Change is now the only environment an American under the age of sixty has ever known.

Malachi, the last book of the Old Testament, was written during a time of change. In addition to the Israelites returning from their exile in Babylon to rebuild Jerusalem, new political powers would soon emerge. No longer would political threats be coming from the East (Assyria and Babylon), but from the West (Greece and Rome). Even more significant would be the coming of the Messiah, the Christ, whose life and teaching would be documented in the New Testament. A new order was about to unfold. God would take on flesh and enter human history. A major expansion was just around the corner, as thousands—followed by millions—of Gentile converts would soon embrace the God of Israel. Indeed, much was about to change when the prophet Malachi wrote these words that conclude the Old Testament.

At that critical historical moment, when change was in the air, the Almighty LORD declared: "I the LORD do not change" (3:6). Theologians refer to this as the immutability of God. In other words, God's essence, character, and purpose are constant and unchanging.

Author John H. Parker, in his 2009 book *Abide with Me*, tells the story of nineteenth-century preacher and hymnwriter Henry Lyte. His ministry in England coincided with the end of the country's Industrial Revolution. Changes in manufacturing and the economy had rippled throughout society over the preceding century, altering how people worked, interacted, and viewed life. During these unsettling times Lyte was a steadying influence among those in his church and community in the village of Brixham, located along the southwest coast of England. Lyte faithfully ministered there for twenty-seven years. By 1847, however, poor health and failing eyesight told him the end was near. No longer able to endure the tuberculosis that wracked his body, on the first Sunday in September he preached his last sermon to the congregation he had long loved and served. That same afternoon, back in his room, his final prayer was expressed in these words he had written:

Abide with me! Fast falls the eventide
The darkness deepens; Lord, with me abide
When other helpers fail and comforts flee
Help of the helpless, Oh, abide with me

Swift to its close ebbs out life's little day
Earth's joys grow dim; its glories pass away

Change and decay in all around I see
O Thou who changest not, abide with me

Hold Thou Thy cross before my closing eyes
Shine thro' the gloom, and point me to the skies
Heav'n's morning breaks, and earth's vain shadows flee
In life, in death, O Lord, abide with me

Though Henry Lyte witnessed significant social change and experienced debilitating bodily decay, he knew the God he had preached about for nearly thirty years was the Changeless One who would abide with him despite life's unpredictable and shifting circumstances. Lyte's hymn closed with lyrics of hope and promise: "In life, in death, O Lord, abide with me!" Henry Lyte died two months later.

The hymn writer Lyte and the prophet Malachi had much in common. Each represented God to a people living through a season of great change, and each shared the message that God does not change despite what takes place in the surrounding environment. In fact, Malachi's name means "my messenger." It was as if God said, "Listen to this prophet. I have a message for you through him." What we have here in Malachi, then, is a fitting title and book to wrap up the 12 minor prophets, a fitting conclusion to the 22 books that form the Old Testament's appendix, and a fitting close to the entire 39 books that comprise the Old Testament. Malachi is God's exclamation mark. God's message through the prophet is this: *I'm not kidding! My message has not changed over thirty-nine books and over the thousand years I have been inspiring authors to contribute to these sacred Scriptures.* What God said from the beginning—back in Genesis and in the other early books of the Bible—still held true a millennium later.

Three themes are dominant in Malachi. Those themes combine to make up the prophet's message and, arguably, summarize what God was saying throughout the whole Old Testament. Let us consider each of the three topics here.

I the LORD do not change: my design for marriage and family still matters. If you had been given editing privileges, how might you have chosen to close the Old Testament? What would your final written word have been while the people waited another four hundred years for the Messiah to come and the New Testament era to begin? Malachi ended with an emphasis on the family, the theme we noted when we opened the book of Genesis. The Old Testament closes with

Malachi's concern about fathers and their children (4:6)—a concern so serious that the neglect of this primary relationship would bring a curse on the land. Earlier in the book, God spoke in equally strong terms about marriage and divorce (2:10–17). One cannot read Malachi without being impressed by the fact that God still cared about the design and purpose of marriage and the family with which he began at the time of creation. Though they lived in a changing world, God's people were not to change the design and priority of these fundamental institutions. God claims ownership of them. He holds the patents and intends for them to be honored and used in the way he planned.

I the LORD do not change: obedience, holiness, law and order still matter. The expectations God set forth in the other early books of the Old Testament, beyond Genesis, were also still valid in the last book of Malachi. The importance of obedience (Exodus), holiness (Leviticus), order (Numbers), and law (Deuteronomy)—all emphasized within the first five books of the Bible—were to continue guiding the behavior of God's people centuries later. God had not changed his mind on these. And yet, sadly, the people had failed to take God's plan seriously. They had not obeyed God in their religious practices but had grown slack in their offerings and sacrifices (1:6–9; 3:8–10). They had not distinguished "between the righteous and the wicked," between the holy and the unholy (3:18). They had not taken seriously the order of the marriage covenant (2:10–16) but instead had inverted good and evil (2:17); thus, God's plan for an ordered society had turned to disorder. They had not been faithful to "matters of the law" (2:9). They had neglected what was foundational. No wonder God reminded them: "I the LORD do not change" (3:6). If such a reminder was needed then, how much more do we need the reminder today? Obedience, holiness, law, and order have not been rescinded by God but by a cancel culture that disapproves of God and has withdrawn from him to follow its own ways.

I the LORD do not change: you are my treasured possession, and you still matter. We dare not miss this final message, for to do so would jeopardize a proper understanding of the entire Old Testament. God calls his people "my treasured possession" (3:17). This is an expression that communicates priceless value. That is how God feels about his children. Though they had rebelled against him, struggled, complained, and prostituted themselves before other gods down through the centuries, when all was said and done, the Old Testament closed with these words from God: "They will be mine . . . my treasured possession" (3:17). This rare description was first used back at Mount Sinai just before God gave his people the Ten Commandments (Ex 19:5). As the people of God were coming out of Egypt and beginning their journey with the Lord, he wanted them to know how he felt about them. Periodically thereafter, God would remind them that they were his "treasured possession" (Deut 7:6; 14:2; 26:18; Ps 135:4). The themes we have covered throughout the Old Testament—themes such as promise, character, conversation, songs, wisdom, romance, and mercy—have reminded us how much God treasures his people. Even the uncomfortable themes we have considered—such as disaster, consequences, evil, woes, mourning, judgment, and anger—are God's way of saying: *I care so much about you that I want you to know the truth about my created world and how life works within it. Because you are my treasured possession, I have provided these thirty-nine books with their themes to instruct, guide, and bring you fulfillment.*

God does not change. Psalm 136 reminds us: God's love and mercy endure forever. He still looks at his people and says, "They will be mine . . . my treasured possession" (3:17).

Whether it be the curtain closing on Israel's turbulent history in the Old Testament, or Henry Lyte's failing body signaling the end of his work in England, or the unsettling changes of our day, perhaps there is no better prayer than this: O Thou who changest not, abide with me!

When we turn the page to the New Testament, we will find that prayer answered.

PRAYER

O Sovereign Lord, you are our Rock. When the world, its ideas, and its patterns all change, we can count on you to be constant and secure. With the songwriter Henry Lyte we sometimes feel that "change and decay" are all around us, but our trust is in You, "thou who changest not." Our prayer is that you would indeed "abide with" us. And then help us to abide with you. Thank you for the truth, instruction, and encouragement we find in your Word. Help us to be people who read, study, memorize, meditate on, and live out your Word in our daily lives. Continue to teach and lead us, we pray. AMEN.

QUESTIONS

1. What is one of the biggest changes you have personally experienced in your lifetime? How did you navigate, or cope with, that change?

2. What makes it hard to believe that you are really God's "treasured possession?" What might you do to change that faulty perception and begin believing God cherishes you?

3. Malachi means "my messenger." Which of his messages do you most need to hear? Reflecting back over the Old Testament as a whole, what primary message have you heard God speak to you? What are you doing to respond to that message?

4. How does the New Testament answer the prayer, "O Thou who changest not, abide with me!"?

SUGGESTED READING

Malachi 1–4

NEW TESTAMENT
THEMES

ജ ര

40

MATTHEW: Kingdom

*From that time on Jesus began to preach, "Repent, for
the kingdom of heaven is near." (Matthew 4:17)*

*Blessed are the poor in spirit, for theirs is the
kingdom of heaven. (Matthew 5:3)*

*Our Father in heaven, hallowed be your name, Your kingdom come,
your will be done on earth as it is in heaven. (Matthew 6:9–10)*

*But seek first his kingdom and his righteousness, and all
these things will be given to you as well. (Matthew 6:33)*

The book of Matthew, likely written nearly five hundred years after
Malachi closed the Old Testament, marks the beginning of the New
Testament and a new kingdom. The New Testament refers to a new
covenant, or a new relationship, between God and his people; the new
kingdom refers to a new reign or regime. A kingdom implies both a king,
or ruler, and a territory over which the king operates with authority.
The birth of Jesus—which Matthew reports was announced by an angel
(Matt 1:20, 24), acknowledged by Magi (Matt 2:1–2), and despised by
King Herod (Matt 2:3, 16)—was the event that signaled the arrival of
that new king and kingdom.

No New Testament writer mentions the word *kingdom* more than
Matthew, and no Old Testament writer does so more than Daniel. Both
writers make over fifty references to the idea of a kingdom. Daniel's ref-

erences are primarily about human kingdoms on earth with their kings and officials—kingdoms such as Babylon, Media, and Persia. Matthew, on the other hand, emphasizes the heavenly kingdom where God reigns supreme (Matt 6:33; 7:21). Thus, a new type of kingdom emerges when one turns from the Old to the New Testament. Understanding that new kingdom opens the door to the entire New Testament and its teaching. There are five central characteristics of this kingdom described in Matthew: it was anticipated, it is ruled by Jesus, it brings heaven to earth, it is everlasting, and it begins now.

The kingdom was anticipated. The Old Testament prophets (e.g., Isa 7:14; 9:6–7; Jer 31:15; Mic 5:2) spoke repeatedly of this coming kingdom. Matthew quotes from or references the Old Testament more than any other gospel writer, often reminding us that the events surrounding the life of Jesus "fulfill what the Lord had said through the prophet" (1:22; 2:15, 23; 8:17; 12:17; 21:4; 27:9). He goes to great lengths to show the relationship between Jesus's life and all that came before him. The kingdom that Jesus ushered in was expected and described by the prophets across many centuries. What that means is that one part of the Bible cannot be fully understood without the other part. Alone, either the Old Testament or the New Testament provides only a partial picture of God's plan for humanity. Both parts are inextricably linked. Both parts demand our attention. Matthew makes that clear at the outset of the New Testament. To be a citizen of the kingdom is to recognize the value of and need for both Testaments.

The kingdom is ruled by Jesus. Every kingdom has a king—one who reigns and has dominion over its citizens and their activities. Jesus is that ruler here. Matthew opens his book by explaining how Jesus came from the royal line of King David (1:1). Magi came from the east to worship the one "born king of the Jews" (2:2). Just before his crucifixion, Jesus responded affirmatively when Pilate asked (27:11), "Are you the king of the Jews?" Only John's gospel references Jesus more than the 170 times Matthew speaks his name. Matthew is very intentional and explicit when he states that Jesus was virgin born, would be known as "Immanuel—which means, 'God with us'" (1:23), and would be the one to "save his people from their sins" (1:21). Not only did Matthew want his readers to know a new kingdom was underway, whose king was Jesus, but also he wanted them to know precisely who Jesus was. Jesus was the Son of God, the Savior of the world. His coming into the world inaugurated a new kingdom, the likes of which had never been seen. To be a citizen of the kingdom is to give allegiance to the person of Jesus Christ and believe in his saving power.

The kingdom brings heaven to earth. Matthew speaks of heaven more than any other biblical writer. Though John, in Revelation, provides unparalleled detail about heaven, it is Matthew who whets the reader's appetite with his eighty-four references to heaven. As noted earlier, every kingdom has a territory—a domain over which a king rules. Heaven represents the territory of the kingdom that Matthew clearly associates with Jesus. I find it interesting that Satan, when tempting Jesus in the desert, offered him "all the kingdoms of the world" (Matt 4:8–9). Of course, Jesus rebuked Satan and sent him away, for the Son of God had a bigger and more marvelous kingdom than what Satan could provide. Jesus had come from heaven, and he brought that heavenly kingdom to earth. Anyone who received him—the Son of God from heaven—entered that kingdom. All the great kingdoms of the world pale in comparison. To be a citizen of the kingdom is to value heaven above the allures of this world.

The kingdom is everlasting. Unlike the kingdoms of earth—whether Babylon, Rome, America, or any other kingdom—the kingdom over which Jesus rules will never end. It is a timeless kingdom. Daniel, pointing ahead to the Messiah that Matthew presented, said, "His kingdom will be an everlasting kingdom, and all rulers will worship and obey him" (Dan 7:27). Peter spoke of "the eternal kingdom of our Lord and Savior Jesus Christ" (2 Pet 1:11). Thus, the testimony of other biblical writers is clear on the subject: the kingdom of Jesus is unique in that it is here to stay. The well-known twentieth-century Methodist missionary to India, E. Stanley Jones, was a prolific author. At the age of eighty-seven, Jones pointed to Hebrews 12:28—"we are receiving a kingdom that cannot be shaken"—and wrote his final book, *The Unshakable Kingdom and the Unchanging Person* (1972). The book highlights the eternal nature of the kingdom that Jesus represented when he came from heaven to earth. That kingdom did not collapse at the end of Jesus's earthly life and ministry, nor will it—ever. To be a citizen of the kingdom is to build one's life on what is unshakable.

The kingdom begins now. Another emphasis of E. Stanley Jones' *The Unshakable Kingdom* is that the kingdom is present with us now. Jones declares the kingdom "is something to be lived, lived now, not merely hereafter" (p 69). We do not have to wait until we die to enter it. While it is true that the kingdom is both heavenly and eternal, it begins in this world. Of course, that has consequences. Jones is quick to note that because the kingdom exists in the present it "upsets everything that doesn't conform to the Kingdom now" (p 69). Coming to Jesus, trusting him as Savior and Lord, and embracing his life, death, and resurrection bring the kingdom into the present. The result is that life gets completely altered. That is the message of Matthew and the entire New Testament. When Paul said, "our citizenship is in heaven" (Phil 3:20), he used the present tense. The kingdom is a present reality, available now and extending throughout eternity, that changes us from the inside out. To be a citizen of the kingdom is to embrace that life-changing work right now.

What is that change? What does life look like inside the kingdom? No one need search far to find the answer, especially if the person has access to a red-letter edition of the Bible that highlights the words spoken by Jesus. Matthew sets forth the teaching of Jesus, the one who rules the kingdom, in an organized fashion. In doing so, he describes two primary characteristics of kingdom life. First, that life is marked by moral and ethical behavior, as seen in the Sermon on the Mount. Second, surprises, or unexpected outcomes, occur along life's way in the kingdom, typically illustrated in parables told by Jesus.

Just five chapters into the New Testament, where a new kind of relationship with God and a new kingdom are presented, the reader comes to the Sermon on the Mount (Matt 5–7). The sermon lays out moral (i.e., our response to God) and ethical (i.e., our response to others) standards of conduct. The former is depicted in how one prays, fasts, and trusts God rather than worrying about life's basic needs. The latter is seen in how we treat other people. It involves such behavior as loving one's enemies, giving to the needy, and avoiding hypocritical judgments toward others. Life in the kingdom demands that its citizens develop habits of taking the high road and building their lives wisely on the firm foundation of Jesus Christ. To operate in such a way—morally and ethically—is to live out the creed of the kingdom. Christians, living as kingdom citizens, are different from their neighbors.

The second characteristic of kingdom life, the claim that it contains a series of surprises, is found in the parables of Jesus. Eleven of those parables include the phrase, "The kingdom of heaven is like" (Matt 13:24, 31, 33, 44, 45, 47; 18:23; 20:1; 22:2; 25:1, 14). Each parable then proceeds to turn the head of the listener because what follows is unanticipated. For example, each of the six parables in Matthew 13 has an unexpected message:

- One is cautioned about eagerly pulling up weeds lest the harvest of wheat also be destroyed in the process (13:24–30).
- A small seed can produce a disproportionately large plant (13:31–32).
- A little yeast can expand a lot of dough (13:33).
- Finding a treasure in a field is worth selling everything in order to buy the field (13:44).
- Finding a pearl drives one to a similar response (13:45–46).
- At the end of the age the wicked will be thrown into a fiery furnace (13:47–50).

All these outcomes are rather stunning. Other "kingdom of heaven" parables surprise us with their teaching on justice and mercy (18:23–35); what seems to be unfair compensation for work (20:1–16); the type of guests invited to a wedding banquet (22:1–14); and the seriousness associated with being ready for when the Lord returns (25:1–13; 25:14–30). These parables all contain something unexpected. They leave the audience surprised by the response to, or the consequences of, some action. Life in the kingdom does not follow the ordinary customs, or norms, of the prevailing culture. At times it is radical and extreme. Kingdom citizens astonish others by their audacity to do what no one expected or thought possible.

Acting morally and ethically in a culture of compromise and surprising others by consistently operating with elevated standards are behaviors practiced by kingdom people. That's the kingdom that Jesus brought to earth. That's the kingdom the reader discovers when opening Matthew and beginning the New Testament. Is that the kingdom that defines us? Is that how we live?

Matthew ties together the old and the new, the past and the future. The Old Testament prophets pointed to the coming Messiah and his kingdom. Matthew presents Jesus as the fulfillment of those prophets' message. The kingdom that dominates the New Testament culminates with a vivid description of heaven in the book of Revelation. In essence, then, Matthew serves as the hinge that connects both testaments. When we walk through Matthew we enter a new kingdom, develop an enriched understanding of and relationship with the King, and set our sights on a future filled with limitless possibilities.

Having carefully and colorfully described the kingdom, Matthew closes with this word: "Therefore go and make [kingdom] disciples of all nations . . ." (Matt 28:19). Nothing matters more.

Prayer

"Our Father in heaven, hallowed be your name. Let your kingdom come and your will be done on earth as it is in heaven" (6:9–10). Thank you for this new kingdom. We have witnessed too many kingdoms fail and disappoint us. Thus, it is with delight and optimism that we embrace your kingdom, ruled by your Son Jesus, offered to us now and through all eternity. Help us to live morally, ethically, and open to your surprises along the way. We pray this all in Jesus's name. AMEN.

Questions

1. Review the five central characteristics of the kingdom. Which of these offers you the most hope and encouragement? Why? Which one needs more emphasis today?

2. What moral or ethical changes might you expect to observe in your community if more people lived by kingdom principles and took the Sermon on the Mount seriously?

3. What surprising decision, activity, or behavior have you witnessed from someone who lives (or lived) according to kingdom principles? Describe the surprise.

4. How did your life change once you became a citizen of the Kingdom of Heaven?

Suggested Reading

Matthew 3–7, 13, 18–19

41

MARK: Gospel

The beginning of the gospel about Jesus
Christ, the Son of God. (Mark 1:1)

After John was put in prison, Jesus went into Galilee, proclaiming
the good news of God. "The time has come," he said. "The kingdom
of God is near. Repent and believe the good news!" (Mark 1:14–15)

For whoever wants to save his life will lose it, but whoever loses
his life for me and for the gospel will save it. (Mark 8:35)

He said to them, "Go into all the world and preach
the good news to all creation." (Mark 16:15)

The gospel of Mark is unique in several ways. First, the emphasis on the term *gospel* itself is worth noting. The gospel means "good news," and its inclusion in the opening line of the book communicates that what follows is optimistic, encouraging, and ought not be missed. Second, Mark alone opens his gospel account with a title. That title—"The beginning of the gospel about Jesus Christ, the Son of God"—is only seven words in the original Greek (i.e., beginning the gospel, Jesus Christ, God's son). Those few words, however, are descriptive. The title provides at least three important messages regarding the good news. Those messages pertain to the duration of the gospel (what Mark presents is just "the beginning"), the person responsible for the good news (Jesus Christ), and the relationship that person has with God (the Son of God). Third, Mark's writing style is simple, straightforward, succinct, and fast-moving. He tends to get right to the point. His sixteen chapters take the reader rapidly from one event to another in the life of Jesus, as if the writer cannot get his message out quickly enough. Perhaps that tells us something about the nature of the gospel as well: this good news is too exciting and important to miss an opportunity to share it right now. Nothing should delay its proclamation.

If the gospel is indeed good news, a fair question is this: what makes it so? Why have believers for two thousand years consistently, and without serious debate, accepted and promoted the fact that the Christian faith is good news? There certainly has been no shortage of bad news in the world. History books repeatedly narrate bad news that has resulted from wars, assassinations, genocide, cruel tyrants, and other horrendous atrocities. How, then, have Christians been able to declare that the kingdom described in Matthew is the good news declared in Mark?

In keeping with Mark's straightforward and succinct style, it may be helpful to understand the gospel by focusing on two common words used often by its author: *come* and *go*. These two verbs contain the secret of the good news and serve as bookends for Mark's gospel. The first chapter of the book emphasizes *coming*, mentioning the word there ten times (1:4, 7, 9, 14, 17, 24, 25, 26, 38, 40). The final chapter, on the other hand, shines a spotlight on *going* (16:1, 7, 15). Taken together, these dual themes define the good news of the gospel.

Richard Halverson, a graduate of Wheaton College, served for twenty-three years as the senior pastor at Fourth Presbyterian Church just outside Washington, D.C., and later became the Chaplain of the United States Senate (1981–1995). During his distinguished career, Halverson authored several books, including a book of reflections on Christianity that he entitled *Walk with God Between Sundays* (1965). In one of the book's readings—called "Come! Go!"—Halverson wrote the following (pp 24–25):

> Healthy Christianity is elliptical. It polarizes around
> two opposing harmonious forces. One is centripetal: the
> invitation, "Come." The other is centrifugal: the commission,
> "Go!" Either without the other produces the eccentric.
> Together they put the Christian in orbit. Coming to Jesus
> qualifies [one] to go to others, but until [one] comes to
> Jesus, his going is useless and purposeless. Some [people]
> are always coming—never going anywhere. Spiritual sops,

they are dominated by finicky spiritual appetites, constantly feeling their spiritual pulses—busy keeping score on themselves—preoccupied with the condition of their own piety. They are like spiritual hypochondriacs. Some are just busy going. Theirs is the religion of the "do-gooder." They are busy-bodies, generally in the way—a nuisance, playing amateur providence with others' lives, interfering, managing their friends. They are spiritual vacuums! But the [one] who comes to Jesus and abides in Him, and then goes in His strength and love to others is a blessing to everyone within his orbit.

Halverson and Mark agree that both actions—coming and going—are central to understanding and living out the gospel. Together they form the twin pillars that bring good news to a fallen or needy world, or as Halverson said, "they put the Christian in orbit."

Four significant uses of the word *come* appear in the opening chapter of Mark. First, **the Savior has come**. Mark begins by pointing to "Jesus Christ, the Son of God" (1:1). Using this extended name for Jesus at the outset establishes his identity as the Savior (Jesus), the long-anticipated Messiah (Christ), and God himself—deity—in the flesh (Son of God). The savior for whom God's people had long been waiting had arrived. That was great news to a people who had been waiting for centuries.

Second, **the time has come**. Mark tells us that Jesus came "proclaiming the good news of God. 'The time has come,' he said" (1:14–15). The wait was over. The opportune moment was at hand. Out of an apparent disaster—the imprisonment of John—came the seed for inaugurating the spread of the gospel. What the enemy intended for evil, God used to launch his greatest work. God's timing is always perfect and that is good news.

Third, **the kingdom has come**. Jesus went on to declare, "The kingdom of God is near" (1:15). As we noted in Matthew, Jesus Christ, the Savior of the world, brought the kingdom to Earth. Those who "repent and believe the good news" (1:15) have access to that new kingdom right now; they become citizens of that kingdom and life takes on new meaning and bursts forth with good news.

Fourth, **we can now come**. The Savior, the time, and the kingdom all point to this singular fact: people are now personally invited to embrace the gospel. The invitation to Peter and Andrew—"Come, follow me" (1:17)—has been repeated countless times to others since then. The gospel, by nature, extends an invitation; it always draws people. There is a yearning in the human soul for good news.

No wonder Mark's first words are about the gospel, or good news! No wonder he cannot move beyond his opening paragraphs without describing the excitement exploding in his chest: *The Savior has come! The time has come! The kingdom has come! Therefore, we too ought to come!* The gospel is not a drab, boring, take-it-or-leave-it proposition. Shame on anyone who dares present it that way. The gospel is life-giving and life-changing. It is good news to anyone who will receive it, benefitting the individual and all society.

Throughout the book of Mark, however, and especially at the end of the book, the emphasis changes from *come* to *go*. The gospel is good news not only because of what has come but also because of what goes when one encounters Jesus Christ, the Savior. As with the word *come* above, let us consider four uses of the word *go* that result from the gospel.

First, **our past can go**. Jesus told the woman who "had been subject to bleeding for twelve years" (5:25) to "Go in peace and be freed from your suffering" (5:34). The gospel—the good news that Jesus brings— sets people free from bondage to past suffering. Throughout Mark, and down through history, the gospel has liberated scores of individuals from their past.

Second, **our sin can go**. Jesus told another woman, one caught in the act of adultery: "Go now and leave your life of sin" (John 8:11). The implication was that the adulteress need no longer be defined by her sin. Rather, she could let go of the sin and chart a new course. Only the power of the gospel can do that.

Third, **our guilt can go**. A wonderful redundancy occurs in the closing chapter of Mark that illustrates this. On resurrection morning an angel spoke to a small group of alarmed and distraught women with these words: "[G]o, tell his disciples and Peter, 'He is going ahead of you into Galilee. There you will see him, just as he told you'" (16:7). Peter, of course, was one of the disciples; he already would have been included in the command to the women. So why was he singled out in this directive? Why the redundancy? Could it be that the compassionate Christ knew the guilt Peter would be carrying after his denial? Lest Peter succumb to his overwhelming guilt and risk missing the good news of the resurrection, Jesus made a special point of arranging to meet his friend in

Galilee. Perhaps no story in all Scripture better reflects the good news of the gospel.

The reference to guilt reminds me of a recent incident with one of our grandsons. Our family has a tradition of gathering for Sunday dinner at our house. Our sons, their wives, our grandchildren, and occasional guests enjoy a meal together. One Sunday after all the other cousins and relatives had left, our three-year-old grandson, Benny, came bolting out of the spare bedroom designated as the kids' play area. He slammed the door behind him and came running down the hall, crying: "I want to go home right now!" Through his sobs and tears he repeated himself three or four times. His daddy, Luke, picked him up and asked what was wrong. Benny typically cried—probably like many children his age—because he had to leave his grandparents' house and go home. Now he was crying and protesting because he could not leave soon enough.

A bit of adult logic told us that something had happened behind the closed door. Sure enough, when we entered the room the reason for his desperate cry became clear. Benny had found some children's paint, applied it to the walls, and then accidently tipped over the paint jar onto the carpet in the process. Only later did we learn he had done something similar the prior week at his own home—decorating white walls with markers—and had suffered appropriate consequences. As a repeat offender at his grandparents' house, he wanted "to go home right now!" The guilt was too much to bear, even for a three-year-old.

As only a grandma can do, my wife quickly got some damp towels and completely removed the paint from both the walls and the carpet. No permanent damage was done. In Benny's young eyes, his grandma delivered good news. His sobbing stopped. That is a picture of the gospel of Jesus Christ. The past, the sin, and even the guilt are cleaned up and wiped away.

A fourth and final observation from Mark's gospel is this: **We can go**. No, we *must* go. The book of Mark concludes with these well-known words from Jesus: "Go into all the world and preach the good news to all creation" (16:15). Is there any other option for one who has been the recipient of such good news? The gospel is not to be kept a secret, nor is it intended for private use only, but is to be shared enthusiastically and hopefully with others.

Come, hear, and receive the gospel. Then go, live, and declare the gospel. For it is the good news that changes everything. Just ask the apostle Peter, or our grandson Benny.

Prayer

Our Father in heaven, thank you for the gospel, the good news! Thank you for sending your Son, Jesus, for our salvation. What He *came* to give and what he empowers us to let *go* of have transformed our lives and the entire world. We are eternally grateful. Help us to be ambassadors of the gospel in our generation, taking the good news with us and declaring and demonstrating it every chance we get. We offer this prayer joyfully, in the name of our Savior, Jesus Christ, the Son of God. AMEN.

Questions

1. Can you remember a time when you received particularly good news? What was that news? And what was your response?

2. What came into your life when you encountered Jesus and received the gospel?

3. What did you let go of when you encountered Jesus and received the gospel?

4. Why is guilt so hard to eradicate at times? What factors make this a challenge?

Suggested Reading

Mark 1–3, 5, 8, 10, 15–16

42

LUKE: Account

Many have undertaken to draw up an account of the things that
have been fulfilled among us, just as they were handed down to us by
those who from the first were eyewitnesses and servants of the word.
Therefore, since I myself have carefully investigated everything
from the beginning it seemed good also to me to write an orderly
account for you, most excellent Theophilus, so that you may know
the certainty of the things you have been taught. (Luke 1:1–4)

Then he opened their minds so they could
understand the Scriptures. (Luke 24:45)

My parents were high school sweethearts from rural central Michigan. They married at age eighteen and had three children by the age of twenty-three, with another child to come four years later. Two of their four children were born deaf; I grew up between those two. Not surprisingly, I suppose, I became the family interpreter and have spent much of my life associating with and working among members of the Deaf community.

Church was central in my upbringing. My first recollection of making a spiritual decision was when I knelt at a camp meeting altar at the age of seven. However, it was the 1970 Asbury College revival—when a college student came to our church and the revival fires spread there—that marked the pivotal movement of God in my early years; I was fifteen at the time. The event influenced my high school experience and set the trajectory of my life thereafter.

At different stages of my journey, I was a high school athlete, a college-age preacher, a determined graduate student, and then for thirty-four years a university professor at two distinct institutions. Along the way I married my college chapel partner, we had two sons, and lived on both coasts of the United States. Our family of four has now expanded to a family of eleven, with two daughters-in-law and five grandchildren added to the number. Two of our grandchildren are girls and three are boys; two of them—a granddaughter and a grandson—have cystic fibrosis, resulting in challenges and investments in treatments and care that once were never on our family's horizon. I am deeply indebted to God for his grace, strength, and guidance across the years of my life. He has made, and continues to make, all the difference.

What I have shared above might be called a brief *account* of my life. The details, while admittedly sketchy, include information about my roots, my family, a formative revival, my career pursuits, and how both deafness and cystic fibrosis have shaped me. All these are woven together to provide a record or explanation of who I am and how I arrived at this point. Anyone could do the same. Every account, of course, would be different. There are unique elements and influences that define each of us and shape our experiences. Scripture tells us about a "written account of Adam's line" (Gen 5:1), of Noah (Gen 6:9), of Noah's sons (Gen 10:1), of Abraham's father Terah (Gen 11:27), of Abraham's sons Ishmael (Gen 25:12) and Isaac (Gen 25:19), of the family of Aaron and Moses (Num 3:1), and of many others. A written account—whether detailing a family's history or one's financial assets in a bank—provides a record of important information that can be referenced when needed.

Back in 1777, John Wesley, widely recognized as the father of Methodism, wrote *A Plain Account of Christian Perfection*. The title comes from the opening words of Wesley's writing on the topic: "What I purpose in the following papers, is, to give a plain and distinct account of the steps by which I was led, during a course of many years, to embrace the doctrine of Christian perfection" (p 9). Wesley proceeded to describe the development of his views, leaving behind an account that has been studied by theologians for the past 250 years.

The New Testament writer Luke began the book that bears his name by following this same pattern: he provided "an account" (1:1, 3)—not of his own life, nor of financial assets, nor of a favorite theological topic, but of Jesus Christ. Luke composed a detailed narrative of the one Matthew pointed to as ushering in the kingdom and the one Mark defined as being central to the gospel. Luke was careful to ensure his account was credible, orderly, intentional, and purposeful.

Evidence of this fourfold concern is seen in the verses that comprise the introduction to the book. Luke references "eyewitnesses" (1:2) and how he "carefully investigated everything" (1:3). He had *credible* sources and applied meticulous methods in completing his report. Luke also wanted to leave an *orderly* record. He acknowledged preparing an "orderly account" (1:3), lest any reader be left confused or uncertain. We know the entire narrative was *intentional* because Luke indicated it was written for the benefit of a specific person, Theophilus (1:3). Though little is known about the identity of this individual, we do know that Theophilus means "one who loves God." After reading Luke's account, few would argue that the producer and the recipient of this account both could be described this way, as lovers of God. Finally, what Luke wrote was *purposeful*, designed "so that you may know the certainty of the things you have been taught" (1:4). Information was quickly beginning to circulate regarding Jesus and Luke wanted to set the record straight, fill in any gaps that he could, and respond to unanswered questions. Luke was on a mission to produce an account worthy of God's Son that would stand the test of time.

The content of Luke's account can be summarized in seven general themes, or categories, all of which have inspired additional books and discussions over the years. Each theme adds important information to the whole account:

1. **Birth**. Luke begins his book with an extended narrative of the events associated with the birth of Jesus. No other biblical writer provides the rich detail surrounding the pregnancies of Elizabeth and Mary, and the witness of angels and shepherds. We are indebted to Luke for his thorough narrative regarding how Jesus entered the world.

2. **Healings**. More stories of healing appear in Luke than in any other New Testament book. Though some of these are also recorded in Matthew or Mark, others are unique to Luke—such as the healing of the ten lepers (17:11–19) and the healing of the high priest's servant's ear that was cut off when Jesus was arrested (22:50–51). The prominence given to healings in Luke's

account are likely due to the author being a doctor (Col 4:14), one who would naturally be interested in physical conditions and their cures.

3. **Teaching**. No New Testament writer references teaching more than Luke. All twenty-four chapters, except the first, either mention the word *teach* or *teacher*, or contain significant teaching from Jesus himself. Luke alone tells us that as a young boy Jesus was found in the temple "sitting among the teachers" (2:46), attributes his arrest and death specifically to those who disliked "his teaching" (23:5), and describes Jesus after the resurrection as traveling to Emmaus and explaining Scripture (24:27). Luke makes clear that Jesus was the Master Teacher.

4. **Relationships**. Jesus interacted with a wide variety of people and Luke wants his readers to notice those relationships. The synagogue ruler Jairus (8:41), sisters Mary and Martha (10:38–42), the tax collector Zacchaeus (19:1–10), the thief on the cross (23:39–43), and Cleopas and his friend on the road to Emmaus (24:13–35) are only a few of the relationships highlighted in Luke. Several parables found only in Luke—such as the Good Samaritan (10:25–37), the Prodigal Son (15:11–32), the Rich Man and Lazarus (16:19–31), the Persistent Widow (18:1–8), and others—also emphasize relationships. Luke's account focuses on real-life interactions.

5. **Death**. Like all the other gospel accounts, Luke leads us to the unjust and despicable death Jesus suffered on the cross. Despite his virgin birth, miraculous healings, authoritative teaching, and compassionate relationships, Jesus came to die for the sins of the world. Luke points readers to that astounding historical event (23:44–49).

6. **Resurrection**. Only Luke includes the story of the two travelers on the Emmaus Road and specific details regarding the ascension (Luke 24:50–53; Acts 1:9–11). Neither Jesus's death nor resurrection was the end of the story. These events changed lives and communities and then paved the way for the ascension, wherein Jesus returned victoriously to his Father. Luke's account culminates with heaven.

7. **The Holy Spirit**. In Luke's sequel, the book of Acts, he makes clear that the account of Jesus did not end once the four gospel writers finished their parallel books. The work and ministry of Jesus continued through the power and guidance of the Holy Spirit, given on the day of Pentecost (Acts 1:8; 2:1). The implication is clear: the account of Jesus, through the presence and influence of that same Holy Spirit, stretches to us today and will extend throughout all eternity. Luke provides a picture that is focused and rare. No other account matches his depth and breadth; no other account so clearly emphasizes the twin themes of history and hope.

When the blind American hymnwriter, Fanny Crosby, wrote "Tell me the story of Jesus, write on my heart every word" in 1880, one wonders whether she had in mind Luke's gospel account. We know that the detailed focus on the birth of Jesus, his healing and teaching ministry, and his meaningful relationships with all types of individuals has inspired countless people through the centuries. Furthermore, Luke's unique insights regarding how Jesus's death and resurrection were understood by his contemporaries, as well as Luke's later writings on the coming and work of the Holy Spirit, have instructed and encouraged Christians around the world. Everyone, everywhere, over the past two thousand years—regardless of the person's knowledge or depth of faith—seems to know something about Luke's version of the gospel. Whether referencing the virgin birth, the angels' proclamation of that birth, the good Samaritan, the prodigal son, or Jesus's reply to the thief on the cross, literature has borrowed extensively from Luke's careful and thorough account. The timeless and universal cry of the human heart has been, "Tell me the story of Jesus." Luke answers that cry.

How carefully have we considered the full story, or account, of Jesus? What difference has it made in our lives? Our response to those two questions foreshadows the future event that Paul described when he said one day everyone "will give an account of himself to God" (Rom 14:12). Maybe we should follow Luke's example and become more credible, orderly, intentional, and purposeful in our own account of Jesus right now. The world needs our witness, our account. Let us tell the story.

Prayer

Lord, you are calling us to give an account. One day we will do so when we stand before you at the judgment. But may we not wait until then. The world needs to hear a credible, orderly, intentional, and purposeful account today. Over the years you have repeatedly used this method to draw others into your kingdom. So, help us to be faithful, honest, and bold in communicating our account of your Son, our Savior, Jesus Christ. AMEN.

Questions

1. What four or five topics would you want to include if you were writing an account of how Jesus has influenced your life? Why would you choose those topics?

2. Why do you think Luke highlighted so many relationships in the life and parables of Jesus? What message is Luke trying to communicate by doing so?

3. What is a favorite topic, story, or pattern you find in the book of Luke? Why? What does that message tell you about Jesus?

4. Think back to Matthew's emphasis on the kingdom, Mark's emphasis on the gospel, and Luke's emphasis on giving an account. Which of these emphases do you find most relevant, or needed, in our world today? Explain.

Suggested Reading

Luke 1–2, 4, 10, 15, 19, 24

43

JOHN: Love

*For God so loved the world that he gave his one
and only Son, that whoever believes in him shall
not perish but have eternal life. (John 3:16)*

*A new command I give you: Love one another. As I have loved
you, so you must love one another. By this all men will know that
you are my disciples, if you love one another. (John 13:34–35)*

*Greater love has no one than this, that he lay
down his life for his friends. (John 15:13)*

Has any idea been more distorted and abused over the years than love? What the Apostle Paul described as "the fruit of the Spirit" (Gal 5:22) has apparently fallen off the tree and rotted. The noblest of virtues has been reduced to a feeling concerned with personal pleasure. Love has become so sexualized that we hardly know any other way to talk about it today. While in some ways modern society has elevated love, there is evidence that what has been elevated is only a caricature of the real thing. We have lifted sexual desire—and called it "love"—above every other right and sensibility in our world. The result has been devastating, producing both moral chaos and intellectual absurdity. There is no shortage of irrational and illogical behavior tolerated today, and even legalized in our courts, because playing the "love" card always results in the reasonable question: How can anyone argue with love?

Back in 1967, Dusty Springfield popularized a song composed by Burt Bacharach and Hal David, "The Look of Love." What is that look? What does true *love* look like? A line in the song suggests love is more than mere words: "The look of love is saying so much more than just words could ever say." Indeed, it is. Love goes deeper, has more substance, stretches farther, and demands broader understanding than the flimsy emotion widely promoted and accepted in society today. Again, Paul contributed to the discussion when he described "how wide and long and high and deep is the love of Christ" (Eph 3:18). There are dimensions and features that get overlooked when love is reduced to the pursuit of a pleasurable feeling.

The gospel writer John had a great deal to say about love and its characteristics. In essence, he described "the look of love" long before the 1967 pop song hit the music charts. John's first reference to love is found in the Bible verse that probably has been more widely memorized than any other: John 3:16, "For God so loved the world . . . ." Once the idea of love is introduced there, John cannot stop talking about it. Love keeps creeping back into his narrative. None of the other gospel writers emphasizes love to the degree that John does. In fact, only Paul, among all biblical writers, comes close to referencing love as often as John. The topic of love is so compelling to John that he later writes an entire letter—1 John—given to its further explanation. In that letter, he boldly asserts that "God is love" (1 John 4:8). One cannot understand God without grasping love; and, conversely, one cannot understand love without grasping God.

Because John so clearly championed love, it is worth exploring "the look of love" from his perspective. What are the characteristics, or features, of the love that so captivated him? While it would be impossible to exhaust our understanding of love—for remember, God himself is love, and no one can ever fully exhaust God—there are some important themes provided in the book of John that inform us.

The nature of love. The love that John describes has a twofold nature having to do with both action and quality. When John speaks about love, he almost always does so by making it a verb. Nearly ninety percent of his references to love use the verb form of the word, highlighting a deliberate action. John sees love as something one does rather than what one says or feels. Author Bob Goff's 2012 book title, *Love Does*, while succinct, lends support to John's understanding. Love is a choice to act a particular way, regardless of feelings or circumstances.

That relates, of course, to the quality of love. John, like other New Testament writers, primarily uses the word *agape* when speaking about love. The Greek word implies deep and unconditional concern for another's wellbeing, even when that individual is unworthy. Love, then, is a choice to *act* even when feelings are absent and even when the object of love is not deserving of affection. The world has strayed far from this biblical "look of love." John described the nature of love as "so much more than just words could ever say" and more than self-centered feelings of pleasure. Love is an audacious and unconditional act that intentionally puts others ahead of oneself.

The scope of love. Love knows no boundaries; it encompasses the whole world (3:16). Is it mere coincidence that the first time John references love he speaks of its magnitude? There is no one in all creation who falls outside God's vast canopy of love. The whole world—including the culturally-despised Samaritans (4:4–9), the physically-disabled outcast (5:1–9), and the morally-depraved adulteress (8:1–11)—is loved by God and, by implication, by those who claim to follow God. Those whom society marginalizes or rejects are the very ones whom God loves. The scope of love found in John is wide, reaching those who may be hard to love and those who may offer little in return. Unfortunately, that look of love has grown increasingly rare in the world today.

The witness of love. John records these words from Jesus: "all men will know that you are my disciples, if you love one another" (13:35). Love, then, is the primary witness to the world of one's devotion to Jesus. Across the years Christians have been led to believe, by zealous yet sometimes misguided spiritual leaders, that religious ritual, the paying of penance, church attendance, and other dutiful activities signal one's devotion to Christ. Though these behaviors may help focus our attention and provide needed discipline, none of these was highlighted by Jesus as the primary evidence of discipleship. The true witness of the disciple of Jesus is love. The simple act of love communicates "so much more than just [pious] words could ever say." So much is at stake in how we understand or look at love. Stretching far beyond my own personal comfort or pleasure, love has implications for the witness and spread of the gospel. Nowhere in the Bible are we told that love is a pleasurable feeling, but we are told it is a winsome witness of our commitment to Jesus Christ.

The sacrifice of love. Jesus zeroed in on the essence of love when he tied it to what we do for others rather than what we seek for ourselves. After washing his disciples' feet (13:1–17), illustrating how love sacrifices position and status, Jesus went a step further and said sometimes the sacrifice requires even more—one's very life. He put it this way: "Greater love has no one than this, that he lay down his life for his friends" (15:13). Of course, that is exactly what Jesus did when he died for us on the cross. His love was so deep that he sacrificed his life for our eternal salvation. The look of love that John described, in contrast to today's shallow version of love, was not self-centered; it was sacrificial. True love still is, though few recognize this characteristic of love in a society that emphasizes individual rights.

The proof of love. An interesting story unfolds in the last chapter of John that is only told there. One day after his resurrection, Jesus was waiting for his disciples to return from an all-night fishing trip. When they came to shore, they were surprised to find Jesus there with breakfast prepared (21:12). Jesus used the early morning occasion to ask Peter, who days earlier had denied being a follower of Jesus (18:15–27), whether he "truly" loved him. In fact, he asked the question three times (21:15–17), perhaps purposely corresponding to Peter's three earlier denials. What is certain is that after each question Jesus followed with an admonition for Peter to prove his love by feeding or caring for the Lord's "sheep." The message seems to be that the proof of love is found in service to others. Words, without supporting acts of service, are hollow and meaningless. The look of love John describes entails caring for those for whom Christ died, not seeking one's own pleasure.

The identity of love. A descriptive phrase, repeated in the second half of the book of John, is only found in John. Five times there is reference to "the disciple whom Jesus loved" (13:23; 19:26; 20:2; 21:7, 20). Most biblical scholars agree this was John's humble way of identifying himself. His life was so transformed that it only had meaning in relationship to Jesus and the love that Jesus offered. John was so smitten by this love that it became a reference point for the remainder of his life. We know that because even when John was exiled to the island of Patmos in his later years (Rev 1:9), he still referred to Jesus as "[he] who loves us" (Rev 1:5). Adverse circumstances did not diminish the deep love John recognized as coming from his Lord and Master. John was loved by Jesus—no one and no circumstance could take that love from him. He knew the reality of which Paul wrote: "[Nothing] will be able to separate us from the love of God that is in Christ Jesus our Lord" (Rom 8:39). John's identity was secure and squarely established on the fact that Jesus loved him. O, that we would recapture *that* look of love today—knowing we are loved by Jesus—rather than chasing after superficial loves and passions that serve only as temporary identities.

Charles Wesley, writing sixteen centuries after John penned his gospel, was captured by the same love that moved the apostle. Wesley's well-known lyrics now echo in song throughout Christendom:

> *Amazing love*
> *How can it be*
> *That Thou, my God, shouldst die for me*

The time has come to correct the numerous harmful distortions surrounding love and emphasize the "amazing love" of Christ. A sane, balanced, and biblical understanding of love has the power to change the world—one person at a time. It always has been that way. May we be a people restored *by* and restored *to* such love.

When all is said and done, "these three [will] remain: faith, hope and love. But the greatest of these is love" (1 Cor 13:13). In other words, the look of love knows no end.

PRAYER

O loving God, we are humbled and even overwhelmed by your unconditional and sacrificial love that has reached down to this world. Thank you for initiating that love to undeserving sinners such as us. Forgive us for the ways we have confused and corrupted the love that you so graciously designed and have so generously shared. Help us to follow your example. May those around us know that we are your followers because we love like you. Deliver and keep us from a false and superficial substitute. We offer this prayer in the name of the One who incarnated love, Jesus, our Savior and Lord. AMEN.

QUESTIONS

1. How would you define love? What does that love look like?

2. Why has love grown so distorted across the years? What might we do to restore love to a more biblical understanding?

3. What example of sacrificial human love have you seen or experienced in your life? What was the sacrifice? What was the impact?

4. Who comes to mind from your social circle of family or friends when you think of a "disciple whom Jesus loved" or, conversely, one who is known to be in love with Jesus? What evidence does the person give of his or her love relationship with Jesus?

SUGGESTED READING

John 1, 3–4, 13–15, 17, 21

44

Acts: Witness

But you will receive power when the Holy Spirit comes on you; and you will be my witnesses in Jerusalem, and in all Judea and Samaria, and to the ends of the earth. (Acts 1:8)

God has raised this Jesus to life, and we are all witnesses of the fact. (Acts 2:32)

You killed the author of life, but God raised him from the dead. We are witnesses of this. (Acts 3:15)

But God raised him from the dead, and for many days he was seen by those who had traveled with him from Galilee to Jerusalem. They are now his witnesses to our people. (Acts 13:30–31)

In the early 1970s, when I was between the ages of fifteen and twenty, telling others what I had personally seen Christ do in people's lives became a common activity. My friends and I had experienced a powerful outpouring of God's Spirit upon our church, its youth group, and our families. It was only natural that we wanted to tell others about what had happened. Thus, in the summer of 1970 I joined other youth and took to the streets of Flint, Michigan, in search of people with whom we might share the good news. We called it *witnessing*—telling others about what Jesus had done for us and assuring our oft-startled audience that Jesus could do the same for them. The following year, in 1971, a group of my friends and I traveled to northern Georgia at the invitation of a small church and gave our collective witness there over a period of several days. During the next few years, I found myself giving a public witness to the saving work of Christ in several locations around Michigan, back in Georgia a second time, out in British Columbia, and then in Kentucky. A bold and public proclamation of the gospel seemed the only reasonable response to the transformative work of God we had witnessed in the lives of both friends and strangers, young and old. For five years or more, we looked for opportunities to head to the streets, a parking lot, or across the country in search of an audience with whom we might share the good news.

To be a witness means to give a credible report regarding something a person has seen, heard, or experienced firsthand. In our case, we wanted to give witness to what we had seen God do in our young lives when the 1970 Asbury revival fires swept through our church and community. In a similar fashion, the book of Acts—a history of the early church—emphasizes the witness of those who personally encountered the resurrected Lord, Jesus Christ, and then experienced the infilling of the Holy Spirit at Pentecost (2:1–4). There was a story to tell and those who knew it could not be silenced. Luke's second volume, like his first, addressed Theophilus (Acts 1:1; cf. Luke 1:3) and focused on the ongoing influence of Jesus through the witness of his followers. The word *witness* is found nearly thirty times in Acts; throughout Scripture only John uses the word more. The earliest followers of Jesus gave eyewitness accounts of his life, death, resurrection, and the subsequent coming of the Holy Spirit.

The Greek word for witness is the word *martus*, from which we get the English word "martyr." A witness, then, is one willing to give his or her life for what is known to be true. Such a person is so sure of what has been seen or heard that he is willing to stake his life on the veracity or truthfulness of his claim. In our legal system, we require courtroom witnesses to swear an oath that they will tell "the whole truth and nothing but the truth." To be a witness is a serious matter requiring integrity, reliability, and certainty.

God has raised up witnesses in every generation who have pointed people to Jesus and his work of salvation for a lost and needy world. In fact, a careful investigation of Acts and a study of the entire history of Christendom combine to indicate that it is often through someone's witness that others are drawn to consider the claims of Christ. That witness tends to manifest itself in one of three ways, all of which are noted in the book of Acts and illustrated in more modern history as well.

First, **there is the witness of a spoken word**. As teenagers, that is how my friends and I understood witnessing. We were not wrong to think so, for that is the picture that unfolds in Acts. Consider Peter, who addressed the crowd in Jerusalem at Pentecost (2:14), the crippled beggar at the temple gate (3:1–6), the religious leaders who had jailed him (4:1–12), and the Roman centurion Cornelius (10:24–46). In each case, Peter's witness included the spoken word that contained the good news about Jesus, almost always referencing his resurrection. The need for a spoken word of witness has not diminished over time. People still need to know the hope that is found in Jesus. However, I fear what has diminished is our willingness to share such a word. In a world of pluralism, hyper criticism, and social media, we recognize our reputation may be at risk if we dare give such a bold verbal witness regarding Christ. While the concern is understandable, we would do well to remind ourselves that Peter faced the same risk. Peter was jailed for his word of witness on more than one occasion (4:3; 5:18; 12:3–5), which presumably tarnished his reputation among various members of the local community. Nonetheless, Peter was compelled to keep speaking because of his conviction that "salvation is found in no one else" other than Jesus (4:12). That fact drove him to the twofold conclusion that "we cannot help speaking about what we have seen and heard" (4:20) and "we must obey God rather than men" (5:29).

Yes, a word of witness may be misunderstood, ridiculed, or despised. Stories throughout the book of Acts make that clear. However, the primary concern of the devoted follower of Christ is *his* reputation, not ours. The world may threaten us, but Jesus thrills us to the point that we cannot keep silent. If we do, the very "stones will cry out" in praise and witness to the glory of God (Luke 19:40). When was the last time we spoke a word of witness to a friend, family member, or office colleague? A spoken word of witness is still needed today.

Second, **there is the witness of a steady example**. While words matter if we are to be a witness for Christ, there is another type of witness that I did not understand very well when I was a teenager. A witness also occurs when one lives a consistent and steady life of devotion. A holy example becomes a powerful exhibit of what God can do in an individual's life. Who has not been inspired by the model of another? Whereas Peter provides a case study of one who boldly spoke words of witness on behalf of the risen Christ, Barnabas represents one whose life was an exemplary witness. Barnabas is mentioned twenty-four times throughout the book of Acts, and we are the beneficiaries of that repetition. The name Barnabas means "Son of Encouragement" (4:36), and so he was. It was Barnabas who encouraged Saul and brought the one-time persecutor into the apostles' circle (9:27); it was Barnabas who encouraged the early believers in Antioch (11:19–24), once the church began to spread beyond Jerusalem; it was Barnabas who stood by Paul at the Jerusalem council and encouraged the early Jewish church to open its arms to the Gentiles (15:2, 12); and it was Barnabas who encouraged and teamed up with Mark when Paul no longer trusted the young man (15:36–39). I suspect we may be surprised by how many people are in heaven due to the steady example and witness of Barnabas and those just like him—those who lived behind the scenes, modeled a godly life, and quietly encouraged others. There is power in such a witness.

During my four years at Asbury College in Kentucky, I was blessed to become acquainted with the Brabon family. I arrived at college shortly after Margaret Brabon, herself a 1942 Asbury graduate, had moved back to the community. Her husband of twenty-nine years, Harold, had died the year before I enrolled as a freshman. I was captivated by what I learned about the Brabons. As a young man, Harold worked as a chemist for the Ford Motor Company, where he was considered one of the top young minds in the expanding auto industry. However, in the 1940s God called Harold and Margaret to the country of Colombia, South America, where both their words and their exemplary lives of service—often carried out under threats and duress—became the seeds that led many Colombians into the kingdom of God (Margaret Brabon's 1993 book *What Now, Lord?* provides more details). Henry Ford let Harold know that his decision to exchange a promising career for a life of uncertainty in a far-off country made absolutely no sense. Ford, of course, was correct. A steady life of exemplary and winsome witness for Christ never makes sense to the outsider focused on achievement, advancement, and material gain. Yet the witness of such a life always has been an effective way to spread the gospel of Jesus Christ. Harold Brabon's obedience to God influenced others, including all four of his children who became missionaries after him. The witness of his steady example continues to bear fruit today.

Third, **there is the witness of a surrendered life**. In addition to words and examples, there remains another type of witness. Whereas the former types forfeit reputation and opportunity for personal gain, the latter type forfeits longevity in that it sacrifices life itself for the cause of Christ. We often speak of the experience as martyrdom. This is fitting, of course, since we noted earlier that the Greek word translated as "witness" is *martus*. A martyr is a powerful witness to the person or principle for which one has died. Acts records the martyrdom of early believers, such as Stephen (7:59–60) and James the brother of John (12:2). The sixteenth-century English historian, John Foxe, later chronicled the stories of numerous other Christian martyrs across the early centuries of Christendom. His 1563 volume became popularly known as *Foxe's Book of Martyrs*. A predictable pattern surrounds martyrdom: the rise of "persecution" results in the death of some, which in turn results in the "scattering" of God's people, providing further opportunity for them to "preach the word" as they go and point to the witness of the one who surrendered his or her life for the sake of Christ (8:1, 4; cf. 11:19; 13:50–51). At the end of the New Testament, John, while writing details regarding his heavenly vision, noted that there were residents in heaven who had overcome the enemy "by the word of their testimony" (the Greek word there is *martus*, or witness) and because "they did not love their lives so much as to shrink from death" (Rev 12:11). A surrendered life to Christ, even when the result is death, has always inspired others and served as a clear witness of the unsurpassed value of the gospel.

Being a witness is no less important today than it was during Bible times or at any period in history. Whether it is a spoken word, a steady example, or a surrendered life, God is looking for those who will be his willing and winsome witnesses. It may mean forfeiting reputation, opportunity, and long life. However, each of those is a small price to pay. The central message of the gospel is that what Jesus offers is of more value than any competing pursuit in this world.

May our words, our example, and our lives bear witness to Jesus Christ. When the disciples asked Jesus on this side of the resurrection if the time had now come for him "to restore the kingdom to Israel" (1:6), the implication—and perhaps the hope—was that the work was finally done. Jesus redirected their focus when he replied: "[Y]ou will be my witnesses . . . to the ends of the earth" (1:8). Translated, there is work that remains to be done. A witness is needed in every generation.

PRAYER

O Lord, we bow in recognition of your Son's saving work on the cross and the victory he won through his resurrection. Thank you. However, we recognize the work is not done. For you call every new generation of followers to be your witnesses in the present world. So, with Isaiah the prophet and with the earliest disciples our humble prayer is: "Here am I. Send me" (Isa 6:8). Make *me* a witness. Make *me* a light for you in an otherwise dark world—a witness who consistently points to Jesus Christ. Grant wisdom, winsomeness, boldness, persistence, and assurance that the calling is worthy and noble. We pray this in the name of Jesus. AMEN.

QUESTIONS

1. Who do you know to be an effective witness for Christ? To what do you attribute that person's effectiveness? What characteristics does he or she possess?

2. Why do you think we hear so little about being a witness today? Why is so little attention given to teaching or helping others become witnesses in our world?

3. What are some common challenges, or obstacles, every generation faces when trying to be a witness? What are some challenges unique to our present generation?

4. Review the three types of witnesses referenced in this chapter. What example can you provide of each type of witness from your own experiences, observations of others, or readings?

SUGGESTED READING

Acts 1–3, 9–10, 13, 15–16

45

ROMANS: Faith

*I thank my God through Jesus Christ for all of you, because
your faith is being reported all over the world. (Romans 1:8)*

*I am not ashamed of the gospel, because it is the power of God
for the salvation of everyone who believes: first for the Jew, then
for the Gentile. For in the gospel a righteousness from God is
revealed, a righteousness that is by faith from first to last, just as
it is written: "The righteous will live by faith." (Romans 1:16–17)*

*This righteousness from God comes through faith in
Jesus Christ to all who believe. (Romans 3:22)*

*Therefore, since we have been justified through faith, we have
peace with God through our Lord Jesus Christ, through whom we
have gained access by faith into this grace in which we now stand.
And we rejoice in the hope of the glory of God. (Romans 5:1–2)*

Neil Armstrong and Buzz Aldrin became household names after they
were the first two humans to walk on the moon on July 20, 1969.
On the other hand, relatively few people know the name Michael Collins.
However, had it not been for Collins, the story of Armstrong, Aldrin,
and the entire Apollo 11 mission would have been very different. Collins
was the commander of the spaceship that orbited the moon numerous
times while his comrades left their footprints on its surface. Sometimes
referred to as the "forgotten astronaut," Collins was cut off from com-

munication with both NASA and his fellow astronauts for nearly fifty minutes every time he circled the dark side of the moon. Yet he was responsible for ensuring the spaceship performed optimally and was in position for the all-important rendezvous with the lunar module once it exited the moon. Then after the three astronauts were reunited above the moon's surface, Collins navigated the crew safely back to Earth.

The entire project demanded significant amounts of faith at every step. The crew had faith in the laws of physics, the laws of gravity, the laws of aerodynamics, advanced technology, and the scientists and engineers back at NASA's mission control in Houston. Armstrong and Aldrin also had faith that Collins would return from his repeated orbits of the moon; likewise, Collins had faith that Armstrong and Aldrin would be able to launch their uniquely crafted module successfully from the moon and join him for the return trip home. Make no mistake about it, faith infused every aspect of the Apollo 11 mission. In fact, without it there would have been no lunar landing, no safe return, and no victorious story to report. Little wonder that *Apollo 11* was released as a movie in 2019, commemorating the historic event from fifty years earlier.

Just like one cannot tell the story of Apollo 11 and its unlikely journey to the moon without reference to the faith of its crew, one cannot tell the story of the New Testament and the unlikely journeys of its heroes without noting the prominence of their faith. Every book of the New Testament—except for the short letters of 2 and 3 John—highlights faith. In fact, the term, whether in its noun or verb form (i.e., to believe, or to have faith), is found nearly five hundred times throughout the New Testament. In the apostle Paul's letter to the Romans, the terms *faith* or *believe* are found over sixty times. The centrality of faith is impossible to miss. What do we learn about this faith from the book of Romans?

First, **faith has an object**. Too often people talk about faith as a nebulous abstraction. That was not the kind of faith practiced by the Apollo 11 crew, nor is it the kind of faith described by Paul and other biblical writers. For faith to exist, it needs an object. Faith must be anchored to something or someone reliable. In Romans, Paul emphasized "faith in Jesus Christ" (3:22), later referring to "faith in his blood" (3:25). Thus, Jesus is the object of our faith. His blood—his death on the cross—atoned for our sins. "Faith in Jesus" (3:26), rather than keeping the law, justifies and redeems us (3:21–31). Scripture repeatedly points to faith in the person, death, and resurrection of Jesus Christ; to miss this is to miss the most fundamental principle of life. Furthermore, to have faith is to know Jesus personally, not just to know *about* him.

Second, **faith has a history**. The faith demonstrated by the Apollo 11 crew was based on information gained from thirty-four previous human spaceflights—twenty-two of those were American flights, twelve were Soviet flights—as well as numerous unmanned space missions. Paul, recognizing the value of history when it comes to faith, takes his readers all the way back to the patriarch Abraham (4:1–22), noting that he too was an individual of faith. Faith did not originate with us, nor even with Paul. Its history is long and colorful. Later, in Hebrews 11—a chapter commonly referred to as the Bible's "Hall of Fame" or "Hall of Faith"—we are provided a long list of men and women remembered for their faith. However, there is even more to our history of faith. Paul links the faith of believers to "God's faithfulness" (3:3). The faithfulness of God makes our faith possible. We have faith because our God has proven himself faithful to us. He then provided examples and witnesses of humans with faith throughout the centuries. Faith that looks to the future is built on God's work in the past.

Third, **faith has ultimate victory**. The victory of Apollo 11 was widely celebrated, though there were struggles and setbacks that preceded the mission. In fact, Apollo 1 astronauts never made it off the launch pad, where three of them died in a preflight test on January 27, 1967. There were other setbacks and failures with the Apollo program as well. Christians often tell a similar story. For example, Paul described how sin wants to reign and be our master (6:12–14); he followed that with a description of his own struggle with sin (7:14–20). Nonetheless, immediately thereafter Paul wrote one of the most eloquent and victorious messages found in any of his writings. For in Romans 8, he declared faith in Christ results in "no condemnation" (8:1), the possibility of a Spirit-controlled life (8:10, 26), a new perspective on all life's circumstances (8:28), and victory despite challenges and adversity (8:37–39). The clear message is that faith ultimately triumphs, leading to unimaginable conquests.

Fourth, **faith has consequences**. Faith, by its very nature, does not signal an ending but a turning point. That turning point, or consequence, is captured by the connecting word *therefore* (12:1). Though the use of *therefore* is not unique to Romans, there are arguably few uses that are more strategic or meaningful. Because of faith, we are compelled to live differently. Paul opens his letter by saying that "obedience . . . comes from faith" (1:5). So, after eleven chapters that describe such faith, Paul takes a breath and says *therefore* (12:1) we ought to live a certain way. The end of his letter provides a summary of what that means. Just as the aftermath of Apollo 11 was a turning point for space exploration and technological advances—for example, ten other astronauts would walk on the moon and a variety of new space vehicles were designed—according to Paul, faith culminates in a turning point as well. The word *therefore* in Romans 12:1 is a way of saying there are some changes expected to follow. Because of faith, one ought to live differently. The last five chapters of Romans offer what Paul suggests are reasonable consequences of the faith he has described in the first eleven chapters: total commitment, total love, total submission, total selflessness, and total concern.

Total commitment (12:1–7). Evidence of being people of faith comes in the form of sacrifice, surrender, and service. Because our faith is in the resurrected and victorious Lord, no sacrifice is too great, surrender defies popular understanding in that it results not in loss but in gain, and service is embraced as a way of enriching both oneself and others in the body of Christ. Faith calls for total commitment, a devotion that transforms attitudes and activities. Allegiance to Jesus affects what we think and what we do. It is comprehensive.

Total love (12:9–21; 13:8–14). Another consequence of faith is love. This is no ordinary display of affection. Paul urges people of faith to:

- "Be sincere" in their love (12:9).
- "Honor one another above yourselves" (12:10).
- Be "patient in affliction" (12:12).
- "Bless those who persecute you" (12:14).
- "Associate with people of low position" (12:16).
- "If it is possible . . . live at peace with everyone" (12:18).
- "Overcome evil with good" (12:21).
- Do "no harm to [a] neighbor" (13:10).
- "Behave decently" (13:13).

Faith makes one love the unlovable and undeserving. Faith-motivated love goes above and beyond what is humanly expected, responding to difficult situations in ways that benefit others more than oneself.

Total submission (13:1–7). Faith results in submission to authorities. In contrast to our media-saturated world where we see daily images of those who ridicule and reject authority, and often get rewarded for doing so, Paul declares that people of faith ought to respond differently. For example, those who govern, those who collect taxes, and those to whom we owe bills are to be treated with godly respect. Paul goes so far as to say we should submit "not only because of possible punishment but also because of conscience" (13:5). Faith in Christ changes one's thinking. We can submit to another because we know that Jesus already has triumphed. Our faith recognizes that the battle, the outcome, has been won. Total submission becomes a powerful witness to the fact that our God reigns.

Total selflessness (14:1—15:13). People of faith are considerate of and encouraging toward others. They willingly withhold judgment and give the benefit of the doubt when it comes to disputable matters of faith. Paul suggests that arguments regarding food (14:2–3, 14–21) and sacred days (14:5–6) are not battles worth fighting. Rather, he encourages us to "stop passing judgment on one another" and to avoid putting "any stumbling block or obstacle in your brother's way" (14:13). The implication is that faith leads to a rare selflessness that acknowledges God's unique work in another, even when the individual does not think or act exactly as we do. The standard of faith becomes "mutual edification" (14:19), not "pleas[ing] ourselves" (15:1). After all, "even Christ did not please himself" (15:3). Only a strong faith can produce such a selfless perspective.

Total concern (15:14—16:27). Faith results in a deep concern expressed through hospitality. Paul illustrates this outcome of faith autobiographically. In Romans 9, he describes such sincere concern for his people, the Israelites, that he speaks of his willingness to forfeit his own relationship with Christ for their sake (9:1–4). Later he identifies a parallel interest in the Gentiles, noting that God has called him to minister to them (15:15–16). In his final chapter, Romans 16, Paul references a long list of people with whom he has established relationships—commending some, while sending personal greetings to others. These references illustrate Paul's compassion and concern for others. The outcome of faith is an expanding interest in the wellbeing of our brothers and sisters in Christ.

In the final analysis, faith is central to life and changes it. All major human endeavors require faith of one kind or another. Whether heading to the moon, heaven, or more mundane places like the office, university, or marketplace, faith is needed. That simple fact raises at least three important questions:

1. In whom will we place our faith?
2. What will that faith look like?
3. What difference will it make in our lives?

A good time to answer those questions is right now.

PRAYER

Our Father in heaven, you have made us to be people of faith, people who follow you. Help us on that journey. We confess there are distractions and obstacles along the way that tempt us to divert our attention away from you and your design. Deliver us from such temptation. May our faith remain strong in the various seasons of life. May our lives be a clear witness to the faith our lips proclaim. This we pray in the name of your Son, our Savior, Jesus Christ. AMEN.

QUESTIONS

1. When have you had to demonstrate mature faith? What were the circumstances? What was the outcome?

2. In addition to the Apollo 11 space mission, what other events or accomplishments have required significant faith? Describe some of the elements or evidence of that faith.

3. What are some common obstacles to faith today? How might these be overcome?

4. How has the "therefore" (12:1) of faith played out in your life? What changes have occurred in your life because of your faith? Are there other changes still needed? What are those changes?

SUGGESTED READING

Romans 1, 3, 5, 8, 10, 12–14

46

1 CORINTHIANS: Christ

*We preach Christ crucified: a stumbling block to Jews
and foolishness to Gentiles, but to those whom God has
called, both Jews and Greeks, Christ the power of God
and the wisdom of God. (1 Corinthians 1:23–24)*

*For I resolved to know nothing while I was with you except
Jesus Christ and him crucified. (1 Corinthians 2:2)*

*Follow my example, as I follow the example
of Christ. (1 Corinthians 11:1)*

*For what I received I passed on to you as of first importance:
that Christ died for our sins according to the Scriptures,
that he was buried, that he was raised on the third day
according to the Scriptures, and that he appeared to
Peter, and then to the Twelve. (1 Corinthians 15:3–5)*

Every New Testament theme we have discussed thus far points to
Jesus Christ. The *kingdom* of Matthew, the *gospel* of Mark, the
account of Luke, the *love* of John, the *witness* of Acts, and the *faith* of
Romans all find their meaning in Christ. The Old Testament prophets
anticipated Christ and the New Testament apostles were ambassadors
for Christ. Without him there would be no Christianity, no church, no
Bible, no salvation, no hope of eternity. Christ is the central figure of
history; we divide time into BC and AD in reference to his coming to

earth. No other individual has been so revered and yet so divisive as Jesus Christ.

The title *Christ* occurs 69 times in 1 Corinthians, more than any other single book of the Bible. Romans comes next with 68 references, followed by 2 Corinthians with 49. Altogether, the name of Christ appears over 560 times in the New Testament. Except for the short letter of 3 John (which does not mention Christ at all), every New Testament book references Christ multiple times. It would be impossible to read the New Testament and miss this title and its impact.

In Greek, the word *Christ* literally means "the anointed one." Biblical writers used the term to translate the older Hebrew word "Messiah." Of course, throughout the New Testament the designation is associated with Jesus. Thus, "Jesus Christ" became the standard expression identifying the Son of God (e.g., Matt 1:1; Mark 1:1). Paul often reversed the order of the names and spoke of "Christ Jesus" (e.g., Rom 1:1; 1 Cor 1:1; 2 Cor 1:1; Eph 1:1; Phil 1:1; etc.). One can only conjecture whether this was a stylistic preference by Paul or whether he was trying to draw particular attention to the anointed and anticipated Messiah who represented the hope for all humanity. What is not conjecture is that Paul speaks of Christ more than any other biblical author. Paul, once a zealous Jewish Pharisee (Phil 3:5–6), had an encounter with the resurrected Christ and then could not stop talking about him.

We, too, ought to be talking about Christ—more than we do. However, we have a problem. It is primarily a problem of misunderstanding. While it is true that some people completely reject or deny Christ, the bigger concern is with those of us who think we are honoring him but who make one of several common mistakes when it comes to our understanding of him.

Knowing about Christ but failing to truly know and be like Christ. Dennis Kinlaw, in his daily devotional *This Day with the Master* (2002), begins his November 9 entry this way: "What Western Christianity needs first and foremost is not more Christians, but for Christians to be much more Christian than they are." There are numerous bright people—many of them in our churches, Bible schools, and seminaries—who can converse intelligently *about* Christ, his teachings, and doctrines pertaining to him. Sadly, too many of these same people show little evidence of having an intimate knowledge and relationship *with* Christ. Too few live like Christ; too few regularly operate as a Christian. Paul was one of the most learned men of his day, and yet he did not promote mere mental comprehension when it came to Christ. On the contrary, Paul wrote, "we preach Christ crucified: a stumbling block to Jews and foolishness to Gentiles . . . Christ the power of God and the wisdom of God" (1 Cor 1:23–24). The power and wisdom of God are not gained through intellectual pursuits but through encountering and becoming like the crucified and risen Christ. Such teaching struck many people as foolishness; it still does. Yet our call is to know him and live as he lived, "to be much more Christian than [we] are."

Growing up in Michigan in the 1960s, I knew quite a bit about several state celebrities such as Henry Ford II, the long-time CEO of Ford Motor Company; Detroit Tiger Hall-of-Famer Al Kaline, one of the few baseball players to become a star while never playing a game in the minor leagues; and Motown singer Diana Ross, who rose from her Detroit roots to enjoy unparalleled success with her vocal group the Supremes. Everyone in Michigan knew *about* these local shining stars. However, most Michigan residents at the time—myself included—did not actually *know* any of them. I never exchanged a word or personally communicated with one of those three personalities. I only knew about them, heard of their achievements, and observed them from a distance. Tragically, that describes too many people when it comes to their relationship with Christ. Paul, in another letter, was emphatic when he wrote: "I want to know Christ and the power of his resurrection and the fellowship of sharing in his sufferings, becoming like him in his death" (Phil 3:10). He was not content with information *about* Christ; he sought intimacy *with* Christ. Paul desired to be like Christ. That remains the standard for every Christian.

Substituting the church for Christ. There has been a centuries-old tendency among followers of Christ to substitute the church, the bride of Christ, for Christ himself. The shift is subtle yet idolatrous. Such people honor Jesus Christ with their lips, but their lives indicate he has lost his lofty position as "head of the church" (Eph 5:23; cf. Eph 1:22; 4:15; Col 1:18). Allegiance to the church—the institution, with its programs, activities, and upkeep—has replaced allegiance to Christ. The former demands support; the latter demands submission. The one invites attendance; the other invites adoration. The one emphasizes ritual; the other emphasizes relationship. The one wants us to give something for the cause of ministry; the other wants us to give everything for the cause of the master.

Let me be clear: supporting, attending, participating in, and giving to a local church's ministry are all good. There never has been a time in my life when I have not done these things out of loyalty and commitment. But these acts dare not take the place of submission, adoration, relationship, and surrender of everything to Christ. When the church and its activities come before Christ we are in trouble. Anything that we substitute for Christ—even when it is his bride—misses the reason for which he came and misses the intent of the gospel. The result is a misguided devotion that too often becomes life-draining rather than life-giving. Paul left no room for ambiguity when he wrote: "For I resolved to know nothing while I was with you except Jesus Christ and him crucified" (1 Cor 2:2).

Acknowledging the principles of Christ while rejecting the person of Christ. Many people in our day, as well as throughout history, have been impressed by the teaching and example of Christ. The principles he promoted—meekness, love, forgiveness, concern for the poor, and virtuous ethics—have become timeless and universal standards of conduct. However, the principles without the person of Christ are not enough. Christ did not come to urge people to endorse a petition or support a ballot measure; he came so that fallen humanity might develop a relationship with God incarnate. If we miss the person, we miss the point. Paul identified what was of "first importance" when he wrote "Christ died for our sins according to the Scriptures" (1 Cor 15:3). The person of Christ and his sacrifice for our sins confront each of us. Accepting his principles without embracing his life and death is an affront to God. We dare not confuse noble principles with the noted person of Jesus Christ.

E. Stanley Jones, in his autobiography *A Song of Ascents* (1968), discussed his cordial relationship with Mahatma Gandhi, one of India's leading political figures in the early 1900s. Jones spent most of his life as a missionary in India, where he had great respect for and several exchanges with Mr. Gandhi. Once, when Jones asked Gandhi how Christianity might become more naturalized in India, the Indian leader responded by saying, "Christians, missionaries and all, must begin to live more like Jesus Christ" (Jones, p 132). Gandhi, a Hindu, spoke highly of Christ, his teaching, and his example. However, after multiple conversations and years of friendship, Jones one day wrote a letter to Gandhi wherein he soberly communicated the following: "I . . . thought you had grasped the center of the Christian faith, but I'm afraid I will have to change my mind. You have grasped certain principles which have molded you and made you great. But while you have grasped the principles . . . you have missed the Person" (p 133). Unfortunately, what was true of Gandhi has become the experience of far too many people in our world today. It is easier and more socially acceptable to endorse the principles of Christ than to embrace the person of Christ.

All three of these behaviors fall short of God's intention. He did not send Christ—the anointed one—so that we might only know about him, substitute the church and its activities for him, or merely follow his principles and example. These are all tragic mistakes that the Enemy is happy for us to make. There are other mistakes as well. For example, some people add to Christ and create a form of syncretistic religious experience rather than finding sufficiency in Christ alone. Others strip Christ of any backbone or muscle, leaving nothing but a spineless caricature of a good religious leader who offends no one. Still others make of Christ a magician or good luck charm, to whom they turn for help during times of trouble. All miss the mark. All fail to recognize Christ for who he truly is and the reason for which he came.

How, then, are we to understand Christ and what ought to be our response to him? The message of the New Testament consistently calls us to a personal relationship with the revealed, righteous, and risen Lord Jesus Christ. We see this clearly in the opening chapter of 1 Corinthians. Several observations are worth noting. First, Paul acknowledges that both he and the church to whom he writes have been *invited*, or called (1:1–2, 9). Second, he makes clear the call is to a personal relationship, or *fellowship*, with Christ (1:9). Fellowship implies a degree of intimacy and interaction. Third, Jesus Christ is *revealed* (1:7) by God, not the product of human initiative or fantasy. Fourth, Christ is *our righteousness* (1:30), meaning we are only made right through him and are only capable of doing right because of him. Fifth, Christ is the *risen and living Lord*. So foundational is this point that Paul devotes an entire chapter to an eloquent description of the resurrection (1 Cor 15). Sixth, addressing God's Son with the threefold title "Lord Jesus Christ" (1:2, 3, 7, 8, 9, 10, etc.) became the common way to identify him as absolute *master*, *savior* of our sins, and the *anointed* one sent from God.

When all is said and done, Christ alone stands as the centerpiece of human history and existence. Nothing in this world matters more than embracing and following Christ.

PRAYER

Almighty God, Creator of heaven and earth, thank you for sending us your Son, Jesus Christ, to be our Savior and Lord. That in itself would be enough reason to praise you for all eternity. However, in addition to saving and overseeing us, you made it possible for us to have a personal relationship with him—the righteous, resurrected, living Christ. In fact, it is your initiative that has called us into that relationship. Thank you. May we live our lives in a way that others see Christ in us and are drawn to him. Make us Christlike today, we pray. AMEN.

QUESTIONS

1. What is the biggest obstacle to accepting or believing Christ today? Why do more people not turn to him?

2. How and when did you come to know Christ personally? What difference has your relationship with him made in your life over the years?

3. Which of the common mistakes noted above do you think is most prevalent in our society and churches today? What are the harmful effects of that mistake?

4. How would you summarize who Christ is, why he came, and why any of it still matters today? How would you state that in just a sentence or two?

SUGGESTED READING

1 Corinthians 1–2, 5–6, 11–13, 15

47

2 CORINTHIANS: Apostle

*Paul, an apostle of Christ Jesus by the will of God, and Timothy
our brother, To the church of God in Corinth, together with all
the saints throughout Achaia: Grace and peace to you from God
our Father and the Lord Jesus Christ. (2 Corinthians 1:1–2)*

*The things that mark an apostle—signs, wonders and miracles—were
done among you with great perseverance. (2 Corinthians 12:12)*

*I urged Titus to go to you and I sent our brother
with him. (2 Corinthians 12:18)*

Paul begins his second letter to the Corinthians, as he does nine of
his thirteen letters, identifying himself as an apostle. Both Paul and
Luke, travel partners in spreading the gospel, use the term *apostle* frequently. Each author mentions the word over thirty times in his writings. For Paul, the word is found sprinkled throughout most of his letters; in Luke's case, the term dominates the book of Acts.

The root word of *apostle* in Greek means "to send out from." An
apostle, therefore, is a person sent out from another on a special mission. Three distinct individuals are implied by the term: someone in
authority does the sending, the one who is sent carries a special message on the appointed mission, and there is the one who receives the
sent messenger and his or her message. In the early church, God, or his
representatives, sent out individuals to take the gospel to the expand-

ing world. For example, the church at Antioch, prompted by the Holy Spirit, "placed their hands on [Barnabas and Saul] and sent them off" (Acts 13:1–4) on what became known as the first great missionary endeavor of the church.

That initial send-off has been copied and repeated countless times since then. To illustrate, let us consider what many church historians refer to as "the modern missions movement" that began near the outset of the nineteenth century. William Carey (1761–1834) is often referred to as "the Father of modern missions." In 1792, while serving as a Baptist pastor in England, he preached a sermon wherein he said: "Expect great things from God. Attempt great things for God." Shortly thereafter, as if in response to Carey's own message, the Baptists sent him to India. For the next forty years Carey devoted his life to spreading the gospel there. The work was not easy. Seven years passed before he saw his first convert. Nonetheless, in the decades that stretched before him he gave himself to translating the Bible into several languages in India, establishing a Christian presence there that still exists to this day. Shortly before his death in 1834, Carey advised a young missionary following in his footsteps: "Do not speak of Dr. Carey. Speak of Dr. Carey's Saviour." Carey, like the early apostles, heard God's call and responded by representing Christ among the people of India. Had Carey not been sent, God's kingdom would be poorer today. (See Elgin S. Moyer, *Great Leaders of the Christian Church*, Moody Press, 1951, pp 435–39).

One of the first great Americans sent as a missionary was Adoniram Judson (1788–1850). Though Judson was originally headed to India in 1812, resistance there redirected him to the nearby country of Burma. For nearly forty years he served the Lord among the Burmese, often under very oppressive and challenging conditions, including spending many months in a crowded, deplorable prison. Despite the hardships, by the time of his death Judson was responsible for over seven thousand baptized Christians in Burma. Had "the Apostle to Burma," as Judson became known, not been sent, thousands of Burmese people and their offspring might never have heard the gospel of Christ (Moyer, 1951, pp 439–42).

The sending of Carey and Judson marked a renewed emphasis in the church. Following the apostolic model of the New Testament, more and more nineteenth-century believers began listening to see where God might send them as a witness to those who did not yet know Christ. Three other missionaries from this era became well known and inspired future generations to consider where God might want to send them. David Livingstone (1813–1873) was sent from London to the continent of Africa in 1840. Facing adventure and danger, Livingstone was known for praying and preaching the gospel as he explored the interior of Africa.

Hudson Taylor (1832–1905), also from England, was sent to China in 1854. For the next fifty years he adopted much of the Chinese culture—eating and dressing like the Chinese—and tirelessly gave himself to translating the Bible into the Chinese language. He is buried in China, the land to which he was sent, with the words "'A man in Christ' (2 Cor 12:2)" etched on his tombstone. Taylor, known for his bold faith and relentless work ethic, formed the China Inland Mission and inspired many others to take up the cause of Christ on the mission field.

One of those influenced by Taylor was a young woman, Amy Carmichael (1867–1951). At the young age of nineteen, Carmichael heard Hudson Taylor speak at a convention about the need for missions. A few years later, in 1895, Carmichael found herself in India. Like Taylor in China, Carmichael adopted the dress and many customs of the Indians among whom she lived and served. She founded an orphanage and gave the next fifty-five years of her life to rescuing young girls from temple prostitution, sharing the gospel and love of Christ with countless numbers of abandoned and abused children.

The impact of these sent ones—apostles—will be fully known only once we are gathered around heaven's throne. The work of Carey, Judson, Livingstone, Taylor, and Carmichael was inspired by the apostle Paul who dared take the gospel beyond the comfortable and familiar borders that marked his early life. God has raised up messengers of grace and hope in every generation, sending them out to a hurting world.

A closer look at 2 Corinthians reveals a great deal about what Paul meant when he identified himself as an apostle. Four observations are worth our attention.

1. Paul was "an apostle of Christ Jesus" (1:1). Every time Paul began a letter identifying himself as an apostle—which, as noted earlier, he did nine times—he referenced Christ. After his Damascus Road encounter with the resurrected Jesus (Acts 9:1–6), Paul became an ambassador for Christ Jesus alone. Everything he did the remainder of his life was done on behalf of Christ. This raises an important question: Who do we represent when we go out into the world? Is it ourselves? Is it a company or an organization? Or do we primarily see ourselves as representing Christ? Paul explicitly and consistently identified himself in relationship to Christ, doing so both in word and deed. The apostle wrote: "For we do not preach ourselves, but Jesus Christ as Lord, and ourselves as your servants for Jesus's sake" (4:5). As noted earlier, Christ was central in the early church.

2. This was "the will of God" (1:1). Paul connected his apostleship to the will of God no fewer than five times (e.g., 1 Cor 1:1, 2 Cor 1:1; Eph 1:1; Col 1:1; and 2 Tim 1:1). God intended that Paul be sent out to represent his Son, Jesus. Paul's recognition of that fact gave him the boldness to declare: "Follow my example, as I follow the example of Christ" (1 Cor 11:1). Later, he boldly asserted that he was one of "God's fellow workers" (2 Cor 6:1). Paul operated with clarity and confidence that he was carrying out God's will. Today the American church seems to be busy with nonstop activity. Some of its leaders and people work at a frantic pace trying to juggle all their ministry responsibilities. My fear is that we sometimes become so busy with our good works that we struggle to discern whether what we are doing is really the will of God. God's will is to send us out to represent Christ, a calling that too easily gets confused with planning and executing another program that leaves us exhausted. Exhaustion resulting from church work is not synonymous with doing God's will. Are we people who seek his will? Can we declare with certainty, like Paul, that we have been sent "by the will of God?"

3. Some are guilty of "masquerading as apostles of Christ" (11:13). Paul identified the existence of "false apostles"—*pseudo-apostles* is the term used in the original Greek—who deceived others by pretending to be "apostles of Christ." What were the characteristics of these people who conned their fellow citizens? Chapter 11 provides some clues. First, they led people away from Christ rather than promoting "devotion to Christ" (11:3). Second, the implication is they were trained speakers, slick with their words (11:6). Third, the false prophets apparently charged for their services, seeking to benefit from sharing the gospel (11:7–9). Fourth, they openly boasted about their greatness (11:12, 18–23), whereas Paul boasted of his weakness and dependence on God (11:30–31). The church has always had false apostles and teachers—those who deceive, boast, use smooth and impressive-sounding words, find ways to profit financially off others, and ultimately lead people away from Christ. So how does one recognize a legitimate apostle, or representative, of Christ? What is the difference between a true and false apostle? Paul answered that question in the next chapter.

4. There are "things that mark an apostle" (12:12). Because there were false apostles operating among the early community of believers, Paul made sure his readers knew "the things that mark" a trustworthy apostle. Three features are mentioned: "signs, wonders and miracles," displaying "great perseverance" (12:12), and "never a burden" (12:13). In other words, an apostle does what Jesus did, with power and anointing. An apostle perseveres as Jesus did, even amidst suffering and adversity. An apostle resists the temptation to become a burden to others, choosing instead to "spend" and "expend" his or her resources for others (12:15). Those are still markers we should look for when evaluating anyone who claims to have been sent by God. Simply stated, the identifying characteristics of an apostle are consistently looking and acting like Jesus Christ.

By the way, in a certain sense, Jesus himself was the first apostle (see Heb 3:1). He was the one sent by God—a point noted multiple times in the book of John (e.g., 4:34; 5:24, 30, 36, 37; 6:38, 39; 17:3, 8, 18, 21, 23, 25; 20:21; etc.). When God sent his Son into the world a pattern was established. So, the reader is not surprised when near the end of his life Jesus prayed to his Father: "As you sent me into the world, I have sent them into the world" (John 17:18). That same pattern has been repeated thousands of times since Jesus's prayer.

The question we need to consider is this: Will we be his apostles—his sent ones—in a world that desperately needs Christ today? God sends people not only to India, Burma, China, and Africa but also to the downtown office, bank, factory, school, PTA, university, hospital, marketplace, construction site, neighborhood, civic club, library, courthouse, concert hall, laboratory, fitness center, stadium, restaurant, and the local church.

May we adopt the willing and enthusiastic response of the prophet Isaiah, who said: "Here am I. Send me!" (6:8). For every generation needs apostles.

PRAYER

Our Father in Heaven, thank you for sending your Son to be our Savior and Lord. Thank you for also sending men and women across the years who were willing—sometimes at great personal risk—to share the gospel with people like us. Now send us. May we go into the world as your ambassadors, representing you to those who need to see a clear picture of Christ. We acknowledge the task will not always be easy, and the Enemy will seek to defeat, discourage, and destroy us. So, grant us courage, consistency, compassion, and character that reflect your image as we go. We pray all this, and we go, in the name of Jesus Christ. AMEN.

QUESTIONS

1. Who do you know that has clearly been sent by God to carry out a specific mission? Who comes to mind? What do you know about that person's story?

2. Do you remember a time when God sent someone into your life at a particular time of need? Who was it? What was the experience? What were the results?

3. What is a favorite missionary story that gives you inspiration and encouragement? (It may or may not be one of the stories mentioned in this chapter.)

4. Think about the week ahead. Where might God be sending you? How might he want to use you to represent him in the ordinary and mundane places you will be this week?

SUGGESTED READING

2 Corinthians 1, 4, 6, 10–13

48

GALATIANS: Freedom

Some false brothers had infiltrated our ranks to spy on the freedom
we have in Christ Jesus and to make us slaves. (Galatians 2:4)

There is neither Jew nor Greek, slave nor free, male nor
female, for you are all one in Christ Jesus. (Galatians 3:28)

It is for freedom that Christ has set us free. Stand
firm, then, and do not let yourselves be burdened
again by a yoke of slavery. (Galatians 5:1)

You, my brothers, were called to be free. But do not
use your freedom to indulge the sinful nature; rather,
serve one another in love. (Galatians 5:13)

When I was a teenager, I once overheard an elderly man at an altar of prayer exclaim, "I'm free! I'm free!" He had knelt and publicly confessed to Jesus Christ a lifetime of sin and disobedience. What captured his imagination immediately following his prayer of contrition as a new believer was the thought of freedom. He was free from being a slave to sin. He was free from incessant guilt. He was free from future condemnation. He was free from the torment of not being the man he was created to be. He was overwhelmed by his newfound freedom.

Several years prior to the event mentioned above, on August 28, 1963, Martin Luther King, Jr., stood at the Lincoln Memorial and gave his "I Have a Dream" speech before thousands of civil rights supporters gathered in Washington, D.C. While King's address did indeed outline a noble dream, arguably the more dominant theme that day was freedom. Not only was the term *freedom* referenced twice as often as *dream* in the speech but freedom began and ended the memorable oration. Nearing his conclusion, King's voice reached a crescendo when he repeated the refrain "let freedom ring" several times. Finally, he closed with the lyrics of an old spiritual: "Free at last! Free at last! Thank God Almighty, we are free at last."

Freedom—the ability to come, go, and do as one pleases—is a universal desire. It is the birthright of every human being created in the image of God. The desire for freedom might be best understood as a reference to emancipation that is either physical, social, psychological, or moral in nature. *Physical* freedom, perhaps the most fundamental type of freedom, is the longing typically associated with slaves and prisoners who want to be liberated from the chains and bars that hold them. *Social* freedom pertains to breaking through oppressive and unjust societal structures that prohibit advancement and equality. While having freedom of movement, people seeking social freedom are tormented by limited opportunity and by what seems unfair, intolerant, and discriminatory. *Psychological* freedom is sought by those desiring to escape the inner turmoil that often results from a past traumatic experience, addictive behavior, or abusive relationship. Outwardly, such people appear to have unlimited potential, but inwardly they are prisoners to fears and insecurities. Today a new kind of *moral* freedom is sought. This relates to the yearning to cast off any moral authority that might restrain, restrict, or limit individual expression. People fight for the right to do as they please, without reference or concern for wider social health or the public good. Regardless of its specific form, everyone craves freedom from what enslaves, imprisons, or torments.

The book of Galatians, Paul's letter that was likely circulated among several churches scattered throughout the region of Galatia, emphasizes *freedom*. The word is found eleven times in the six-chapter letter. Galatians is thought to be one of the earliest books written in the New Testament. As Christianity was beginning to take root in the first century, just decades after Jesus's crucifixion and resurrection, Paul wanted to make sure new believers understood what was at stake. Jesus's death and subsequent victory made possible a whole new type of freedom: spiritual freedom. It was available to all who chose to "live by the Spirit" (5:16, 18, 25). Such freedom comes whenever an individual experiences the new birth that results by placing his or her faith in Christ. Galatians is Paul's attempt to provide insights into the spiritual freedom made accessible to all believers. Each of the six chapters highlights an aspect of that spiritual freedom.

First, **there is freedom to step aside, wait, and prepare**. In chapter 1, Paul described how his life once had been characterized by "advancing" (1:14). However, his encounter with Jesus changed all that. The result was three years away in Arabia before Paul returned to Jerusalem and met with the disciples Peter and James (1:15–19). One can only assume that for Paul this was a time of quiet reordering of his priorities and preparing for the ministry to which God was calling him. Paul had been "extremely zealous" (1:14) in his support of Judaism and was accustomed to being in charge. The time away from the public spotlight likely helped him realize there was now another one in charge: the Spirit of God. Thus, Paul's new goal was to learn to "keep in step with the Spirit" (5:25). There is great freedom when one learns that he or she is no longer in charge. There is freedom in stepping back, waiting, and letting the Lord direct the affairs of this world. If we are honest, many of us struggle here. Three hours for meaningful reflection is difficult, three days disconnected from our phones and social media is nearly impossible, and three weeks away from our work is out of the question. And yet Paul spent three *years* in barren Arabia. He had found a freedom that allowed him to step aside, do some soul-searching, and prepare himself for a new kind of work that God had planned for him.

Second, **there is freedom to surrender to a crucifixion**. Because Paul had already yielded his life and future to the Spirit of God, crucifixion no longer held the horror it once did. Paul concludes chapter 2 with these words: "I have been crucified with Christ and I no longer live, but Christ lives in me" (2:20). Paul was free to surrender to the cruelty of death itself because, in a sense, he had already died. He had denied himself and forfeited any rights in his new relationship to Christ. An incredible freedom results when one completely surrenders. No longer need one worry about personal offenses or unfair treatment. No longer need one worry about being passed over for an honor or recognition. No longer need one worry about reputation, misunderstanding, or ridicule. A crucifixion has a way of setting one free from those common human concerns that so often consume us.

Third, **there is freedom to rise above popular social categories**. Sociology has long emphasized the categories of race, class, and gender. These three groupings are routinely investigated by social scientists, who point out their inequities. Belonging to the wrong race, class, or gender can lead to a life of disproportionate misery, privation, and exploitation. Sociologists document this fact; no serious student doubts it. And yet here Paul implies there is a freedom wherein "there is neither Jew nor Greek, slave nor free, male nor female, for . . . all [are] one in Christ Jesus" (3:28). Paul has the audacity to dismantle these social categories that define and divide us. He suggests that the Spirit of God, because of what Christ did for us on the cross, breaks down these categories and sets us free from restrictive social labels. We are free to elevate one another and see every human being as worthy of respect and goodwill. We are free to believe every person—regardless of label—is a valued creation of God to be honored and treasured. We are free to care for one another as brothers and sisters in Christ, despite our differences.

Fourth, **there is freedom to receive God's promised inheritance**. In chapters 3 and 4 Paul focuses on God's *promise* that believers will *inherit* (3:29). We are "no longer a slave [to the law], but a son; and since you are a son, God has made you also an heir" (4:7). We are now "children of promise" (4:28) who will "inherit the kingdom of God" (5:21). Our relationship with God results in freedom and assurance. God has taken us into his family and made us his heirs. This is unheard of in other world religions; it is a dream come true. God, the creator of the universe, offers us all that is his. We receive this gift freely—there is nothing we can do to earn it—and in receiving it we are launched into a new kind of freedom. Worries and fears about the future fade when we know such an inheritance is ours. Material goods and possessions lose their luster when we accept our inheritance from God Almighty, for anything we possess here will pale in comparison with what we are about to receive. Death itself loses its "sting" and surrenders to "victory" (1 Cor 15:54–57). Realizing one is an heir of God changes everything, leading to freedom from the need to possess. Worries, stuff, and even death need not concern the child of God. Why do so few of God's people live as if they believe this?

Fifth, **there is freedom to serve others in love**. Near the end of Paul's letters, he typically turns to several practical matters. These matters are generally communicated in straightforward ways. That is certainly the case in Galatians. While promoting freedom, Paul cautions his readers: "do not use your freedom to indulge the sinful nature" (5:13). Later, he gives a catalog of harmful behaviors that flow out of one's sinful nature: sexual immorality, idolatry, hatred, fits of rage and more (5:19–21). Freedom, according to Paul, is not a license to engage in selfish acts. Our freedom in Christ is so that we might "serve one another in love" (5:13). Freedom is to be used to benefit, assist, and serve others. There is no limit to the possibilities here. Paul encourages us to look around and find ways to serve. It is as if he says: *Go ahead. There is no need to wait for someone to ask you. Your newfound freedom in Christ sets you free to serve anyone, anytime, anywhere.* One is always free to serve others in love.

Sixth, **there is freedom to do good to all people**. Related to the previous observation, Paul extends his encouragement to serve others in love by saying: "let us do good to all people, especially to those who belong to the family of believers" (6:10). Service is needed, but so are other acts of kindness and goodness. We can do good by speaking a gentle word of inspiration, by listening to a discouraged soul, by offering moral support to one going through a difficult season, or by welcoming another with a warm smile and pleasant greeting. Freedom is not intended to be focused on ourselves; it is not an invitation to exert our rights. Our freedom is so that we might live to benefit others. Anything less is a misuse and corruption of the freedom for which Christ died.

Three final thoughts are worth considering. First, the freedoms noted above are not the result of self-effort but of *surrender*. Only those who "live by the Spirit . . . [and] keep in step with the Spirit" (5:25) will know these freedoms. Second, no one, other than ourselves, can take these spiritual freedoms from us. They are matters of the human heart to which no one else has access. Third, these freedoms are exceedingly *rare*. The fact is that too many of us have "let [our]selves be burdened again by a yoke of slavery," even after "Christ has set us free" (5:1). What a needless shame. May God help us claim the freedom that is ours.

That elderly man at the altar during my youthful days said: "I'm free! I'm free!" Martin Luther King, Jr., declared: "Free at last! Free at last! Thank God Almighty, we are free at last!" Both were echoing Paul.

Freedom is available to every child of God. It has the power to change our lives and our world. Therefore, "let freedom ring." To live otherwise is to deny the work Christ came to do.

PRAYER

O Lord, we humbly confess that we too often live as slaves in bondage, when you have created us for freedom and victory. Set us free so that freedom unmistakably rings throughout our lives. We are asking neither for license nor for indulgence of our sinful desires. Rather, we are asking that you make us free to be different, free to take a back seat, free to surrender all to you, free to see ourselves and others through your eyes alone, free to receive our inheritance from your good hand, free to lovingly serve others, and free to do good to all the people we can. Yes, let that kind of freedom ring loud and clear in our lives and relationships. AMEN.

QUESTIONS

1. Consider the various types of freedom: physical, social, psychological, moral, and spiritual. In your own words, how would you define each of these?

2. Can you remember a time when you were set free from an adverse situation, addiction, or destructive pattern? What was that like? How did that freedom come?

3. Review the six spiritual freedoms found in Galatians. Which of these is most challenging to embrace? Why? Which do you wish was more evident among believers? Why?

4. What examples come to mind of ways to "do good to all people?" Who do you know who routinely exhibits such behaviors? To whom might you do good this week?

SUGGESTED READING

Galatians 1–6

49

EPHESIANS: Riches

In him we have redemption through his blood, the forgiveness of sins, in accordance with the riches of God's grace that he lavished on us with all wisdom and understanding. (Ephesians 1:7–8)

I pray also that the eyes of your heart may be enlightened in order that you may know the hope to which he has called you, the riches of his glorious inheritance in the saints. (Ephesians 1:18)

And God raised us up with Christ and seated us with him in the heavenly realms in Christ Jesus, in order that in the coming ages he might show the incomparable riches of his grace, expressed in his kindness to us in Christ Jesus. (Ephesians 2:6–7)

Although I am less than the least of all God's people, this grace was given me: to preach to the Gentiles the unsearchable riches of Christ. (Ephesians 3:8)

Ephesians is the first of Paul's four letters written from prison. Philippians, Colossians, and Philemon are the other three. The reader would never know these were prison letters unless Paul explicitly mentioned the fact each time. The respective themes of the four letters—riches, joy, hope, and brotherhood—are not what one might expect from one unjustly imprisoned. However, as noted in the last chapter, Paul has discovered a freedom that the nonbeliever cannot comprehend. Thus, as he unjustly sits "in chains" his primary concern is that he be a fearless "ambassador" for Christ (6:20). Paul's relationship with Christ resulted in him living on a plane far above the ordinary human experience. Have you ever known someone like that? Have you ever aspired to be someone like that? If not, why not?

Paul's emphasis on riches while stripped of his dignity and bound in prison, reminds me of the life of Evelyn Harris Brand. Born in 1879, Evelyn was part of a large, affluent family that valued education. By the time Evelyn was in her thirties, however, she had left the comforts and fashions of her London upbringing for missionary work in southern India. She fell in love and married the missionary Jesse Brand, though his death sixteen years later left her and their two children heartbroken. Crushed but undeterred, Evelyn spent the next several decades pouring herself into the people of India. She taught them, dispensed medicine, prayed and shared Christ at every opportunity. Evelyn, who continued serving the people of India until her death at age ninety-five, was affectionately known as "Granny" by those in her circle. Her son, Paul Brand, became world renowned as a surgeon, specializing in the repair of bodies devastated by leprosy. One day before his mother's last birthday, in 1974, Paul wrote the following:

> What can you give to someone who has EVERYTHING? I was with my mother earlier this year. As always I began to be ashamed that I have a fine house with electric current and water from a tap. I tried, as I have tried before, to find what I could give her that she would not regard as a luxury or not immediately give away to somebody who has less than she has. Mother insists that she has everything . . . She has her treasure where her heart is, and her heart is in the work that God has given her to do. (*Dorothy Clarke Wilson, Granny Brand: Her Story*, 1976, pp 218–19.)

Granny Brand, like the apostle Paul, possessed riches that were unseen and unknown to the rest of the world—riches not held in a bank account, nor evident by where one sleeps at night, nor measured by one's associates, nor known by any other customary standard. To be *rich*, of course, means one has plenty of that which is valuable, an abundance of goods, or an ample supply. "Saints" (Eph 1:1, 18)—a repeated term found in every chapter of Ephesians—inherit "incomparable" (2:7), "unsearchable" (3:8), and "glorious riches" (3:16) unavailable to others. In fact, these riches are "lavished on" (1:8) saints. Anyone who believes in the saving work of Christ Jesus is heir to the unique riches of God.

The problem with us humans is that we seek the wrong kind of riches. We seek to be rich in money, possessions, popularity, and fame. People give themselves tirelessly, wearing themselves out, chasing careers they hope will result in the accumulation of such wealth. In the process, the pursuit of these earth-bound riches blinds us to the greater riches God wants to lavish on us. What are those riches? Paul gives us some clues in his Ephesians letter.

Rich in grace and mercy (1:7; 2:4, 7). Paul delighted in the riches of God's grace and mercy for he knew it took a big supply of both to cover his sins. Fortunately, God's grace and mercy are inexhaustible. Those riches are available to every generation. If it were not so we would be lost without hope today. God's boundless supply of riches of grace has reached down and forgiven sins across the centuries, including ours. Nothing less would cover the debt that we owe due to our disobedience and rebellion. How often do we pause to consider how rich we really are when it comes to the grace and mercy God has bestowed on us? We have far more riches than we realize.

Rich in descriptive language. No letter quite matches Ephesians when it comes to language. There is a richness here in both word choice and sentence structure. Paul used colorful and descriptive words to talk about the gospel and its provisions. Many of those terms have already been noted. To these might be added descriptive expressions that include "the heavenly realms" (1:3, 20; 2:6; 3:10; 6:12); "his good pleasure" (1:9); the width, length, height, and depth of Christ's love (3:18); and reference to the one "who is able to do immeasurably more than all we ask or imagine" (3:20). Beyond the words themselves, however, Paul began his letter with three lengthy sentences in the original Greek. These three sentences—totaling 495 Greek words—form the passages of 1:3–14, 1:15–23, and 2:1–7. It is almost as if Paul could not bring himself to pause as he eagerly sought to communicate the riches of God. The thought left him breathless. What about us? Does our language adequately describe the riches of God? Are we ever left breathless while searching for elevated language befitting the gospel? Our language ought to correspond to the matchless blessing experienced by having a relationship with Jesus Christ.

Rich in lofty prayers. Paul's emphasis and reliance on prayer is unmistakable in Ephesians. Twice he expressed his prayer for others (1:15–23; 3:14–21) and once he encouraged those at Ephesus to pray, including a request that they pray for him (6:18–20). Paul's prayers extended far beyond the issues of health, physical well-being, and safety that constitute so many contemporary prayers. His concern was that others "may know [God] better" (1:17); "know the hope . . . riches . . . and . . . power" available to those who believe (1:18–19); and "know this love that surpasses knowledge" (3:19). Furthermore, Paul's request for himself was not a prayer for release from prison chains but for fearlessness in proclaiming the gospel while he was in chains (6:19–20). Paul modeled lofty prayers while seeking the same from those who prayed for him. There is a richness and depth that exceeds the focus of far too many prayers today. Paul prayed for spiritual growth, vitality, and influence. Would those who listen to us pray describe our prayers as lofty, noble, and exalted? Do our public prayers exhibit a spiritual richness that attracts others and welcomes them into the presence of God?

Rich in explosive power. The idea of *power* is dominant throughout the letter of Ephesians. Not only is there "incomparably great power for us who believe" (1:19) but also "his glorious riches" are available to "strengthen [us] with power" (3:16). Paul acknowledged the centrality of God's power when he concluded his letter with this encouragement: "Finally, be strong in the Lord and in his mighty power" (6:10). The Greek word that most often gets translated "power" is *dynamis*, from which we get the English word "dynamite." Such is the power God has for us. It is large in both magnitude and supply. In reality, however, few people access this power. Instead, we often live as if we are powerless victims of circumstances rather than powerful victors over those same circumstances. God's power did not explode and break the chains that constrained Paul; the explosion was bigger than that. The explosion blew apart Paul's preoccupation with himself and his comforts, blasted his narrow thinking that once only focused on his Jewish roots, and burst open his constricted heart until all he could do was "live a life of love" (5:2). How are the riches of God's power evident in our lives? What has his divine dynamite exploded around us? Have we tapped into that "incomparably great power?"

Rich in meaningful relationships. The last half of Ephesians is essentially focused on the rich and meaningful relationships possible when one lives in obedience to Christ. Paul began this section by calling himself "a prisoner for the Lord," urging others "to live a life worthy of the calling [they] have received" (4:1). The implication is that when people live this way—"completely humble and gentle . . . patient, bearing with one another in love" (4:2)—life and its relationships begin to change. One's relationship with Christ matures, one's relationship with others becomes more respectful and wholesome, and one's relationship with his or her spouse (5:22–33) or other family members (6:1–4) is transformed. In fact, there is not a relationship that goes untouched. In the last three chapters of Ephesians, Paul offered practical advice on how all relationships might be enriched and deepened. In a world that desperately seeks, and needs, meaningful relationships today, Paul showed us the way forward. What are our relationships like? Are they as rich and meaningful as they could be? Have we embraced God's plan for our relationships?

No wonder Paul ends his letter with a strong warning against "the devil's schemes" (6:11). The Enemy of our souls seeks to rob us of all these riches and leave us in spiritual poverty. That's why Paul encourages his readers to "be strong in the Lord" (6:10), "put on the full armor of God" (6:11), and prepare for battle (6:12–18). Dennis Kinlaw, in *This Day with the Master* (Nov 30), makes the following observation: "If I were the devil, I would do my best to corrupt every loving human relationship that I could find . . . [so people] would never know the wealth of reality outside their immediate conscious existence." That is the tragedy of the Fall: God's intended wealth is squandered. Incomparable and glorious riches are regularly forfeited. Instead of gaining real, eternal wealth, we humans spend inordinate amounts of time and energy chasing artificial, temporary riches that do not satisfy.

May the riches of Christ become our daily reality. Granny Brand was correct when she told her son that she had everything she needed. Let us be more like Granny and Paul—both of whom pursued riches that last—even if that means we have to borrow a dollar now and then.

PRAYER

Lord Jesus, we recognize you as the One who has "adopted" us (1:5) and "lavished on us . . . the riches of [your] grace" (1:7–8). You are the One "who is able to do immeasurably more than all we ask or imagine, according to [your] power that is at work within us" (3:20). You are the One with wealth that the world cannot see or comprehend. We confess our need of you and your provision in our lives. Bestow upon us the riches of inexhaustible grace, elevated language, thoughtful prayers, immeasurable power, and rewarding relationships. Help us to embrace the riches you have designed for our flourishing. We pray in the name of Jesus Christ, our Savior and Lord. AMEN.

QUESTIONS

1. Who do you know that is rich in Christ? What makes it obvious? How does that person exhibit those riches?

2. Look honestly at your life as a believer. Which of these riches— grace, language, prayer, power, relationships—needs to be re-supplied? How might you do so?

3. Why do so many who chase after this world's riches, power, or fame ultimately report such dissatisfaction in their lives? Are riches and satisfaction ever compatible? When?

4. What is your greatest battle when it comes to riches? When or where do you most need to "put on the full armor of God" (6:11) and prepare for battle in this area?

SUGGESTED READING

Ephesians 1–6

50

PHILIPPIANS: Joy

*In all my prayers for all of you, I always pray with joy because
of your partnership in the gospel. (Philippians 1:4–5)*

*Therefore, my brothers, you whom I love and long
for, my joy and crown, that is how you should stand
firm in the Lord, dear friends. (Philippians 4:1)*

*Rejoice in the Lord always. I will say it again: Rejoice! Let your
gentleness be evident to all. The Lord is near. Do not be anxious
about anything, but in everything, by prayer and petition, with
thanksgiving, present your requests to God. And the peace of God,
which transcends all understanding, will guard your hearts and
your minds in Christ Jesus. Finally, brothers, whatever is true,
whatever is noble, whatever is right, whatever is pure, whatever
is lovely, whatever is admirable—if anything is excellent or
praiseworthy—think about such things. Whatever you have learned
or received or heard from me, or seen in me—put it into practice.
And the God of peace will be with you. (Philippians 4:4–9)*

During my college days in the 1970s, in the little town of Wilmore,
Kentucky, I observed two people who operated with unusual expressions of joy. Julian C. ("JC") McPheeters, in his mid-eighties, had
retired from a career as a minister and seminary president. Earl A.
("Tata") Seamands, also in his eighties, was a retired missionary engineer who had built churches, schools, and hospitals throughout south-

ern India. Near the end of their respective lives, these octogenarian friends occasionally had encounters on the streets of Wilmore that resulted in the duo spontaneously and enthusiastically bursting into song:

> Christ gives joy unspeakable and full of glory
> Full of glory, full of glory
> Christ gives joy unspeakable and full of glory
> And the half has never yet been told

JC and Tata became the talk of the town. Anyone who saw them on the sidewalk would smile, pass by without disturbing the pair, and go tell a neighbor about the odd public scene they had just witnessed: the former seminary president and former missionary joyfully singing together. Their shared expression was rooted in the reality of their experience. "Joy unspeakable" was the natural outgrowth of their relationship with the risen Christ. (See Chilton C. McPheeters, *Pardon Me, Sir . . . Your Halo's Showing*, 1984, p 139.)

Joy has always been a hallmark of the Judeo-Christian faith. However, something has gone tragically wrong in recent years. Our towns and streets tell a different story. "Joy unspeakable" has been replaced by violence, fear, anxiety, depression, bitterness, hurt, handwringing, and despair. Our communities—including, unfortunately, too many communities of faith—are marked by stress, suspicion, and sadness. We need a revival of joy. A collective cry is needed that echoes David's prayer: "Restore to me the joy of your salvation" (Ps 51:12).

Joy is a theme found in over half of the books of the Old Testament, being especially prominent in Psalms and Isaiah. The theme is repeated in two-thirds of the New Testament books. As central as joy is to faith and as pervasive as it is across the Bible's pages, perhaps no book highlights it more clearly than Philippians. The book references joy and its verb form, *rejoice*, in all four of its chapters and fourteen times altogether. This is remarkable, considering Philippians is another of Paul's prison letters, written while he was imprisoned by the Roman government for the proclamation of the gospel. Many Christians over the years have turned to this book to find encouragement and to have their joy bolstered and restored.

The reader of Philippians is introduced to Paul's fourfold understanding of joy. He defines the term in a way that runs counter to common experience and exceeds ordinary human expectations. There are four characteristics, or truths, of joy found in Philippians.

First, **joy is defined by a Person, not a plan**. That person, of course, is Christ. It is not coincidental that in this letter of joy Paul references "Christ" thirty-eight times, the vast majority of which are found in the first half of the letter. Joy has it source in Christ, a Person. Biblical joy does not come from a plan to be achieved but from a Person to be adored. Paul is consistent with other writers in this regard. For example, Luke records the Christmas angel's announcement: "I bring you good news of great joy that will be for all the people. Today in the town of David a Savior has been born to you; he is Christ the Lord" (2:10–11). Joy has its roots in Christ.

The English writer and clergyman Isaac Watts captured this theme when he wrote the much-beloved Christmas song "Joy to the World" in the early 1700s:

> *Joy to the world! The Lord is come*
> *Let earth receive her King*

Watts, like the angel and Paul centuries earlier, associated joy with the Lord, Jesus Christ. He alone is the universal source of joy in our broken world. Without Christ, sorrow and despair would have the last word. Watts recognized that when he continued:

> *No more let sin and sorrow grow*

Joy is neither an abstraction divorced from a person nor something to be planned and strategized to overcome life's sorrows—as if we can discipline ourselves and work hard to become more joyful in the face of difficulty. Rather, joy is the natural response that bursts forth when one knows the Person who is the fountain of joy. Biblical writers and hymn writers agree: a Person, not a plan or strategy, makes joy possible; and that joy transforms life.

Second, **joy is defined by a perspective, not a place**. Paul was "in chains"—a fact mentioned four times in the first chapter (1:7, 13, 14, 17)—but that did not diminish his joy. Paul had learned the secret of joy and contentment (4:11–12) regardless of the place he occupied or the restrictions that limited his movement. The secret rested on a twofold perspective: God rules and heaven awaits. Though imprisoned, Paul recognized that "it is God who works in you to will and to act according to his good purpose" (2:13). Further, Paul declared with confidence, "my God will meet all your needs according to his glorious riches in Christ

Jesus" (4:19). The hymn writer Watts noted: "He rules the world with truth and grace." Joy looks beyond circumstances and understands that God is the ruler of all.

However, a truly joyful person also is one who has his or her sights set on heaven. The secular world scoffs at the idea of heaven or considers it irrational or even delusional. In sharp contrast to such a view, Paul's heavenly perspective provided joy that defied place and human-imposed restrictions. Paul had the audacity to declare: "For to me, to live is Christ and to die is gain . . . I am torn between the two: I desire to depart and be with Christ" (1:21–23). Later he boldly claimed, "our citizenship is in heaven" (3:20). The lines of this familiar southern gospel song capture Paul's thoughts well:

> *This world is not my home*
> *I'm just a-passing through*
> *My treasures are laid up*
> *Somewhere beyond the blue*

So it was with Paul; and so it is with anyone who exhibits joy while in a wretched and miserable place. Joy is possible because one's perspective stretches far beyond the place one occupies today. God rules and heaven awaits the believer in Christ. To believe so is not to be delusional but to recognize the source of deep and abiding joy.

Third, **joy is defined by persistence, not a plane**. Paul instructs his readers to "rejoice in the Lord always" (4:4). Joy is to be a constant expression and state, an impossibility unless one knows the Person of Christ and has the perspective that he rules and heaven awaits. One cannot conjure up incessant joy on one's own. Paul, however, points to a Source that is underutilized, whose name is Jesus. Life does not unfold on a smooth, flat surface. Life's trajectory is not a straight line or what we might call a level plane. To the contrary, bumps, highs and lows, rough days, and steep challenges make up the human experience. If anyone knew that reality, it was Paul, who on more than one occasion described his own hardships (Rom 8:35–39; 1 Cor 4:10–13; 2 Cor 4:8–12; 6:4–5; 7:5; 1 Thess 2:9; 2 Tim 2:3). His joy was not the result of living carefully on a geometric plane but the result of persistence and perseverance despite trials and adversity (Rom 5:1–5; 1 Cor 4:12). All of this was made possible by his relationship with Christ and the promise and anticipation of eternity.

No life exists on a steady and secure plane; life has ups and downs, good times and bad, delights and disappointments. Paul speaks into this fact by encouraging his readers to: "Rejoice in the Lord always" (Phil 4:4). He is so adamant on this point that he repeats it: "I will say it again: Rejoice!" It is the persistence of joy through unspeakable hardship that distinguishes the follower of Christ from others. This does not imply giddiness, nor a perpetual smile plastered on one's face. Both of those usually reveal a lack of maturity and understanding. Persistent joy comes from deep within, where Christ resides and keeps directing us onward and upward.

Fourth, **joy is defined by peace, not a plaque**. The latter is something we hang on a wall and point to as a reminder of a past accomplishment. A plaque can encourage us because it commemorates what we have *done*. Peace, on the other hand, characterizes who we *are* right now and dwells deep within our souls. The word *peace* opens every one of Paul's thirteen letters, and in ten of those letters he returns to the topic of peace later in the body of his writing. Peace is more than the standard greeting found in New Testament writings; it is the standard attribute of the follower of Jesus Christ. The prophet Isaiah pointed to it (9:6–7) and Jesus delivered it (John 14:27). Peace is mentioned in twenty-six of the twenty-seven New Testament books (the exception being 1 John). In Galatians 5:22, "love, joy, [and] peace" are grouped together and identified as the initial "fruit of the Spirit." In fact, joy and peace are nearly indistinguishable, serving as the flip side of the same coin. Thus, we are not talking about something to be mounted and displayed on a wall to help us remember a significant past experience. Rather, joy and peace are twins that pervade a human heart when Christ assumes control, resulting in a deep delight that can be known no other way.

As so often seems to happen when attempting to describe biblical truth, these thoughts on joy were written during a week when the message was put to the test in my own life. My daughter-in-law and grandchildren were in a car accident that totaled their vehicle, a routine doctor's visit took twice as long as expected on a day already packed with too many other commitments, some hard conversations were required at the office, an honest mistake led to an overdrawn bank account and subsequent penalty, and both family and work needs were particularly demanding and stressful. There was much I did not like this past week.

Then I read Paul's words again: *Rejoice in the Lord always! I will say it again: Rejoice!*

Prayer

Lord, you have called us to rejoice. You intended neither for it to be a burden nor that we would muster up the resources to do it on our own. Rather, you designed that joy would be the natural outgrowth of a life surrendered to you and your Lordship. Thank you for making joy one of the outcomes, or fruits, of a life lived under the control of your Spirit. Restore to us the joy of our salvation. May that joy result in inner peace, influence those around us, and bring delight to your heart. We pray this in Jesus's name. AMEN.

Questions

1. Is there someone you know who exhibits joy on a regular basis? How do you feel when you are around him or her?

2. Is there a difference between joy and happiness? If so, how would you distinguish between the two?

3. Why is joy so rare in the world today? Why does it also seem to be rare among God's people in the church? How might we change that?

4. Music is known to bring joy into a person's life. What particular song inspires joy in you? Why?

Suggested Reading

Philippians 1–4

51

COLOSSIANS: Hope

We always thank God, the Father of our Lord Jesus Christ,
when we pray for you, because we have heard of your
faith in Christ Jesus and of the love you have for all the
saints—the faith and love that spring from the hope that
is stored up for you in heaven . . . (Colossians 1:3–5)

But now he has reconciled you by Christ's physical body through
death to present you holy in his sight, without blemish and free from
accusation—if you continue in your faith, established and firm, not
moved from the hope held out in the gospel. (Colossians 1:22–23)

To [the saints] God has chosen to make known among
the Gentiles the glorious riches of this mystery, which is
Christ in you, the hope of glory. (Colossians 1:27)

Hope, like joy, is all too rare today. We are witnessing hopelessness on a grand scale. Social scientists now talk about "deaths of
despair"—a phrase popularized by two Princeton University econo-
mists—describing those who die from alcohol, drug overdoses (opioids
being the major culprit), or suicide. These deaths, which were already
on the rise as the twenty-first century dawned, increased even more
with the COVID pandemic and the isolation and financial downturn that
accompanied the pandemic. School shootings, riots and chaos in the
streets, smash-and-grab robberies, distrust of politicians and police officers, and increasing gender confusion have added to the despondency.

Is it any wonder that someone would write a song entitled "Despair," with the following lyrics?

> *Oh despair, you were there through my wasted days*
> *You're there through my wasted nights*
> *You're there through my wasted years*
> *You're there through my wasted life*
> *You've always been there*

Not only is the haunting message of this 2013 pop song unusual, but so is the name of the New York City rock band that wrote and performed it. The band is known as the "Yeah Yeah Yeahs." Ironically, the lyrics elicit a response within me that shouts: *No, No, No! One need not surrender to despair!* While it is true that social unrest, widespread pessimism, and national division threaten this generation's hope, there is an answer.

The loss of hope, witnessed in our streets and schools and heard in our music, stands in sharp contrast to what Paul describes as he begins his third prison letter, Colossians. Three times in the first chapter, Paul—who was still "in chains" (4:3, 18)—emphasizes *hope* (1:5, 23, 27). Interestingly, each time hope is mentioned Paul personalizes it by using the second-person pronoun, *you*. The hope that Paul knew and wrote about was available to his readers. It was not an abstraction to be discussed or debated but a reality to be experienced. The message is clear: *You*, like Paul, can have hope despite dark days of adversity.

Many years ago, I heard a Free Methodist bishop, Elmer Parsons, describe hope as a combination of desire and expectation. I have always liked that definition. More than mere wishful thinking, hope sincerely desires something and reasonably expects to obtain it. One might buy a lottery ticket because one wants to become an instant millionaire, but the same person has very little expectation of that happening. The desire does not translate into a realistic hope. Another might fully expect to be selected to lead a major project at work but have little desire to do so because of the added time and stress the project will entail. The expectation is closer to a nightmare than an aspiration. Neither of these scenarios reflects the kind of hope being discussed here. Hope requires both desire and expectation, want and anticipation. Yet there is more if we are to understand the biblical hope described by Paul.

Three key components are necessary if hope is to be experienced in any generation: *a promising future, a dependable guide*, and *a mean-*

ingful relationship. Tragically, all three of these elements are eroding at an alarming rate around us. Their disappearance helps explain
why hope has become so rare these days. Seven words from Colossians
1:27—"Christ in you, the hope of glory"—point to the importance of all
three elements and define biblical hope. Losing any one of the three
ingredients results in a parallel loss of hope.

First, **hope is lost when one looks ahead and realizes there
is no future**. Paul captured that future in the phrase, "the hope of
glory" (1:27). This is consistent with his earlier reference to "the hope
that is stored up for you in heaven" (1:5). Heaven gives us hope. The
writer of Hebrews described Abraham as "looking forward to the city . . .
whose architect and builder is God" (Heb 11:10), noted how other people
of faith "were longing for a better country—a heavenly one" (11:16), and
explained that Moses was "looking ahead to his reward" (11:26). Hope
is always found by looking forward to a promising future. The opposite
is also true. When one looks ahead and sees no future but misery and
dread, hopelessness results.

When I was a twenty-five-year-old fresh seminary graduate serving
as a pastor in western Oregon, I immediately encountered several situations for which no theology book or classroom lecture had adequately
prepared me. I had only been in my new pastoral role a few months
when word came that a young man in his thirties had taken his life. I
found myself on my way to visit the grieving wife and her two young
children. The husband and father shot himself above his garage, in the
family's pool room, where his horrified wife later found him. Though
from others' perspective he had so much to live for—a beautiful wife and
two of the cutest kids one would ever lay eyes upon—in his own eyes,
clouded by a drug addiction, the future looked bleak and unwelcoming.
I have no recollection of what I said that afternoon so many years ago.
However, I do remember the deep sadness I felt for the young man who
looked down the road, saw a dark and impossible future, and determined the best response to his hopelessness was to end his life. Over the
years since then, I have seen that tragedy repeated far too often.

Paul's response was different, and he wanted to let his readers in
on the secret, or what he called the "mystery" (1:26, 27; 2:2; 4:3). Hope
springs from the promise of eternity, from "that [which] is stored up for
you in heaven" (1:5). Though Paul was unjustly chained in a prison, "the
hope of glory" (1:27) beckoned him on to a brighter day. God's people
always have a future, no matter how dark they find the present. That

theme is consistent across the pages of Scripture. Abraham, Moses, the prophets, and the apostles—despite their circumstances—all looked ahead with hope. Hope is only lost when one fails to see the future possibilities and promises that God has in store.

Second, **hope is lost when one looks around and realizes there is no guide**. We all need a guide to help us navigate life's uncertainties. Regardless of our upbringing or natural abilities, we are ill-equipped to master the multiple perplexities that confront us in our world. No amount of talent, education, training, practical experience, or self-sufficiency will sustain us through life's rough times. A guide is needed—one who knows the territory and has the resources and competency to lead us through the maze. Christ alone is that guide. "Christ," whom Paul mentions twenty-six times in Colossians, is "the hope of glory" (1:27). We noted earlier how often Paul points to Christ. In fact, Paul is responsible for seventy percent of the nearly six hundred times Christ is named in the New Testament. He wanted one thing perfectly clear: Christ is our guide; our hope is in him.

The need for a guide came into sharp focus after my freshman year of college when I spent two months with a handful of other students on a summer mission trip to Colombia, South America. One of our adventures was travelling down the Magdalena River—one of the major waterways in South America—in order to reach a remote village to share the gospel. The missionary we accompanied pointed out his reliance on the native guide who knew the river well. With thick vegetation creating endless green walls along the broad river's banks, and with floating islands that shifted without warning, only a veteran guide was able to navigate the Magdalena. I still remember his eyes carefully studying the shoreline terrain while also alertly monitoring the flow of the river ahead. After a long, hot journey, the guide delivered us to our destination. We would have been hopelessly lost without him. A competent guide is indispensable; hope vanishes without one.

The same principle holds true in life. Many social analysts suspect that today's rampant hopelessness is, in part, the result of the high rate of fatherlessness that plagues society. When nearly forty percent of children in the U.S. today are born out of wedlock, one can only assume that leaves large numbers of youth searching for a reliable guide. Fathers have traditionally assumed that role. Their absence from the home has made hope a casualty. The evidence is in the despair so prevalent in our country's streets and schools.

Third, **hope is lost when one looks within and realizes there is no meaningful relationship**. In addition to looking ahead in search of a promising future and looking around in search of a dependable guide, human nature is such that people tend to look within their souls for meaning—meaning that comes from a deep relationship with another. When none is found, hopelessness results. Paul declared real hope comes from a relationship with Christ. "Christ in you [is] the hope of glory" (1:27). It is reassuring to be able to *approach* Christ when you need a guide; it is even better to have an intimate relationship with Christ who is *in* you. The prophet Isaiah pointed to the coming of Immanuel (7:14). Later, the gospel writer Matthew made sure his readers knew Immanuel means "God with us" (1:23). Then the apostle Paul extended the thought further. Not only is God *with* us, but Christ is *within* us. This is a relationship that knows no limits and has no end. Long before modern technology made it possible for relationships to sustain 24/7 contact, the Christ who came down from heaven promised a relationship wherein he would reside within us. That would mean immediate access, inexhaustible resources, and eternal fellowship—all seeds of hope. We were made for relationships, and the one that gives hope to all others is our relationship with Christ.

Paul sat in prison proclaiming hope to the world. How could he do that, given his circumstances? The answer comes in those seven words—"Christ in you, the hope of glory." Therein is found a future, a guide, and a relationship like no other.

Do not be deceived. Alternatives have been tried in every generation and have failed. Paul described some of these in Colossians when he talked about intellectual-sounding philosophies (2:8), religious rituals (2:16–23), personal pleasures (3:5–8), and identity politics (3:11). All promise to satisfy human longing. However, the result is always the same: these alternatives eventually disappoint and end in despair. Christ alone is the hope of the world.

PRAYER

Our Father in heaven, thank you for sending your Son, Jesus, to be our Savior and our Hope. There is no other who cares so deeply for us today while gently calling us into a promising future. When the world deals despair, your Son responds with hope. Though undeserving, we are richly blessed. Remind us often that things are not as bleak as they appear, for when we have Christ we have a future, a guide, and the one relationship we need. Thank you for your provisions that lead us onward toward victory. Thank you for our hope in Jesus Christ. AMEN.

QUESTIONS

1. When you face a situation in life that tempts you toward hopelessness and despair, what do you do? What strategies have you found helpful to restore your hope?

2. Review the three components of hope: a future, a guide, and a relationship. Which of the three most inspires hope in you? Explain why.

3. Why is hope so rare these days throughout society? What needs to be done to restore hope, especially among our youth?

4. What excites you about the future? As you look ahead, what encourages you, gives you hope, and keeps you moving forward?

SUGGESTED READING

Colossians 1–4

52

1 THESSALONIANS: Encouragement

For you know that we dealt with each of you as a father deals with his own children, encouraging, comforting and urging you to live lives worthy of God. (1 Thessalonians 2:11–12)

Therefore encourage each other with these words. (1 Thessalonians 4:18)

Therefore encourage one another and build each other up, just as in fact you are doing. (1 Thessalonians 5:11)

And we urge you, brothers, warn those who are idle, encourage the timid, help the weak, be patient with everyone. (1 Thessalonians 5:14)

My dad grew up on a farm and was a self-taught mechanic. He liked to work on old cars and trucks—models that were not yet computerized. Dad enjoyed the challenge of figuring out how to get a stalled engine running. For many years he operated a used car dealership on the west side of Flint, Michigan, known as "Olney Sales." He bought, repaired, and sold used cars. A related interest was his desire to help motorists stranded alongside the road with engine problems. On more than one occasion my dad played the Good Samaritan by stopping to help get a stranger back on the road again.

Long after I had left home and had a family of my own, Dad told me a story I shall never forget. One cold morning, my dad came upon an intersection south of Flint and saw a motorist with a stalled vehicle. A closer look revealed a middle-aged woman behind the wheel of a beat-up car. Dad pulled over and jumped out to see if he could help. He popped open the hood and began his usual assessment by checking for loose battery cables, looking at the engine belts, fiddling around with the choke and carburetor, and performing a few other tricks of the trade. Nothing he did helped; the car would not start. The woman was understandably agitated; she was trying to get her young son, who was in the car with her, to school that morning.

Dad, the problem solver, quickly hatched a plan on the spot. He suggested the woman take his car—another used car, but one in far better shape than hers—and deliver her son to school. "In fact," he continued, "let's just trade cars. I'll give you mine and I'll take yours. Meet me back here at this corner tomorrow morning at the same time—inside that restaurant right over there—and I will bring you the title to the car. I am giving it to you. It's yours to keep." The woman was stunned and a bit suspicious, but she soon took his keys and headed down the road with her son. Her stalled car left her with few other options.

Eventually my dad got the old car running well enough to drive it home. The next morning, as promised, Dad headed out to keep his appointment at the restaurant, secretly wondering if the woman would show up. She did, bringing a male friend with her to make sure she was not being scammed or taken advantage of in some way by the roadside stranger she had met the previous day. As I recall, she had even made several phone calls to see if this "Mr. Olney" was a reputable and trustworthy man. What if he was pawning off on her a lemon? Or worse, what if he had given her a stolen car? Apparently, the phone calls satisfied her because there she was. At their brief morning meeting Dad signed off on the title and wished her well. They never saw each other again, but I suspect she never forgot the stranger who helped during her hour of distress and traded his car for hers. I have often wished I could meet this woman and hear the story from her perspective.

An appropriate word to describe this event is *encouragement*. My dad was an encourager. Strangers along the roadside or in restaurants were often recipients of his encouragement, as were friends, co-workers, and family members. Many people over the years have told me how much my dad helped them during a time when they needed direction or inspiration. I, too, was the beneficiary of Dad's encouragement on many occasions. It came in the form of an optimistic attitude when things looked bleak, humor and laughter even during dark days, believing in me when I did not always believe in myself, a word of inspiration that instilled a dream, a well-timed financial gift when he suspected things might be tight, and the numerous times he helped with a household or automobile need.

Such encouragement was characteristic of early Christians. Over half of the 150 references to encouragement found in the New Testament come from the pen of Paul. First Thessalonians is one of his letters that frequently highlights its importance (2:12; 3:2, 7; 4:18; 5:11, 14). The New Testament was originally written in Greek, and the term that commonly gets translated "encouragement" comes from a Greek compound word that combines two ideas: being positioned alongside another and being called. Thus, an encourager is one called alongside another to offer help. The New Testament sometimes renders the word as "comforter," "counselor" (John 14:16, 26; 15:26; 16:7), or "advocate" (1 John 2:1 KJV).

My dad came alongside a stranded motorist in a stalled car and encouraged her. In doing so, he was merely following an established historical pattern. God did the same but on a grander scale. He sent his Son, Jesus, to come alongside a stalled world that needed a Savior. Deliverance and encouragement were the result. Before Jesus left this world, he promised to send the Holy Spirit to come alongside us and be our teacher and encourager. The Good Samaritan illustrates one who came alongside a beaten and dying man and offered hope (Luke 10:33). Barnabas, known as the "son of encouragement" (Acts 4:36), came alongside the new convert Paul and helped his entry into the early Christian community. That act of encouragement has resulted in generations being blessed by Paul's writings. Paul himself came alongside numerous fledgling churches and offered words of encouragement in his visits and letters. Paul's companions—Silas, Timothy, and others (1 Thess 1:1)—came alongside him to help carry the load of ministry and offer encouragement in the process. The pattern is clear. Encouragement is the lifeblood of the church, from one generation to the next.

Who might God be calling us to come alongside and encourage? And how might we do it? At least three time-tested ways are available—all of which are needed and, if done more, would transform our homes, churches, and communities. Encouragement can be given when we *speak a word, give a smile,* or *do a kind deed.* These acts need not cost a penny, yet their value exceeds all the assets held in the world's largest financial institutions.

Speak. I am sometimes amazed at how often God brought about good by just speaking a word. I am equally amazed at how often we fail to do so. For people who have such advanced communication technology available, we have become woefully inept at the art of pleasant conversation. We have forgotten the basic courtesy of communicating when another person is in the room. A cheerful word of greeting or an inquiry into one's day sends a message of respect and acknowledges the other person's worth. That alone can be an encouragement. In our world of increasing isolation wherein we only communicate via electronic devices, we are losing our ability to speak. I see it far too often among college students in hallways and on sidewalks. Some act stunned and dazed when a word is spoken to them. This is not a call for introverts to become extroverts. Rather, this is a call to engage in the basic and common courtesy of speaking a word of encouragement to a fellow human whose greatest need may be just to know that another individual is interested enough in his or her life to share a word. Encouragement comes when a word of goodwill is spoken.

Smile. Is there a greater and more economical gift? A smile has the potential not only to lift another soul but also to communicate friendliness, trustworthiness, and optimism—all of which should mark the follower of Christ. Too many proceed through life with intensity, anxiety, anger, or even horror written on their faces. No needy individual seeks out such people, because they look like they have too many troubles of their own. But the winsome smile of a family member, neighbor, or friend is attractive and draws people who need encouragement.

When our boys were young, we used to observe what we called people's "neutral face"—what people look like when they do not realize others are observing them. We would notice complete strangers in a shopping mall or pastors and choir members seated on the church platform. A smile—not a plastered-on, cheesy grin, but a natural and pleasant smile—always stands out and uplifts others. A scowl, on the other hand, drives people away either out of pity or fear. Marathon runners report that the smiles and cheers of onlookers along the route buoy their spirits and keep them motivated to finish the race. The same is true in the race of life. The smiles of winsome people along the route encourage us to keep going. Not surprisingly, encouragers often find encouragement themselves in the process, as others seek to be in the presence of good-natured people. A smile pays rich dividends to everyone.

Act. Doing something for another has the dual benefit of encouraging the recipient and inspiring the giver. The act may be one of kindness, service, or generosity. The options are as endless as the creativity and abilities of individuals. Raking leaves, writing a letter, preparing a meal, visiting or calling a lonely friend, fixing a leaky faucet, delivering groceries, performing music, surprising someone with a cash gift, providing childcare, helping clean up a yard or garage, giving a ride, or helping a stranded motorist are all acts that can encourage another. Using one's own unique gifts is paramount in God's kingdom. Paul said by doing so "the body of Christ may be built up" (Eph 4:12). That is another way of saying people will be encouraged. We need not do what *another* has been called to come alongside and do, but we ought to do what God has called *us* to come alongside someone and do. When that happens, we become encouragers and the entire body of Christ benefits.

We would do well to rethink how we respond to others. The world is desperately in need of encouragement today. There are signs all around us that people are weary and discouraged. We may not be able to change everything that is wrong in our community, but what if we seized the opportunities right in front of us to make a positive difference? What if we spoke a compliment or offered a word of thanks to someone? What if we intentionally smiled, perhaps even when we think no one is observing us? What if we engaged in an act for which we expected nothing in return? I suspect such encouragement would not only change those around us but also would change us.

What happens when we encourage another? The English word itself gives us a clue: the infusion of *courage* takes place. An encourager is ultimately a dispenser of courage. Let us find someone who needs a dose of courage today. What a splendid gift that would be!

PRAYER

Dear Lord, thank you for being our Encourager. Long ago you knew that we would need much encouragement. We would need someone to instill courage in our timid and fearful souls. So, you sent your Son, and then your Holy Spirit. Thank you. You also sent us other people, many of whom have encouraged us in a variety of ways over the years. And now you are sending us to encourage others. Help us to do so. Whether by word, by smile, by deed, or by some other means—make us encouragers to those in our circles. Our fallen and broken world needs a boost. May we, through the guidance and power of your Spirit, bring encouragement and hope to those around us. This we pray in Jesus's name. AMEN.

Questions

1. Thinking back over your life, when did someone's encouragement make a difference for you? Who encouraged you? How? Why did it matter just then?

2. Which form of encouragement noted above—a word, a smile, or a deed—is the easiest, for you? Which do you find most difficult? How might you change that?

3. What biblical or historical story of encouragement has inspired you? Why does the story move you as it does?

4. Who comes to mind that might need encouragement right now? Is there someone you might come alongside to encourage? What might you do to encourage that individual?

Suggested Reading

1 Thessalonians 1–5

53

2 THESSALONIANS: Warning

He will punish those who do not know God and do not obey
the gospel of our Lord Jesus. (2 Thessalonians 1:8)

They perish because they refused to love the truth
and so be saved. (2 Thessalonians 2:10)

If anyone does not obey our instruction in this letter, take
special note of him. Do not associate with him, in order that
he may feel ashamed. Yet do not regard him as an enemy,
but warn him as a brother. (2 Thessalonians 3:14–15)

There are always people who think warnings are for someone else. Does that describe you? I confess there have been times in my life when that has been true of me. My first recollection of ignoring a warning occurred when I was five or six years old. Ritchie was my neighbor, and his family had an impressive garden each year. Though we had been warned to stay out of the garden, one day the temptation got the best of Ritchie and me. The colorful peppers growing there appealed to our innocent eyes. It was my first experience with peppers, and the introduction did not go well. Not only did the peppers unexpectedly set my young mouth on fire but also their juice somehow got in my eyes. The more I rubbed them, the worse the condition. I remember running home across three yards, wailing, rubbing, and blinking as I went. That was an unforgettable and unpleasant day that I never wanted to repeat. Warnings about gardens ought to be taken seriously.

Unfortunately, it was far from the last warning I ignored. A few years later—somewhere around the age of ten or twelve—I remember attending a week-long children's church camp in northern Michigan. On the very first afternoon—while registration was still taking place and before the scheduled program began—my friend Paul and I thought it would be fun to do some exploring on our own. Though the camp leaders had warned everyone to stay within the clearly marked boundaries of the campground, we saw no harm in heading off through a wooded area toward the nearby lake. We promised one another that we would not get too near the lake's edge; and we kept our word. However, little did we know that the wooded area adjacent to the lake was nothing but a swamp. We soon found ourselves thigh-deep in mud and muck that worked like quicksand. We struggled to pull each other out, and the more we struggled the deeper we seemed to find ourselves in trouble. We eventually made it back to the campground and our cabin, but our shoes and whatever clothes we were wearing were pretty much out of commission for the rest of the week. It was a lesson in understanding that camp warnings are given for a reason.

I wish I could say that second lesson stuck with me and I have been a wise and mature individual ever since, one who has diligently paid attention to every warning. Some of us just seem to have to learn the hard way. Though I have managed to avoid garden peppers and quicksand since those early traumatic experiences, I have unfortunately found myself ignoring yet new kinds of warnings. One that comes to mind is when I was a high school senior taking my ACT in preparation for college. Today those tests usually occur at a computer, but I took the test by pencil and paper with a teacher carefully monitoring a room full of students, serving as timekeeper, and giving verbal instructions as we moved through each distinct part of the test. After completing several test sections on subjects such as math and vocabulary, it became obvious to me that I was routinely running out of time at the end of each section. As the teacher gave the order, "put your pencil down," I was leaving too many blank answers. It bothered me to the point that I determined to get started early on a section of the test that followed an extended break, even though we had been warned clearly to wait for the instructions each time. I chose not to wait, deciding instead to get a head start on a series of challenging history questions. Those questions were tough! I remember wondering to myself: *Were new college students really supposed to know this information?* I hardly knew any of it. Nonetheless, by the time the instructions came, I was pleased to be nearly half done responding to the questions—though admittedly I was less than satisfied with my answers. Only then did I realize all the questions I was attempting to answer were based on a lengthy and detailed narrative we were supposed to read prior to responding to the questions. That part of the ACT was designed to test reading comprehension, not my knowledge of history. Needless to say, my subsequent reading comprehension score was far from impressive. Asbury College must have admitted me based on potential or pity, or perhaps a combination of both. I learned the embarrassing lesson that test instructions matter.

Yes, I have had my share of warnings. Like so many people I observe today, however, I have struggled to generalize one warning and its consequences to the next scenario in life. Warnings are intended to impart wisdom. Their purpose is to protect us from harm and promote health and well-being. When we ignore warnings, we take unnecessary risks that someone else—often one more experienced—wants to help us avoid. We act as if we are smart enough to figure out things on our own, only to find ourselves in a mess—rubbing our eyes, stuck in the mud, or failing to reach our full potential. Warnings are given for a reason.

The Bible is a book of eternal hope and good news. However, it is also a book containing several warnings. The wise individual will embrace both the hope and the warnings. Regarding the latter, it is worth noting that a warning begins and ends the Bible. Immediately after the creation of man, God warned him: "you must not eat from the tree of the knowledge of good and evil, for when you eat of it you will surely die" (Gen 2:17). Though the instruction was clear, Adam ignored the warning, and the problem of death has plagued humanity ever since. The warning that closes the Bible comes from the Apostle John, when in the last chapter of Revelation, he writes:

> I warn everyone who hears the words of the prophecy of this
> book: If anyone adds anything to them, God will add to him
> the plagues described in this book. And if anyone takes words
> away from this book of prophecy, God will take away from
> him his share in the tree of life and in the holy city, which are
> described in this book. (22:18–19)

The Bible, then, begins and closes with a warning, each carrying dire consequences. The first warning suggests that disobedience will result in death. The final warning suggests that manipulating or altering God's Word to suit oneself will result in forfeiting eternity with God. These warnings have significant and eternal implications, as so many do. The nature of warnings is such that we heed them or ignore them at our own peril. In either case, life itself is in the balance.

In 2 Thessalonians, Paul said believers have an obligation to "warn . . . a brother" (3:15) who responds to instruction with disobedience. Thus, a warning is not only a gift to be received but a gift we share with another. In essence, that is what Paul does in this short, three-chapter letter sent to the church in Thessalonica, a bustling Greek seaport city. Three primary warnings are highlighted, all of which continue to have relevance today. Each is worth pausing to consider.

Punishment of disobedience. Consistent with teaching found elsewhere in Scripture, Paul warns his readers that punishment awaits "those who do not know God and do not obey the gospel of our Lord Jesus" (1:8). Over the years, people have argued whether this is fair, have sought to reinterpret and soften the warning, and have taken a variety of positions on the matter. Warnings often lead to such debates. Human nature is such that we prefer to justify our present actions rather than acknowledge we may need to change, or repent. Paul chooses not to argue the point. He simply states the fact that has been evident in the fifty-two preceding books of the Bible: persistent disobedience to God leads to "everlasting destruction." In other words, God finally grants what is sought. The individual who insists on operating on his or her own terms is ultimately "shut out from the presence of the Lord" (1:9). This is a tragic and needless outcome that results when one chooses to ignore God's warning.

Delusion of lawlessness. Humans have long struggled with truth—a point Paul makes with clarity and force in this letter (2:9–13). Paul warns that the struggle often ends in "a powerful delusion" (2:11), or deception (2:3, 10), that rejects truth and leads to lawlessness. In every generation there are people who think they would be better off with fewer restrictions and laws. They seek freedom but are deceived in their search. Such a delusion operated in Thessalonica during Paul's day, and we have witnessed similar delusions in our country in recent years. For example, in 2020 a movement to "defund the police" was promoted as the answer to the problems rampant in America's cities.

Sixty-Six

Many reasoned that fewer laws and restrictions would liberate the oppressed and marginalized and lead to social utopia. Several months of lawlessness followed, and the delusion was revealed for what it was: a dead-end experiment that brought more harm and destruction than good to the citizens it purported to help. Whenever people reject "truth" and believe a "lie" (2:10–11), needless tragedy follows.

Burden of idleness. A final warning raised by Paul has to do with those who are idle (3:6–13). Though the thought of idleness being a burden may initially sound like an oxymoron—after all, idleness frees one from the burden of work, does it not?—the description is fitting. Those who are idle find that their inactivity and indolence boomerang and create serious problems. Idleness reduces the possibility of obtaining needed food and material resources, making one a burden to others. The same posture tempts people to become busybodies, meddling in others' business. Idleness sets a poor example for others, including one's children. No wonder Paul adds this warning to his list of cautions. Idleness burdens society in that it turns people into *takers* rather than *givers*. No community, business, church, or family can thrive if its people are idle. Paul warns that such behavior is unbecoming for the people of God. The burden of idleness is a heavy one to bear, leaving many casualties along the way.

These warnings and more are given for our good. There is wisdom in heeding a warning, especially when it comes from the Word of God. The intent is not to limit or hinder a person, but quite the opposite. A warning that is taken to heart can catapult an individual toward great achievement and reduce disturbances along the way—disturbances like pepper in one's eyes, mud-covered shoes, and a disappointing entrance exam score.

Our Enemy—the devil, "the father of lies" (John 8:44)—is a master at minimizing, or even ridiculing, warnings. He has a long history of doing so, beginning with Adam and Eve in the garden. He is still on the prowl (1 Pet 5:8) which, in and of itself, is a warning to us all.

PRAYER

Our Father in heaven, you love us so much that you refuse to leave us or forsake us. Rather, you have chosen to guide and advise us as we conduct our daily lives. Thank you for being such a caring and gracious God. Would you give us hearts and minds that find it easy to lean in and heed your warnings? We recognize that your written Word, in large part, was produced so that we might have a roadmap for life. Help us to search its pages, know its teachings, embrace its promises, heed its warnings, and live out its principles. In doing so, may we reflect and honor you in the world today. We pray this in the name of your Son, Jesus Christ. AMEN.

QUESTIONS

1. As you look back over your life, what warning did you heed for which you are now thankful? What warning did you ignore that you now wish you had heeded?

2. Why is it that some people act as if no warning applies to them? What makes those people defy every warning and think they know best? Do you know someone like that?

3. How does one strike a balance between heeding a warning and yet not living in fear and paralysis? Is there a way to know whether a warning is legitimate?

4. If you—from your life experience—could offer two or three words of warning to an individual, what would those words be? Why?

SUGGESTED READING

2 Thessalonians 1–3

54

1 TIMOTHY: Godliness

*I urge, then, first of all, that requests, prayers, intercession
and thanksgiving be made for everyone—for kings and
all those in authority, that we may live peaceful and quiet
lives in all godliness and holiness. (1 Timothy 2:1–2)*

*Physical training is of some value, but godliness has
value for all things, holding promise for both the
present life and the life to come. (1 Timothy 4:8)*

But godliness with contentment is great gain. (1 Timothy 6:6)

*But you, man of God, flee from all this, and pursue
righteousness, godliness, faith, love, endurance and gentleness.
Fight the good fight of the faith. (1 Timothy 6:11–12)*

Does anyone aspire to be godly these days? There was a time when godliness was the goal of mature believers. It was spoken of and identified in another person as a sign of maturity in the faith. To be godly was considered both desirable and attainable. Yet I rarely hear reference to the word or idea today, which causes me to wonder why. Has godliness gone the way of the hula hoop and transistor radio? Has it been cast on the dustbin of artifacts from a bygone era? Is it something we sentimentally smile at but never expect to see again in an advanced, fast-paced world like ours? Those are all fair questions worthy of serious reflection.

The word *godliness* is used only by three New Testament writers: Luke, Paul, and Peter; and of the three no one used it more than Paul. Even so, Paul's use of the term was confined to three New Testament books—1 Timothy, 2 Timothy, and Titus—often called "The Pastoral Letters." These letters are so named because they were written to individuals who had pastoral care of churches. Paul, then, in addition to providing practical advice regarding several church matters, encouraged these young leaders and their followers to be godly. Apparently, godliness is an attribute that describes individuals, not institutions or organizations. At least that is the way the three New Testament authors consistently used the term.

If godliness is indeed a characteristic of individuals, what does it take to become such a person? What are the ingredients that make a person godly? Minimally, three qualities seem to be necessary: *desire, time*, and *a teachable spirit*. Godliness will not exist without all three.

Desire. Godliness has to do with devotion and piety, both of which grow in the soil of desire. To be devoted, or committed, to another is an expression of desire for that individual. Likewise, the virtue of piety implies a desire or longing for God. The psalmist said: "As the deer pants for streams of water, so my soul pants for you, O God. My soul thirsts for God, for the living God" (Ps 42:1–2). This vivid description borrows an image from the natural world to reveal the depth of the writer's longing for God. Godliness develops when one's chief desire is to know and please God. Paul seemed to think the fulfillment of that desire was possible for he encouraged Timothy, his young protégé, to avoid chasing after money and to "pursue righteousness, godliness," and other fruits of the spirit (1 Tim 6:11). Timothy was urged to evaluate his desires and make an adjustment if necessary. One will never be godly without first and foremost desiring God and seeking to be devoted to him above all else.

One of my favorite books, and one to which I have found myself returning often, is the little volume written by A. W. Tozer in 1948, *The Pursuit of God*. Tozer associated himself with the Christian and Missionary Alliance and served thirty-one years (1928–1959) as pastor of the Southside Alliance Church in Chicago. While speaking about "full Lordship" and "complete submission" to God, Tozer noted that "millions call themselves by [God's] name, it is true, and pay some token respect to him, but a simple test will show how little He is really honored among them. . . . the proof is in the choices [an individual] makes day after day throughout his life" (1982 edition, pp 102–3). The true measure of godliness is not in mouthing religious words but in the day-to-day choices that reflect an uncompromised devotion and desire to honor God.

Time. Another factor that contributes to godliness is the use of one's time. It is impossible to imitate a person unless one spends time with the individual, studying his or her character and behaviors. That is how sons and daughters grow to become like their parents. Significant time together results in shared mannerisms and responses. So it is with godliness. If we are to become *like* God we will have to spend time *with* God. There is no shortcut. Time reading God's Word, time in prayer, time intentionally listening to God's voice and seeking his direction are how one becomes known for being godly. I have never met a godly person who did not do these things. Never. Godliness is a product of time spent with God. It is also the case that godliness usually springs from time spent with other godly people who model what it looks like to pursue God. Tozer wrote, "Come near to the holy men and women of the past and you will soon feel the heat of their desire after God" (p 15). Associate with and get close to other devoted followers of God and their desires will soon rub off on you and become your desires. Indeed, there is no substitute for time in the presence of God and his saints if one is seeking a life of godliness. That means, of course, that overly busy and frantic schedules stand as the enemy of godly people, making exorbitant demands on their time and leaving little opportunity for quietness in the presence of the Lord.

A teachable spirit. The final ingredient required for godliness to flourish may initially surprise some, though both Scripture and experience point to the fact. Anyone who digs deep to discover what lies underneath the surface of a godly person will ultimately find a teachable spirit. The Old Testament prophets were teachable, as were the New Testament disciples. It is impossible to find a godly person in history who did not have a hunger to learn more from and about God. That is, in part, what makes Paul's letter to Timothy fascinating. First Timothy emphasizes two related themes: godliness and teaching. A case could be made that the former cannot exist without the latter. "Sound doctrine" (1:10), "sound instruction" (6:3), and "godly teaching" (6:3) were expressions used to communicate the importance of seeking and maintaining a proper understanding of God's ways. That implies an ongoing openness to learning indispensable truths from our Lord. Paul urged Timothy to "teach" (4:11, 13; 6:2), said that a church leader must be "able to teach" (3:2), and highlighted the importance of following "good teaching" (4:6; 6:3). Those who pursue godliness are eager to learn about the faith and how they might think and behave more like Jesus. They are humble enough to admit their need of understanding and courageous enough to put into practice what they have learned. In a word, they are teachable.

Godliness will result only when all three ingredients operate together. Desire that is not acted upon by the additional commitment of time and being teachable becomes little more than wishful thinking. An investment of time that exhibits neither desire nor a teachable spirit becomes wasted effort. Being teachable without desiring God and spending time with him may produce a conversant person on several topics, but godliness will not be one of them. All three of these attributes working together contribute to godliness. The problem, however, is that each of these three ingredients is countercultural in the twenty-first century. Desire has been hijacked and twisted so that it focuses almost entirely on personal pleasure and comforts in our world. Who desires anything that includes hardship and suffering or that demands perseverance? Time, despite all our technology and gadgets, is a rare commodity. While giving lip service to the wonders of our time-saving devices, evidence suggests we feel busier and more stressed than ever. Who has time to slow down, quiet oneself, and listen to God? Being teachable is a foreign concept in a world where information is at our fingertips. We believe everything we need can be found on our phones and computers. Why, then, would someone submit to learning from another, even if that other is God himself? Consequently, godliness is rare.

When and where godliness does exist, however, it still looks like the description Paul provided in his letter to Timothy. A walk through 1 Timothy will reveal that godly people tend to be characterized by the following attributes:

- Advancing God's work (1:4).
- Promoting sound doctrine (1:10), particularly as it relates to one's understanding of Jesus (3:16).
- Engaging in meaningful prayer (2:1–2, 8).
- Living peaceful and quiet lives (2:2).
- Demonstrating exemplary moral leadership (3:1–13).

- Committing to training that is designed to help one persevere (4:7–16).
- Caring for family members and community widows (5:1–16).
- Not showing partiality or favoritism (5:21).
- Living with contentment (6:6–10).
- Pursuing God and his attributes and pointing others to do the same (6:11–12).

While this list is far from exhaustive, it offers a good starting point. This is what godliness looks like in the everyday lives of God's people.

Three final thoughts strike me as I ponder the topic of godliness; one comes from Paul, one from A. W. Tozer, and one from the writer of this entry. First, Paul makes clear that **godliness is not something reserved for, or only to be found among, the elderly**. Timothy, to whom Paul was writing these things, was a young man. In fact, Paul made a point of warning him, "Don't let anyone look down on you because you are young, but set an example for the believers" (4:12). The call to godliness (4:8; 6:11) is made to young and old alike. There are no exceptions.

Second, Tozer concludes *The Pursuit of God* by making clear that **godliness does not permit the popular sacred-secular divide in life**. To the contrary, he notes, "The sacred-secular antithesis has no foundation in the New Testament" (p 119). Godliness, or the pursuit of God, influences every area of life. "Whatever [we] do, whether in word or deed, [we] do it all in the name of the Lord Jesus, giving thanks to God the Father through him" (Col 3:17; cf. 1 Cor 10:31). Godliness tears down the arbitrary distinction between the sacred and the secular. One cannot turn on or turn off godliness at will; it permeates the totality of life, erasing our man-made categories in the process.

Third, **godliness is more than mere goodness**. While the latter is laudable and even scriptural (e.g., Gal 5:22; 2 Pet 1:5), the two are not synonyms. Good people make nice neighbors who lend a helping hand; godly people make sincere saints who lay down their lives for another. Good people speak politely to others; godly people speak prayerfully to God on behalf of others. Good people touch the world; godly people touch heaven in a way that changes the world. What if more of us sought to be godly rather than just good? I suspect our families, neighbors, and associates would sit up and take notice. I suspect our churches would become known for their fervor and vitality. I suspect heaven would rejoice.

Godliness need not be rare. Let us pursue it with passion.

PRAYER

O God, our Creator and Lord, you have called us to follow you and become like you. Too often we have failed at both. Forgive us. Plant within us a deep desire to pursue you, and you alone. Make us godly people who look and act like you. Help us to live that way consistently, wherever we find ourselves—at home, at work, at church, or in our neighborhood. May we live humbly, with a single focus that seeks to please and honor you. We pray this is the name of your Son, our Savior and Lord, Jesus Christ. AMEN.

QUESTIONS

1. Who comes to mind when you think of godliness? Is there a person that exemplifies that attribute? What are the characteristics that make that person godly?

2. What are some of the primary obstacles to godliness? Why does it seem to be so rare among Christian believers today?

3. How can one make more time for God in a busy world like ours? What are some practical ways that you have observed in others or experienced yourself?

4. A. W. Tozer wrote a book entitled, *The Pursuit of God*. What are some examples of ways that people might pursue God? How have you pursued God in your own life?

SUGGESTED READING

1 Timothy 1–6

55

2 TIMOTHY: Hardship

But join with me in suffering for the gospel. (2 Timothy 1:8)

*Endure hardship with us like a good soldier
of Christ Jesus. (2 Timothy 2:3)*

*Remember Jesus Christ, raised from the dead, descended from
David. This is my gospel, for which I am suffering even to the
point of being chained like a criminal. (2 Timothy 2:8–9)*

*But you, keep your head in all situations, endure
hardship, do the work of an evangelist, discharge all
the duties of your ministry. (2 Timothy 4:5)*

A young father in his thirties, whose wife had just lost their baby during pregnancy, expressed their shared grief and heartache in the following poem:

*Dear Little One
When mommy and daddy heard that there would be you
It caught us off guard for a moment or two
We thought in our minds our family was set
But you seemed to say that we weren't done yet
So we started to plan for all that would be
Our kids were excited to add you to their three
Would you be a girl? Autumn hoped it'd be so
Of course, the boys had other ideas you know*

But before we knew it, your heart beat no more
It was over so quick, tell us what was that for
We never knew your name or the color of your eyes
Your death, like your life, was also a surprise
Now you're teaching us more than we'll get to teach you
But through all the pain we know this much is true
God is still good, yes His love shines bright
And up there in heaven He is holding you tight
We love you, Dear Little One

The poem's author was my son, Kyle. As he sat down one evening in 2021 to reflect on their fresh and unexpected loss, the words came to him quickly. He, Amber, and their three young children embraced one another in their sorrow. The raw pain seared their hearts, threatening to overwhelm their young family that was already too familiar with hardship.

Hardship comes in a variety of ways. Sometimes it comes as loss during pregnancy; other times it comes as loss of a job, financial security, or even a spouse. Hardship can result from unfair treatment, ridicule, slander, or rejection. At times it looks like a rare and tormenting disease, a severe disability, or paralysis from an accident. Hardship is known during pandemics, wars, terrorist attacks, city riots, and school shootings. Such adversity can influence one physically, mentally, socially, emotionally, or spiritually; often it touches all these areas simultaneously. No one seeks hardship, but everyone has seen it—if not in one's own life, then in the life of a family member or friend. Hardship is all too common everywhere.

Recognizing that fact, in the letter of 2 Timothy Paul twice admonishes Timothy to "endure hardship" (2:3; 4:5). Two other times, in 1:8 and 2:9, the same Greek root word is translated "suffering." The word used here is rare—found only a few times in 2 Timothy and James—and literally means "to suffer evil." While the word may be rare, the experience is not. Hardship, or suffering, always has been common among Christian believers. It is noteworthy that Paul did not advise his young partner in the gospel to do all he could to avoid hardship, run from anything that could be difficult, or even to seek professional help in dealing with it. Instead, he spoke a word that was wise, sound, and straightforward: "endure hardship." Acknowledge it, face it head on, and hold steady despite the challenges. Paul could offer such advice because few individuals had more personal experience with hardship, or more to say on the topic, than he did. His lessons on the subject are instructive and timeless.

First, **hardship is inevitable**. The Fall ensured it (Gen 3:16–19); now we must endure it. Sin's entry into the world guaranteed human hardship on this side of heaven. Not until "a new heaven and a new earth" (Rev 21:1) have become a reality will we be free from hardships and suffering. Those who think they can somehow escape the effects of the Fall—perhaps by working hard or accumulating wealth as a security buffer—are deluding themselves. Hardship is one experience every human shares at one time or another. Paul knew that; his word was rooted in reality. It was his way of saying: *Timothy, you will face difficulties. When they come, endure them "like a good soldier" (2:3) and know that Christ Jesus stands with you.*

Second, **hardship even comes to those who live right and make good choices**. Timothy was a remarkable young man. Paul thought so highly of him that he assigned Timothy to provide leadership in the church at Ephesus (1 Tim 1:3). Timothy's mother and grandmother were both believers (2 Tim 1:5). Thus, he came from a solid family of faith. He traveled with Paul and became a partner in the early missionary enterprise of the church (e.g., Acts 16:1–3; 2 Cor 1:1; Phil 1:1; Col 1:1; 1 Thess 1:1; 2 Thess 1:1; Philem 1). Timothy was an exemplary young man with a strong work ethic and a solid reputation (Acts 16:1–2). He was the kind of person others wanted their sons and daughters to emulate. He lived well and was wise and mature beyond his years; and yet Paul recognized there would be hardships for Timothy, too. No one is exempt, not even those of high character.

Third, **hardship often comes because people live right and make good choices**. We like to think that wise decisions will prevent difficulties and problems, but Paul and others in the Bible are proof that hardship at times *results from* making right choices and obeying God. Paul knew this from experience and spoke often of the hardships he endured for preaching the gospel (e.g., Acts 20:23; 2 Cor 1:8; 4:8–9; 6:4–10; 12:10; 1 Thess 2:9). His story was not unique. Other biblical heroes suffered hardship for doing right as well. "Blameless" Job (1:8) lost everything; David, "a man after [God's] own heart" (Acts 13:22), wrote many of the Psalms while in the pits of life (e.g., Ps 40:2; 69:15; 103:4); and three loyal Hebrew young men found themselves in a fiery furnace in Babylon (Dan 3). All these giants of the faith, and many others like them, knew hardship as a direct result of their faith and virtues.

Fourth, **hardship need not separate one from Christ and his love**. Paul was explicit about this fact (Rom 8:35). There is a choice to be made when pain and difficulty arise: the experience can catapult one into the loving arms of our Lord or cause one to abandon him. I have seen both. Some people grow sweeter when they are squeezed; others become bitter. The difference is one of perspective. Those who see Jesus Christ as both the Sovereign Lord and the Suffering Servant who knows human pain draw close to him for solace and strength. On the other hand, those who have a distorted, inadequate, and unbiblical view of Christ—perhaps seeing him as little more than a cosmic Santa Claus—are disappointed that he has allowed hardship to touch them. They conclude that he is cruel, uncompassionate, or incapable and sadly distance themselves from the very One whose love they most need.

Fifth, **hardship endured is how Christ's power is made known**. Those who use hardship as a springboard to greater intimacy with Christ come to an amazing realization: Christ gets exalted and glorified in their struggle. Human weakness paves the way for the display of divine strength. Paul went so far as to say: "[F]or Christ's sake, I delight in weaknesses, in insults, in hardships, in persecutions, in difficulties. For when I am weak, then I am strong [in Christ's power]" (2 Cor 12:10). Paul had surrendered all his rights to the Lord. His only concern, therefore, was Christ and his glory. Once a person comes to that place in his or her spiritual life, hardships and difficulties become the very instruments through which Christ is honored. That which would ruin another becomes the very platform by which Christ is exalted and made known. Such has been the case countless times down through history. The same option exists today. Is there a hardship we need to see differently "for Christ's sake" (2 Cor 12:10)?

As noted above, my son and his wife, Kyle and Amber, were already familiar with hardship when they unexpectedly lost their fourth child in pregnancy. Two of their first three children were born with cystic fibrosis (CF), a genetic condition that damages the lungs and digestive system and for which there is no cure. That has meant several things for their family—hard things that no parents or grandparents would wish for their kids. CF is an *isolating* problem. There are places and people that the family has to avoid for the sake of health. Further, CF is an *intense* and *incessant* problem. Rigorous treatments are done multiple times a day, sometimes followed by sleepless nights with fits of coughing. Daily medication, mealtime enzymes, diets and hygiene, and regular doctor visits are all carefully monitored. The task is wearisome, to be sure. There are no days or weeks off from the demanding regimen. Good health demands diligence. Thus, the pattern and needs are repeated day after day. Finally, CF is *invisible*, meaning the problems are internal rather than external, requiring ongoing explanations to others as to why certain actions are taken or prohibited. The hardship of CF—never anticipated and certainly never desired—has changed the lives of Kyle, Amber, their children, and those around them.

Yet they are not alone. There are other families dealing with CF and a host of other challenges. Hardship is no respecter of persons. The sun rises "on the evil and the good," and the rain falls on "the righteous and the unrighteous" (Matt 5:45). The evidence of faith or spiritual maturity, then, is not the absence of hardship. Rather, mature faith is seen in the lives of those who *endure* hardship and who, in their personal pain, reach the conclusion that "God is still good." They are not alone because the Lord is with them (2 Tim 4:22). Job, who universally has come to represent human hardship and pain, made this unyielding declaration: "Though he slay me, yet will I hope in him" (Job 13:15). Though hardships abound, so does the hope of which Job spoke.

Yes, God is still good. Let us place our hope in him.

PRAYER

Our Father in heaven, we confess that sometimes we grow weary and discouraged with what seems to be relentless hardships. We turn to you just now and ask for your grace to endure. Help us to trust that your sovereign hand is at work in the affairs of our lives, even when everything seems hard. Strengthen our faith, bolster our resolve, and sweeten our disposition so that others may be attracted to you when they observe us. Remind us that Jesus Christ, in whose name we pray, became our model when he endured the hardship of the cross. AMEN.

QUESTIONS

1. Who do you know in your life who has endured much hardship, and yet continues to express great faith in God? What do you think has been that person's secret?

2. Why do you think an all-powerful, loving God allows hardships and unbearable pain to touch his children? What might be the purpose of it all?

3. What are some practical and helpful ways to come alongside one who is experiencing hardship? What do you find most encouraging during your own times of hardship?

4. What hardship are you currently facing for which you need God's help? What steps might you need to take to face your current challenges in a way that honors God?

SUGGESTED READING

2 Timothy 1–4

56

Titus: Example

They claim to know God, but by their actions
they deny him. (Titus 1:16)

Encourage the young men to be self-controlled. In everything set
them an example, by doing what is good. In your teaching show
integrity, seriousness and soundness of speech that cannot be
condemned, so that those who oppose you may not be ashamed
because they have nothing bad to say about us. (Titus 2:6–8)

Our people must learn to devote themselves to doing
what is good, in order that they may provide for daily
necessities and not live unproductive lives. (Titus 3:14)

Everyone has heard the adage, "a picture is worth a thousand words." If that is true—if a simple image has such great value—imagine the value and potential of a living example. Being an example to others may be one of the most underestimated and underutilized tools in existence for shaping the next generation, though it is available to everyone. Any individual can choose to live his or her life as an example. In fact, we do so whether we are conscious of it or not. The younger generation—our sons and daughters, grandsons and granddaughters—watch us and pick up our words, mannerisms, and habits regardless of our intentions. That means, of course, that the question is never really: Will I choose to be an example? Rather, the question is always: What kind of example will I choose to be?

Paul spoke often about being an example, as did other New Testament writers. The early church understood the value and power of modeling Christlikeness to one's neighbors. The recipients of Paul's pastoral letters—Timothy and Titus—were encouraged to "set an example" (1 Tim 4:12; Titus 2:7) in their respective communities. Timothy was serving in Ephesus (1 Tim 1:3), one of the most important and populated Mediterranean port cities at the time, whereas Titus was responsible for ministry on the island of Crete (Titus 1:5), located some two hundred miles southwest of Ephesus. Both places, Ephesus and Crete, were known for paganism and immorality that contradicted the Christian ethic. Neither area would have been hospitable to the gospel and its influence. Fully aware of these antagonistic environments, Paul unequivocally instructed these two young men to live as models in their respective communities.

Paul knew that being an example was an effective leadership strategy. Leaders lead by modeling behaviors they want others to follow. Jesus did that when he washed his disciples' feet and then said to them: "I have set you an example that you should do as I have done for you" (John 13:15). He demonstrated serving his followers and encouraged them to do the same. Words alone have limited appeal, but words that take on flesh and become an example are a different story. The example of a life wherein one practices what he preaches is the most effective way to influence others. That is why teaching or preaching—whether in the home, the classroom, or the church—that is rich with illustrations is more effective than instruction that relies only on words, concepts, and abstract thoughts. Anyone who wants to lead and instruct others needs to provide an example, beginning with his or her own life.

Becoming an example, or model, is not restricted by age. The expectation is not that one should experience all of life's good pleasures and hard knocks first and, thereby, become qualified to serve as an example for the next generation. To the contrary, Paul encouraged modeling as the pattern for youth. He wrote, "Don't let anyone look down on you because you are young, but set an example for the believers in speech, in life, in love, in faith and in purity" (1 Tim 4:12). The emphasis was clearly on taking initiative to set patterns that others might emulate even while one is still young. Far too few value living that way today.

The Peter Pan Syndrome, popularized by Dan Kiley's 1983 book bearing that title, describes the desires and behaviors of those who do not want to grow up and take on adult responsibilities. A decade later, author Robert Bly, in *The Sibling Society* (1996), took up the same theme when he highlighted the growing tendency of prolonging adolescence. The term *perpetual adolescence* eventually became popular, defining the phenomenon wherein adult responsibilities are pushed back further and further so that people in their mid-adult years still act like irresponsible adolescents. In such a world, narcissism and hedonism—self-absorption and seeking pleasure—are values that trump the kind of concern for others that would result in setting an example. Paul had a different idea. He believed young men like Timothy and Titus had a golden opportunity to model mature and godly behavior, and then show how one might endure hardship for the sake of Christ. Being an example in one's youth is a powerful influence and has the potential to inspire an entire generation.

Paul was so convinced of the value of an exemplary lifestyle that he invited others to follow his own example. Today not many people would have the audacity to extend such an invitation. We reason: *Who am I to think someone should follow me? I am such a flawed person.* That thought was apparently foreign to Paul. Was he arrogant? No. He labeled himself "the worst" of sinners (1 Tim 1:15), yet he was confident that Jesus, the One who "began a good work" in him, would continue the transformation process and "carry it on to completion" (Phil 1:6). Therefore, on more than one occasion Paul invited entire groups of people to follow his example (1 Cor 11:1; Phil 3:17; 2 Thess 3:7). Paul often used the Greek word from which we get our English word "mimic." The idea communicates imitation. He lived his life in such a way—mimicking, or imitating, Christ—that he had confidence he could then turn and invite others to mimic or imitate his lifestyle, which reflected Christ. What a standard he set. Do we live our lives close enough to Jesus, imitating him, that we can confidently turn to others and invite them to copy or imitate us, knowing that by doing so they will become more like Jesus? That is what Paul envisioned and encouraged among those in the early church.

The specific instruction Paul offered Timothy and Titus pertaining to how they ought to be an example was very similar. Our focus here will be primarily on Titus, but the fact that Paul offers parallel advice to both young men is noteworthy and strengthens what he had to say on the matter to each one. Paul suggested three ways that Titus could be an example to those living on the island of Crete. These same three ways have relevance in our world as well.

First, **set an example by being self-controlled**. This is what Titus was supposed to "encourage" (2:6) and model among the young men under his influence. The Greek word translated "self-controlled" means to be sober. In other words, life was to be marked by moderation and seriousness. Balance is implied, along with good judgment and the avoidance of extremes. When urging Timothy likewise to be an example in his youth, Paul said, "set an example . . . in life" (1 Tim 4:12). One's entire life is to be well-balanced and self-controlled. Paul suggested that since others were watching, no area of life should become unmanageable. God wants his people to be self-controlled, for it is the best way to demonstrate that God himself is in control. If God is indeed Lord of all, people will come to recognize that fact when they observe that we have surrendered control to him in every area of life. Such surrender manifests itself to observers as self-control when in reality it is *God*-control. Paul encouraged Titus to be that kind of example to those around him. That same standard exists for all who follow Christ in any generation. The social value of modeling self-control cannot be overstated.

Second, **set an example by doing good**. Paul was straightforward when he said, "In everything set them an example by doing what is good" (2:7). The expression—"doing what is good"—comes from two Greek words: good works. Every action, every deed, and every work ought to be motivated by the desire to do good. While this sounds easy enough on the surface, the challenge comes from the verse's first two words: "in everything." When we have been wronged, hurt, or disrespected, doing good is usually the last thing on our minds. Sinful human nature wants to retaliate and even the score. However, Paul includes no exception clause. Doing good should be evident "in everything." In his parallel instruction to Timothy, Paul's instruction was to "set an example . . . in love" (1 Tim 4:12). Unconditional love—*agape*—was to mark Timothy's behavior, doing good regardless of the treatment of others. That kind of example is still called for today. Jesus said the demonstration of love—choosing to do good despite the circumstances—was how people would identify his followers (John 13:35). No less an example is needed in a world like ours.

Third, **set an example in teaching and speech**. Setting an example in self-control and in doing good are projects that could occupy most of us—me included—for a lifetime. Yet Paul continued by noting the way one teaches and talks should also be exemplary. The teaching of Titus was to be characterized by "integrity," by "seriousness," and by "soundness of speech that cannot be condemned" (2:7–8). Translated, what is spoken matters. Paul prioritized this when he wrote his list of the ways that Timothy was to be an example, placing it first on the list. Paul wrote, "set an example for the believers in speech" (1 Tim 4:12). Speech reveals those things hidden in the heart. What we say and how we say it serve as models to those who listen. Children, students, neighbors, friends, and those who attend our churches notice how we teach and communicate. Some are winsome and attractive; they teach and speak with grace, gentleness, relevance, and application. Others are negative, cynical, or even scathing; they speak in ways that are critical, harsh, manipulative, and insensitive. Whether we pause to realize it or not, every time we open our mouths to teach or speak, we serve as a model for others. The writer of Proverbs reminds us that "he who loves a pure heart and whose speech is gracious will have the king for a friend" (22:11)—and I suspect many other friends as well. For setting a good example in teaching and speech is appealing and encouraging to everyone.

In summary, our habits, actions, and words all matter. The habit of self-control, the action of doing good, and the words spoken when we teach and converse with others are all on display. When we take these behaviors seriously enough to set a noble example for others, we honor Christ. Ultimately, that was Paul's personal desire and charge to those young leaders under his influence. His goal was that he and others might honor and live like Christ. Therefore, Paul's invitation was bold, clear, and universal: "Follow my example, as I follow the example of Christ" (1 Cor 11:1).

Whose example are *we* following? What example are *we* setting?

PRAYER

Our loving Lord, you have called us into fellowship and invited us to live, act, and talk like you. In fact, you have made us in your very image. As if that were not enough, you also have provided us human examples in history and in daily life of people who have walked closely with you. Help us to observe and imitate those godly men and women who reflect you. Then help us to so live our own lives that others might see our example of self-control, good works, and elevated speech and thereby be drawn to you. Forbid that we would ever be a stumbling block to anyone who watches us. Make us more like your Son, Jesus, in whose name we pray. AMEN.

QUESTIONS

1. Looking back on your life, who set an example for you? Are there two or three people who modeled behaviors that you now practice? What did they model?

2. Why are we so hesitant today to think that we might be a model for others? Do we need to change that mindset? If so, what needs to take place for that change to occur?

3. Of the three ways to set an example noted above—self-control, doing good, and teaching or talking—which do you find most challenging? Why?

4. What specific changes are needed in your life to be a more attractive example of a follower of Christ? What is stopping you from getting started right now?

SUGGESTED READING

Titus 1–3

57

PHILEMON: Brothers

Your love has given me great joy and encouragement, because you, brother, have refreshed the hearts of the saints. (Philemon 7)

Perhaps the reason he was separated from you for a little while was that you might have him back for good—no longer as a slave, but better than a slave, as a dear brother. He is very dear to me but even dearer to you, both as a man and as a brother in the Lord. (Philemon 15–16)

I do wish, brother, that I may have some benefit from you in the Lord; refresh my heart in Christ. (Philemon 20)

Family language fills the pages of Scripture. God relates to us as Father; we relate to him as sons and daughters. People within the community of faith relate to one another as brothers and sisters. In fact, the word *brother* is found some 350 times in the New Testament alone, occurring in 25 of its 27 books (only the brief letters of Titus and 2 John fail to mention the word). How we relate to one another apparently matters; and the predominant model given to us in Scripture draws on a family relationship. In Paul's letter addressed to Philemon (thus, the name of the book), the apostle uses the term *brother* to identify three people: Timothy (v 1), Philemon (vv 7, 20), and Onesimus (v 16). Such relationships implied certain obligations and commitments. Before exploring those relationships further, however, it would be helpful to know a little more about the letter itself.

Philemon is intriguing and unique in many ways. First, **it is a personal letter pertaining to a private matter**. Most New Testament letters were general in nature, intended for wide public circulation. Of Paul's thirteen preserved letters, nine contain a combination of doctrinal and practical advice intended for entire church communities. Three other letters addressed church leaders Timothy and Titus, providing instruction and principles to guide those responsible for local church ministries. Philemon is unique in that its message was personal, targeting a solitary individual with a specific plea.

Second, **Philemon is a very short letter**. Like a handful of other New Testament letters—2 John, 3 John, and Jude—and the Old Testament book of Obadiah, Philemon consists of only one chapter. Remarkably, each of these small books still has a big message, perhaps underscoring the fact that word count is not nearly as important as clarity and straightforwardness. A few words can still pack a powerful punch.

Third, **the content is endearing and heartwarming**. Philemon has had great human appeal over the years because it tells the story of Paul coming to the aid of a runaway slave, Onesimus. In the process, Paul encouraged grace and forgiveness on the part of Philemon when it came to receiving Onesimus back into his care. Tenderness, inspiration, and hope form a threefold thread that runs throughout the story.

Fourth, **the message is socially radical**. The message of Philemon encourages us to see others through a new lens that is countercultural. The invitation is to see each other for what we have in common rather than defining an individual by socio-economic status or some arbitrary category derived from identity politics. The new lens transforms our perspective until we see each other solely as brothers—valued, loved, and sharing mutual concerns and goals.

This short letter mentions *brother* several times (e.g., vv 1, 7, 16, 20). A brother is one who shares common origins, ties, or interests with another. Together the individuals possess tremendous potential for good or evil. For example, in the early 1900s, brothers Wilbur and Orville Wright helped people take flight with their pioneering aviation efforts in North Carolina. Just a few decades earlier, in the late 1800s, Missouri-born brothers Frank and Jesse James terrorized frontier communities by robbing banks and holding up trains. One set of brothers *lifted* others—literally and figuratively—whereas the other set of brothers *lowered* others into fear and suspicion. The influence of brothers can be powerful and often becomes legendary.

However, what is it that brothers actually *do* for each other? Attempting a comprehensive list would be impractical and result in such a lengthy catalog as to be of little value. Nonetheless, Paul highlighted a few attributes of brothers in Philemon that help us understand the term and provide insights as to a brother's worth. It is to those brotherly attributes that we turn next. Four characteristics stand out here.

1. Brothers stick together when times are tough (v 1). Paul began his letter by identifying himself as "a prisoner of Christ Jesus," adding the fact that "Timothy our brother" was also present with him. While this was not the only time Paul began a letter referring to his companion Timothy as a "brother" (e.g., 2 Cor 1:1; Col 1:1), it is the only time that Paul did so while also noting that he himself was "a prisoner" (vv 1, 9). A prisoner, by definition, is bound, limited, and constrained by outside forces. Timothy, observant and fully aware of Paul's circumstances, did not abandon his ministry partner, for they were brothers. A brother does not jump ship when storms arise. Proverbs 17:17 reminds us that "a brother is born for adversity." Paul had a brother like that in Timothy. Though at times Paul also referred to Timothy as his "son" (1 Tim 1:2, 18; 2 Tim 1:2), here he saw him as a brother. Perhaps that is because when times are tough, a brother is needed to help shoulder the load. Whereas one might seek to lighten the load for a son, one typically will rely on a brother to help him carry it. Timothy was that person for Paul during some challenging seasons of life. He was a brother in ministry who remained loyal when days grew difficult and demanding.

2. Brothers encourage each other when one of them is down (vv 7, 20). Timothy was not the only brother Paul referenced in the letter. Paul acknowledged receiving "joy and encouragement" from his brother Philemon, who apparently had also "refreshed the hearts of the saints" elsewhere (v 7). Later in the letter, Paul expressed his hope that his brother Philemon would continue to bring "benefit" and "refresh [his] heart in Christ" (v 20)—something Paul was "confident" Philemon would do. After all, that is what it means to be a brother. Brothers encourage each other when life looks bleak and the road ahead is dreary. A well-timed visit, word, gift, promise, act of service, or memory communicated by a brother can indeed bring "joy and encouragement." Paul was blessed to have such a brother in Philemon. However, he was not the only brother who brought Paul encouragement. A careful reading of Paul's letters will reveal that he often closed them by expressing his gratitude to numerous brothers and sisters in the faith who encouraged him. There are seasons in everyone's life when discouragement and dejection threaten to overwhelm. At such times, encouragement from another proves priceless. That is what brothers and sisters do: they encourage one another, giving hope and reason to continue the journey. When Paul encountered Christ on the road to Damascus (Acts 9:1–31), he discovered and then cultivated a new network of brothers and sisters who would encourage him the rest of his life. In short, he was adopted into a family.

3. Brothers see value that others may miss (v 11). An individual's usefulness and strengths may not be apparent immediately to the casual observer. Sometimes it takes a brother to point them out and appreciate them. That was certainly evident in the events described in Philemon. Paul appealed to Philemon, "on the basis of love" (v 9), to respond with grace and kindness to his runaway slave, Onesimus. Paul explained the matter this way: though Onesimus once "was useless to you . . . now he has become useful both to you and to me" (v 11). The author is using a play on words here, for the Greek name "Onesimus" means useful. Up until this time, Onesimus had never lived up to his name. However, all that apparently changed through an encounter with Christ and subsequent mentorship by Paul. Therefore, Paul recommended Onesimus be seen "no longer as a slave, but better than a slave, as a dear brother" (v 16). Paul discovered that the one who was once *useless* was now transformed and had become *useful*. Onesimus ministered to Paul while he "was in chains" (v 10), causing Paul to witness and appreciate the value of personal tender service. It often takes a brother to notice, encourage, and help develop the potential that lies dormant in another. What Barnabas had once done for Paul—introducing him to the brotherhood of apostles (Acts 9:26–30)—Paul did for Onesimus. The result was a valuable new brother added to the family of God.

4. Brothers sacrifice for one another for the greater good of all (vv 15–16). Paul communicated a remarkable expectation, wherein both brothers—Onesimus and Philemon—were asked to sacrifice for the other. The fact that this short letter made its way into the New Testament, combined with a parallel reference to Onesimus in Colossians 4:9, make it reasonable to assume that these sacrifices were indeed made. It is easy, even natural, for today's reader to miss the call for mutual sacrifice here because the message of slavery looms large in the story.

In a world like ours, where individual rights are promoted above all else, the temptation is to see nothing but an injustice that needs a remedy. However, if we interpret the events of Philemon only through our current cultural lens, we miss a central and universal point. Paul was asking both Philemon and Onesimus, as brothers in the Lord, to sacrifice for each other—Onesimus by returning to Philemon; Philemon by elevating his former slave to a brother. Both were asked to see each other in a new light; both were asked to give up some of their personal rights, privileges, and comforts for the sake of the other. It was a bold request, and yet that is what brothers do; they sacrifice for one another. John put it this way: "Jesus Christ laid down his life for us. And we ought to lay down our lives for our brothers" (1 John 3:16).

The truth is that Scripture tells the stories of many sets of brothers. Some were flesh-and-blood brothers, whereas others were brothers in mission and calling. Yet they all shared the common experience of relying on one another during significant seasons of life. Moses had Aaron; David had Jonathan; and Shadrach had Meshach and Abednego. Peter had Andrew; James had John; and Paul had Barnabas, Silas, and Timothy. Working as a team, these sets of brothers accomplished more than any of them could have done alone. They faced hardship together, sacrificed for one another, and offered encouragement in times of duress. That is what brothers do.

The history of brothers advancing the work of God, however, is not confined to our favorite Bible characters. The Methodist revival that influenced England and America in the eighteenth and nineteenth centuries would have looked very different had John Wesley not had Charles. The former was known for his preaching; the latter was known for his hymns. Together they communicated the gospel and its central doctrines to a needy world. In the twentieth century, it was Billy Graham and his brothers who moved the world for God. For half a century, Graham enjoyed the brotherly advice, support, and partnership of the Wilson brothers, T. W. and Grady. The three of them grew up together in North Carolina and all became effective evangelists who worked closely together. Musicians Cliff Barrows and George Beverly Shea rounded out the Graham team. These five brothers in the faith prayed with and for one another, traveled together to six continents as ambassadors for Christ, and advised each other on an untold number of occasions. That is what brothers do.

"How good and pleasant it is when brothers live together in unity" (Ps 133:1).

PRAYER

Our Father in heaven, you have called us into a family relationship. That means we live *as*, and *with*, brothers and sisters. Thank you for these people who encourage, support, and help us along life's way. May we find and be the kind of brothers and sisters that point to you and serve those in need. We pray this in the name of our brother, your Son, Jesus Christ. AMEN.

QUESTIONS

1. What has a "brother" in the Lord done for you? Can you identify something specific that a brother has done to help you along the way? What difference did it make in your life?

2. Is there someone you know who could be far more useful than he or she is? How might you, as a brother or sister, help that individual embrace his or her value and usefulness?

3. When have you witnessed brothers supporting each other during a tough time? What was the effect—on them—of their doing so? And on others around them?

4. What example do you know of one who has significantly sacrificed for another individual? How has that act of sacrifice inspired you, or perhaps others?

SUGGESTED READING

Philemon

58

HEBREWS: Better

*Even though we speak like this, dear friends, we
are confident of better things in your case—things
that accompany salvation. (Hebrews 6:9)*

*Because of this oath, Jesus has become the guarantee
of a better covenant. (Hebrews 7:22)*

*If they had been thinking of the country they had left, they would
have had opportunity to return. Instead, they were longing
for a better country—a heavenly one. (Hebrews 11:15–16)*

God had planned something better for us . . . (Hebrews 11:40)

Few people realize, let alone reach, their full potential. Sadly, too many people never become all that they could be. Perhaps this fact is most observed in athletes and artists who regularly perform in public. A young ballplayer may have all the natural tools needed to become a star yet fail to reach the heights predicted of him. A promising musician may impress others with her talents but never quite make the big stage expected of her. The reasons for falling short are many: a poor work ethic, insufficient opportunity, lack of proper coaching, an unteachable spirit, performance anxiety, inability to get along with others, distractions, injury or illness, fear of success, or unresolved hurts from the past may all be barriers to achievement. Only those who "throw off everything that hinders and . . . entangles, and . . . run with perseverance the race marked out for [them]" (12:1) reach their God-given potential. The truth is that most of us could do much *better* than we do.

The word *better* is significant for three reasons. First, it implies there is a level to be attained above and beyond just being good. The word pushes us not to settle for mediocrity but to press on to something greater. Thus, there is a subtle power in the word itself, pulling and pushing one forward to a higher standard. Second, the word can be used in a wide variety of ways in the English language. For example, the word often occurs as an adverb (e.g., she writes *better* than her sister) or adjective (e.g., this is a *better* car than my last one). However, it can also be used in verb form (e.g., he did all he could to *better* his position) or as a noun (e.g., I expected *better* from him). The word *better* obviously has a great deal of utility and versatility in our language. Third, the word is found several times in the book of Hebrews, the only New Testament book whose author is unknown. The original Greek word—*kreitton*—that gets translated "better" is found twenty times across the pages of the New Testament; thirteen of those occurrences are right here in Hebrews (1:4; 6:9; 7:7, 19, 22; 8:6, 6; 9:23; 10:34; 11:16, 35, 40; 12:24). Clearly, the author—whose name remains a mystery—left little mystery regarding the point of writing: God has something better in store for us; it would be a shame to miss it. There is a better way to live that we dare not overlook.

There is a better way of salvation: Jesus. One cannot read Hebrews without immediately being struck by the number of references to the Old Testament. There are numerous quotes from the Law, the Prophets, and the Psalms—all of which point to Jesus. There are also references to a variety of themes that dominate the Old Testament. For example, Hebrews repeatedly mentions priests (31 times), offerings (25 times), sacrifices (17 times), the covenant (17 times), the law (14 times), and the tabernacle (10 times). The author's primary purpose, however, is not to highlight these themes as a way of preserving their value but to use them as a context and comparison for pointing to something better. Those former ways of pleasing and satisfying God were replaced by a new and better way; that way was found in Jesus. The way of salvation, the way to God, had been transformed from a religious system to a reliable person: Jesus. Rituals of a covenant gave way to a relationship with Christ. The call was to move from a sacred formula to a strong faith in Christ (ch 11), from Jewish liturgy to daily living for Christ (ch 13), from the sacrifice of animals to the "sacrifice of praise" (13:15) that confessed and honored Christ. Indeed, references to "Christ" (13 times) and "Jesus" (14 times) are found throughout the thirteen-chapter book. He is presented as the better way.

Sadly, there are many pious people today who have not yet discovered or embraced this better way of salvation. Instead, they cling to a religious system of rules and obligations while exhibiting little evidence of having a relationship with Jesus. They *do* good things and have good habits, but their lives lack power and joy. Gritting one's teeth while persevering through another religious sacrifice misses the whole reason Jesus came to earth. This is a tragedy that has led untold numbers of people away from the faith in disillusionment and disappointment. Jesus came to give us "life . . . to the full" (John 10:10). Therefore, our calling is to "fix our eyes on Jesus, the author and perfecter of our faith" (12:2). When a daily and vital relationship with Jesus replaces religious ritual in one's life, everyone takes notice. Life takes on meaning and purpose, hollow prayers give way to connecting with divine and dynamic power, drudgery becomes opportunity, what once was annoying is seen in a new light, and love and compassion replace animosity toward others. There truly is a better way of salvation. Jesus is his name. We should not settle for less.

There is a better hope for the future: heaven. The hope of a bright future is what carried our forefathers and foremothers onward during their most challenging times. One of the longstanding favorite chapters in the entire Bible is Hebrews 11, wherein a roster of heroes is listed. Eighteen individuals or groups are remembered there for "looking forward to the city with foundations, whose architect and builder is God" (11:10) and "longing for a better country—a heavenly one" (11:16). Story after story is told in this single chapter to illustrate the author's point that a better future awaits those who have faith. The chapter concludes with these words: "These were all commended for their faith, yet none of them received what had been promised. God had planned something better . . ." (11:39–40). That "something better" is heaven, a place that awaits all those who endure and stand strong in the faith.

During this period of my life, I find my social activities increasingly include funerals. I suspect my age and the recent COVID pandemic have both contributed to the trend. Perhaps no social event lends itself more easily to human observation than does a funeral, where everyone gathers to mourn, share memories, and observe the responses of others who also mourn. Never have I been more aware than during these recent days of the sharp distinction that exists when it comes to hope expressed at gatherings like these. Some funerals signal the end, while other funerals mark a new beginning. Some are sad; some are joyful. Some are mournful tragedies; some are promising celebrations. Some point only backward to a life that once was lived; some point confidently forward to a new life yet to come. Some are anchored in the past alone; some are anchored in that future known as eternity. The difference is tied to the hope of the believer, to the hope of the one who has found the better way in Jesus. Those who know and have fixed their gaze on Jesus, "the author and perfector of [their] faith," are those who "will not grow weary and lose heart" (12:2–3) even when passing through the valley of struggle and sorrow. Nothing—not even death itself (Rom 8:38–39)—can steal one's hope when heaven beckons and promises eternal life, love, and fellowship with Christ. The better way of Jesus leads to the better hope of heaven.

There is a better promise for today: rest. Once Jesus is embraced and heaven is expected, today will look much brighter. Present circumstances begin to look much better when Jesus and heaven are in clear view. The anxiety and stress witnessed in so many lives today are, in part, spiritual in nature. At least that is what the writer of Hebrews implies in chapter 4: "Therefore, since the promise of entering his rest still stands, let us be careful that none of you be found to have fallen short of it" (v 1). Two observations are noteworthy here.

First, the reference to *rest* takes the reader back to the Old Testament where God promised rest to his people once they entered the Promised Land (Ex 33:14; Josh 1:13). God's promise to his followers has always included rest. How ironic and sad, then, that today so many of his people have been enculturated into western civilization's busy and exhausting way of life that provides little time for adequate rest. One might argue that exhaustion has become a badge of honor, reflecting the importance of our work and how indispensable we think we are to that work. There is a better way; it is the way of rest. God modeled it at the time of creation, promised it to his people throughout Scripture, and continues to offer it today.

Second, it is worth noting that *rest* occurs a grand total of eleven times in the first eleven verses of Hebrews 4. The author apparently thought the topic was significant enough to repeat it several times. Every parent and teacher know that repetition is purposeful, serving to drive home important messages that dare not be overlooked or ignored. Such is the case here. The primary Greek root word that gets translated "rest" is *pausis*, from which we get our English word "pause." The writer implies that we are to stop, cease our efforts, and rest. The picture is one wherein we are invited to push the pause button on all activity and let God be God. We are not indispensable after all. When we pause, or rest, we acknowledge that God—not us—is in control and we trust his sovereignty over the affairs of life. This kind of response makes today, and every day, go better. Too many of us forfeit the promise of God to provide what is needed this day. In our flurry of activity and worry, we lose the physical and mental rest that would make today so much better. Those who have found the better way in Jesus and cling to the better hope awaiting us in heaven are able to seize the better promise of rest today.

The message here is clear: we really can do better. Jesus, heaven, and rest are available to those who will receive them. The book of Hebrews is a timeless and universal invitation to lift our sights, surrender our struggles, and stop resisting the plan of God. Those who accept the divine design will soon discover that all of life works better that way.

Pale, tasteless, and mediocre religious practice is not our destiny. God has a better plan.

Prayer

Almighty God, we acknowledge that you have prepared a better way for us to live. We confess that the voices of the world around us constantly seek to lure us toward its competing agenda. But we know that alternate agenda ultimately leads to disappointment and even despair. So, help us to accept your way—the better way of Jesus, the better hope of heaven, and the better promise of rest today. May we place our full trust in you, and in you alone. AMEN.

Questions

1. Looking back over your life, how has Jesus made things better for you? What specific changes has he brought that have improved daily living?

2. Is there a particular area of your life that still needs improvement? What changes are needed? What steps do you need to take to do better in that area?

3. What makes religious rituals so attractive to people? Why do people often confuse rituals with a relationship with Jesus? What is the outcome of that confusion?

4. Why do so many people seem to struggle with rest? What is there about human nature that makes us feel we cannot rest or that we don't really need to rest?

SUGGESTED READING

Hebrews 1–4, 10–13

59

JAMES: Actions

*Suppose a brother or sister is without clothes and daily
food. If one of you says to him, "Go, I wish you well; keep
warm and well fed," but does nothing about his physical
needs, what good is it? In the same way, faith by itself, if it
is not accompanied by action, is dead. (James 2:15–17)*

*You foolish man, do you want evidence that faith without deeds
is useless? Was not our ancestor Abraham considered righteous
for what he did when he offered his son Isaac on the altar? You
see that his faith and his actions were working together, and his
faith was made complete by what he did. (James 2:20–22)*

*You see that a person is justified by what he does
and not by faith alone. (James 2:24)*

*Anyone, then, who knows the good he ought to
do and doesn't do it, sins. (James 4:17)*

At the end of the twentieth century, we Americans became increasingly fascinated with lifestyles. The general rise in economic prosperity, the elevation of individual rights, and the promotion of identity
politics likely all contributed to the trend. For example, beginning in
1984 and continuing for the next decade, the television show "Lifestyles
of the Rich and Famous" took us into the opulent homes of celebrities
and allowed us to enjoy their extravagance vicariously. Alternate life-

styles also became popular. The hippie culture, living single in the city, RV travelers, veganism, various LGBTQ groups, the anti-technology Luddites, and body modification with its tattoos and piercings were just a few of the expressions, or lifestyles, with which we became familiar to one degree or another. What all these individuals had in common was that each adopted ways of behaving that defined their particular group. Certain actions, repeated until they became habit, came to identify the respective lifestyle.

Though the particulars often seemed strange, the pattern itself was not new. The earliest followers of Jesus were called to repeat certain actions, or exhibit a lifestyle, by which others might easily identify them. Several characteristics of the new religious movement that gradually became known as "Christianity" were based on actions that demonstrated faith. Most prominent among those action characteristics were love, forgiveness, service, joy, and peace. Jesus himself said, "All men will know that you are my disciples, if you love one another" (John 13:35). Consistent acts of love mark the community of believers. Bob Goff captured the essence of this sentiment when he entitled his engaging 2012 book, *Love Does*. Goff is correct. Love is a decision to act for the benefit of another; it is what Christians do. Driven by love, believers also forgive. Peter asked Jesus, "How many times shall I forgive my brother?" He thought he was being generous by offering to do so "up to seven times" (Matt 18:21). Jesus responded in a way that made it clear there was to be no limit, or cap, on forgiveness. Rather, forgiveness is an action that is to become a lifestyle, a pattern that sets us apart and marks us as his followers. Service, likewise, is part of that lifestyle. Jesus told his disciples that he "did not come to be served, but to serve" (Matt 20:28). Later, he told the same group that they should follow his example by serving one another (John 13:14–17). This is an action that communicates that we belong to Jesus. Joy and peace, the final ingredients of this short list of prominent characteristics, go together. The early Christians puzzled and disturbed their adversaries when, despite their circumstances, they demonstrated a rare and supernatural joy and contentment. All these actions became so common that they began to identify the lifestyle of believers everywhere.

No book in the Bible emphasizes actions and deeds more than the book of James. Written by the brother of Jesus (Matt 13:55), who also became a leader of the notable Jerusalem council (Acts 15:13), James is thought to be one of the earliest of the New Testament books. As new believers suffered "persecution" (Acts 8:1) and were "scattered among the nations" (Jam 1:1), James sought to underscore the importance of their actions. Wherever they found themselves, they would be carefully observed by their new neighbors. This provided an opportunity for God's people to let their work and actions reflect an undying commitment to their "glorious Lord Jesus Christ" (2:1). James knew that "faith by itself, if it is not accompanied by action, is dead" (2:17). A set of doctrines without a corresponding life of discipline would be useless. Talk without the requisite walk is a charade.

Unfortunately, the history of Christendom has witnessed seasons wherein actions have been marginalized. The argument is sometimes raised that if one thinks and believes correctly, how he or she lives and the practices one keeps do not matter. In the process many dismiss actions and behaviors as irrelevant. Labels such as "Pharisaical legalism" or "works righteousness" have been used as shields against behavioral demands or expectations. While we certainly ought to guard against becoming enslaved to legalism or thinking that our works can somehow save us or endear us to our heavenly Father, we do harm to the gospel and cause of Christ when we minimize the value of actions. Work and actions have always mattered in the Christian community. What we do—our conduct—ought not be trivialized. To be sure, actions are a response to faith, not the basis of faith, yet deeds of service are natural and valued expressions that flow from a life of gratitude. In addition to expressing gratitude, there are three other reasons actions matter in the life of every believer.

This is the way of Jesus. Actions matter because they mattered to Jesus. As noted above, God's Son declared he had come into this world to serve the world (Matt 20:28). The Incarnation itself was an act of service. Jesus was not a passive member of the Trinity, doted on by the Father and protected from doing hard work. Instead, his life was an exhibit of meaningful work and intentional actions. Introduced to the world as "the carpenter's son" (Matt 13:55), Jesus performed acts of healing, engaged the crowds, and served meals to others on several occasions. He conducted his life with compassion and respect toward those who despised him. His surrender to the cross was his greatest act, ensuring the salvation of the world. Make no mistake about it, Jesus modeled work and actions; we are called to imitate his example. Actions matter because they are the way of Jesus.

Others have needs. Actions are the avenue through which we respond to others' needs. The book of James references "orphans and widows" (1:27), "a poor man in shabby clothes" (2:2), "those who are poor in the eyes of the world" (2:5), "a brother or sister . . . without clothes and daily food" (2:15), one who is "in trouble" or "sick" (5:13–14), and one who might "wander from the truth" (5:19). All underscore the numerous needs that exist in a fallen world. These needs are present all around us and call for our attention. Sadly, we in the church are prone to one of two mistakes when it comes to responding to needs. The first mistake is *romanticizing* foreign missionary efforts. Whether thinking of short-term or career missionaries, we assume they are better positioned and equipped in a far-off land to serve human needs than are we here at home. The second mistake is *compartmentalizing* life so that we delegate such work to the professionals—whether they be clergy, social workers, food banks, or soup kitchens. In the process, we rationalize our own limited actions by pointing to, and even supporting, professionals serving the needy elsewhere in the world. James counters both these mistakes by noting there are needs awaiting action on every doorstep.

I need to be saved from myself. Actions matter because they move me beyond myself and my own concerns. Doing something for another is a time-tested way to prevent self-centeredness and self-absorption. Our cultural propensity to promote personal rights—turning the spotlight on *me* and *my* pleasures and desires—was identified by social historian Christopher Lasch in his 1979 book entitled, *The Culture of Narcissism*. The antidote for narcissism is work and activity that turns toward benefitting others—whether they be family members, neighbors, or strangers in wider society. Failure to engage in such work leads to social breakdown characterized by isolation from one another, fear and anxiety, and widespread depression. Tragically, these trends describe our social climate today. God-honoring, other-oriented actions are needed to save us from ourselves. James may have been hinting at that very fact when he combined "look[ing] after orphans and widows in their distress" with "keep[ing] oneself from being polluted by the world" (1:27). Perhaps one of the best ways to prevent the world's pollution is to engage in activity that is focused on caring for others. Later, James encouraged his readers to "submit yourselves, then, to God" (4:7). This is James's way of reminding us to move beyond ourselves and acknowledge God's sovereignty.

Few people would recognize the name of Agnes Gonxhe Bojaxhiu, an Albanian born in North Macedonia in 1910. After a year of study in Ireland, Agnes headed to India at the young age of nineteen and never saw her family again. She spent the rest of her life working in India, eventually caring for "the poorest of the poor" on the streets of Calcutta. The world would eventually know Agnes as Mother Teresa, the woman who addressed the needs of homeless orphans and society's outcasts who suffered with leprosy, AIDS, tuberculosis, and other ailments. For nearly seventy years she gave herself tirelessly to a work that few others were willing to do, serving and bringing comfort to those who could never repay her. Half of those seventy years her efforts were largely unknown; not until the 1960s did her name begin to symbolize and motivate acts of charity around the world. By the time of her death in 1997, few doubted that Mother Teresa's actions were a testament to following the way of Jesus, caring for human needs, and sacrificing one's own interests for the sake of others.

Mother Teresa, however, had her share of critics. Some attacked her work before she died; others have done so after her death. Her motivations, intentions, qualifications as a medical caregiver, and positions on a variety of political issues all have been questioned. Detractors have doubted both the sincerity and value of her deeds. That is the problem with those who dare take action: they open themselves up to misunderstanding, opposition, and criticism. The same attacks were leveled at Jesus. Because he did not operate the way the religious leaders expected, some questioned his authority and credentials. He associated with disreputable people, was suspected of having ties to the devil (Mark 3:22), and angered several leading people with his views on important political and moral issues of his day. The only way to avoid offending others is to remain inactive, to do nothing. Actions, by their very nature, provoke reactions, and those reactions are not always encouraging. The only way to avoid the kind of reactions that Jesus and Mother Teresa experienced is indolence and refusing to act or work altogether. James erased any doubt about that being a viable option in the early church. "Believers in our glorious Lord Jesus Christ" (2:1) were to engage in noble actions, whether or not others approved. That expectation has not changed.

Actions really do matter. Repeating those actions on a regular basis will form a lifestyle. When that lifestyle is one of godliness and service that then gets "scattered among the nations" (1:1), Christ is honored and the world is influenced for good.

What actions are we exhibiting? What characterizes our lifestyle?

Prayer

Dear Lord, you have made us in your image and have called us to act like you. Help us as we respond to that calling. On our own, we know that we fall short. But with your help, grace, and guidance, we dare to believe that our actions and lifestyle can bear testimony to you and influence others to receive you. May we adopt the way of Jesus, serve others in need, and keep ourselves from selfish pursuits. We offer this prayer in the name of "our glorious Lord Jesus Christ," whose actions changed the world. AMEN.

Questions

1. What actions identify you as a follower of Jesus Christ? What are you intentional about doing because you belong to him?

2. Who in your life has modeled an attractive lifestyle as a believer? What are the traits that make that person's lifestyle so appealing?

3. How does a person engage in acts of service (doing good things) without expecting something in return or thinking that the efforts somehow make one more righteous?

4. Why are good works and noble efforts so often criticized by others? Has that kind of criticism ever been leveled against you? If so, how did you respond?

Suggested Reading

James 1–5

60

1 PETER: Suffering

In this you greatly rejoice, though now for a little while you
may have had to suffer grief in all kinds of trials. (1 Peter 1:6)

But if you suffer for doing good and you endure it, this
is commendable before God. To this you were called,
because Christ suffered for you, leaving you an example,
that you should follow in his steps. (1 Peter 2:20–21)

But even if you should suffer for what is right,
you are blessed. (1 Peter 3:14)

If you suffer as a Christian, do not be ashamed, but
praise God that you bear that name. (Peter 4:16)

And the God of all grace, who called you to his eternal glory in
Christ, after you have suffered a little while, will himself restore
you and make you strong, firm and steadfast. (1 Peter 5:10)

Do you know anyone who has suffered terribly for the cause of Christ? I remember a fellow seminary student in the late 1970s who came to America from Indonesia. He had a noticeable limp, the result of his family members beating him when they discovered he had converted from Islam to Christianity. His hip was permanently injured. Every time the young man walked to class or his mailbox, he carried with him a vivid reminder of the cost of following Christ. I also remember the young female student from India who sat in several of my sociology classes. She confided in me that her father considered her dead for the same reason. He no longer spoke of her, communicated with her, or acknowledged her existence because she had left the family's religion to embrace and follow Christ. For many people around the world suffering has been, and continues to be, a consequence of their faith in Jesus Christ.

Suffering has a long history. The ancient character Job still universally symbolizes the human suffering that is common in every generation. The theme of suffering is prominent in Peter's first New Testament letter; in fact, every chapter in the letter speaks of it. "Peter, an apostle of Jesus Christ" (1 Pet 1:1), had watched closely as his Lord suffered betrayal, humiliation, and crucifixion. The apostle knew that the "scattered" followers of Christ would likewise suffer and he wanted to make sure they were not caught off guard by their experiences. Perhaps remembering how Jesus had warned his followers by saying, "All men will hate you because of me" (Mark 13:13; cf. John 15:18–21), Peter wanted to prepare new believers for what was inevitable. Suffering was not only in their past but in their future. Consequently, Peter wrote a general letter to God's people that provided instruction pertaining to the affliction and distress they were likely to endure.

A careful reading of 1 Peter reveals that four words dominate the author's thoughts, each word occurring several times throughout the letter: *suffering* (15 times), *glory* (15 times), *good* (14 times), and *grace* (10 times). Taken together, these words offer important insight and help the reader develop a healthy understanding of suffering. However, there is another word, found only once in 1 Peter and just two additional places in the New Testament, deserving of attention. That word is "Christian" (1 Pet 4:16; Acts 11:26; 26:28), the label that would gradually become the most popular way of talking about people with an allegiance to Christ. Peter connected the label to suffering when he referenced those who "suffer as a Christian." He wanted his fellow disciples, those who bore the name "Christian," to know what awaited them. Peter's observations might be summarized as follows.

The Christian can expect to suffer for doing good. Somewhere along the way, a faulty teaching began to spread the idea that suffering is what happens to bad people, not to good people. Suffering became associated with punishment for one's wicked deeds. Such an idea was completely foreign to Peter. Instead, he pointed to those who "suffer for doing good" and described the ordeal as "commendable" (2:20). Then he talked about those who "suffer for what is right" and called them "blessed" (3:14). He suggested that those who "suffer as a Christian" have a unique opportunity to "praise God that [they] bear that name" (4:16). How can that be? How is it that doing good could possibly result in suffering? Peter gave us a clue when he noted the activities of our "pagan" neighbors—"living in debauchery, lust, drunkenness, orgies, carousing and detestable idolatry" (4:3). These very people then "think it strange that you do not plunge with them into the same flood of dissipation, and they heap abuse on you" (4:4). Human nature is such that people do not like it when others make decisions or act in ways that put their own choices and behaviors in a negative light. There are social consequences for failing to follow the crowd and refusing to join one's peers in their decadence. No one wants to look bad by being compared to another person's righteousness.

Harry Moore was a good and godly man who supported his family by working in the exploding automobile industry in the 1930s. Moore lived in rural, central Michigan and drove with a group of other men over forty miles to the auto factory south of Flint. At the end of each work week, on late Friday afternoons, all the men in the carpool liked to celebrate by stopping for some drinks at a tavern conveniently located along the route—all except Harry Moore, who would sit in the car praying while his peers imbibed their beer inside the bar. When they finally came out an hour or so later, having consumed too much alcohol, they heaped ridicule and scorn on the solitary man patiently waiting in the vehicle. The pattern was repeated on most Fridays, with Moore silently suffering the verbal attacks and abuse of his drunken co-workers. I knew Harry Moore as a young child, though I knew him by the affectionate name of "Brother Moore." In fact, I suppose it would not be an exaggeration to say I am a Christian today because of him. He was the man who picked up my dad from his family's farm and took him to Sunday school when my dad was just a young boy. Brother Moore introduced my dad to Jesus; years later my dad introduced me to Jesus. There have been many individuals down through the years who, like Brother Moore, have suffered for doing good. Only heaven will reveal the blessings that resulted from their suffering.

The Christian can expect suffering to be accompanied by God's grace. *Suffering* is not the only word, or theme, the reader finds in every chapter of 1 Peter; *grace* also fits that category. If any disciple knew and experienced the amazing grace of Jesus, it was Peter. Grace, the unmerited love and favor of God, made such an impression on Peter that he could not stop talking about it. He began (1:2) and closed (5:12) his letter with the theme and highlighted its importance throughout the body of his writing (e.g., 1:10, 13; 3:7: 4:10; 5:5, 10). Peter noted that grace alone could sustain us and help us endure when we suffer for doing good (2:19–20; 5:10). Peter knew such grace, as did his contemporary Paul. The latter had the audacity to write, "I want to know Christ and the power of his resurrection and the fellowship of sharing in his sufferings" (Phil 3:10). No ordinary person talks like that or expresses a desire like that. Thus, there are only two options in our attempt to understand a statement like Paul's: either he was crazy or he had fully embraced and daily relied on the grace of God. It is grace alone that attracts one to the suffering Christ and equips the person to "follow in his steps" (2:21).

Though our English translations do not make it clear, the reference to imitating Christ and walking "in his steps" comes after Peter has described God's grace to the one who suffers. Twice in the preceding verses, the Greek word for grace gets translated "commendable" (2:19–20), making it easy to miss Peter's intent. He says, "it is commendable [grace] if a person bears up under the pain of unjust suffering" (2:19). In case the reader missed it, Peter repeats himself: "But if you suffer for doing good and you endure it, this is commendable [grace] before God" (2:20). Peter linked grace and suffering. Suffering was not evidence of the lack of grace (i.e., what happens to the ungodly), but enduring suffering was only possible *because of* grace. That same grace explains how the earliest believers looked upon the suffering Christ and sought to "follow in his steps" (2:21).

Charles Sheldon's 1896 book, *In His Steps,* was based on this passage from 1 Peter. The novel became one of the most popular books ever written, eventually selling over fifty million copies. The book's subtitle— *What Would Jesus Do?*—would one day become a familiar acronym as WWJD adorned T-shirts, bracelets, and other items. *In His Steps* tells the story of a minister and a small group of his parishioners who dared make decisions and engage in behaviors based on what they discerned Jesus would do in the same situation, even if the consequences were unpleasant. Near the end of the book come these words: "our definition of Christianity . . . [is] a long way from following the steps of him who trod the way with groans and tears and sobs of anguish for a lost humanity" (p 185). Indeed, Sheldon pointed to the crux of the problem. Over the years we have redefined and revised the Christian faith until it no longer includes suffering. In our desire to make Christianity more attractive, we have lost the wonder of God's grace that sees us through suffering. Therefore, we know little of Paul's experience when Jesus reassured him with the promise: "My grace is sufficient for you, for my power is made perfect in weakness" (2 Cor 12:9). We have become unfamiliar with the grace one draws upon when suffering for doing good and yet choosing to walk in the steps of Christ anyway. May we rediscover what yesterday's saints knew so well: the one who suffers, while walking "in his steps," will be sustained by bountiful grace.

The Christian can expect suffering to result in glory. Suffering does not signal the end for the Christian but points to future glory and splendor. Peter emphasized this point numerous times in his letter. The reference is not to a hero's glory for overcoming the odds, but to a heavenly glory for overcoming our Enemy—the Accuser—"by the blood of the Lamb" and by not clinging to our "lives so much as to shrink from death" (Rev 12:10–11). Peter wrote about "the sufferings of Christ and the glories that would follow" (1:11). Later he was even more direct when he wrote: "But rejoice that you participate in the sufferings of Christ, so that you may be overjoyed when his glory is revealed" (4:13). Then he wrapped up his letter by pointing to "the God of all grace, who called you to his eternal glory in Christ, after you have suffered a little while" (5:10). Glory—being in God's presence forever—was a reward for those who followed Jesus Christ, walking "in his steps" and suffering as he did. No wonder early believers did not run from or succumb to suffering. No wonder persecution, prisons, lions' dens, stakes, and crosses did not deter these men and women. They anticipated and awaited the glory yet to come.

Of course, Bible writers also used *glory* in another way, as a synonym for praise and honor. The common Greek word for "glory" is *doxa*, from which we get the word *doxology*—signifying a word of praise to God. When Peter associated the dual themes of suffering and glory, it was his way of saying that, rather than inhibiting praise, suffering ought to increase it. Glory was understood as both a present reality to be expressed and a future goal to be enjoyed by those who suffered on behalf of Christ. May our suffering, likewise, result in lips that communicate glory (praise) and eyes that are fixed on glory (heaven).

Suffering always elicits a response. What will our response be?

Prayer

Our Father in heaven, we join with Peter in acknowledging you as "the God of all grace" (5:10). In doing so, we dare to believe that you have grace for the difficult seasons of our lives—those times of suffering, affliction, and discouragement. So, we call on you to help us, sustain us, and lead us on to glory. Despite unpredictable circumstances that sometimes lead to misery and woe, may we be steadfast—knowing the blessing that comes from doing what is right (3:14) and praising you for the opportunity to bear your holy name (4:16). We offer this prayer in the name of Jesus Christ, the one who suffered that we might be saved. AMEN.

Questions

1. Do you know anyone personally who has suffered for his or her faith? What is the person's story that has led to such suffering?

2. Why is it so hard to accept the fact that suffering is often experienced by those who do good? What factors contribute to our struggle to believe this?

3. In your own words, how would you describe the relationship between grace and suffering? Between glory and suffering?

4. What would it mean for you if you determined to walk "in his steps" today? What changes might you need to make? What difference do you think others would notice?

Suggested Reading

1 Peter 1–5

61

2 PETER: Knowledge

His divine power has given us everything we need for life
and godliness through our knowledge of him who called
us by his own glory and goodness. (2 Peter 1:3)

For this very reason, make every effort to add to your faith
goodness; and to goodness, knowledge; and to knowledge,
self-control; and to self-control, perseverance; and to
perseverance, godliness; and to godliness, brotherly
kindness; and to brotherly kindness, love. (2 Peter 1:5–7)

But grow in the grace and knowledge of our Lord and Savior Jesus
Christ. To him be glory both now and forever! Amen. (2 Peter 3:18)

Humans were created with the capacity and curiosity to know. It
should come as no surprise, therefore, that the words *know* and
knowledge combined are found nearly fourteen hundred times across
the pages of the Bible, appearing in sixty-four of the Bible's sixty-six
books (the short Old Testament books of Obadiah and Haggai are the
only exceptions). Furthermore, the Old Testament prophet Daniel
closed his book by pointing to "the time of the end" when "many will go
here and there to increase knowledge" (12:4). Apparently, the curiosity
and appetite for knowledge does not get satisfied over time but will mark
the human condition until the very end.

Perhaps one of the tragedies of our day, however, is the delusion that surrounds knowledge. Many sociologists and historians have used the label "Information Age" to describe social changes that began in the late twentieth century. Computer technology gave us access to a worldwide web that put information at our fingertips. With such capabilities we assumed human knowledge would grow exponentially. While access to information has indeed grown, a strong argument could be made that we have seen a corresponding decrease in knowledge. For example, various reports indicate educational test scores continue to drop in our nation. The problem is that we have confused information and knowledge.

Knowledge requires information, but the two should not be thought of as synonyms. Information is a collection of facts; knowledge presupposes familiarity with those facts. Information can be obtained relatively quickly given our computer capabilities; knowledge requires studied focus over time. Information can be passed on with minimal effort; the process of passing on knowledge is more complicated and demands more commitment. There is no shortage of cultural symbols to illustrate our fascination with information. The internet, social media, smartphones, cable TV with its endless lineup of talk shows, and the longstanding popularity of the TV game show *Jeopardy!* all point to our obsession with information. We have sacrificed deep knowledge and become content with surface information.

Knowledge was an important feature of the early Church. Peter's second letter near the end of the New Testament mentions it sixteen times in only three chapters—nine of those references are in chapter one alone (1:2, 3, 5, 6, 8, 12, 14, 16, 20). In his attempt to instruct believers regarding how they might live a virtuous life, Peter advised, "make every effort to add to your faith goodness; and to goodness, knowledge" (1:5). Knowledge stood as the third in a series of eight characteristics that Peter said should mark the follower of Christ. Other virtues on the list include self-control, perseverance, godliness, brotherly kindness, and love. Before developing those latter virtues, however, Peter wanted it known that believers would not advance far in their faith and good deeds unless they had a solid knowledge of truth. Knowledge was neither optional nor marginal to the faith. Rather, it served as the foundation upon which other noble attributes and Christianity itself would develop and expand.

The perceived value of knowledge is evident in the founding of many of America's earliest colleges and universities. For example, Harvard University, America's oldest and arguably most prestigious university, was founded in 1636 so that ministers could gain the knowledge necessary to make Christianity appealing to seventeenth-century New Englanders. Following Harvard's lead, many other colleges and universities were started by Christians concerned about having educated ministers and citizens. By the late nineteenth century an explosion of evangelical colleges and Bible institutes took place. Those schools included Wheaton College (est 1860); Nyack College in New York City (est 1882); Moody Bible Institute in Chicago (est 1886); my alma mater, Asbury College (est 1890); and Olivet Nazarene University (est 1907), where I have served on the faculty for the past three decades. All these schools, and dozens more like them, were launched with Peter's conviction and vision that faith, goodness, and knowledge form the foundation of a virtuous citizenry. Knowledge has always been considered indispensable to the evangelical thrust and outreach of the church.

Whereas gaining knowledge of multiple subjects in God's creation eventually became the university standard, the early Christian focus was very specific. Knowledge, by definition, requires an object. Peter made it clear that the singular object of knowledge among early believers was "our Lord and Savior Jesus Christ" (2:20; 3:18; cf. 1:2, 3, 8). That knowledge alone would make it possible to "participate in the divine nature and escape the corruption in the world caused by evil desires" (1:4; cf. 2:20). That knowledge alone would prevent one from being "near-sighted and blind" (1:9). That knowledge alone would sustain the mission of Christian higher education centuries after Peter wrote his letters. Knowledge of Jesus Christ was needed. The stakes were high; they still are.

Unfortunately, there are three common errors that plague us when it comes to knowing Jesus Christ. All three errors risk substituting something else for truly knowing Jesus. The first error has already been noted: There is a tendency to substitute information for knowledge. Thus, many people possess facts *about* Jesus without knowing him personally. They know Mary was his mother, he taught and healed people, he had twelve disciples, he was crucified, and many people still claim allegiance to him today. All those facts are true and provide useful information. However, information itself is not the same as knowing him. Over the years my interests have led me to gather information on a wide range of people—from U.S. presidents to professional baseball players to academic sociologists—and yet only rarely have I known any of them. I have known *about* them without knowing them personally. Peter emphasized *knowing* Jesus, not merely gathering facts about him.

A second common error is substituting knowledge about God's world for knowledge about God's Son. Perhaps this is most often seen among those who give their lives to higher education. Colleges and universities—many of which were founded with the best intentions, as noted earlier—foster knowledge of various aspects of the world, while too often ignoring the Creator of the world. The result is that knowing arts, sciences, philosophies, theories, or methods too often become a distraction from truly knowing Jesus Christ, the one by whom "all things were created" and in whom "all things hold together" (Col 1:16–17). Knowledge of a small slice of the world is a poor substitute for knowing Jesus, the Creator and Lord of the world. The error ultimately dead-ends in disillusionment.

A third common error is related to the previous two. We make a serious error when we substitute knowledge of theology, church history, denominational polity, religious rituals, or ministry strategies for an intimate knowledge of—and relationship with—Jesus Christ himself. Over the years I have interacted with far too many people in the church who have impressed me with their intellectual knowledge of religious topics, yet who rarely speak of or give evidence that they know and love Christ. One cannot read 2 Peter without recognizing the author's concern that people know "our Lord and Savior Jesus Christ" (2:20; 3:18). Only knowledge that makes Jesus our object and focus will suffice in this fallen world and lead us to the next. The risk of religious education is always that people might mistake religious creeds, and even orthodoxy, for the resurrected Christ. Peter wanted his readers rooted in the latter.

In addition to needing an object, knowledge demands a source of authority. How does one come to know Jesus when his physical presence on earth was limited to just thirty short years lived some two thousand years ago? Where does one turn to discover and become better acquainted with the Lord Jesus Christ? Scripture is that source; we ought to know it above all else. Knowledge of God's Word is critical if we are to mature in the faith. Peter noted that the sacred texts that make up our Bible came from "men [who] spoke from God as they were carried along by the Holy Spirit" (1:20–21). By way of personal confession, it was the Bible—God's Holy Word—that kept me grounded while in graduate school, studying secular, Marxist ideas. Scripture held me steady. I read it, memorized it, meditated on it, and tried to apply it while being exposed to a body of sociological knowledge that all too often countered God's Word. If we are to know Christ, we need to be students of the Bible. No alternate source exists. Knowledge of another requires time together, interaction, and carefully listening to that individual. The same steps are required if we are to know and then grow in Jesus Christ.

Finally, it is worth exploring *why* "knowledge of our Lord and Savior Jesus Christ" (2:20; 3:18) is so important. What difference does it really make? Why is the Bible—and our knowledge of it—still so valuable in a world like ours, where countless books and limitless information compete for priority and authority? Would it be wiser simply to "live and let live?" There are so many versions of truth that battle for preeminence, why promote such a narrow and ancient view of knowledge? These are all worthwhile questions demanding answers. Peter's response was to associate "knowledge of the Lord Jesus Christ" (1:8) with:

1. Greater effectiveness and productivity (1:8). Human potential is enhanced, not diminished, when we know Jesus. Clearly, we become more useful and fruitful.

2. "False prophets," "false teachers" (2:1), and "lawless men" (3:17). There are those who threaten to mislead us. The Greek word translated "false" is *pseudo*, which often gets rendered as "liar." One needs to know Jesus well to avoid following seductive lies.

3. Scoffers and mockers who seek to derail us. If false prophets and teachers do not succeed in leading us astray, there will be neighbors and associates "scoffing and following their own evil desires" (3:3), who will urge us to join them in doing the same.

4. "The day of judgment" (3:7). Also known as "the day of the Lord" (3:10), this points to the time when we will meet our Lord face to face. The wise person will get ready for that meeting in advance. Only a fool would approach the inevitable unprepared.

Peter closes his brief letter with an important final thought: Knowledge can, and should, grow (3:18). How tragic it is when growth is stunted. If we only know Jesus today as well as we once knew him at some point in the past, we are to be pitied. We were designed for growth.

Creation around us testifies to the fact in that flowers grow, trees grow, and children grow. Likewise, Christians ought to grow.

May it always be said of us that we are "grow[ing] in the grace and knowledge of our Lord and Savior Jesus Christ" (3:18).

PRAYER

Lord, you have called us into a relationship where we might know you well. Forgive us for too often neglecting that possibility. Keep us from substituting mere information for meaningful knowledge. And forbid that we would substitute other types of knowledge—even that which is worthwhile—for knowing you personally. Make us a people who "grow in . . . grace and knowledge," and as we do, may you receive all the "glory both now and forever! AMEN" (3:18).

QUESTIONS

1. What is one subject you know well? How did you become so knowledgeable about it? What lessons from learning that subject might you now use to learn more about Jesus?

2. In your own words, how would you distinguish between information and knowledge? Why is it so easy to confuse the two or think of them as synonyms?

3. Who comes to your mind when you think of someone who knows Jesus well? What characteristics are present that reveal the person's deep knowledge of Jesus?

4. Peter ends his letter by urging readers to "grow in the grace and knowledge of our Lord and Savior Jesus Christ" (3:18). How does one grow in these ways? Are you growing?

SUGGESTED READING

2 Peter 1–3

62

1 JOHN: Life

*That which was from the beginning, which we have
heard, which we have seen with our eyes, which we
have looked at and our hands have touched—this we
proclaim concerning the Word of life. (1 John 1:1)*

And this is what he promised us—even eternal life. (1 John 2:25)

*We know that we have passed from death to life,
because we love our brothers. (1 John 3:14)*

*And this is the testimony: God has given us eternal life, and
this life is in his Son. He who has the Son has life; he who does
not have the Son of God does not have life. (1 John 5:11–12)*

Too few people are fully alive today. True, most individuals breathe,
work, talk, marry, have children, and grow old; yet rarely do they
experience the fullness of life designed by their Creator. They exist and
leave their footprint on the planet but fall short of life that is satisfying and abundant. Many of us know such people. They may be family
members, neighbors, or people at work. Or perhaps this lifeless existence describes us. We may find ourselves going through motions and
movements that have become memorized and routine, yet life is dull,
meaningless, and void of purpose. The secret of life has escaped many
of us. What is that secret and how is it discovered?

Before attempting to answer that question, it is worth noting that a "tree of life" opens and closes the pages of Scripture (Gen 2:9; Rev 22:2). The tree's dominant placement and symbolism in both creation and heaven surely signify that life matters to God, the Creator. Furthermore, the life God had in mind presumably consists of more than mere physical existence characterized by a pulse. Life implies vitality, spirit, enthusiasm, and endurance. Sometimes we speak of one who is "the life of the party" or of an experience that "breathes new life" into an individual or organization. These expressions help us understand that life extends beyond physiology (breathing and blood flow) and includes psychological (outlook and attitudes) and emotional areas (joy and excitement) of our being as well. There are many people who are alive physiologically, but that is about the extent of their existence. A sadness surrounds them. They tend to be emotionally flat, lack drive, contribute very little to others, seem to have endless needs, struggle with day-to-day activities and demands, have little vision for the future, often bring others in their circle down, and are generally void of optimism and hope. Though they walk, eat, and sleep, they are lifeless.

No New Testament writer had more to say about the matter of life than John. The word *life* itself is found repeatedly in the books he authored: John (36 times), 1 John (13 times), and Revelation (15 times). Our primary focus here is the letter of 1 John, wherein "life" bookends the author's thoughts. John began the letter by declaring "this [is what] we proclaim concerning the Word of life" (1:1); he ended the same letter by pointing to "Jesus Christ" and identifying him as "the true God and eternal life" (5:20). Everything the apostle John wanted to communicate in this five-chapter epistle can be summarized in this singular four-letter word: *life*. Those who grasp the message will do more than exist—they are destined to flourish.

Now let us return to the question above: What is the secret of life and how does one discover it? John presented Jesus as the source and secret of life. When one encounters Jesus, life is the byproduct. A review of all John's writings reveals that he not only referenced Jesus more than any other New Testament writer but also associated Jesus with life more than anyone else (e.g., John 6:35; 11:25; 14:6). Meaning and fulfillment in life grow out of a relationship with Jesus Christ. To embrace Jesus, therefore, is to embrace life. First John, in essence, is a manual for how to get the most out of life, and John presents Jesus as the key.

Life is maximized by listening to Jesus. The letter opens with a confession that what John is about to proclaim *regarding* Jesus is what John first heard *from* Jesus (1:1–3). John listened to God's "Son, Jesus Christ" (1:3), and it changed his life. The apostle encouraged others to do the same: to pay attention and listen to the message "you have heard from the beginning" (2:24; 3:11; cf. 1:5). The fulfilling life that John points others to embrace begins by listening carefully to Jesus.

Life is maximized by knowing Jesus. The theme of knowledge was the focus of the previous book, 2 Peter. All the early disciples wanted to know Jesus, the Son of God. John made a point of celebrating those who had come to *know* "him who is from the beginning" (2:13–14). Then he concluded his letter with a list of several descriptive statements declaring *what* "we know" regarding Jesus (5:15–20). The word *know* occurs forty times throughout this brief letter, indicating just how central knowing Jesus is to a meaningful life. We listen to him in order to know him, and in knowing him life takes on purpose.

Life is maximized by loving like Jesus. Whereas the word *know* is found forty times in the text of 1 John, the word *love* (the Greek word is *agape*) occurs over fifty times. Such extraordinary repetition reminds us that life never reaches its potential when one is self-absorbed. Only those who look outside themselves and love others discover the riches of life that come through relationships. "Since God so loved us, we also ought to love one another" (4:11). When we do, life gets enlarged and enriched in ways we never dreamed possible. Expressing love toward others reaps dividends that come no other way.

Life is maximized by confessing our sins to Jesus. Another repeated theme in John's letter is the problem of sin. Every chapter of 1 John speaks of the problem, and the word *sin* itself is found twenty-seven times throughout the letter. The solution to the problem is to "confess our sins" (1:9) to "Jesus Christ, the Righteous One" (2:1). He alone is "the atoning sacrifice for our sins" (2:2; 4:10). When sin is acknowledged and confessed before God, it leads to purity (1:7–9; 3:3), "victory" (5:4), and "life" (5:16). On the other hand, sin that is ignored controls, entangles, and deceives us (1:8), eventually leading to "lawlessness" (3:4) and "death" (5:16). Life in its fullness—the life God intended—is only possible when one confesses and then stops sinning (3:6–9). The major problem with sin is that it inhibits life designed by the Creator. Those who keep sinning forfeit the richness and fullness of life that could be theirs.

Life is maximized by anticipating eternity with Jesus. No biblical author so constantly keeps "eternal life" before his readers as does John. In 1 John, these references (1:2; 2:25; 3:15; 5:11, 13, 20) serve to remind us that God's design for life contains both a quality and a quantity. The new quality of life that begins here on earth continues beyond the grave, becoming endless days of delight in the presence of Jesus. This quality and quantity of life—known as eternal life—is God's gift of love to the world and the hope of every Christian.

When one makes Jesus the model and focal point of life, a depth and vibrancy develop that can be experienced no other way. Such a life is far from the mundane existence witnessed among so many people in our world today. Life centered on Jesus is marked by incredible quality and infinite quantity. It becomes an abundant, lasting, joyful, sacrificial, and surrendered life that elevates an individual and attracts others in significant ways.

Consider what this means. For example, an *abundant* life is a full life. Jesus came to ensure that kind of life to all who receive him (John 10:10)—life full of opportunity and optimism, life full of relationships and refreshment, life full of purpose and perspective, and life full of courage and contentment. A *lasting* life is one that does not end. What is experienced here is only the beginning, for God has "set eternity in the hearts of men" (Eccles 3:11). We were made to yearn for abundant life that continues beyond the eighty years so commonly experienced today. In Jesus, we are promised permanence that extends life throughout eternity (John 3:16).

A *joyful* life, once the standard characteristic of all followers of Christ, has become increasingly rare in our consumer-driven world. Yet it is still available to those who embrace Jesus. Peter described it as "inexpressible and glorious joy" (1 Pet 1:8) or what an older translation rendered as "joy unspeakable and full of glory" (KJV). This life—abundant, lasting, and joyful—is available to every child of God, without exception. It elevates human existence far above the din of the world and attracts those so desperate for hope.

Yet there is more to this life in Christ. A *sacrificial* life is our calling. As noted earlier, we were not created to turn inward and care only about ourselves and our personal needs. A life of sacrificial service to others is the hallmark of one who follows Jesus. We were designed for others; our bodies, minds, and spirits all testify to that fact. Thus, we sacrifice for the sake of another in marriage, in friendship, and in countless other relationships. Jesus went so far as to say, "Greater love has no one than this, that one lay down his life for his friends" (John 15:13). Sacrifice marks the life of those who dare live like Jesus, the One willing to "lay down [his] life for the sheep" (John 10:15–19).

A *surrendered* life is related to a sacrificial life. We do not sit at the controls of our lives; that position is reserved for the Lord Jesus Christ. We submit to him and his lordship. Certainly, that is the overarching call and message of the Bible. After all, its writers repeatedly used the term *Lord* to refer to God and his Son. The designation is found over seven thousand times in the Old Testament and nearly seven hundred additional times in the New Testament. God the Father was called "Lord"; Jesus the Son was likewise called "Lord." The name refers to one who is in charge. It implies we have a boss, one who supervises life, one to whom we answer and are accountable. Our life is not our own to live as we choose, but it is ours to surrender to the lordship of Jesus Christ.

The American gospel musician William McDowell captured the essence of the sacrificial and surrendered life well in his 2009 worship song, "I Give Myself Away." The following lyrics underscore the life described by John and so many other Bible writers:

> *My life is not my own*
> *To you I belong*
> *I give myself, I give myself to you*

It is a prudent sacrifice, a reasonable surrender. After all, "the fear of the LORD is a fountain of life" (Prov 14:27). In him alone does one find ultimate meaning and destiny. "He who has the Son has life; he who does not have the Son of God does not have life" (1 John 5:12).

The message of the gospel is clear and twofold: Jesus lives, and we find life in him. Why would anyone not give himself or herself to Jesus and this life?

PRAYER

Dear Father and Lord, we recognize you as the fountain, or source, of all life. Help us to embrace you fully, so that we might live. Keep us from falling for the cheap and misguided counterfeits of life offered by the world. Give us the real thing. Give us life that is abundant, lasting, joyful, sacrificial, and surrendered. May your Son, Jesus Christ, be our focus and our model. It is in his name that we offer this prayer. AMEN.

QUESTIONS

1. Looking back over your life, what would you identify as three highlights? How was God active in your life during those times?

2. What obstacles hinder people from believing and acting that Jesus is the key, or secret, to a fulfilling life? What might we do to help remove those obstacles?

3. In your own words, how would you describe the quality and quantity of life we enjoy as followers of Christ? Which of these has the greatest appeal to you? Why?

4. Who do you know who seems to live life to the full under the Lordship of Jesus Christ? What is the evidence? What would it take for you to live that same way?

SUGGESTED READING

1 John 1–5

63

2 JOHN: Walk

*It has given me great joy to find some of your children walking
in the truth, just as the Father commanded us. (2 John 4)*

*And this is love: that we walk in obedience to his
commands. As you have heard from the beginning, his
command is that you walk in love. (2 John 6)*

Have you ever observed how people walk? Some always seem to be in
a hurry. Some walk with confidence. Others walk with their heads
down, purposely avoiding interaction with passersby. Some saunter,
some stroll, some skip, and some sashay. There are those who know
another person so well that they can identify the individual by the way
he or she walks. Years ago, when I was a high school athlete, my parents
always claimed they could immediately spot me among my teammates
by the way I walked. Now I see what they meant, for I observe the unique
ways my children and grandchildren walk. We human beings are known
by how we walk. One's walk communicates a great deal: identity, health,
strength, confidence, mood, purpose, and more.

The apostle John was interested in how people walked. All his writings had something to say on the subject, but nowhere is the topic emphasized more than in his brief letters known as 2 and 3 John. Both
letters—the two shortest books in the entire Bible—begin with a focus
on the importance of one's walk. While writers use the term to note

the physical activity of moving from one location to another, as when describing the two who "walked" to Emmaus after the resurrection (Luke 24:17), the word also is often used figuratively. In the latter case it refers to how a person conducts the daily affairs of his or her life. To say a person "walks what he talks" is to say that his conduct is consistent with his claims. That was John's concern for the early believers; it should be our concern as well. How we walk—how we conduct our daily lives—sends a message to those around us.

That was true of my father-in-law. Born in 1919, the Minnesota Norwegian George W. Olson was a good Christian and churchman who cared and provided for his family. His personal conduct and ethics—including his work ethic—were exemplary to all who knew him. George was a man whose word could be trusted and who took pleasure in helping his neighbor. These characteristics eventually landed him a prominent position overseeing finances and stewardship for his denomination. One of George's greatest sources of joy and pride was the family cabin he built on a beautiful lake west of the Twin Cities. Today his four children and their families still enjoy the cabin and walk the grounds that he once walked. In many ways, George epitomized the American Dream in the late twentieth century. He took pleasure in his family, his work, his church, and weekends at the lake. At the turn of the century, however, in George's last few years, family members watched with sadness as Parkinson's disease made it increasingly difficult for their strong and capable father to walk. What was once so effortless and taken for granted became labored steps—feeble, uncertain, and tentative. George grew frustrated and confused regarding movements that had once been so natural.

As a young boy, George had walked back and forth to school on many frigid Minneapolis winter days. As a teenager on the high school gymnastics team, strength and balance helped George achieve various physical feats; coordination and walking were second nature. As a young man in his early twenties, he served alongside other American comrades in France during World War II. Pressed into service as a medic, he often found himself racing to rescue others and carrying soldiers who could no longer walk themselves. Though he rarely talked about it, the mundane act of walking had served him and others well on countless occasions. Over his lifetime the ability to walk allowed George to trudge over ice and snow, climb ladders and crawl over roofs, hike while carrying soldiers and later his own children and grandchildren on his back, and escort two lovely daughters down the aisle on their wedding days. Walking was what he knew until Parkinson's caught up with him in his eighties. Then his walk became compromised and reduced to a shuffle.

The value, utility, and power of walking ought not be underestimated or taken for granted. Those without the ability to do so forfeit more than movement; they lose influence, possibilities, and sometimes their dignity. Perhaps that is why John wrote: "It has given me great joy to find some of your children walking . . . just as the Father commanded us" (2 John 4). Walking indicates health, strength, development, and maturity. Whether celebrating the first steps of a toddler or the incremental strides of a stroke survivor, walking implies one is making progress and moving forward. That kind of development is what John desired for the "children" (2 John 1, 4, 13) under his care—those newborn believers in Jesus Christ. He rejoiced to see them walking and defined three primary ways they did so.

These children were "walking in the truth" (2 John 4). That fact resulted in "great joy" (2 John 4), a theme repeated twice in 3 John (vv 3, 4). Truth points to honesty and integrity. The early believers conducted their lives (they walked) so that integrity was evident to all observers. Truth's prominence in the New Testament, where the word is found over 180 times in 25 of the 27 books (half of those occurrences are in the writings of John), suggests we ought to pay attention to it. Biblical writers recognized that people in the surrounding culture all too easily dismissed truth if it meant they could gain an advantage over others. In fact, John warned about "deceivers" in the world (2 John 7) who would compromise what was genuine and try to lead people astray. Truth and integrity were nonnegotiable to this upstart group of Christian believers. Deception of any kind was to be avoided. Perhaps John had in mind the words of Jesus who said: "Simply let your 'Yes' be 'Yes,' and your 'No,' 'No'" (Matt 5:37). The point was for an individual to walk in such a way that no one could question his or her integrity. The same standard ought to exist today. The same walk is demanded. When there is a choice to be made for the child of God, the honest and righteous choice is to be made every time, for "walking in the truth" defines the follower of Jesus Christ.

These children were walking "in obedience to his commands" (2 John 6). At least two principles are implied by this statement: first, the very fact that God gave commands suggests he had a design and order by which he wanted his people to operate; and second, one would have to listen to God to know what those commands were.

Walking "in obedience to his commands," then, means one becomes intentionally tuned in to God's design for life. This presupposes a seriousness and focus that is too rarely witnessed in a fallen world wherein people take pride in independence and innovation. The measure of greatness in the kingdom of God is neither self-discovery nor self-expression but crucifixion of the self that permits faithfulness to God and his design. That is why John wrote: "Anyone who runs ahead and does not continue in the teaching of Christ does not have God" (2 John 9). When any of us dare "run ahead" and reject "the teaching of Christ"—whether it be in regard to our understanding of authority, our cavalier attitude toward and acceptance of sin, our disregard for the miracle of conception and life, our redefining of marriage or gender, our disrespect for brothers and sisters of other races and ethnicities, or a host of other possibilities—we minimize the design of the Creator God and do harm to the order he established. Children who walk "in obedience to his commands" seek to follow God's blueprint rather than usurping his authority and forming their own patterns. We will only know the divine blueprint if we listen carefully to God's voice and heed his word. In our walk, we dare not "run ahead" and miss the instruction and plan God has for us.

These children were walking "in love" (2 John 6). To walk in love means to conduct one's life with an eye toward the welfare of others. Daily activities are less about concern for oneself and more about caring for others. The one who walks in love thinks less about self-preservation and more about providing for his or her neighbors. One's vision gets adjusted from inward observation to outward observation, and one's priority moves from convenience to compassion. The most common Greek word for love in the New Testament, *agape*, is found there more than three hundred times, indicating how much it shaped the Christian environment of that era. Love was the defining characteristic of the early church. The walk of believers was noticeable—it was the walk of love demonstrated toward neighbors and community members, whether they be fellow believers or enemies of Christ. That same walk ought to define us still today.

Make no mistake, the follower of Jesus Christ always has been known by his or her walk. It is a walk of integrity, a walk that honors God's design, and a walk of compassion toward others. "Many deceivers" (2 John 7) will suggest a different kind of walk, one that may appear more attractive, self-serving, and promise greater immediate utility.

Like so many other areas of life, how we walk demands a choice: we can walk the way of Jesus—following "in his steps" (1 Pet 2:21)—or we can walk the way of our peers and follow the godless icons of culture. Either way, we will be remembered for how we walk.

My father-in-law, George, was known for more than his physical walk that took him from tumbling on gymnastics mats as a teenager to carrying the wounded across French battlefields in World War II to stubborn and immobile feet near the end of his life due to Parkinson's. When he died in 2003, people said little about his physical walk. It was another kind of walk that mattered then: his conduct and character. You see, George also was known for walking in truth, in obedience to God's commands, and in love. Integrity, the design of God, and compassion toward others were hallmarks of his life. The legacy of his walk remains in subsequent generations of family members today.

What will people be saying one day about the way you and I have walked? What legacy will we leave?

PRAYER

Our loving Father and Lord, help us as we seek to walk *with* you and *like* you, for you alone are "the way and the truth and the life" (John 14:6). We acknowledge that all we need is found in you. Yet we confess that at times our walk grows week, wobbly, and wayward. Forgive us. Help us to walk in truth, in obedience to your commands, and in love. May our walk give us away, clearly identifying us as those who belong to you. This we pray in the name of your Son, our Savior, Jesus Christ. AMEN.

QUESTIONS

1. Who do you know who has a distinct walk? What makes it so? How would you describe that person's walk?

2. Why is it that people want truth and integrity in their leaders, while often compromising their own personal integrity? Why is there such inconsistency, or a double standard?

3. What commands, instructions, or designs of God need greater attention today among God's people? Why do certain teachings of God get neglected or distorted at times?

4. Why is it so rare to find people today who walk in integrity, follow God's design, and operate out of love? Which of these three do you think is the most challenging?

SUGGESTED READING

2 John

64

3 JOHN: Truth

It gave me great joy to have some brothers come and tell about your faithfulness to the truth and how you continue to walk in the truth. I have no greater joy than to hear that my children are walking in the truth. (3 John 3–4)

We ought therefore to show hospitality to such men so that we may work together for the truth. (3 John 8)

Demetrius is well spoken of by everyone—and even by the truth itself. (3 John 12)

A strange phenomenon has occurred over the past half-century. As information and the speed with which we obtain it has increased exponentially, truth has become scarce. In fact, we might call truth a casualty of the Information Age. Previously, we noted truth's prevalence throughout the New Testament, the word appearing in twenty-five of twenty-seven books. Truth—both its pursuit and embrace—was a distinguishing mark of the early Christian community. However, it seems to have lost its lofty position in our society today, once known for being formed and guided by Judeo-Christian principles. Tragically, an argument could be made that truth also has lost its place in our churches. Evidence of its demise is plentiful.

First, consider a few examples from society. Fact checks have become a standard follow-up to news stories and statements made by public officials here in the twenty-first century. The reason for these checks extends beyond technology making them possible; the trustworthiness of our officials in handling truth is also a factor. Plagiarism has become so rampant in education that every university in America—faith-based or secular—has faculty committees and policies to address the problem. Software has been designed to detect writing that takes from another author without giving due credit. Numerous, and often complicated, forms of verification are now demanded before one can access various personal accounts and records. No one is quite sure whether a person is really who he or she claims to be. Hiring has moved from a gentleman's handshake—symbolizing the veracity of his word—to a thorough background check to investigate any acts of dishonesty or impropriety. Truth cannot be counted on. Therefore, great measures are taken to ensure its existence as best we can.

The church, sadly, also has lost its grip on truth. In its attempts to be popular, positive, or political, the church too often compromises. When the desire to fill pews and increase attendance becomes the priority, certain difficult topics that need to be addressed with truth and clarity are ignored. Popularity is not won by taking on controversial topics that are sure to upset people. Closely linked to popularity is positivity. There are those who are averse to anything that might be interpreted as negative. Some church leaders operate by trying to be positive at all times. They have convinced themselves that people are more attracted to optimism and feeling good than they are to truth. Consequently, focus is placed on creating feel-good worship experiences, while how one lives during the week is largely ignored. The problem is that such an approach is neither realistic nor biblical. Life demands a balance of optimism and hard truth. Some churches and their leaders are driven by politics. Political positions on either side of the political spectrum can interfere with declaring the truth of the gospel of Jesus Christ. Political correctness suppresses truth, elevating human ideas from the prevailing culture above the eternal truth of God found in his Holy Word. In short, what is safe, rather than what is true, has come to define the message of western Christianity in our day. The institution that once stood as society's bastion of truth is in danger of losing its purpose and relevance.

The problem, of course, is that truth, by its very nature, is offensive. It demands of us what few are willing to give. The Baptist minister Wilbur E. Rees in his 1971 devotional book with the provocative title *$3.00 Worth of God* had this to say about truth:

Your speech is offensive, Lord. If you have to speak the truth, why can't you soften it a bit for delicate ears and tender tastes? Reality is vulgar. We hide our garbage in plastic cans and bury our cesspools beneath our lawns. We cover our sweat with aerosol spray and our bourbon breath with peppermint. When you speak, take a lesson from the professionals. Turn on the background music and avoid naked honesty as you would obscenity. Call sin an inadequate perception and call the morgue a slumber room. Fish do not enjoy reading seafood menus nor do canaries enjoy movies of cats. If you insist on stating the truth, you may run out of an audience. (p 94)

Ironically, however, truth is the basis of civilization. Without it, society disintegrates. When public leaders can no longer be trusted, when financial institutions become corrupt, when businesses market and sell compromised products, and when education promotes an agenda based on social preferences rather than historical facts, the foundations of a nation begin to crumble. The absence of truth is a cancer that destroys civilization from within. Deception corrodes and sabotages community life that is built on pillars consisting of trust in shared truth. That is why our forefathers insisted that the first amendment to the U.S. Constitution, ratified in 1791, include a statement on the freedom of religion, of speech, and of the press. These freedoms underscored the importance of the right to pursue and express truth. The thought of suppressing, silencing, or twisting it was seen as detrimental to a free and prosperous nation. Truth matters. Without it, society and its social institutions, including the church, become mere caricatures. Civilization falters, digresses, and ultimately fails.

Perhaps that is why the apostle John had so much to say about truth near the end of the Bible. The word is mentioned sixteen times in 1 John (in every chapter), five times in 2 John, and seven times in 3 John. The two other New Testament books authored by John—the Gospel of John and Revelation—contain the word another sixty-six times combined. Clearly, John was concerned that believers understand and embrace truth. What is there about this concept that makes it so fundamental to the Christian faith? Why is it repeated so often? How is it that civilization and social order itself rest on truth? John offers several clues in his last short letter.

Truth points to Jesus. As Jesus was nearing the cross, he told his disciples that he was "the way and the truth and the life" (John 14:6). It was a bold claim. Just a few days later Jesus was arrested and brought before the authorities. The topic came up again when the Roman governor Pilate asked him directly (John 18:38), "What is truth?" Pilate's question revealed he had no idea that he was staring Truth in the face that day. In contrast to Pilate, the apostle John saw Jesus as the embodiment and representative of truth. There is an interesting observation worth noting here: 3 John is the only New Testament book that includes neither the name Jesus nor the title Christ. One might speculate as to the reason for the absence, but what is more important is that truth always points to Jesus. Where there is truth, there is Jesus. Consequently, though his formal and proper name is not mentioned in this letter, Jesus is represented there by truth. That is still the case today. Those who promote truth, knowingly or unknowingly, point to Jesus, of whom it was said: "no deceit was found in his mouth" (1 Pet 2:22; Isa 53:9). Because Jesus is the embodiment of truth, all expressions of truth point to him.

Truth is associated with faithfulness. John rejoiced when he heard about those who practiced "faithfulness to the truth" (v 3). Truth has its roots in faithfulness. Or is it vice versa? What we know for sure is this: Those who "are walking in the truth" (v 4)—making it part of their daily conduct and pattern—stand out among their peers. Their faithfulness and determination to uphold truth, no matter what, make them trusted community pillars. Furthermore, there is a recognition that someone who is faithful to the truth in one area is likely to be truthful and faithful in other areas as well. Integrity begets integrity, whatever the circumstances. That is why those who establish an artificial dichotomy between their private and public lives are suspect. Faithfulness to the truth cannot be compartmentalized in such a way. One either walks in the truth, or does not; one can be trusted to be faithful, or not. If a boundary has been breached in one area, we should not be surprised to see a similar breach in another area. Truth tends to mark one's entire life, or none of it at all. Integrity of character grows out of faithfulness and consistency.

Truth needs a cooperative effort. John urged the church to "work together for the truth" (v 8). The beauty of truth is that it invites others to partner with it. Truth becomes a cultural, or community, norm that people intentionally work together to uphold. It brings people together, rallying them around shared values of honesty, transparency, dignity, and respect. Truth is the glue that permits social order. The opposite is also true. Where there is deceit and distrust, people withdraw and live isolated lives of suspicion. The absence of honesty and integrity—whether in elected officials, local businesses, or neighbors—results in social chaos rather than order. When lies replace truth in a nation or a family, bitterness and breakdown follow. Without cooperative efforts to operate based on truth, there is nothing to hold people together. No wonder the apostle John encouraged early believers to "work together for the truth." The Christian community could not exist without it. A careful historical study of fallen nations, failed business enterprises, or fractured families reveals the abandonment of truth. Let us work together, then, to raise and maintain a high standard of truth in our generation, just as John advocated for his day.

Truth accompanies a good reputation. John noted that Demetrius, of whom we know little else, was "well spoken of" among members of his community (v 12). Even "the truth" came to his defense. Though the meaning of this remains somewhat vague, what is not vague is the fact that truth and a good reputation always go together. They are partners. Truth leads to a good reputation, and a good reputation leads others to the truth. People known for truthfulness and honesty will always have a good reputation. Such people, like Demetrius here, also have a winsome witness. May God grant us more people like Demetrius in our world today—people who do not need or seek the spotlight, but of whom others consistently speak well and with whom truth gets associated. When truth is incarnated, we call it integrity. When integrity exists in a humble servant like Demetrius, the whole surrounding community benefits.

There are two timeless truths about truth. Both were emphasized by John. First, as noted earlier, truth is offensive. It cost Jesus his life (John 18:37–19:18). Second, truth sets people free (John 8:32). Living in delusion, rather than accepting reality, is a form of slavery and oppression. One's full potential can only be reached when truth prevails.

May God grant us a revival of truth and integrity today. The cost is great, but the benefits are greater.

PRAYER

Dear Lord, grant us a hunger for truth. Help us understand that your Son, Jesus, *is* truth. Then draw us ever closer to him. Forgive us for acting as if we can navigate life on our own, for we cannot do so apart from you. Forgive us for being so easily offended by the claims of truth, for we need the guidance that your truth provides. Forgive us for too often running from the truth that can set us free, for we end up in bondage when we do so. May truth be elevated in our nation, our community, our workplace, our church, our family, and in our daily personal lives. And may Jesus—the way, the truth, and the life—be glorified as a result. AMEN.

QUESTIONS

1. What examples can you think of that illustrate how we have lost the shared value of truth and integrity in our society today? How might we restore truth and integrity?

2. Why is truth so often offensive? Is there any way to make it less offensive without compromising the truth itself? If so, how?

3. Who do you know—like Demetrius—whose good reputation is associated with his or her faithfulness to the truth? What else do you admire about that person?

4. Have you ever stood for truth even though it was unpopular? What were the circumstances? What did it cost you? What did you learn from the experience?

SUGGESTED READING

3 John

65

JUDE: Persistence

Dear friends, although I was very eager to write to you about the salvation we share, I felt I had to write and urge you to contend for the faith that was once for all entrusted to the saints. (Jude 3)

> *But you, dear friends, build yourselves up in your most holy faith and pray in the Holy Spirit. Keep yourselves in God's love as you wait for the mercy of our Lord Jesus Christ to bring you to eternal life. (Jude 20–21)*

To him who is able to keep you from falling and to present you before his glorious presence without fault and with great joy—to the only God our Savior be glory, majesty, power and authority, through Jesus Christ our Lord, before all ages, now and forevermore! Amen. (Jude 24–25)

Persistence is the ability to focus and stay on course despite distractions, opposition, disappointments, and adversity along the way. This characteristic is needed by anyone pursuing a goal. No meaningful accomplishment will be achieved without determination and the ability to persist. Persistence is what helped one person complete twenty-nine years of formal education on his way to becoming a university professor. Persistence helped that same individual continue in his work as a classroom professor for thirty-four years. Persistence saw that man reach forty-six years of marriage and keep going. Persistence undergirded the man's faith for more than sixty years after he made a commitment to follow Christ as a young child. I know these facts to be true because I am that man. With the Lord's help, persistence has served me well over the years. The road has not always been easy. Discouragement has come in many forms: failure to pass a major doctoral exam in the field of sociology, the disappointment of not being selected for a sought-after job, watching close family members suffer with debilitating diseases such as cancer or cystic fibrosis, and more. Yet I am writing today as one who gives testimony to the fact that God has provided the grace to persist and prevail. I have found that God not only desires but specializes in persistence; the pages of Scripture make this abundantly clear.

Jude, another single-chapter book tucked in at the end of the New Testament, emphasizes the believer's need for persistence. The author and his brother James (v 1) were younger brothers of Jesus (Matt 13:55; Mark 6:3). Jude's purpose in writing seemed to be to encourage early believers to be on their guard, to not give up, to show some grit and determination, and to persist on "to eternal life" (v 21). In fact, as brothers of Jesus both James and Jude initially may have experienced their share of doubts regarding Jesus being the Christ (e.g., Mark 3:21). However, that was early in their lives. After the resurrection, those doubts apparently vanished and James and Jude persisted in their faith, making significant contributions to the spread of Christianity through their writings and leadership. The Church of Jesus Christ would not exist today were it not for those who have demonstrated persistence in their faith down through the years. Resolve and tenacity sustained the Church; they still do.

Jude encouraged his readers "to contend for the faith" (v 3), implying they could expect a struggle due to opposition. He then went on to describe both the present source and historical nature of the struggle that would require their persistence. The present source of their struggle consisted of godless peers. The terms *godless* or *ungodly* are found six times in the short book of Jude (vv 4, 15, 18), more than in any other New Testament book. Those godless peers were described as those who "have secretly slipped in among you" (v 4), "who change the grace of our God into a license for immorality" (v 4), "shepherds who feed only themselves" (v 12), and "grumblers and faultfinders" who "boast about themselves and flatter others for their own advantage" (v 16). Persistence always is required—in every generation—to maintain one's faith while living among godless and immoral people such as these. The historical nature of the struggle is evident in the multiple references Jude makes to Old Testament events. Several distinct stories are noted (see vv 5, 6, 7, 9, 11, and 14), all of which serve to provide background context and warning. The point is that those who came before us also had to endure challenging times and hardship; persistence was no less needed then than now. History confirms and godless peers remind us of our constant need for persistence.

So how does one do it? How does one persist and make it to the end of life with his or her faith intact? In addition to contending, or fighting, for the faith, which is Jude's emphasis as he begins his brief book (v 3), the author offers additional tips near the end of his writing—tips that sound similar to the advice one might receive when preparing for a marathon. The persistence needed to cross the finish line, whether in a grueling physical race or a demanding spiritual battle, comes from three central responses: remembering, building oneself up, and keeping oneself on target. These same responses, or words, will help us persevere.

Remember. "Remember what the apostles of our Lord Jesus Christ foretold" (v 17). Remember what others have told us; remember what the coach said and stick to the game plan. The problem with many of us is not how or what we have been taught. Most of us were taught well, but we struggle to *remember* what we were told. Godly people have tried to speak into our lives along the way. Have we listened? Do we remember their sage advice? When times become challenging and the temptation is to quit, we need to remember what yesterday's "saints" (v 3) foretold: there will be days of doubt, distress, disappointment, and discouragement. Do not give up. We are not alone. God walks with us. Others have passed this way and prevailed; we can, too. If we are to persist in the faith through the dark valleys of life—through pandemics, famines, storms, terror, wars, and personal loss—it will be the result of remembering what the apostles have told us. The first apostles left us a written record to encourage us: the Bible. Those who persist are those who know this book. Later "apostles"—those representatives of Christ sent out in every generation—have left us testimonies of words and lives to encourage and guide us in the faith. Let us pause and remember what all the apostles and saints have experienced and communicated to those who follow in their steps.

Build. "Build yourselves up in your most holy faith and pray in the Holy Spirit" (v 20). A marathon runner trains to build up endurance. Paul alluded to that in his first letter to the Corinthians when he wrote, "Everyone who competes in the games goes into strict training" (9:25).

He went on to say that athletes do this to gain a temporary crown, or trophy; "but we do it to get a crown that will last forever." Our training is designed to build spiritual muscle that will see us through hard times. Unlike developing physical muscle that results from active movement, however, developing spiritual muscle occurs primarily when we are inactive—quiet and still, on our knees before God, "pray[ing] in the Holy Spirit" (v 20). What we learn today through unpleasant trials and prayer, and the commitments we make in response to these experiences, all work together to develop within us a faith that will endure. To be sure, such experiences are neither easy nor comfortable; if they were, they would have little lasting value. The late gospel songwriter Andraé Crouch put it this way in his popular 1971 song, "Through it All:"

> *I've had many tears and sorrows*
> *I've had questions for tomorrow*
> *There've been times I didn't know right from wrong*
> *But in every situation*
> *God gave me blessed consolation*
> *That my trials come to only make me strong*

Persistence is learned by going through fiery trials and being made strong in the process. Building up our muscles of faith and endurance can happen no other way.

Keep. "Keep yourselves in God's love as you wait for . . . eternal life" (v 21). Finally, persistence is the result of keeping our lives on track, keeping important matters of life the priority they should be. Remaining properly positioned in relationship to God and staying focused on the ultimate goal are both mandatory. A top-level runner learns to stay focused. Again, Paul helped us when he said, "I press on toward the goal to win the prize for which God has called me heavenward in Christ Jesus" (Phil 3:14). Keeping oneself on target is required. Staying focused on "God's love" and our eternal destination in heaven is the key to persistence. The problem is we humans have a tendency to wander off course. Thus, we find ourselves moving away from God's love, his design, and the destiny he has planned for us. Now and then a realignment is necessary, wherein we reprioritize life and reorient ourselves to God's great love and plan. Persistence is a product of staying close to God, keeping ourselves in the center of his will, and keeping our focus on what lies ahead: eternal life in heaven with our Lord, Jesus Christ.

Interestingly, persistence has become a dominant theme in higher education these days. University administrators and accreditation bodies are concerned about persistence as it pertains to students. Too many young people enroll in college and yet do not finish their education. They begin, secure large loans, amass a sizeable debt, and then leave without having completed their degree. Consequently, there is little hope they will ever be able to pay off their debt. The reasons for the lack of persistence that create this problem are multiple. Some find the rigors of their studies to be tougher than they anticipated. Others leave one college for another, thinking the fit will be better elsewhere, only to repeat the pattern. Still others are influenced by their peers who seem to have found an easier and shorter path to their career goals. Regardless of the reasons, higher education has made persistence one of its priorities here in the twenty-first century. This should not surprise us, for the life and sustainability of universities depend on students who persist.

In the same fashion, the sustainability of the early church was seen through this lens. The reasons for abandoning the faith were, and still are, similar to what we are witnessing at universities today. Some find the rigors of the journey to be too demanding, some leave Christianity and go elsewhere because they are attracted to another god or faith that ultimately disappoints, and some follow their peers along what seems to be an easier or more appealing road for reaching their goals. Thus, too many who begin their journey of faith end it prematurely. They fail to persist—the very thing that so concerned the writer, Jude.

The brief book of Jude appropriately ends with what has become one of the best-known doxologies in all Scripture. It is a declaration of praise that points to Jesus Christ, who alone "is able to keep [us] from falling" (v 24). Since Jesus modeled persistence when he endured the trials and suffering associated with the cross, to him "be glory, majesty, power and authority . . . now and forevermore! Amen" (v 25).

Let us remember what Jude and other biblical writers sought to teach us. Let us build up our faith in Jesus Christ. Let us keep our eyes focused on what is yet to come. Then let us end our lives with a loud and clear doxology of praise to our Lord Jesus Christ (vv 24–25).

PRAYER

O Lord our God, we recognize and confess our propensity to give up too easily. Forgive us and keep us faithful. Help us to remember well what the apostles and saints have taught us over the years. Help us to continue to build up our faith by our daily practices. And help us to keep ourselves in your love, focused on you and our eternal reward with you. May we persist until faith becomes sight, trials cease, and we are found forever in your presence. We offer this prayer in the name of our Lord Jesus Christ, who alone is able to keep us from falling. AMEN.

QUESTIONS

1. How would you advise someone who is struggling—in any area of life—to hang in there and persist to the end? What word of advice might you offer?

2. Why is quitting such a common experience in so many areas of life today? People quit jobs, quit school, end relationships, and more. What makes people give up so easily?

3. Who do you know who persisted through very difficult circumstances and yet came out victoriously, with his or her faith intact on the other side? What made the difference?

4. What strategies have you found effective when going through hard times? How do you persist and keep going when circumstances are difficult?

SUGGESTED READING

Jude

66

REVELATION: Heaven

*"I am the Alpha and Omega," says the Lord God, "who is, and
who was, and who is to come, the Almighty." (Revelation 1:8)*

*After this I looked, and there before me was a door standing
open in heaven. And the voice I had first heard speaking
to me like a trumpet said, "Come up here, and I will show
you what must take place after this." (Revelation 4:1)*

*Then I saw a new heaven and a new earth . . . I saw the Holy City, the
new Jerusalem, coming down out of heaven from God, prepared as
a bride beautifully dressed for her husband. And I heard a loud voice
from the throne saying, "Now the dwelling of God is with men, and
he will live with them. They will be his people, and God himself will
be with them and be their God. He will wipe every tear from their
eyes. There will be no more death or mourning or crying or pain,
for the old order of things has passed away. (Revelation 21:1–4)*

We come to the last of the sixty-six books that comprise our Bible,
the book of Revelation, with its emphasis on heaven. The word
heaven is found over fifty times here; only Matthew, of all the books
in the New Testament, mentions the term more. Thus, the New Testament begins and ends with language that draws the reader's attention to
heaven. The same is true in the book of Revelation itself, opening with
a personal invitation to heaven (4:1) and closing with a description of

heaven (21:1–22:17). Apparently, God wants us to be familiar with this place he has designed us to inhabit for all eternity.

John, the New Testament author who also emphasized the important themes of *love* (John), *life* (1 John), how we *walk* (2 John), and *truth* (3 John), now concludes with thoughts on *heaven*. No one provides more detailed information pertaining to this place—where God dwells eternally with his people—than does the apostle John in the final book of the Bible. We owe him a debt of gratitude for providing written pictures of our eternal home.

I also owe a debt of gratitude to another individual named John, who now resides in this eternal, heavenly home. John Canfield and I met in 1979 when my wife and I moved to Salem, Oregon, to pastor a deaf congregation. John, a deaf man, and four years older than I, worked as a computer programmer for the Oregon Department of Transportation. He drove a sporty Chevrolet Camaro and loved photography and travel. He also loved his Lord and the church. With a winsome smile, a twinkle in his eyes, and a ready laugh, John communicated easily with people—whether they knew sign language as he did or not.

Shortly after we met, I learned that John had a physical condition far more serious than his deafness; he had developed diabetes in his youth. Whereas deafness cut John off from communicating with some people, diabetes would cut off more significant functions and eventually take his life. Initially it was just an inconvenience, but as time passed the inconvenience grew into an incapacity. His eyesight began to fail, leading to the complete loss of vision in his right eye. When John began experiencing kidney failure, it meant countless hours at the kidney dialysis center and the hospital. These setbacks did not deter John. He held his job as long as he could and continued his excursions with his Camaro and camera whenever he had a few days off. Eventually, however, John's diabetes progressed, his vision grew worse, and he was no longer able to keep working.

Those familiar with diabetes know that it often cruelly leads to other physical complications. In John's case, it led to the amputation of a leg before the age of forty. I was with him in the hospital—as his pastor, interpreter, and friend—when the doctor told him that to save his life, they would need to remove his infected leg. It was an agonizingly dark and difficult hour as John had to face yet another loss. His body responded well after the amputation, but the eyesight remaining in his left eye further diminished and blurred. Soon he could only see very narrowly out of the corner of his eye. Not long thereafter, John's other leg was also amputated. This once active photographer, traveler, and Department of Transportation employee had his world reduced. He was unable to hear, could barely see out of only one eye, and had lost both legs above his knees.

I visited John often during those days, hoping that I might encourage him. Remarkably, he ended up encouraging *me* with his spirit that remained vibrant and strong despite his losses. We sat together in his parents' living room near the big picture window so that the incoming light would help John see with his limited remaining eyesight. To my amazement, John had his sights set on yet another trip—one that he knew would be his last. He was focused on his journey to heaven. Week after week, we talked about his eternal destination. John was not shy about the topic; he initiated the discussions every time I visited. In fact, he grilled me with questions regarding heaven: What would it be like? Are the streets there literally made of gold? Will we each have our own beautiful home? What will our new bodies be like? Do you suppose sign language will be used there? What will it be like to live forever and not grow old? Who will we see there? Why don't more people make plans to go there? Yes, John was busy preparing for his next big trip. He would not need his Camaro and camera for this journey. He would not even need his legs and eyes there because he knew Revelation promised there was one "seated on the throne [who] said, 'I am making everything new!'" (21:5).

John Canfield took that trip and went to heaven on January 17, 1996. He was forty-four years old. One day I plan to join him. Perhaps our roles will be reversed then. Instead of John asking me, a young minister at the time, what heaven might be like, I wonder if I will be asking him.

Thoughts and talk about heaven have certainly fascinated people over the years. Libraries contain books that have been written on both Revelation and heaven. Classes and seminars have been taught on these dual subjects. Sermons and songs have been crafted to inspire people to look heavenward. Artists have tried to depict it on canvas. Bumper stickers, lapel pins, and T-shirts remind us of heaven's invitation and possibility.

My friend John asked the question: "What will heaven be like?" The apostle John tried to answer that question in the last book of the Bible. While recognizing that human words and expressions fall short in adequately describing this divine, other-worldly place, there are nonetheless several characteristics of heaven worth noting. Observations from the writer John reveal many features, five of which will be noted here

1. Jesus is there. One cannot get far in the book of Revelation without encountering Jesus. In our English translations, "Jesus" is the fourth word of the book; in the original Greek, his name is the second word, coming only after the word *revelation*. John intentionally began and ended his description of heaven with a focus on Jesus (1:1; 22:21). Then repeated throughout the book is reference to Jesus as the Lamb—the one "who was slain" (5:12), whose "blood . . . purchased" our salvation (5:9), and who now is positioned victoriously on heaven's "throne" (5:6, 13; 7:10–17). The picture could not be clearer. Jesus, the Lamb of God, is the central attraction of heaven. Over the years, numerous books pertaining to heaven have gained popularity because their authors highlighted other dramatic scenes or events. In John's book of Revelation, however, heaven simply would not be heaven without Jesus. Everything that follows throughout the book—every description, every detail, and every enticement—is secondary in importance to Jesus. John wanted his readers to know, first and foremost, that heaven is where we will enjoy the uninterrupted presence of our Savior, Jesus Christ.

2. Splendor dominates the place. The student of Revelation cannot help but be struck by the beauty of heaven. Streets and crowns of gold, walls of jasper, gates made of pearls, and other magnificent sights grab our attention (4:1–6; 21:15–27). Though we are told "the kings of the earth will bring splendor into it" (21:24), I suspect their contributions will pale in comparison to what they will find already there. Some might even shrink in embarrassment. For we who spend so much time and effort beautifying our homes, yards, and images will no doubt be amazed at the unparalleled splendor that awaits us in heaven. We surely will marvel at the sights and majesty all around us there. John seems to have run out of words in his attempt to describe the glory and grandeur he observed on his tour of heaven.

3. Delight defines the experience. Heaven is universally desired because of the delights that are promised there. All that is broken will be made new (21:5) and "a new song" (5:9; 14:3) will fill the air. "Praise" to the Lamb will be the dominant expression heard in heaven (5:12, 13; 7:12; 19:5). This should not surprise us, for heaven is the place wherein God "will wipe every tear from their eyes. There will be no more death or mourning or crying or pain, for the old order of things has passed away" (21:4). What unspeakable joy will result, giving way to natural and spontaneous praise to the one who has made it all possible. Furthermore, these delights will not occur periodically after isolated special occasions but will be the common experience and environment enjoyed by all heaven's inhabitants.

4. Eternity marks the calendar. We know that heaven's delights will be ongoing because the phrase "for ever and ever" dominates Revelation (e.g., 1:6, 18; 7:12; 22:5). What takes place in heaven continues throughout eternity. There will be a new order without boundaries marking time. "There will be no more night" (22:5); nor will there be months or seasons. Heaven "does not need the sun or the moon to shine on it" (21:23), for seasons and months—which are governed by those celestial bodies—will have no meaning there. Eternity will usher in a whole new way of understanding and experiencing time. Heaven is not only where the "throne of God and of the Lamb will be" (22:3) but also where his servants "will reign for ever and ever" (22:5). There will be no end, as time gives way to eternity.

5. Entrance is restricted. As wonderful as heaven promises to be, we ought not be deceived. Not everyone will enter. Ironically, though all are invited, not all choose to accept the invitation (Rev 3:20; cf. John 3:16). Entering is conditioned upon receiving and believing in Jesus (John 1:12)—as the Lamb of God whose "blood . . . purchased" the redemption of those who look to him (5:6–10; cf. 7:9–10). Despite those well-intentioned people who have tried to make heaven the destiny of all, that message runs counter to what we find in Revelation and in the rest of the New Testament. Sadly, Revelation closes with reference to those who remain "outside" heaven (22:15; cf. 21:8, 27) because they have refused to bow and submit to the eternal Lord, his design and truth, and have demanded to live their own way.

The apostle John could not have been clearer than he was in describing these particular features of heaven. Sure, there is still much we will not know until we get there. However, what we do know communicates a message that is both attractive and urgent. I think my friend John Canfield had it right when he began anticipating and talking about his trip there.

What is keeping us from more seriously planning our own trip to heaven?

PRAYER

"Our Father in heaven, hallowed be your name" (Matt 6:9). This model prayer from the lips of Jesus reminds us of the appropriateness of acknowledging, anticipating, and prioritizing heaven—that place wherein Your Spirit dwells eternally. May we think and live that way today. Thank you for calling us heavenward and wanting us to live there with you for all eternity. Thank you for your Son, Jesus, whose death on the cross and subsequent resurrection made the way to heaven possible. We give you praise, both now and forevermore. AMEN.

QUESTIONS

1. How does one keep his or her sights on heaven when there are so many distractions? What advice would you offer?

2. Why do we hear so little about eternal life—heaven or hell—in our churches these days? What factors influence the topics or themes that get emphasized in a generation?

3. Who do you know—like my friend John—who arrived at the place in life where he or she sincerely longed for heaven? What do you remember about that individual's faith?

4. What feature or aspect of heaven from the book of Revelation do you most anticipate? Why? What do you think it will be like when you enter heaven?

SUGGESTED READING

Revelation 1–5, 19, 21–22

References

Aitken, Jonathan. *John Newton: From Disgrace to Amazing Grace.* Wheaton, IL: Crossway, 2007.

Antonson, Rick. *Route 66 Still Kicks: Driving America's Main Street.* New York: Skyhorse Publishing, 2012.

Benge, Janet and Geoff. *Jacob DeShazer: Forgive Your Enemies.* Seattle, WA: YWAM Publishing, 2009.

Bennett, William J., ed. *The Book of Virtues.* New York: Simon & Schuster, 1993.

Bennett, William J. *The Death of Outrage.* New York: The Free Press, 1998.

Blankenhorn, David. *Fatherless America: Confronting Our Most Urgent Social Problem.* New York: Basic Books, 1995.

Brabon, Margaret. *What Now, Lord?* Greenwood, IN: OMS International, 1993.

Bly, Robert. *The Sibling Society.* New York: Vintage Books, 1996.

Dedek, Peter B. *Hip to the Trip: A Cultural History of Route 66.* Albuquerque, NM: University of New Mexico, 2007.

Durkheim, Émile. *The Elementary Forms of the Religious Life.* New York: The Free Press, 1965 (1915).

Eberstadt, Mary. "The Fury of the Fatherless," *First Things,* December 2020.

Engels, Friedrich. "The Origin of the Family, Private Property, and the State," in *The Marx-Engels Reader,* 2nd edition. Edited by Robert C. Tucker. New York: W.W. Norton & Company, 1978 (essay originally written in 1884).

Foxe, John. *Foxe's Book of Martyrs*. Newberry, FL: Bridge-Logos, 2001 (1563).

Goff, Bob. *Love Does*. Nashville, TN: Thomas Nelson, 2012.

Goldstein, Donald M. and Carol Aiko DeShazer Dixon. *Return of the Raider*. Lake Mary FL: Creation House, 2010.

Halverson, Richard C. *Walk with God Between Sundays*. Grand Rapids, MI: Zondervan, 1965.

Jones, E. Stanley. *A Song of Ascents: A Spiritual Autobiography*. Nashville, TN: Abingdon, 1968.

Jones, E. Stanley. *The Unshakable Kingdom and the Unchanging Person*. Nashville, TN: Abingdon, 1972.

Kiley, Dan. *The Peter Pan Syndrome: Men Who Have Never Grown Up*. New York: Avon Books, 1983.

Kinlaw, Dennis. *This Day with the Master*. Nappanee, IN: Francis Asbury Press, 2002.

Krim, Arthur. *Route 66: Iconography of the American Highway*. Santa Fe, NM: Center for American Places, 2005.

Lasch, Christopher. *The Culture of Narcissism: American Life in an Age of Diminishing Expectations*. New York: W.W. Norton & Company, 1979.

McPheeters, Chilton C. *Pardon Me, Sir . . . Your Halo's Showing: The Story of J.C. McPheeters*. Wilmore, KY: Francis Asbury Society, 1984.

Merriam-Webster's Collegiate Dictionary, 11th edition. Springfield, MA: Merriam-Webster, 2011.

Mills, C. Wright. *The Sociological Imagination*. New York: Oxford University Press, 1959.

Moyer, Elgin S. *Great Leaders of the Christian Church*. Chicago: Moody Press, 1951.

Parker, John H. *Abide with Me: A Photographic Journey through Great British Hymns*. Green Forest, AR: New Leaf Press, 2009.

Phillips, J. B. *Your God Is Too Small*. NY: MacMillan, 1961 (1952).

Rees, Wilbur E. *$3.00 Worth of God*. Valley Forge, PA: Judson Press, 1971.

Sheldon, Charles. *In His Steps*. Old Tappan, NJ: Fleming H. Revell Company, 1976 (1896).

Steinbeck, John. *The Grapes of Wrath*. New York: Penguin, 2002 (1939).

Sixty-Six

Tozer, A. W. *The Pursuit of God*. Camp Hill, PA: Christian
	Publications, 1982 (1948).
Wallis, Michael. *Route 66: The Mother Road*. New York: St. Martin's
	Press, 1990.
Watson, C. Hoyt. *DeShazer: The Doolittle Raider Who Turned
	Missionary*. Winona Lake, IN: Light and Life Press, 1950.
Wesley, John. *A Plain Account of Christian Perfection*. Kansas City,
	MO: Beacon Hill Press, 1966 (1777).
Wilson, Dorothy Clarke. *Granny Brand: Her Story*. Chappaqua, NY:
	Christian Herald Books, 1976.
Young, Sarah. *Jesus Calling*. Nashville, TN: Thomas Nelson, 2014
	(2004).

About the Author

Kent R. Olney, Ph.D., has had several roles and titles over his career. Those include sociologist, college professor, department chair, college dean, pastor, Sunday school teacher, public speaker, sign language instructor, sign language interpreter, husband, father, grandfather, and student of the Word of God. The last one has influenced all the others.

Kent currently serves as dean of the College of Arts and Sciences at Olivet Nazarene University. Prior to his current position he taught sociology at Olivet for twenty-six years. For twenty of those years, he also taught an intergenerational Sunday school class called Scripture & Society. The class focused on studying entire books from the Bible, noting their relevance to contemporary social life and making practical application for daily living. The weekly class gatherings often numbered seventy or more individuals and included university students, faculty, and administrators, along with many individuals from the local community.

Kent is an ordained minister with ten years of experience as a local church pastor. His credentials are with the Church of the Nazarene. He is a graduate of Asbury University and Asbury Theological Seminary, both in Wilmore, Kentucky. Kent also holds a master's degree in counseling from Gallaudet University, in Washington, D.C., and both a master's degree and doctorate's degree in sociology from the University of Oregon.

Having grown up with deaf siblings, Kent is fluent in American Sign Language (ASL). Prior to serving on the faculty at Olivet Nazarene University, he taught ASL at Western Oregon State College for eight years and worked extensively as a freelance interpreter. During his tenure at

Western Oregon, he was the faculty sponsor for Campus Crusade for Christ. All these experiences helped shape how he views the world.

Kent married his college sweetheart, Beth, over four decades ago. They have lived together in four different regions of the United States— the South, the East Coast, the West Coast, and the Midwest. Kent and Beth have two married sons and five grandchildren. In addition to his writing and university responsibilities these days, Kent enjoys backyard baseball, laughing, storytelling, reading biographies, and passing on the faith to his grandchildren.

Made in the USA
Monee, IL
17 November 2023

46774691R10236